Madonna as Postmodern Myth

Madonna as Postmodern Myth

*How One Star's Self-Construction
Rewrites Sex, Gender, Hollywood
and the American Dream*

GEORGES-CLAUDE GUILBERT

McFarland & Company, Inc., Publishers
Jefferson, North Carolina, and London

Library of Congress Cataloguing-in-Publication Data

Guilbert, Georges-Claude
  Madonna as postmodern myth : how one star's self-construction
rewrites sex, gender, Hollywood and the American dream / by
Georges-Claude Guilbert.
      p.   cm.
  Includes bibliographical references and index.

  ISBN 0-7864-1408-1 (softcover : 50# alkaline paper) ∞

  1. Madonna, 1958– — Criticism and interpretation.   I. Title.
ML420.M1387 G85   2002
782.42166'092 — dc21   2002015002

British Library cataloguing data are available

Manufactured in the United States of America

Cover photograph ©2002 PhotoDisc

*McFarland & Company, Inc., Publishers
  Box 611, Jefferson, North Carolina 28640
  www.mcfarlandpub.com*

Acknowledgments

I wish to thank, for the support and inspiration they provided, the following people: Michel Bandry, Jacqueline Bardolph, Sonia Bardy, Caroline Béchet, Julie Bezzi, Myriam Boussahba, Pat Browne, Kelly Bunyan, Marc Chénetier, Robert Conrath, Maurice Couturier, John Dean, Chantal Delourme, Jean-Claude Dupas, Régis Durand, Cécile Fouache, Catherine Bresson Galliani, Anthony Guilbert, Georges Louis Guilbert, Yvette Guilbert, James Helgeson, Régis Hélie, Thierry Lanlard, Susan Larkins, Gilles Lévêque, Nicolas Magenham, Marcel Marcellesi, Valérie Marchisio, Kristin Swenson Musselman, Corinne Ors, Olivier Payelle, Gérard Poncin, Paul Ponder, Laetitia Robache, Philippe Romanski, Sylvie Roger, Margaret Sidbon, Robert Springer, Marc Stewart, Denise Terrell, and Anne Wicke.

Very special thanks to Francis Bordat.

Contents

If Madonna shows a predominant vice, it is that she always stands for something. It is usually rich enough, or by her detractors' estimates, gamy enough to be on the very edge of the public's digestive powers.

— Norman Mailer, 1994

It is true that I did not initially think of Madonna in that way, it did not seem attractive to me at all, but something else is at stake, there is a strategy, it is offensive. She does obtain a mix, a multiculturalism, and also a questioning of sexual difference, by shuffling the cards, all the cards. Maybe that's what post-modern means.

— Jean Baudrillard, 1994, p. 29

Preface

It's flattering to me that people take the time to analyze me and that I've so infiltrated their psyches that
they have to intellectualize my very being. I'd rather be
on their mind than off.
                                                        — Madonna[1]

The polyvalent artist Madonna, born in 1958, made an impact on a few
hundred New Yorkers in 1982, penetrated America's collective consciousness in 1983, and took hold of the world's in 1984, notably with the song
Like a Virgin. Since then, she has never let go of it. Businesswoman, theater and movie actress,[2] producer, musician, songwriter, writer, journalist,
model and camp[3] pop singer, she colonizes the Western media landscape.

She has released fifteen albums (all of which have been top 10 best-
sellers in the majority of the countries on the planet). She has also acted
in three plays and eighteen movies, written the book *Sex* as well as several articles, and published her *Private Diary*. Many singles have been
extracted from her albums, most having reached the top 5 (often number 1). The videos that promote those singles have become classics of the
genre. By October 2002, at the beginning of a new century, Madonna had
sold about 140 million albums.

I consider the whole of Madonna's work *and* the whole of her person

1

as a sum of signs lending themselves to analysis. Her songs, her videos, her movies, her book, her interviews, her TV appearances, as well as the outfits she wears, her hairstyles and her makeup constitute a vast text that I read, as much *ex professo* as possible. Such an ambition is largely semiotic — it borrows from literary criticism as well as from pop music criticism, art criticism or film criticism — but certain aspects of my study naturally have to do with sociology, as they concern Madonna's impact on American (and Western) society. My bibliography illustrates the interest she has raised in numerous universities, which sometimes have gone as far as to propose Madonna courses. Princeton, Harvard, UCLA, the University of Colorado and Rutgers were among the first. Even Amsterdam followed suit in April 1997, creating an optional course within the Musicology department entitled "Madonna: The Music and the Phenomenon."

The discourse of Madonnologists is generally marked by left wing ideology, radical antiracism, extreme feminism lesbian or gay militancy. Some, as we'll see, even seek to appropriate the Madonna text in order to serve an ideology, and reproach Madonna for her failures to promote this or that cause. Two "political" positions in particular are frequently attached to Madonna studies: pro-choice, and safe sex campaigns which encourage the use of condoms.

As I do not intend to expand on the imprecise nature of the borders between high art and low art, I'll merely classify Madonna in the second category, and remind the reader that American cultural studies (the domain of most Madonnologists) are more and more preoccupied with low culture (or popular culture or even mass culture — depending on definitions). Their work is frequently inscribed in women's studies, feminist studies, gender studies, LGBT (lesbian, gay, bisexual, transgender) studies, or even Queer Theory, which often sees itself as semiotic and psychoanalytic, and does not hesitate to proclaim itself postmodern.

Borrowing from all this and from a couple of French theorists, as well as relying on Hollywood references, I'll try to establish how exactly Madonna can be apprehended as a postmodern myth.

I have examined the whole of the critical apparatus, as well as the works of Madonna, and her person, but I have also consulted a great many press articles, extracted from the most sensationalist tabloids or the most austere dailies.

In the American, British, Australian and French press (my four principal sources), it is generally taken for granted that Madonna is the most famous female in the world.[4] Figures irrefutably show that she is the one (among living artists still working) who has sold the greatest number of records worldwide; they also show that she is counted among the highest paid artists at various times in recording history, with Prince, Michael

Jackson, R.E.M. and Janet Jackson, obtaining enormous sums of money in exchange for a signature. The media constantly mention her, and every individual in the Western hemisphere (practically in the whole world, I suspect) has at least heard of what is commonly referred to as her "provocation," even if one has achieved the improbable exploit of never having heard any of Madonna's songs. Her tremendous fame can be illustrated by a couple of revealing examples for the time being: the birth of her first child in October 1996 was reported by *all* the generalist media, at least in the U.S., the U.K., Australia, and France (and certainly in most other countries), and her garbage cans have been examined by journalists who sold pictures of their contents for a very good price. The garbage itself was sold.[5]

Madonna's capacity to analyze her own creation, her image and her success shouldn't be overestimated. In spite of the intellectual status she is sometimes granted, you can't expect her to have an academic view of everything she stands for.[6] In the following pages, I regularly evoke the cultural appropriations that characterize her work, and it's impossible not to wonder to what extent those are deliberate and conscious. Two mistakes must be avoided: you may easily consider that Madonna does not understand much of her own discourse and plays with references she does not really grasp. Just as simplistically, you may be tempted to imagine that she masters more elements of her creation than is really the case. The problem does not arise when dealing with David Bowie, with whom I frequently compare her. It is established that he is well read, having read every line of John Rechy, William Burroughs and George Orwell; he knows German philosophy and German expressionism well, and he is capable of commenting upon today's society very coherently. The singer Annie Lennox provides another useful comparison: she seems for her part to accept the intellectual label, and when she deals with matters of feminism, gender-bending or drag queen politics, as in the video of the song *Beethoven (I Love to Listen to),*[7] the audience presumes that it is the result of authentic reflection.[8]

With Madonna, in this and in many other domains, it is harder to hold a fixed opinion. In some interviews, she seems practically brainless, she utters verbless sentences, swears like a fishmonger, lacks vocabulary, and gives the impression that she has never read a book in her life. On such occasions, even her voice and accent are nasal and vulgar. On others, she expresses herself in a refined manner, she is distinguished, mature, poised.[9] Her voice is transformed, she speaks of psychoanalysis,[10] of arty films, of painters,[11] of highbrow writers, all very convincingly.[12] On this point as on many others, I suppose we'll never know the truth — supposing there might be such a thing as a "true" Madonna. "The truth is rarely pure, and never simple."[13] In a postmodern context, it is in the order of things. I myself am convinced of Madonna's superior intelligence: you do not reach such a degree of stardom without it.

First, I'll attempt to define the terms of my title. What is a myth? What are the connections between myth and stardom? What is the postmodern in general? What is the postmodern in popular culture?

Secondly, I'll show how Madonna methodically discovered and constructed herself. It seems very much as if she had planned her interventions in the numerous artistic domains that interested her, ticking boxes as she went along. I'll look at the nature and extent of her ambition, the domains in which it manifests itself, and the means she uses to reach her goals. I'll illustrate the way in which she organized her own cult, single-handedly devising her artistic output, and craftily targeting different publics. I'll also examine the ubiquity of the Madonna discourse, and the way it is recuperated by different agents. Thirdly, I'll study the duality that her career rests on, the deep contradiction that fuels it. Is Madonna a nun or a femme fatale? A good girl or a bad girl?

My fourth part, the one most concerned with old Hollywood, will be devoted to the study of the different masks Madonna wears, the drag strategies she exploits, and her constant rewrites of dead stars.

Finally, I'll describe the way in which Madonna seems to reflect today's America, its contradictions and worries, its attitudes toward sexuality and religion. Is Madonna an avatar of the American Dream? And I'll conclude with another fundamental question: can Madonna be viewed as a feminist heroine?

I hope that the still skeptical reader will be convinced by the end of this book of the cultural importance of Madonna, or simply her artistic value. David Tetzlaff encourages us to take it seriously:

> *Inside Edition* even did a story on college professors who study Madonna or discuss her work in class. When tabloid journalists start presenting the activities of academics to their sensation-seeking audiences, it is obvious that some very large cultural power is at hand.[14]

For all that, this work by no means constitutes a hagiography, even if I do not intend to hide my attraction to its subject. "We are all in the gutter, but some of us are looking at the stars."[15]

The very nature of the said subject explains why my chapters sometimes crisscross; obviously certain ideas keep creeping up as soon as you start exploring the Madonna universe: ambiguity, quest for power, Hollywood references and provocation, to name but four. I hope I'll be forgiven for this. I also hope I'll be forgiven for writing every song title in italics, instead of respecting the habitual inverted commas: I analyze them as short, self-sufficient works.

ONE

Definitions

Myth

The word myth comes from the Greek *muthos*, which means narrative, fable, or more generally any orally transmitted thing. Dictionaries evoke fabulous narratives, often of popular origin, that involve beings who symbolically incarnate forces of nature, or aspects of the human condition. But they propose as second definitions the ideas of purely imaginary constructions or of expressions of ideas, doctrines or theories in the form of poetic narratives. Lastly they tend to speak of simplified images, often illusory, that human groups elaborate or accept, about an individual or a fact — images which play a determining role in their behavior or judgment.

The critic J.A. Cuddon defines myth as a narrative that is not "true" and that "involves (as a rule) supernatural beings— or at any rate supra-human

5

beings. Myth is always concerned with creation. Myth explains how something came to exist. Myth embodies feeling and concept." He concludes with the notion that "many myths or quasi-myths are primitive explanations of the natural order and cosmic forces."[2]

Roger Fowler sees myths as narratives whose origins or authors cannot be identified with certainty, and which accompany religious beliefs, or help to explain them. They often, but not systematically, deal with the exploits of a god or a hero, exploits that "may be of a fabulous or superhuman nature, and which may have instituted a change in the workings of the universe or in the conditions of social life." He then rejoices in the apparent universality and timelessness of myth.[3]

The theologian Don Cupitt, for his part, defines it thus:

> [Myth] is typically a traditional sacred story of anonymous authorship and archetypal or universal significance which is recounted in a certain community and is often linked with a ritual; [...] it tells of the deeds of superhuman beings [...]; it is set outside historical time in primal or eschatological time or in the supernatural world, or may deal with comings and goings between the supernatural world and the world of human history.[4]

The critic Laurence Coupe, however, points out that this is an excessive generalization. "This 'family-resemblance' approach avoids the inevitable dogmatism of any mythography which emphasizes only one paradigm [...]. Exceptions to, and contradictions of, any particular paradigm are endless."[5] She adds that the mythographer will necessarily have to establish hypotheses, since "few people can claim to have been present when a myth was invented."[6] We'll see that this is true even of modern or postmodern myths.

At the beginning of the twentieth century, the Scottish anthropologist J.G. Frazer explained myths as exclusively linked to rituals destined to guarantee the fertility of the vegetal and animal world. He exerted considerable influence on authors such as D.H. Lawrence or T.S. Eliot, as well as on literary critics like Northrop Frye.[7]

Mircea Eliade writes in *Aspects du mythe*: "It would be difficult to find a definition of myth that would be accepted by all scholars as well as accessible to non-specialists." He also wonders if it is possible to find a definition that fits all the types and uses of myth, before suggesting the now classic description:

> Myth tells a sacred story; it relates an event that took place in primordial time, the fabulous time of "beginnings." In other words, myth tells how, thanks to the exploits of the Supernatural Beings, a reality came to exist, whether it be a total reality, the Cosmos, or only a fragment: an

island, a vegetal species, a human behavior, an institution. So it is always the narrative of a "creation."[8]

Most mythographers agree to differentiate between myth and legend or tale, between the powers of mythic characters and those of fairies or witches—even if the distinction is not always perfectly clear, notably in Bruno Bettelheim[9] or Edgar Morin.[10] Peter Graves for his part makes sure that he does not confuse myth with philosophic allegory, sentimental fable, moral legend or heroic saga.[11]

But everyone's definition mentions the grounding of myth in popular narrative. It is clear, however, that describing myth is not enough; you must also wonder about its function, which characterizes it as much as its nature.

Myth also has etiological, ethological, sociogenetic, cosmogonic and eschatological roles. It has an etiological function in as much as it tries to provide satisfactory explanations for the "diseases" that plague humans. In Genesis, the original sin thus accounts for most of the horrors that befall Adam and Eve's descendents.

Myth also fills an ethological part, in that it seeks to provide mankind with a history of mores, of the social facts of a given human group, so as to make it accept, assimilate or imitate them.

Those etiological and ethological functions of myth are to be linked to what we may call its sociogenetic functions, as myth stages the foundations that are indispensable to any sociogenesis, the basic data that serve to organize relationships between individuals—for example, the moral rules that govern them. If you take as a premise the not-very-Rousseauist idea that in the absence of taboos, men would all be rapists, murderers and cannibals, you will easily conceive how myth can be necessary at the dawn of a society. Roger Caillois writes: "It is indeed in myth that one best grasps, vividly, the collusion of the most secret postulations, the most virulent postulations of individual psyche, and the most imperative and puzzling pressures of social existence."[12] Myth channels passions, be they negative or positive.

It is widely admitted that myth has a cosmogonic role. In ancient societies and in so-called primitive societies, myths find their origin in the fear of a world man does not understand. Man is by essence afraid of the unknown and the unexplained. Finding himself incapable of giving meaning to the universe around him, he imagines a formation of the said universe, generally involving some demiurge. However, that is not enough. A reason must also be found, a cosmic aim to existence, linked to its eventual transformation; hence the eschatological aspect of myth, the answer it gives to the fundamental questions regarding the ultimate ends of man and the world. Myth is forged by mankind to elucidate mystery, to solve the unsolvable, to give meaning to individuals' lives, "to explain, to reconcile, to guide action or to legitimate," writes Cupitt.[13]

Myths are, as Claude Lévi-Strauss,[14] Roger Caillois[15] or Mircea Eliade[16] put forth, imaginary solutions to contradictions. Myth reassures, makes sense, explains, protects. Roland Barthes also believed that myth participates in the organization of a world free of contradictions. Thanks to myth, the universe around us appears decipherable.[17] Myth provides reassuring explanations to natural phenomena. However, according to Paul Ricœur, it is necessary to go beyond that modern vision of myth as false explanation, and examine its exploratory signification, and its contribution to our understanding of the world. Coupe reminds us that Ricœur observed the symbolic function of myth more than others, its power of discovery, and of revelation.[18]

For Lévi-Strauss, myth is a language that has been conceived to communicate thought. He studies it as a linguist studies an idiom. He warns his reader against simplistic religious phenomenology and ethnology, and asks: "To understand myth, have we no other choice than platitude and sophism?"[19]

He remarks in *Anthropologie structurale*: "If we want to account for the specific characteristics of mythic thought, we must [...] establish that myth is simultaneously within and beyond language."[20] In *La Potière jalouse*, he shows that mythic thought does not by any means constitute an outmoded kind of intellectual activity.[21] Besides, we must all bear in mind the use that Sigmund Freud, and even more Carl Gustav Jung, made of myth.[22] Caillois severely condemns their work as "lamentable psychoanalytic attempts."[23] Without going quite as far, Fowler deems Lévi-Strauss's work superior to Jung's in that field.

It is important to note, moreover, that different myths observed in distant regions of the world frequently mirror one another, and that myth is present wherever organized society exists. Charles Baudelaire notes in an essay on Wagner that he was struck by the moral analogies which he had found in myths elaborated in different countries:

> Myth is a construction that springs up everywhere, in every climate, under any sun [...]. The religions and poetry of the four corners of the world provide on this subject abundant evidence. As sin is everywhere, redemption is everywhere, myth is everywhere.[24]

Carlos Fuentes says that "myth is the prêt-à-porter of imagination [...], the imagination of the tribe."[25] In Marshall McLuhan's global village,[26] today's myth is the star, as we shall see. In newspapers and magazines, the word "myth" is attributed to various celebrities every day, with no sense of restriction. Its use should, I believe, be restricted to real stars, mythic stars, such as Madonna.

Myth and Stardom

Here again, I have looked in dictionaries. Looking up the definitions of "star," I have been directed to other words, such as "idol," "glamour," and "superstar."

The majority of cultural commentators who investigate the notion of stardom have restricted their research to movies. The old star-system, intimately linked to the might of the old Hollywood studios, no longer exists. Yet it remains the central reference of stardom theorists. It is easy to widen the reflection to the movies of the late twentieth century, as well as to pop music. To my mind, authentic stardom is akin to myth. It requires eight conditions:

Fortune. The true star, at the same time divinity and luxury product, enjoys a very high income, which is justified by the almost guaranteed success of anything that star appears in. Edgar Morin writes that "fabulous fees distinguish stars from other actors."[27]

Stars own princely palaces, private jets and priceless paintings. Their earnings and acquisitions are chronicled in magazines, and the public gasps at the exhibition of such wealth. If I limit myself to female celebrities, in 1997, the best paid actresses were Jodie Foster, Michelle Pfeiffer, Sharon Stone, Sandra Bullock, Nicole Kidman, Meg Ryan, Meryl Streep, Winona Ryder, Barbra Streisand, and Julia Roberts. Roberts was apparently still the most powerful woman in Hollywood in January 2002.

Beauty. The star is beautiful. Her beauty is constructed. Morin writes: "The star-system does not limit itself to the scouting for natural beauties. It has given rise to or renewed the arts of makeup, costumes, allure, manners, photography and if necessary surgery, that perfects, maintains, or even fabricates beauty."[28] Of course, a deformed woman[29] would suffer a handicap, but "natural beauty" constitutes nothing more than a basis— it can even be a hindrance, if you understand natural in the sense of simple, fresh, non-sophisticated, etc. Some supermodels, such as Christy Turlington, exemplify this: without makeup, they are but blank pages, neither aesthetic, nor unaesthetic, since the cosmetic writing has not yet been undertaken. Drag queens who cover their face with a thick layer of pancake before drawing the face of their choice on it are the extreme expression of that sort of phenomenon.

Ambivalence. The first stars were vamps,[30] i.e. whores, as opposed to pure virgins. There is no mythic stardom without some form of ambivalence, as there is no myth without those inconsistencies Cupitt discusses.

In a sexist society, the dominant culture often needs to reduce woman to such secular and reassuring dichotomies, and it is not surprising that stars should exemplify them. Moreover, the vamp is an object of desire, but she is untouchable, like a virginal divinity. A star is by definition impossible to possess. A star is an art masterpiece, an icon, a fetish.[31] The stars whose work depends to a large extent on eroticism (vamps) are even more inaccessible (virgins) each time they take another step in the offering of their bodies to the public. Some, like Madonna, are acutely aware of that aspect of stardom.

Transgression. The mythic star transgresses the traditional boundaries between genders. She is fundamentally androgynous, like any number of divinities. Morin writes that stars, "mistresses of fashion [...], transgress its taboos as they please. Before anyone else, they crossed over the barriers of sartorial sexuality."[32] But the star is not content with mere sartorial daring: she questions established gender roles. As L. Segal writes: "It becomes hard to propose a single Western icon, from Valentino to Elvis, from Mae West to Madonna, who does not emanate a type of sexual ambiguity."[33] Marlene Dietrich and Mae West are constant references in that field, but Greta Garbo or Tallulah Bankhead did not do badly either.

Construction. The authentic star is a construction, never the product of some spontaneous generation, as the popular press regularly tries to have us believe. No star ever suddenly pops up in show business completely and naturally formed. A star is elaborated with care, using artifice (the fabrication of beauty mentioned above), various strategies, and gimmicks. But it is important to distinguish between individual and collective creations: some stars are self-constructed, like Mae West, others are the toys of Pygmalions whose inspiration varies in quantity and quality, like Rita Hayworth who for years was but the plaything of her mentors. Grace Jones, who reached an impressive degree of notoriety between 1977 and 1983, was basically the creation of the designer Jean-Paul Goude. He turned an obscure and slightly gauche model with an Afro haircut into a stunning performer with an unforgettable look, inventing in particular the cropped hairstyle that was to be imitated by thousands of Blacks around the world. Some supermarket starified products of the Spice Girls variety, recruited via classifieds, are very visibly the result of efforts thought up by brilliant marketing experts.

Amalgam. The mythic star and the personae she interprets are amalgamated in the media and the mind of the public. You believe in the personae of the star, you need them and you project yourself onto them. Morin evokes the difference between spectacle and life, and then writes: "As far as stars are concerned, that difference is blurred: the mythology of stars is situated in a confused and mixed zone, between belief and entertainment."[34] TV magazines constantly use the names of fictional characters to refer to the stars who play them. One of the best illustrations of the phenomenon is Joan Collins, who played Alexis Carrington in NBC's *Dynasty* from 1981 to 1989. TV magazine covers always spoke of Alexis, not Joan. Indeed people *still* see Joan Collins as the conniving Alexis. Morin states that when it comes to stars, "their private life is public, their public life is publicity, their screen life is surreal, and their real life is mythic."[35] We'll see that this amalgam between personae and star is particularly interesting in Madonna's case.

Longevity. Jean Cocteau noted: "Movie stars, like genuine celestial stars, continue moving the public long after they have played their part. They are speaking dead bodies, moving dead bodies. They can become actual corpses and this does not hinder their stage entrances."[36] The true star can never be extinguished, even when she dies or retires; it is the same with myth. Ingrid Bergman or Ava Gardner can vouch for it. Old films shown in arty theaters, video sales and recurring classics on TV bear witness to the longevity of some stars. Many TV channels around the world program movie cycles that are centered on stars such as Garbo. In this context, the intrinsic qualities of the films matter little; it is the star you want to look at, notwithstanding the possible mediocrity of the vehicle. In the same order of things, Marlene Dietrich's records have been constantly re-released, especially since the invention of CDs.

Cult. The mythic star is the object of a cult, a religion. In *Les Stars*, Edgar Morin quotes George Bernard Shaw: "The savage worships wood and stone idols; the civilized man flesh and blood idols."[37] In his preface to the third edition he writes: "Stars are beings that partake at once of the human and the divine, they are analogous in some respects to the heroes of mythologies or the gods of Olympus, generating a cult, or even a sort of religion."[38] And he adds:

> The dialectics of actor and role can only account for the star if the notion of myth intervenes. Malraux, before anyone else, threw light on this: "Marlene Dietrich is not an actress, like Sarah Bernhardt, she is a myth, like Phryne."[39]

The comparison that Malraux establishes here is particularly appropriate: Phryne was a fourth-century B.C. Greek courtesan. It is said that she was the model for the Aphrodite of Cnidos by Praxiteles. Madonna is at once Great Prostitute and Love Goddess, like Marlene Dietrich, like Phryne, like Aphrodite.[40]

The mythic star is the object of a pagan cult. Jean Domarchi says of stars: "No wonder legend seizes those exceptional creatures while they are still alive, I cannot help thinking they are all that's left of pagan antiquity.

Their annals will one day be told as those of Assyrian kings or Roman Cae-
sars."[41] A modicum of talent, I may add, can be quite enough. As Richard
Dyer puts it, "Not all highly talented performers become stars, nor are all
stars highly talented."[42]

Stardom or Superstardom?

If a superstar is to a star what a supermarket is to a market, or a
superhero to a hero, if you are entitled to talk about football stars or speak
of a car as the star of automobiles, then it would be tempting to use the
term "superstar" to refer to certain artists. But things are not so simple.
The word was coined by Andy Warhol or someone in his Factory
entourage — possibly Ingrid Superstar.[43]

Of course, as is frequently the case when you deal with Warholian
legend, the available reminiscences are more or less apocryphal. The same
kind of doubt subsists as regards the miniskirt: was it really invented by
Mary Quant, or did Warhol come up with it, pretending that his friend
Taxi was its originator? To better sidetrack the public, like Madonna,
Warhol appropriated other people's ideas, and allowed members of his
crew to appropriate some of his.

There is undoubtedly, whatever the case may be, a basic ambiguity
in the word "superstar." In Warholian terms, a superstar was initially an
unknown person who, in the groove of the sixties New York underground,
bestowed the title upon herself or himself. This was done at once out of
derision (with reference to Hollywood stars) and to generate reality: word
preceded being. The Factory superstars have not branded the general public forever, but some of us remember them very well.[44]

If you are to believe the definition of the prefix "super" given by the
dictionary (Webster's), the term "superstar" seems to fit, say, the Elizabeth Taylor that Warhol admired, as "greater in quality, amount, or degree
than; surpassing," as compared to other celebrities the press calls stars. If
you think that some stars are self-created, like Barbra Streisand or Annie
Lennox, you may equally call them "superstars," according to Warholian
precepts. But have those women proclaimed themselves stars by anticipation, the Ingrid Superstar way, or have they waited for the public and
the media to confer the title onto them, as a reward for their effort? To
Stephen Koch, (Warholian) superstars are less real than stars, they are
lightweight. He opposes them to "real movie stars."[45]

I myself was tempted to call Madonna a "superstar"; but what is the
point? Why try to outbid the press?

Sensationalist nomenclature presents another idea of stardom. TV
magazines and tabloids constantly overuse the two words "star" and

"superstar." I do not mean to discuss the evolution of language and the way once strong words or prefixes such as "giant," "extra," "super," "hyper," etc., have been weakened, but I must say I find it regrettable that people like for instance Martin Landau or Stephanie of Monaco should be referred to as stars, and Sophie Marceau as a superstar. The two words are hackneyed whereas perhaps they should be deserved. It is hard to determine whether there are actual (female) stars alive today besides Madonna. Elizabeth Taylor? Joan Collins? Sharon Stone? Nicole Kidman?

Now that I have defined myth and its links with stardom, it remains for me to explore the various acceptations of "postmodern." Laurence Coupe provides a valuable transition: "With the emergence of 'postmodernity,' or 'the postmodern condition,' we have witnessed not a retreat from myth, but a much more pervasive sense of myth."[46]

Postmodern: The Story So Far

In a few years Madonna's children Lourdes Maria and Rocco, reading all those essays that refer to their mother as a postmodern icon, will no doubt ask her, "Mom, what does postmodern mean?" Pastiching Jean-François Lyotard, I could call the following lines "the postmodern explained to Lourdes and Rocco."

First of all, the matter of suffixes must be clarified. You find "modern" and "modernist" as adjectives or nouns. You also find "modernity" and "modernism." By the same token, you find "postmodern," "postmodernist," "postmodernity" and "postmodernism," as well as the same words but with a hyphen. Things get worse when you realize that some English-speaking critics translate the French theorists' "*postmoderne*" as "postmodernist," whereas others stick to "postmodern" (about the question of the hyphen, among other things, see "4 1/2 Lectures: The Stuttgart Seminars on Postmodernism, Chaos Theory, and the Romantic Arabesque" by John Barth[47]). I have chosen to use "postmodern" as noun and adjective, as Jean-François Lyotard does, but not before suggesting that the "postmodernist" artist might be a "postmodern" who deliberately strives to correspond to the appellation.

Each theorist has his own conception of the meaning of the phrase "postmodern." There are American acceptations, Italian, Spanish or British nuances, and French definitions. There is the postmodern of the poststructuralists, of the deconstructionists, the postmodern of the novelists and that of the theorists. There is a postmodern for the sociologists, a postmodern for the philosophers, one for each art form; the postmodern of the architects, for instance, may seem to bear little connection to that of the literary critics.

The way a critic conceives of the postmodern frequently signals his theoretic choices. Cornel West wonders if this vague phrase has to do with some crucial aspect of today's world, or if it isn't merely a clever invention of the critics and the artists, meant to promote their personal projects. He even goes further: "The way in which one characterizes 'postmodern culture' reflects one's anxieties, frustrations, allegiances, and visions as a critic. In short, one's very intellectual vocation is at stake in one's conception of 'postmodern' culture."[48]

Indeed, if there are as many definitions as there are users of the concept, it is because each appropriates it to serve his interests; I am presumably no exception. Stephen K. White, in his book on the postmodern and political theory, notes that the term is used in connection with a great variety of phenomena and claims when describing pictorial art, architecture, philosophy and politics. He states in his introduction: "What one decides to emphasize as important within this constellation will, of course, depend on one's interests and intentions." [49] This is true of any theory exploited in the pursuit of personal research, but certainly truer when it comes to the postmodern.

So "postmodern" is a hodgepodge word. Roy Shuker observes that any attempt at defining it with precision is doomed to fail: "The precise nature of postmodernism [...] proves hard to pin down, and there is a marked lack of clarity and consistency in all the varying usages of the term."[50]

Americans are particularly fond of the word. MTV — sometimes deemed globally postmodern (since it broadcasts mostly videos, seen as intrinsically postmodern) — did not hesitate to call one of its programs "Postmodern TV," thus fuelling those who see in "postmodern" nothing more than a pompous euphemism for cultural zapping. The label is so overused that some end up seeing it as pejorative; indeed many artists refuse it even when all the critics grant it to them. John Barth is one of the few writers who more or less accept it. In fact, faced with such a variety of usage, some doubt that it means anything at all, especially when it is applied generously to an entire culture. Thus Cornel West asks: "Has the term 'postmodern' become such a buzz word that it means anything, refers to everything — hence signifying nothing?" [51] On the other hand, David Van Leer describes the postmodern as a practice that seeks to convert "the lack of evidence into a statement about the impossibility of ever knowing anything with certainty."[52]

Consequently, prudence and rigor are necessary. Jonathan Bignell judiciously warns that maybe even more than with other critical terms, "the postmodern requires us to be especially careful about definitions."[53] Linda Hutcheon's first sentence in one of her books devoted to the postmodern also warns: "Few words are more used and abused in discussions of contemporary culture than the word 'postmodernism'."[54] Yves Boisvert confirms:

> It is true that at first one feels at a loss when faced with the diversity, or even the contradictions of the postmodernist corpus. Hence the "normal" feeling that one is facing a discursive melting-pot. However, if one means to study this discourse seriously, one must get over this first impression. Apprehending the postmodern discourse constitutes an extremely complex exercise that requires very detailed analysis.[55]

Those difficulties of definition may be linked to the cultural crisis that the States in particular and the Western world in general seem to be going through, as Cornel West writes:

> These questions exemplify the degree to which the debate about what does or does not constitute "postmodern culture" is not a mere disagreement about the use or misuse of a phrase but rather a raging battle over how we define and conceive of the role of culture in American society (as well as those abroad). More pointedly, it highlights how we interpret the current crisis in our society and [try] to alleviate this crisis.[56]

I believe the term does have a concrete meaning, which I mean to elucidate.

The Modern and the Postmodern

It seems Charles Jencks is to blame for the popularization of the word. He examined postmodern architecture, and opposed it to the modernist work of people like Le Corbusier. According to Jencks, Joseph Hudnut was the very first person who spoke of postmodern architecture, as early as 1949.[57]

He also states that it isn't really possible to speak of postmodern architectural realizations before the fifties, with the Italian Revivalists. Theorists do not all agree with this, but they do agree that one of the essential elements of postmodern practice in architecture is the re-appropriation of history: the achievements of the past are not rejected anymore, they are recycled.[58] That notion of cultural appropriation has then been applied to every postmodern art form: the postmodern creator feels free to reuse (rewrite) any preexisting creation. Moreover, he does not refuse to hybridize his work. For Jencks, modern(ist) architecture consisted in exaggerating a specific constraining language, whereas postmodern architecture means to associate this language to others— vernacular, commercial, or historic(al).[59]

Prior to Jencks, Friedrich Nietzsche and Martin Heidegger have been counted among the originators of postmodern theory, at least in its more strictly philosophical, or even political, aspects.[60] According to Stephen K. White, Heidegger prolonged the Nietzschean examination of the metaphysical writings of various philosophers, and then observed the technical orientation[61] and the dilemmas of the modern, while not losing sight of the nature and use of language. Postmodern thought is also said to have arisen from the investigations about will (*Wille*) that the two philosophers carried out, as well as from the way Heidegger exposed the dangers of a (modern) rationalization of the world.[62]

It is generally reckoned that Derrida, after he had read Nietzsche and Heidegger, then elaborated his own theory, thereby participating in the advancement of postmodern reflection. The basis of his contribution is the way he distanced himself from the pretensions of metaphysical thought and modern metanarratives (or master narratives or grand narratives), as well as his defense of impertinence.[63] The influence of Félix Guattari and Gilles Deleuze must also be mentioned, for their analysis of superimposition, interpenetration and circularity. They showed that different discourses coexist, and that those discourses are in no way fixed, as they never cease to cross and displace each other. The postmodern of Guattari and Deleuze is the abandonment of the linear.[64]

It is, however, with Lyotard's *La Condition postmoderne*,[65] that the postmodern became somehow more respected. Lyotard theorized about the increasing impossibility to still believe in the old metanarratives that I have just mentioned, such as those of enlightenment, Marxism, or others (i.e., of the modern). He demonstrates it in this book and elsewhere, using examples from history that refute or invalidate the metanarratives.[66] Like Gianni Vattimo,[67] he sees in the modern an aggressive attempt at erasing the past (historical amnesia, as Yves Boisvert puts it[68]), at proscribing the old in favor of the new at any price. As Boisvert writes, the modern is linked to a bygone era that was marked by a Big Project associated to a specific kind of thought and a relationship to time that was very particular.

> That type of thought is very metaphysical, hence the might, typical of the modern, of the "great ideas" to put into effect and the metanarratives that guide our destiny toward that realization, which is directly linked to a specific organization of time founded on a unitary history. The latter is characterized by a perpetual movement forward that is obsessed and guided by the idea of realization.[69]

The postmodern is what comes into play when you get rid of that mode of thought. Thinkers like Paul Virilio[70] and Jean Baudrillard (I'll come back to him later) seem to enunciate that we are all living in a postmodern era, following the failure of the modern project; whereas Jean-François Lyotard or Barry Smart[71] tend to think that the modern and the postmodern coexist, the latter constantly pointing out the limitations of the former. The evolution of artistic practices, at any rate, does indeed show the exhaustion of the modern, as well as the need for an alternative. The postmodern is also the product of the technical and scientific progress that was accomplished during the first half of the twentieth century.[72] Boisvert writes that "of all the technological developments, the vertiginous expansion of computing in our societies is what characterizes the postmodern best,"[73] inasmuch as it radically modifies the treatment and transmission of information.[74]

The postmodern is also linked to the extreme development of mass media in our society; each theorist measures its consequences, notably the philosopher Gérard Raulet[75] and the critic Guy Scarpetta.[76] This society of ours is McLuhan's global village, it is Guy Debord's *société du spectacle*,[77] it is also a universe where information (in the widest sense of the word) circulates more and more quickly, and it becomes more and more difficult to tell the real from the unreal or the surreal, the genuine from the fabricated.

The sociologist Jean Baudrillard examined the degrees of saturation reached by our consumer society as far as simulacra and simulations are concerned.[78] His contribution is particularly useful when it comes to the analysis of artistic creation. The moderns' conception of artistic creation was rather rigorous and elitist, inasmuch as they felt it had to meet strict rules of specificity and purity, obey genre laws, and avoid vulgarity. This position is outmoded: there is no more sacred art. In terms of postmodern aesthetics, anything goes. There are only products.

The press often confuses postmodern and avant-garde, whereas avant-garde was strictly speaking the province of the modern. Postmodern endeavors may be perceived, on the other hand, as reactions against the proliferation of somewhat totalitarian avant-garde movements. At the very least the postmodern mocks the avant-garde. One of the paintings of the postmodern artist Richard Tipping proclaims in black letters over a yellow background, in the fashion of a road sign: "CAUTION: THERE IS NO AVANT-GARDE, ONLY THOSE WHO HAVE BEEN LEFT BEHIND."[79]

It would be boring to list exhaustively all the postmodern theorists I have used. I'd like to mention, however, Brian McHale,[80] Charles Newman,[81] Frank Kermode,[82] or Ihab Hassan;[83] and Fredric Jameson, to whom I'll come back later.[84]

The Death of the Author

The postmodern is linked to the ideas of the poststructuralists and deconstructionists, of Jacques Derrida[85] and Michel Foucault.[86] The latter have described "fragmented subjects," now deprived of "center," whose confusion some say echoes the general confusion of the postmodern era.

The postmodern is often (best) tackled via literary criticism. But it is imperative to be wary of the amalgam that has been made in this respect between some deconstructionist theories and postmodern practices. Many critics have yielded to that temptation, especially "young" American critics, whose writings are the product of two decades (the seventies and eighties) when American criticism, primarily at Yale, welcomed deconstruction with enthusiasm. From such criticism stemmed today's cultural studies, which tend to read cultural products with the help of linguistics, anthropology and philosophy. The abandonment of the author notion characterizes that problematic. But as Maurice Couturier reminds us: "Barthes had observed 'the death of the author' in an essay that ten years later was to become the foundation charter to the entire deconstructionist movement when Barthes himself had given up that thesis."[87] Couturier sums up the situation in La Figure de l'auteur. He shows that Foucault and Barthes distanced themselves from some of their initial positions; he explains that in order to evolve and acquire legitimacy, the critics had to radicalize their discourse. Proclaiming the death of the author helped to take a closer interest in the narrator, the reader, the almighty language.

At the same time, the reflection of people like Gérard Genette, Umberto Eco, Julia Kristeva and Paul de Man progressed, but in the course of the past ten years, writes Couturier, "It appeared that research couldn't progress much more if the author was still adamantly excluded from the discursive field: one may multiply the agents of the text at will, one always reaches a dead end at some stage or other."[88]

But I am oversimplifying: what does "author" mean anyway? The present book is obviously not the place for this. I'll retain for my research the way Couturier evokes "the Bakhtinian then Kristevian theory of intertextuality: the author does not invent anything, he merely undertakes the bricolage of texts and obeys the laws of language or genre."[89] We'll see if or how this manifests itself.

Adversaries

The postmodern has many adversaries. The main one is undoubtedly Jürgen Habermas, who links postmodern and neo-conservative.[90] He is the leader in the field of anti-postmodern critical thought, having generated a particularly heated debate in the eighties by opposing Lyotard.[91] Also countering Georges Bataille, Michel Foucault and Jacques Derrida, Habermas considers that the modern project has not yet been taken to its conclusion. He sees in the whole of the Western world a context that is apt to support capitalist processes, accompanied by tendencies to criticize the modern systematically, in terms of culture. To sum up, he sees post-modern enthusiasts as Manichean neo-conservatives who in bad faith use various successful modern practices while parading as antimodern, or fish up from a premodern past elements that make them more conservative than the modern, as well as politically suspect or irresponsible.[92]

The objections of the adversaries of the postmodern might very well rest on misunderstandings. As Boisvert thinks, the systematic confusion that Habermas's disciples spread between the postmodern and conservatism is probably regrettable. Boisvert sees a lack of rigor in their reflection, and deems that this lack "is the basis for everybody's persisting ignorance in intellectual circles when it comes to the postmodern corpus." He even speaks of "intellectual obscurantism."[93] Without going so far, I myself deplore the fact that certain artists, because they have been labeled postmodern, are rejected by many left wing critics.

Fredric Jameson is considered one of the foremost authorities on the subject. In his different articles and books, he does not clearly appear as an adversary of the postmodern, but as an observer; however, as a Marxist intellectual, he sees the postmodern as irredeemably linked to the development of capitalism.[94] The postmodern, he writes, is not only an ideology or a cultural fantasy, "but has genuine historical (and socioeconomic) reality as a third great original expansion of capitalism around the globe (after the earlier expansions of the national market and the older imperialist system)."[95]

Ironically, some see in the postmodern intolerable manifestations of selfishness, egocentrism and individualism, and that obscurantism that Boisvert detects in the adversaries of the postmodern is sometimes precisely what they despise the postmodern for, like Nicole-Claude Mathieu who writes:

> The postmodern seems to me to be a kind of new nominalism, individualistic navel gazing. It is not the death of the subject, it is the death of the political, relational subject. In spite of its claim that it "situates" discourses (of course, it is only in regards to other discourses), it is the death of all sociological and historical thought — in brief, a new obscurantism, which seems particularly worrying to me when the women's situation is concerned.[96]

So Mathieu believes that feminism has no place in the postmodern. Yet many feminists claim it.

Feminism?

The postmodern is also characterized by the way it hails the end of the idea of universality, of unitary history, that was nothing but a screen for the masculine, Western, European, white cultural hegemony.

Vattimo denounced the Eurocentrism of the modern,[97] but its phallocentrism can be denounced in the same way. The postmodern artist on the other hand generally succeeds in freeing herself or himself from the reigning cultural ethnocentrism, and from phallocentrism; hence the frequent but contested association of the postmodern with feminism.

Craig Owens writes: "Women's insistence on difference and incommensurability may not only be compatible with, but also an instance of, postmodern thought."[98] Some speak of postmodern feminism, others of postfeminism, the two phrases often — but not systematically — meaning the same thing (I don't subscribe to the view that postfeminism means no more feminism at all). Sophia Phoca and Rebecca Wright's book *Introducing Postfeminism* features Madonna's famous Jean-Paul Gaultier cone-bra bustier on the cover.[99] It seems logical to suppose that distancing oneself from every ideology, as the postmodern does, leads among other things to an identification and a rejection of the inherent phallocentrism of most modern metanarratives, but also of premodern metanarratives, notably Christianity. As Arthur Kroker writes: "What has feminist theory always been about if not a refusal of the grand metaphysics of Being, of the unitary male subject, of the phallocentric order of the Subject, Species, and Membership; in favor a world of 'multiplicities'?"[100]

In terms of creation, feminist artists may feel drawn to the postmodern, inasmuch as it got rid of macho prejudices. And of course, feminist consumers might enjoy postmodern works more than other kinds.

Yet Another Definition

I had to try and touch upon all the domains to which the postmodern is associated, but I am naturally more interested in the postmodern when it has to do with artistic production, leaving its philosophical, sociological, historical and political manifestations to more qualified researchers. So I have chosen to offer yet another definition, restricted to the domain of creation.

Some might be tempted to deduce from the word itself that the postmodern aims at being more modern than the modern, newer than the new. On the contrary, postmodern artists believe that the modern have (sometimes desperately) innovated to exhaustion, leaving nothing to their successors but this realization and what logically follows, as John Barth evokes in his essay "The Literature of Exhaustion."[101]

A postmodern artist is acutely aware of everything that has been produced before he came along, in his field and others. But it is silly to attribute the label to anyone who indiscriminately plunders the past; the way in which that awareness of the past is used must be observed.

The postmodern artist realizes (more or less intellectually) the following: everything has been said before, there is no point in creating if his work constitutes nothing more than yet another (necessarily boring) example of this or that classified type of artistic creation, obeying this or that set of conventions without distance.

The postmodern artist, writes Lyotard, is comparable to a philosopher. "The text he writes, the work he accomplishes is not [...] governed by pre-established rules, and may not be judged [...] according topredefined categories."[102] Foucault showed that any type of knowledge is socially and politically specific, and thus totally relative.[103] This is true of artistic knowledge as it is true of scientific knowledge. Shuker speaks of a "challenge to the established notions of representation in the verbal and the visual spheres."[104]

Since everything has been said before, the postmodern artist produces while being fully aware of the work of palimpsest (almost always playful) that of course he undertakes. He adroitly handles quotation, allusion, reference, tribute, *mise en abyme*, or pastiche and parody; he manifests at all times distance, irony, derision, often mocking herself or himself. A painting by Richard Tipping warns: "DANGER: POSTMODERNISM DOESN'T GIVE A FLYING DUCK."

Any postmodern writing is hypertextual. The postmodern artist knows he is sailing on an ocean of intertextuality. His discourse ceaselessly refers to or echoes other discourses. In *Palimpsestes*, Genette mentions Barth and states: "No wonder *The Odyssey* is the favorite target of hypertextual writing."[105] More than any other postmodern writer, Barth conveys in his fiction an elaborate reflection upon the origins and the evolution of the novel, from Homer to the English epistolary novelists of the eighteenth century — taking in Cervantes. Rather than speak, as Genette does, of hyperaesthetic practices when outside the field of literature, I'd rather generalize the use of the word hypertextual to any type of artistic creation. In pop and in cinema, one of the predominant sources of hypertextual writing is pre–1962 Hollywood.[106]

So the postmodern novelist writes metafiction, a term that the postmodern writer William H. Gass seems to have coined. For the writer, the practice of metafiction consists in showing he knows that everything has already been said, that all the experiments have already been attempted (by the modern) in terms of form, but that this is in no way saddening; on the contrary, it is more than ever possible to celebrate the "*plaisir du texte.*" The metafictional novelist often conveys a feeling of sheer fun linked to the exploration of language and of the centuries of writing that preceded her or him, as Patricia Waugh thinks:

> [Metafiction is] a celebration of the power of the creative imagination together with an uncertainty about the validity of its representations; an extreme self-consciousness about language, literary form and the act of writing fictions; a pervasive insecurity about the relationship of fiction to reality; a parodic, playful, excessive or deceptively naïve style of writing[...]. Metafiction is a term given to fictional writing which self-consciously and systematically draws attention to its status as an artifact in order to pose questions about the relationship between fiction and reality.[107]

This definition may easily be applied to the metapop or metacinema of postmodern singers and filmmakers. Indeed, even if the term metafiction is usually restricted to literary fiction, I do not hesitate to speak of metafiction in pop or cinema, as they both produce as much fiction as literature does. In the same way, I may evoke metafictional pop and metafictional cinema. Following the same logic, the postmodern painter paints metapainting, and the postmodern fashion designer designs metafashion. In other words these artists—at the time they create and inside their very creation — wonder to various degrees about the mechanisms of creation, and about the way it deploys itself, as regards the processes of creation of their "elders."

But rather than distinguish like Waugh a "pervasive insecurity" as far as the relationship between reality and fiction is concerned, I favor the idea of playful interrogation.[108]

So a postmodern artist doesn't really invent, he arranges recuperated signifiers. My work is largely founded on this notion. Yet I am wary of "floating signifiers" theories, linked to those of "the death of the author" mentioned above. As Couturier shows, the notion of "absence" (*a fortiori* death) of the author must not be exaggerated, nor taken too much at face-value. The concept of floating signifiers is interesting, but precisely, doesn't the talent of the postmodern artist consist in meticulously mastering the floating of his signifiers? Doesn't the artist who sails off remain captain of his float? John Barth or Carlos Fuentes, to mention but two, seem to me to be magnificently present (alive) in their work. Of course, the postmodern rubs elbows with anarchy, but it doesn't mean that absolutely "anything goes," in spite of its frequent associations with chaos. The notion of cultural appropriation, mentioned everywhere in connection with postmodern practices, does not entail that of a random gathering of signifiers. The artist who merely throws without method his borrowings in the cauldron and stirs is not postmodern, he is simply uninspired.

The postmodern artist chooses the elements that suit her/him, but without worrying about the usual criteria of high and low culture. He has rejected the obsolescent distinctions between high and low and doesn't care about the opposition between commercial and "authentic" production.[109] This is true of most postmodern novelists, who do not hesitate to borrow elements from genres traditionally seen as minor; it is also true of postmodern painters who will for instance plunder comic books. Shuker states: "Postmodernism seeks to blur, if not totally dissolve the traditional oppositions and boundaries between the aesthetic and the commercial, between art and the market, and between high and low culture.[110]" In this context, the postmodern artist also plays with Camp and kitsch. What the art critic André Rouillé says about postmodern painters and photographers may just as well be applied to pop music and its now indispensable companions, videos:

> [Postmodern artists practice] narcissistic personalization [...], sexual stereotypes, fetish motifs, creation mystique, popular imagery, simplification of form, kitsch, loud colors, mixture of media, codes, and practices.[111]

Naturally, there are more and more postmodern creators in what is still referred to as popular culture, notably in pop music, which lends itself particularly well to all sorts of hypertextual games. Pop allows musicians and singers to celebrate the findings of the icons of past decades, and is good at conveying the anti-discriminatory attitudes that are inherent to the postmodern, as Steven Connor shows:

> Along with the fashion industry, the rock industry is the best example of the elastic salability of the cultural past, with its regular recyclings of its own history [...]. Most accounts or celebrations of postmodern rock or popular music stress two related factors: firstly, its capacity to articulate alternative or plural cultural identities, of groups belonging to the margins of national or dominant cultures; and secondly (often, though not invariably, related to this) the celebration of the principles of parody, pastiche, stylistic multiplicity and generic mobility.[112]

Fredric Jameson deems that in the sixties, the Beatles and the Rolling Stones are modern, and that in terms of pop, the postmodern only appears at the end of the seventies.[113] But his judgment on punk (as well as that of Connor) is not clear enough. Does he or doesn't he think that punk is postmodern?[114] Dick Hebdige, on the other hand, made up his mind, he thinks it is.[115] I disagree. True enough, the punks practiced bricolage and collage aesthetics; true enough, they recycled connoted images, such as that of sadomasochistic bondage, but their nihilism and their violence, their marked leaning toward self-destruction, prevented them from reaching the detached ironic stance that is indispensable to any postmodern undertaking. I see punk on the contrary as the ultimate gasp of modern rock, the testament of an exhausted music that has become too white, the last try at authenticity of a handful of rebels negotiating with difficulty the passage from the seventies to the eighties. Real punks are dead, like Sid Vicious. The punk spirit was moribund as early as late 1977; those who proclaimed themselves punk after that had more to do with retro than with the postmodern.

On the other hand, the trend that followed, New Wave, which would never have seen the light of day if punk hadn't existed, did announce the postmodern turn. New Wave artists did not worry about rejecting the realizations of their elders of the past decades, on the contrary.[116] Seeing a postmodern mix of signifiers in punk is confusing it with New Wave. Indeed you may even wonder if punk wasn't a specifically British movement, which would make all American punks really New Wavers, and would explain why many American critics tend to equate the two. The idea of a French or Italian punk, for instance, is oxymoronic.

Jameson mentions the void of the postmodern pastiche, implying that the postmodern suffers from a lack of identity;[117] Angela McRobbie answers with the idea of a construction of identities (in the plural), with the help precisely of pastiche, of Camp, of the multiplication of texts. She offers the appropriate examples of Frankie Goes to Hollywood, Boy George, Marc Almond and Jimmy Sommerville.[118]

So postmodern practices are — in popular culture and elsewhere — by definition self-conscious (like postmodern critics), hypertextual, playful and ironic. They may be divided into two categories: on one side artists such as John Barth, accused by Gore Vidal in his essay "American Plastic: The Matter of Fiction"[119] of writing novels that are meant to be taught but not read; on the other side people like Kurt Vonnegut, Julian Schnabel, Robert Rodriguez, Björk, Thierry Mugler or Jean-Paul Gaultier, who delight the exegetes as well as the general public.

In the literary field, it is relatively easy to see Gertrude Stein, Virginia Woolf, Franz Kafka or James Joyce as modern. Those writers can be opposed to Donald Barthelme, D.M. Thomas, Grace Paley or William Gaddis, who are postmodern. Of course, it is hard to place with accuracy the *Nouveau Roman*, Jorge Luis Borges or Vladimir Nabokov *vis-à-vis* the two species; perhaps somewhere in the middle?

The artists Gilbert & George or the photographers Cindy Sherman and David LaChapelle[120] are frequently seen as postmodern. Cornel West mentions John Cage, Laurie Anderson, Philip Glass, Ishmael Reed, Barbara Kruger and Martha Rosler.[121] It is a *priori* less easy to determine who in pop or movies is postmodern, but some names come spontaneously to mind, such as the B52s and R.E.M., or Quentin Tarantino, Pedro Almodóvar,[122] Jim Jarmusch and David Lynch.

As for Madonna, almost all the academics who examine her call her postmodern at some point,[123] but generally without stating what they mean exactly. I felt the gap had to be filled; for as Connor writes, the postmodern condition, notably in popular culture, cannot be limited to a certain number of symptoms spotted in a work, but constitutes a "complex effect of the relationship between [...] practice and the theory that organizes, interprets and legitimates its forms."[124]

T W O

Desperately Seeking Stardom

Even when I was a little girl I knew I wanted the whole world to know who I was, to love me and be affected by me.[1]

— Madonna

The title of this second chapter, "Desperately Seeking Stardom," has already been used, notably by Ilene Rosenzweig[2] (I've also found "Desperately Seeking Fame," and many others). It obviously echoes *Desperately Seeking Susan* (Susan Seidelman, 1985), the only Madonna movie that was well received by all the critics. Beyond the allusion, there might very well have been some desperate element in the way Madonna did just about everything to reach stardom, a world stardom intelligently elaborated by a career woman, set on a power race that nothing seems to be able to stop.

Madonna is self-made. Blessed with limitless supplies of ambition, she gradually developed her mastery of different means of expression, taking what she needed anywhere she knew she could find it, and relying

26

mostly on visual rhetoric to spread her cult. I examine her strategies in this chapter. As Guy Debord has it, "spectacle is the material reconstruction of religious illusion."[3]

Now Madonna is everywhere, even in those places where she did not deliberately set out to go. As a genuine star she "belongs" to the public, which has its advantages and its disadvantages. She meets Morin's criteria: Nordic when she is blond and Anglo-Saxon, Mediterranean when she is dark-haired and suddenly remembers her Italian origins (or when she adopts a Hispanic persona), she is at the same time vamp, Great Prostitute, femme fatale, sex-symbol. At the center of a worldwide Madonna discourse, she reigns on the *société du spectacle*.

Personal and Methodic Construction

In the context of her self-construction, Madonna has been led to rewrite her life. I will first briefly sum up her beginnings in show business, then I'll examine the way she has erased or, on the contrary, highlighted certain aspects of her life and career.

Biographical Elements

A general outline of Madonna's biography will be enough, and I'll stick to the undisputed facts. Madonna Louise Veronica Ciccone was born on August 16, 1958, in Bay City, Michigan (near Detroit). Her family was Italian-American and she had many brothers and sisters. She was brought up in Pontiac and Rochester Hills, also near Detroit. She lost her mother — of French Canadian origin — at the age of five and a half.

At the age of sixteen, Madonna had a passion for dancing; she attended the dance classes of Christopher Flynn, who became her first gay friend.[4] After she got her diploma at Rochester Adams High, she obtained a grant to study dancing at the University of Michigan (Ann Arbor). However, she did not conform to the university spirit, and dreamed of stardom. Flynn, who also left for Ann Arbor, greatly influenced her. She said so in numerous interviews, reminiscing about their nights out in gay clubs, in which she discovered there were other universes than the one her Catholic upbringing had delimitated. He encouraged her to try her luck in New York, and she did, quickly leaving Ann Arbor. She arrived in Manhattan with very little money, and spent months "crashing with friends and living with boyfriends."[5] She managed to get Martha Graham's protégée, Pearl Lang, to recruit her in Alvin Ailey's famous dance school; she mixed with numerous gays, musicians, DJs, and tag-graffiti artists. She worked as a waitress, sold doughnuts, featured in a bad underground movie with a microscopic budget,[6] posed in the nude for photographers and art classes, and sang or played the drums in various bands such as The Breakfast Club, The Millionaires, Emmy, Modern Dance or The System. According to legend, she sometimes found her dinner in trash cans, or ate nothing but popcorn for days on end.

That New York period was interrupted for a few months by a stay in Paris, where she was feted by the producers of Patrick Hernandez, singer of the worldwide disco hit *Born to Be Alive*. Those two men, "the two Jeans," Jean van Lieu and Jean-Claude Pellerin, were particularly shocked when she rebelliously dropped them in spite of all the attentions they lavished on her. The precocity of her determination must be stressed. Madonna set out to mix with useful people, never hesitating to drop them when they did not serve her interests any longer. The manager Camille Barbone, the musicians and DJs Stephen Bray, Mark Kamins or Jellybean Benitez count among those early allies. The minute she arrived in New York she showed unflinching willpower, and an uncommon thirst for success. Her first proper single, *Everybody*, came out in April 1982. It was quite successful, as were the following two singles, but mostly on dance floors.

She had to wait until 1983 for her first real (radio) hit. Entitled *Holiday*, it went up the Top 20, then was followed by the album *Madonna*, which reached number eight in the charts. By 1984 Madonna had sold more than a million records. When the song *Like a Virgin* came out it remained number one for six weeks, a rare feat. Madonna's international stardom really began that year. Soon after the release of that huge hit, she was selling 75,000 records a day, and a T-shirt every six seconds. She once sold more than 17,000 concert tickets in half an hour.

First Rewrites

Golden age Hollywood might have been a dream factory, but Madonna is a one-woman dream factory. Before her first record she was not — according to traditional standards — particularly beautiful. When nude pictures of her resurfaced years later she appeared soft and plain; her hair was dark and drab, and her face uninspiring.[7] So she began by constructing her beauty. Constituting an autonomous star-system, a formidable one-woman stardom machine, she put to good use the lessons of bygone Hollywood studios. She knew which aspects of her past should be erased, and which should be emphasized. She notably minimized her father's earnings, turning him into a workman, when he was really an engineer; this in order to present herself initially as someone from the working classes rather than the middle classes.

In the movie *Truth or Dare* (Alek Keshishian, 1991), known in Europe as *In Bed with Madonna*, the highest grossing "documentary" in history,[8] Madonna evokes the painful loss of her mother and says that she had to fill the void somehow. This more or less seriously psychoanalytic dimension can only add to the myth.[9]

Some commentators harbor a grudge against Madonna for not having really grown up in an underprivileged family. Why be sorry she is not a working-class hero(ine), like John Lennon? So what if she lied? The question is not what she *is*, but what she *says*. Her discourse about her childhood is interesting as part and parcel of her personal construction. No one can seriously doubt that Madonna suffered from her mother's premature demise, but she may conceivably have rewritten its consequences to serve her career.

In the same way, she claims she considered the loss of her virginity "as a career move."[10] This is obviously a joke, but you only have to read her numerous biographies to realize that it is generally taken at face value, and thus partakes of the general rewriting of her past. She apparently trusted a certain Russell Long to undertake that career move in a 1966 Cadillac, in 1973, at age fourteen and a half. The latter has abundantly spoken to tabloids about it. What a remarkable claim to fame for him; was there ever a more interesting and pathetic example of reflected glory?[11]

So Madonna arranged her biography. She did not, however, reach the excesses of some singers, like the rapper Vanilla Ice. The latter, white as his name indicates, built a rocketing career in 1990 on huge fabrications: he claimed that he came from a tough ghetto where he had grown up with African Americans. He made it a point of honor to highlight his scars, mentioning some heroic street knife fight. His first album sold eight million copies. Then journalists discovered he had lied and his career plummeted. Madonna hired him, however, for her book *Sex*, as we'll see.

Madonna did not make the mistake of distorting truth to such an extent. No doubt some fans feel sorry they cannot trust the biographies, mostly "dubious Madonna cartoon-biographies."[12] It is likely, however, that these fans choose to believe in one version of the myth that pleases them, in exactly the same way most people do not question the sacred texts their religions are based on. We are dealing with fiction, not with lies. This work proposes to examine the Madonna fictions.

When evoking childhood memories, everyone more or less rewrites his past, including stars. When Madonna, the most famous woman in the world, mentions her childhood in interviews, it is easy to suppose that she says no more than what she deems profitable, and that she is perfectly aware of the weight of every word she utters. So when a biographer relates—as happens frequently—that this or that declaration of hers backfired, it shows tremendous naïveté. Madonna knows exactly what media storms she can trigger. When she narrates her first kiss, aged ten, with a certain Tommy, or tells how she began to rebel at the age of twelve, while collecting good grades at school; when she speaks of her first sexual games, before Russell Long, with girls her own age, whom she names, she knows exactly what she is doing. It is edifying to watch her in *Truth or Dare*, when she remembers how she used to masturbate with her childhood friend Moira McFarland. McFarland appears in the movie, is shamelessly exploited, and of course cannot deny Madonna's words: this is her only chance ever to grab a modicum of fame! To dodge the issue, she mentions drugs and alcohol, which account for gaps in her memory...

To come up with her first fictions, Madonna borrowed from different genres. Like a postmodern novelist who borrows from noir novels or science fiction, she used elements of rock, punk, funk, disco, and other styles. Her music is best defined as pop, although sometimes it could be called simply dance music. Some commentators, however, insist on calling it rock.[13] But hasn't her music always been too tongue-in-cheek to be called rock? True enough, her early (debatable) street credibility did rest on punkish or rock 'n' rolling attitudes, linked to her first persona.

That first persona is commonly referred to as Boy Toy, a nickname Madonna picked for herself. Promoted by the film *Desperately Seeking Susan*, that persona is very New York, very underground: she wears black leather and silver metal belts with buckles bearing the inscription Boy Toy,[14] superimposed heterogeneous necklaces, beads, crucifixes, cutoff gloves, black leather, black lace, dozens of cheap bracelets, and garish makeup.

That first persona is a fearless girl who displays her navel in a stomach that is not quite flat yet. A desire to provoke is associated to that image: these are the days when she keeps saying that the reason she likes crucifixes is because there is a naked man on them.

It is during that first period (1983-1985) that the much-discussed wannabe phenomenon developed. Many teenage girls wanted to emulate Madonna, or at least to look very much like her. Indeed, the star's look was then easy and cheap to copy. Some say that the wannabe phenomenon disappeared as Madonna and her fans grew up; I'd say there are now more subtle ways to be a wannabe (even for academics)...

So rebellion constitutes an essential part of the initial Madonna image, but she says herself that she "played the part" of the rebel;[15] for example, she tells how during her Parisian period she hung out with Vietnamese bikers, or North Africans, the better to underline the "ordinary racism" of French society: a rocker rebel must hang out with those most rejected by the dominant ideology and various father figures. This tendency is present throughout her work. Of course, she milks it more in her twenties than afterwards, as this type of teenage rebellion doesn't quite fit a maturing billionaire star.

Thus Madonna rewrites her youth, rewrites rock and punk, while the wannabes rewrite Madonna. In chapter 5 I'll come back to her borrowings from African American culture, but we may note already that if she pretended for a long time that she had grown up in downtown Detroit, rather than in a peaceful suburb, it was also to uphold one of her inventions, according to which she grew up listening to Tamla Motown artists.

Programmed Future

Madonna quickly decided that she would try her hand at the greatest number of artistic endeavors. Even inside each domain — singing for example, for which she is best-known — Madonna has programmed a methodic route, whose sometimes surprising turns nevertheless follow a logical career plan.[16]

Madonna's theatrical ventures are rarely mentioned. Her first play was David Rabe's *Goose and Tom-Tom*. It was an invitation-only affair and was only on for a week in 1986 at the Lincoln Center, performed for celebrities like Andy Warhol, Warren Beatty or Liza Minnelli. Madonna's partners were Sean Penn and Harvey Keitel (with whom she was to act again). They played gangsters, she played a gangster moll, as she would in *Dick Tracy* (Warren Beatty, 1990) a few years later. The play itself, most of the audience agreed, was extremely bad, but Griffin Dunne, for one, judged the performance of our actress favorably.[17] According to Mark Bego, she tried for her performance to resuscitate Judy Holliday in *Born Yesterday* (George Cukor, 1950):[18] a choice that can only be seen as postmodern.

Madonna then appeared on Broadway in David Mamet's *Speed-the-Plow*, during nearly five months in 1988. She got good and bad reviews. The New York *Daily News* titled one "No she can't act!" One night she couldn't stop giggling. It happened when Karen, the ambitious manipulative woman she played, reads a book about radiation, and is about to suggest to the character played by Joe Mantegna to adapt it for the screen. "It was a real mindfuck of a script," Madonna would later say. "Brilliant but confusing."[19]

One of Madonna's ambitions, characteristic of the postmodern, is to appear where she is not expected, to sail constantly from one art form to another. Theater was a challenge she wanted to take up. The Royale was packed throughout the duration of the run. This may be explained by the massive presence of Madonna fans, who for the most part had never set foot in a theater before. Indeed most of the audience did not really care about the play. They had paid to see Madonna in the flesh.

As every critic notes, the movie *Desperately Seeking Susan* was a decisive landmark in Madonna's career. Before *Evita* (Alan Parker, 1996), it may be seen as her only genuine movie success,[20] even if *Dick Tracy* and *A League of Their Own* (Penny Marshall, 1992) did not do badly, but without being perceived as Madonna vehicles in the way *Desperately Seeking Susan* was.[21] This comedy by Susan Seidelman is a feminist piece, inspired by a film that was the swan song of the French New Wave, *Céline et Julie vont en bateau* (Jacques Rivette, 1973).[22]

Matthew Rettenmund sums up the plot: a housewife named Roberta (Rosanna Arquette) who lives in a New Jersey suburb with her husband, "a cheesy hot-tub salesman," tries to overcome boredom by following a series of classifieds that a man addresses to a mysterious Susan (Madonna). When the man warns that he is "desperately seeking Susan," Roberta decides to go to the meeting place. "Roberta knows there is trouble, so she goes to the park bench in New York where the lovers are set to meet, only to suffer a konk on the head that leaves her thinking she is Susan. Mayhem ensues."[23]

The mayhem that ensues consists in a succession of extremely comic scenes which revolve around repeated identity confusions. Roberta is mostly motivated by curiosity and fascination — if not obsession. According to Roger Ebert, Rosanna Arquette and Madonna deploy two different kinds of seduction, and this is what makes the movie endearing.[24]

The late Pauline Kael, terror of moviemakers, who did not like the film, saw it as "set in the punk world," and found that there was no subtext in it. "This flatness can make your jaw fall open, but it seems to be accepted by the audience as New Wave postmodernism."[25] So Pauline Kael didn't care for the postmodern, but when she spoke of New Wave, was she thinking exclusively of the post-punk movements I referred to earlier, or was she punning, to show that she identified the tribute to Rivette? If so, how could she possibly assert that there was no subtext there? Not only does *Desperately Seeking Susan* find depth in its postmodern references and rich intertext, but it escapes platitudes through its fundamental questioning of sexuality, gender roles, and other fundamentals. Moreover, Kael certainly never attended a punk party, where people used to dance the pogo on broken beer bottles, or she wouldn't have equated the basically harmless universe Susan inhabits with the punk world — which is hard to define anyway.

Kael did concede: "Nobody comes through except Madonna, who comes through as Madonna (she moves regally, an indolent, trampy goddess)."[26] The two meanings of "trampy" are to be applied equally to Susan and Madonna's image in those days. Indeed, various commentators accounted for the success of the movie in a very simple manner: to them, Susan the dramatis persona is very little different from Madonna the realitatis femina. In her *I Hate Madonna Handbook*, Ilene Rosenzweig writes, for example:

> [Madonna] steals the show with a role that fits her like a fingerless glove: a gum-snapping vagabond who might have crawled out of a thrift shop explosion[...]. Some critics [...] have wagered that Madonna is not acting in the movie at all; that the only character she portrays in the film is her own.[27]

But isn't it naive to thus establish what Madonna might be like in "real life"? I would rather say for my part that Susan the persona borrows a lot from Madonna the persona then to be seen on stage and in videos. The nuance is capital. Kael and Rosenzweig do not steer clear of that naiveté when they think themselves capable of identifying Madonna the realitatis femina, the one that according to them "comes through" in *Desperately Seeking Susan*. They are neglecting one of the essential aspects of stardom, the amalgam I mention in chapter 1.

Rosenzweig quotes Madonna: "I thought I shared a lot with [my character].... She's a clever con artist and she doesn't let you know when you're being conned."[28]

Indeed, Madonna, at the very moment when she pretends she has many things in common with Susan, is mocking herself as well as those who do not see that her part in the movie is — precisely — just a part. Madonna is indeed a con artist, the irony of her comment highlights it. Like Susan, she cons everyone. She is constantly acting, and no journalist can claim that he knows the "real" Madonna. She warns, Susan "doesn't let you know when you're being conned," which also means, naturally, that she doesn't let you know when you're not. And the same is true of Madonna, obviously. So why should we think that she is more sincere when she says that she thought she shared a lot with Susan than at other times?

The critics who thought that Madonna had merely played herself in *Desperately Seeking Susan* may have changed their minds when they saw her radically change her look and behavior along the years that followed. Those reactions to the movie in 1985 did not, at any rate, prevent many newspapers and magazines from proclaiming that a star had been born, nor did they prevent Hollywood moguls from starting to woo Madonna.[29]

In *New York* magazine, David Denby describes the Madonna of *Desperately Seeking Susan* as "a coarse erotic object, [...] a caricature of the movie femmes fatales of the past."[30] I'll show later that rather than caricaturing the said femmes fatales, she rewrites them. It seems to me, however, that in *Desperately Seeking Susan*, she has not yet really begun the process. So strangely enough, Denby seems to be anticipating.

All the critics, at any rate, are aware of the "authority" of Madonna, mentioned in *The Village Voice* and *Films in Review*. The magazine *Variety* addresses "thinking women," feminists irritated by Madonna, telling them they ought to forget their prejudices: "Madonna not only turns in a rounded, interesting performance, but the whole picture reflects the fact that none of the producers, director, or writer is named Joe or Sam."

Indeed, *Desperately Seeking Susan* ridicules ordinary machos, celebrating a woman who rejects her bourgeois education to finally become independent, helped by Susan.[31] It's undeniably a feminist film (more on this in chapter 5). It contributed to the elaboration of Madonna the myth, for it illustrated the way she could help her (young female) fans assert their independence while also focusing on the seduction she could exert over men—far from the prefeminist clichés that reigned (and still reign) in other films in that respect. Susan is indeed totally free, as few movie female characters have ever been.[32]

As Pauline Kael noted, *Desperately Seeking Susan* also has aspects of a "rock video going poetic."[33] This is quite deliberate. Seidelman masters her product, aims it at a rather young audience, fed like her on rock and pop, an audience possibly keen on Madonna to begin with, but not exclusively.[34] When Susan meets up with Roberta's husband in a fashionable nightclub, the DJ plays Madonna's song *Get Into the Groove*. Inevitably, clips from the film were used as the promotional video for the song, an operation that was profitable to both. Susan dances on the dance floor to the beat of the song, which functions of course as a *mise en abyme*, but in no way ruins the diegesis. To conclude with *Desperately Seeking Susan* for the time being, I'll insist as *Variety* does on the fact that this film is the work of four women: two actresses, a scriptwriter and a filmmaker. *Céline et Julie vont en bateau* was on the other hand a man's film, which is enough to discredit it in the eyes of the most radical feminists. But critics like Julia Lesage showed that it too could of course be read as a feminist—if not lesbian—text. The playfulness of Rivette's film and of *Desperately Seeking Susan* (which both feature tacky magic shows in second rate nightclubs) is totally compatible with feminist preoccupations. Lesage sees in those films an empowerment of women viewers and a challenge to compulsory heterosexuality.[35]

Biographers have written at great length about the Boy Toy period that followed. The phrase "boy toy" mustn't be understood only in the sense of (female) toy for boys, even if this is obviously the first meaning that comes to mind. As used by Madonna, the phrase implies an ironic semantic reversal. In 1983 already, she played with signs. A boy toy — the phrase is sometimes used as synonymous with "toy boy"[36] — is also a gigolo (serving men or women). Moreover, if you consider that "boy toy" is constructed like the word "boyfriend," Madonna can only be seen as alluding to the way she plays with boys as much as to the way they might play with her, at least in their dreams. Madonna toys with her public.[37] Although the very idea of a sexy woman describing herself as a boy toy seems antifeminist, for Madonna it was clearly some kind of pun. During her early lean times, she tagged it on New York walls, when she didn't tag her name. Among other things, this nickname was devised to provoke mainstream feminists. She already showed back then that a woman could be a feminist without renouncing an exacerbated sexuality, a highly developed sense of humor and a great power of seduction.

What really matters at this stage is the raging winning instincts upholding a formidable capacity for work that Madonna displayed early in the day. Indeed, she is indefatigable: between 1983 and the birth of her daughter in 1996 she only went on holiday four times.[38] "A tough little lady starving in the East Village uncovers her belly button and grows into Madonna, the Material Girl."[39] This is how Jerome Charyn briefly but lucidly sums up those early years.

In some ways, Madonna is pop's William Blake: they are both devoted to mythopoeic creation. She would certainly endorse the words of the poet: "I must Create a System, or be enslav'd by another Man's."[40]

From Boy Toy to Material Girl to Blond Ambition to Spiritual Girl to Maternal Girl, Madonna has never ceased discovering and uncovering herself. She was not, as opposed to other celebrities, discovered by some producer or talent scout in some bar. That, too, makes her postmodern. She found in herself the stuff stars are made of, and worked hard to starify herself.

In bygone eras, it took decades or even centuries for a myth to develop, involving the agency of hundreds of people, of whole tribes. The Hollywood star system, modern, linked to the studio system, built its myths more rapidly. They — like the former — were founded on popular beliefs and needs; they were named Rudolph Valentino, Judy Garland, Joan Crawford, Bette Davis, and the like.

In the era of postmodern art, myths are self-created, even more rapidly than modern myth, and they come equipped with ironic distance. Madonna devised various means to construct her own myth; she borrowed from different ethnic groups, for example, or pushed sex, the universal weapon. Lisa Frank and Paul Smith write: "*Sex* offered us an unusual opportunity to examine the most basic terms of collective life — what else is there besides sex, race, capital, and power?"[41] The word "*Sex*" here refers to Madonna's book, and "us" to the writers of the collective book *Madonnarama*; but the sentence could just as easily sum up Madonna's strategy in general. She managed to establish her credentials because she made sure to stage the "most basic terms of collective life," in other words "sex, race, capital, and power." In the same way, myths, like those studied by Lévi-Strauss, not only provide reassuring explanations for natural phenomena and present some demiurge, but also stage the "most basic terms of collective life."

However, Madonna accomplished that *mise en scène* in a systematic manner, with a systematic ironic distance. She responds to the anxieties of the public, she stages them, sings about them, acts them out and plays with them. But her distance stops her from being just another artist with a message. In a Warholian way, Madonna is aware of everything that twentieth-century American (and to an impressive degree European[42]) popular culture produced before she came along. She is aware of the influence artists may exert on society, on other artists, on her; she knows how to exploit this knowledge to deploy her power over the public, the power of myth.

John Izod describes Madonna as a trickster.[43] He means trickster as in joke-playing god, magician, illusionist, shaman, not as in confidence trickster (although...), and he endeavors to study the Madonna archetypes in a Jungian way. There are parallels between the rocker and the shaman: a "traditional" rock concert functions as a mass, a gathering of the tribe around the medicine man. The visionary singer takes his audience to another universe, with the possible help of drugs, orchestrating a vast collective trance.[44] Laurence Coupe defined that type of shamanism in the case of Jim Morrison's career.[45] In the case of Madonna, the phenomenon is less immediately perceptible, for she maintains a greater distance between herself and the audience.[46]

Izod recalls that Jung, like Freud before him, was really more concerned with the male psyche, and that the trickster figures he examined were almost all male. Yet Madonna is a perfect trickster figure: like a trickster she "deceives," she never crops up where you expect her, and she shape-shifts constantly. She is inscribed in the collective unconscious, and her detractors sometimes associate the Madonna text to somber black magic practices. Izod wonders how Madonna can be situated *vis-à-vis* the seven classic goddesses who constitute a pantheon of archetypes derived from the original Great Goddess, recalling in passing that some of the latter's incarnations were recuperated by Marian cults (Madonna cults):

Demeter, Persephone, Hera, Hestia, Athena, Artemis, and mostly Aphrodite, the one who fits Madonna best. "Both Aphrodite and Madonna are tremendous forces for change; and this connects not only with their sexual but also their artistic fertility."[47] Trickster or goddess, ever-changing and source of change, Madonna masters her different strategies to perfection.

Madonna did create herself, and propelled herself to the top. Madonna's everywhere. As Greil Marcus has it, she is undeniably part of our culture. Wherever you look, you will find Madonna or a Madonna echo.[48]

Madonna is so much of a star that she faced a dilemma on Oscar night in 1991. Who could possibly escort her? She needed someone whose media omnipresence and wealth equaled hers. She found only Michael Jackson. He hasn't always been tender to her in interviews, but she was ready to forgive him. What she could not tolerate, on the other hand, was his look. All she managed to do was to make him wear white sequined clothes, matching her dress. She had even envisaged once to record an actual duet with him. But she would not appear in a video in his company if he didn't do something about his image. So she asked designers like Jean-Paul Gaultier to come up with sketches of a few outfits for him (some of which were published in magazines), to no avail.

Jean-Paul Gaultier and Madonna have a lot in common. They are both postmodern, the former being very much to fashion what the latter is to pop. Moreover, Madonna is equally accountable for some trends. The journalist Michael Pye nicknamed Madonna "the face that launched a thousand fashions."[49] To a large extent Madonna not only makes fashion, she is fashion. The *Vogue* editor Anna Wintour is convinced of this:

> She's a perfect example of how popular culture and street style now influence the world of fashion. Over the years, Madonna has been one of the most potent style setters of our time. She, just as much as Karl Lagerfeld, makes fashion happen.[50]

Such sartorial precision may appear futile, but it is not. The clothing of myth is just as capital as the basic narrative, it varies from one people to another, even when they are separated by only a few miles; the signs vary and the sense that is produced varies accordingly. And the postmodern is by definition very concerned with form. Clothes are to Madonna what linguistic games are to Thomas Pynchon. That uncanny pairing of stars at the Oscars was very widely commented upon in the media, as well as Madonna's failed attempt at revamping Michael Jackson. Even *she* has to renounce *some* ambitions.[51]

Ambitious Grammar

Every star needs an audience. No myth could exist without solid popular foundations. Madonna's initial ambition was to target teenagers, then she added ethnic minorities, and finally she showed a wish to grow old with her fans while addressing all possible audiences, except reactionaries. She remains true to her aesthetic and political choices, even if she means to sell a lot of records. Besides, she has always been able to rely on a lesbian and gay public, non-old-guard feminists, and postmodern academics.

Let us for a moment examine Madonna's ambitious grammar through the name of her tour *Blond Ambition*, a sophisticated figure of speech if ever there was any. It immediately strikes you as a hypallage, the adjective "blond" being generally applied to a person or to hair, but much more rarely to ambition. But are we talking about a one-shot ambition of Madonna's or about her ambition in general? "Ambition" may of course designate Madonna (metonymy), "blond" then becomes a sort of Homeric epithet.[52] However, "ambition" may also refer exclusively to the tour. Whichever way you interpret it, the phrase is catchy, like an advertising slogan. Needless to say, *Blond Ambition* echoes the set phrase "naked ambition," which fits Madonna marvelously.

Blond Ambition also echoes "blind ambition," which alludes to the incommensurability of Madonna's ambition, just as it may allude to the monocle she wears when she sings *Express Yourself*.[53] In the twenties, politicized lesbians (*mutatis mutandis*) displayed a monocle, to recognize each other and parody powerful men at the same time (bankers and managers and heads of family). Some surviving pictures are there to testify. So Madonna using such a prop signifies lesbianism and protests against patriarchy. "She is considered too ambitious, and therefore too much like a man," writes Susie Bright.[54] "Let's face it, if I weren't as talented as I'm ambitious, I'd be a gross monstrosity," said Madonna.[55]

But Madonna's avowed ambition is also to try her hand at every art form. Her artistic talents may not equal David Bowie's, but she strives to multiply her fields of intervention, as we have seen, and is no less postmodern than the ambitious Bowie, notably in the way she blurs genres and genders.

As with Madonna, it is pointless to try and discover some true identity behind Bowie's personae. One of the key differences between the two is that some of Bowie's incarnations had little human attributes left. Like Grace Jones, he was an alien or an android for a long time, before becoming human again. On the contrary, Madonna's always remained human, despite her self-constructed divinity. She notably never stopped being equipped with visible human sexuality, throughout her successive personae.

Pat Kane comments upon the introduction of Bowie on Wall Street as a stock market asset:

> With the floatation of his name as a corporate entity on the New York Stock Exchange, Bowie has become even more of an abstracted "earthling" than ever before.[56]

By fragmenting himself into so many stock market shares, Bowie was again far ahead of his contemporaries. It is difficult to imagine a more postmodern move. He is the first, but of course not the last.[57] Bowie has often been criticized for his coldness. Andrew Smith states that Bowie is prone to self-mythologizing, and then evokes his huge influence in the pop world, before writing that he is "unable to locate the center of his own being, or to stop watching himself from the outside." [58]

Madonna has been influenced by Bowie, and like Bowie, she now greatly influences others. She may also easily be said to be incapable of locating the center of her own being or to stop watching herself from the outside. Some speak of a centerless being, others of an empty core. Bowie used his fractured identity the better to soak in the zeitgeist, as well as absorb the successes of previous decades that seemed to suit his art. Madonna did the same. Madonna, like him, is a show(wo)man of her selves.[59] Such postmodern practices lead some critics to speak of her Bowie-like coldness and inhuman ambition, but she replies:

> It's all just part of the view the media like to have of me. That I'm not a human being. That I don't have any feelings, and don't really care for people. That I'm just ambitious, cold and calculating.... It's all just part of the image that unhappy people like to construct for me.[60]

This may sound like a complaint, but Madonna is really quite unhampered by such media constructions, as they are part and parcel of the global Madonnology[61] I'll describe later.

In spite of the social impact of her work, Madonna rarely claimed that she wanted to do anything more than entertain. "Girls just wanna have fun."

The "blond" in *Blond Ambition* speaks volumes. It echoes the very American notion that blondes have more fun. It evokes a dozen Golden Age Hollywood platinum blondes. Camille Paglia recalls in an interview: "The woman who really started all this in Hollywood was Jean Harlow, with that platinum blonde look which was so incredibly unnatural. With her it was associated with being a harlot — she was mimicking the slouchy, louche look of someone who's a machine for pleasure."[62] Those blondes are rarely real blondes, and "blondes have more fun" suggests that a woman will enjoy life more fully if she bleaches her hair, but also that she will give more pleasure to others (men, generally). When you visit Los Angeles these days, you are amazed by the number of blond(e)s you see. *Blond Ambition* also alludes to *Gentlemen Prefer Blondes* (Howard Hawks, 1953), that Madonna rewrote for the video *Material Girl.* Her *Blond Ambition* sometimes even calls to mind kitsch Las Vegas showgirls.[63]

With her usual postmodern sense of irony and self-derision, Madonna points to her own ambition and her own recipes; she ostensibly and mockingly confesses that, yes, she does frequently resort to peroxide, giving in to the bleaching rites in order to favor her ascension. She plays with clichés, and nobody should be fooled. Just look at the way she repeatedly appeared as a brunette before and after that tour, or better still, the way she has sometimes appeared in public exhibiting long and unaesthetic dark roots. That is a way of commenting upon her episodic blondness, signifying that her popularity does not depend on it, that she is not the prisoner (as perhaps some other past or present stars) of such gross concessions to beauty criteria imposed by a macho society. Having reached mythic statute, nothing can harm her significantly anyway; she uses stereotypes without being ruled by them. She recently commented upon this again in her 2001 *Drowned World* tour, sporting for some songs a raven black wig that hid her platinum blond hair.

With *Blond Ambition*, Madonna was of course toying with the bimbo concept. A bimbo is not particularly intelligent, a bimbo is young, sexy, good-looking. She is blond, and often — not systematically — escorted by an older and richer man, who ordinarily uses her for sex and status. "Bimbo" is often seen as a synonym of "dumb blonde," another tradition linked to sexual promiscuity and hair bleach. Dumb blonde jokes come to mind, of course. In *Dangerous Game* (Abel Ferrara, 1993) Madonna tells dumb blonde jokes. Madonna enjoys (de)constructing bimbo folklore. Feminists tend to see bimbos as men's creation, deeming that if society ever stopped being founded on phallocentric concerns, bimbos would disappear. Their very existence proves that the feminist fight is far from over. So parodying bimbos is of course a feminist move on Madonna's part: "I may be dressing like the traditional bimbo, whatever, but I'm in charge, and isn't that what feminism is all about ... equality for men and women?"[64] But maybe she means to show in addition that women are also entitled to be stupid: they will only be able to say they have conquered equality the day when incompetent women can get high responsibility jobs.[65] In the thirties, Marlene Dietrich already used blondness with irony.

In the now classic *Black Looks: Race and Representation*, bell hooks quotes Julie Burchill, who remarked that the best movie blondes have always been brunettes and asked what this said about racial purity. Then hooks evokes the desire of the non-blonde Other for "those characteristics that are seen as the quintessential markers of racial aesthetic superiority that perpetuate and uphold white supremacy." This leads her to observe:

> In this sense Madonna has much in common with the masses of black women who suffer from internalized racism [...]. Madonna often recalls that she [...] saw herself as ugly, as outside the mainstream beauty standard. And indeed what some of us like about her is the way she deconstructs the myth of "natural" white girl beauty by exposing the extent to which it can be and is usually artificially constructed and maintained. She mocks the conventional racist-defined beauty ideal even as she rigorously strives to embody it.[66]

Madonna's blond ambition is also to highlight with irony her postmodern deconstruction of the classic blond beauty myth, which is undeniably linked to a subterranean racist discourse. At the same time, she appropriates it to uphold her own myth. The fact that she is originally rather plain (in the sense the white dominant culture gives to the adjective), just like Mae West, Jean Harlow, and others, obviously reinforces the process. It is all the better if she makes a political statement — in passing — but that isn't her principal aim.

Let's ponder for a moment the more or less deep gap that cuts Madonna off from her analysts. One of them, Andrew O'Hagan, writes:

> Many cultural commentators and academics who oppose censorship have reasoned that "the enemy of my enemy is my friend." This has allowed them to look on Madonna as a heroic opponent of the American establishment's cultural and political authoritarianism. Following from this, Madonna's champions now demand that we understand her as political activist and cultural demon, as defender of freedom and the polymorphously perverse.[67]

It is a bit excessive to imply that the admiration numerous academics feel for Madonna is the result of a common hostility to censors. Admittedly, though, most of her defenders are indeed opposed to censorship (traditional censorship and new feminist censorship — see chapter 5). Of course Madonna attracts the enemies of censorship, but to suppose that they are interested in her only because of their common enemy is simplistic, reductive and insulting. Other celebrities have opposed the establishment without fuelling so much university writing, like Roseanne Barr or Sinead O'Connor.

On the other hand, it is easy to agree with O'Hagan when he says that Madonna is no political activist. But why should we begrudge her the "cultural demon" label? Doesn't she manifest a radicalism that is potentially subversive in the way she defends freedom and alternative sexual orientations, if not the polymorphously perverse? According to O'Hagan, she is mostly opportunistic, and makes a lot of money, unscrupulously pillaging popular culture.[68] So what's wrong with that exactly? O'Hagan is no fan of the postmodern, as he states himself. What he calls Madonna's "superficiality" can be interpreted positively with postmodern aesthetic criteria.

Madonna's blond ambition is not militant. She doesn't claim that she is occupying some strategic place in some cultural resistance movement, even if her art does offer all kinds of spaces of resistance.

O'Hagan goes as far as to say: "Whether she likes it or not, [Madonna] is the dominant culture."[69] Well, it all depends on what you call dominant culture. Madonna may sell huge amounts of records, but she remains rejected by millions of Americans on whose moral values she tramples. Anyway, her ambition is to be a star, a myth, and get rich along the way. She was asked in 1984: "What do you really want to do when you grow up?"[70] Rule the world was her answer.

I established in chapter 1 the fact that many theorists associate the postmodern with capitalism or conservatism. Expressing their reproaches, people like Habermas polarized the discussion in a Manichean way and gave the debate an overly passionate tone.[71] Well, this Manichean feud is reflected in Madonna studies, as well as in the media that follow her career. Many people write about Madonna as a greedy inauthentic something or other. So Madonna is a capitalist. So Madonna likes money. So Madonna means materialism. You don't say. And, by the way, isn't that true of anyone pursuing a show business career?

Show Business and Materialism

In her second album, *Like a Virgin* (1984), Madonna creates her own grammar. Her song *Material Girl* illustrates this. *A priori*, the punctilious English teacher sees in that title a double mistake. Judging by the lyrics and the video, we are dealing here with someone who has "the tendency to be more concerned with material than with spiritual or intellectual goals or values" (Webster's). So Madonna should sing "Materialistic Girl." Admittedly, the noun "materialist" is more and more used as an adjective in the States, in lieu of "materialistic," but "material" retains quite another meaning. Curiously, this did not strike the handful of academics who analyzed the song as odd in any way. Not only has Material Girl become another name for Madonna, like Blue Angel for Dietrich, but Material Girl also designates a certain type of liberated woman these days. Clearly enough, choosing "Materialistic Girl" would have posed problems of versification for Madonna and for Peter Brown, who wrote the song. But isn't that Material Girl precisely a girl who is tangible, who may be touched (first meaning of "material")? As for the second meaning of "material" (important, essential, pertinent — as opposed to "immaterial"), it also fits Madonna. So the apparent mistake is really nothing but poetic license, allowing the polysemy, as the lyrics of the song confirm: Madonna is the woman you desire, but also the woman you must respect, otherwise she won't stay around. She is a Material Girl who must be recognized for what she is: an independent, self-made woman who takes initiatives. This is another aspect of her basic feminism, evidently.

Madonna implies in *Material Girl* that she is materialistic only because we live in a materialistic world.

The Mary Lambert *Material Girl* video, like most of Madonna's videos, is at the same time an exegesis and a critique of the lyrics and the singer. Madonna wouldn't be Madonna without the tremendous success of pop videos and MTV, obviously. *Material Girl* is a pastiche of the *Diamonds Are a Girl's Best Friend* scene in the movie *Gentlemen Prefer Blondes*, itself already filled with irony. I'll come back to it when I look at the Marilyn Monroe connection in chapter 4. For the time being, I mean to concentrate on the apparent contradiction between the two languages that are deployed: words and pictures.[72]

Two men in one of the screening rooms of a Hollywood studio are watching a rush. On the screen, an actress played by Madonna sings and dances to *Material Girl*, dressed like Marilyn Monroe in the *Diamonds Are a Girl's Best Friend* scene. One of the men, played by Keith Carradine, falls in love (with the image? with the woman behind the image? with Madonna behind the woman behind the image?). His gaze expresses immediate passion.

This man is a director or a producer, he's rich. But jewels are useless, and he only manages to win the actress when he comes to fetch her with an old pickup truck he buys from a peasant and a bunch of daisies. So the Material Girl is not as material(istic) as all that? But can we suppose for one second that in the meantime her new date donated his fortune to some charity organization?

At the beginning of the video, the Keith Carradine character tells his employee: "She's fantastic, I knew she'd be a star." His employee answers: "She could be. She could be great. She could be a major star." The producer then concludes: "She *is* a star, George." Thus Madonna plays, in

every sense of the verb, while proclaiming her stardom, the better to reinforce it, and all the time ironically alluding to the links between stardom
and wealth.

When she sang *Material Girl* during the *Blond Ambition* Tour,
Madonna replaced the words "experience has made me rich" with "experience has made me a bitch." At this point she produced dollar bills out
of her corsage and threw them up in the air. But the game didn't end there:
a few dollar bills fell among the audience, and the spectators who were
lucky or pugnacious enough to grab one found that they bear Madonna's
face. What does this mean? Madonna, a mother among the fathers of the
nation? Madonna the goddess competing with the dollar god? Madonna
so rich that she can be equated with the dollar? Whichever it is, Madonna's
wealth is an element of the myth. Inevitably, those bills have now reached
a value that far surpasses that of the George Washington bills, which also
functions as a comment on Madonna's stardom.

Visual Language

The pop critic Sacha Reins writes: "Madonna masters her image to
perfection. Or her images. She has learned to manipulate crowds with
mere details."[73] That manipulation is the key to her success. As Martine
Trittoléno says: "Her radical conception is entirely based on a redistribution of power. The artist is no more the manipulated interpreter, but the
chief manipulator [...]. Through her, a new image of glamour has risen,
that is a power phenomenon."[74] This is what we will see now.

Videos. Madonna's videos[75] are abundantly commented upon in the
generalist press as much as in the specialized press. They are pulled apart,
blamed or praised, often by writers who neglect the lyrics and the music
altogether. Of course, Madonna relies on this to maintain herself at the
top.

Videos are postmodern *par excellence.*[76] Their length and function
partly explain this. They are called upon by some critics to prove how
interesting the postmodern is, by others to illustrate its vacuity. Indeed
they may be classified, broadly, in two categories. There are those — the
majority, let's face it — that methodlessly pile up overexploited clichés,
playing into the hands of the enemies of the postmodern. And then there
are videos that are directed by masters of the medium, like Jean-Baptiste
Mondino, Jean-Paul Goude, Herb Ritts or Julian Temple. Working for
people like David Bowie and Madonna, such directors intelligently illustrate the lyrics of the songs, or add meaning to them, when they don't
deliberately contradict them, or add a complementary diegesis.

Cherish. In the Herb Ritts *Cherish* video, Madonna plays in the surf with mermen and a merchild, echoing Deborah Kerr in *From Here to Eternity* (Fred Zinnemann, 1953) — already evoked by Bowie in his *China Girl* video (1983). The mermen are beautiful models whose legs have been encased in delightful fishtails; one of them is Tony Ward, one of Madonna's ex-boyfriends.[77] In a parody of *Splash* (Ron Howard, 1984) Madonna the human falls in love with a merman.

Bette Midler has abundantly used the mermaid-in-a-wheelchair (Delores DeLago) motif in her shows.[78] There is in *Cherish* less humor and more aesthetic concern, but Madonna has definitely been influenced by the Divine Miss M. Of course the video alludes to the well-known Andersen tale *The Little Mermaid*. *Splash* reversed the tale in a vaguely feminist way, inasmuch as the man followed the mermaid in the ocean, developing an underwater breathing faculty. Madonna reverses the situation differently: a merman follows a woman and forsakes the ocean. He tears himself away from his original milieu. Like Andersen's mermaid, he has modified his respiratory capacities and turned — through the power of love — his fishtail into a pair of legs, so as to stay with Madonna, a human who is sufficiently lovable, in the strongest sense, to justify such a sacrifice.

This could seem very innocent if Madonna was not playfully discoursing about sexuality in the subtext. No sexual organs seem to break the line of the mermen's scales. Are their submarine companions provided with a uterus? Do they lay eggs? How are they impregnated? Do they reproduce like fish? Or do merpeople reproduce without sexuality, according to the same magical principles that rule their remarkable ability to transform their bodies? In which case Madonna, inspiring passion in a merman, allows him to discover sexuality and lose his innocence; thus she remains true to her corrupter image. The true mermaid (siren) is Madonna, she debauches men; leads them astray, seduces them. She charms them with her singing voice, like the dangerous mermaids of maritime myths and Homer. A Hollywood Lorelei, Madonna makes men go overboard. Doesn't one of the companies she controls bear the name Siren? She once said: "Some people would say that I hate men and that I like to do things to take power away from them, but you don't have to get that analytical."[79]

Open Your Heart. The *Open Your Heart* video[80] was banned on some television channels, and even MTV nearly refused to broadcast it. It caused an avalanche of complaints from various feminist and moral movements, perfectly timed as it was with the anti-porn campaign that was raging in the U.S.[81] Truly enough, some feminists, reading the *Open Your Heart* video at face-value, accused Madonna of setting back history. One of the reproaches she faces is that she promoted the return of bustiers and corsets. This is how Christopher Andersen describes the video:

> Surrounded by a Felliniesque[82] assortment of voyeurs gazing at her from windowed booths, the bustier-clad Madonna struts, prances, and slithers her way through a sufficiently suggestive routine. For added measure, the video ends with her kissing a twelve-year-old boy full on the mouth, then happily skipping off with him into the sunset.[83]

Ilene Rosenzweig writes that she "lasciviously" kisses a child.[84] It begins with a traveling over the gigantic peep-show sign, the reproduction of a Tamara de Lempicka showing three women in the nude. The central woman's nipples have been replaced by lightbulbs. This peep-show establishment is located in a suburb and reminiscent of *Paris, Texas* (Wim Wenders, 1984). Under the sign is the old boss in a ticket booth. A twelve-year-old boy (Felix Howard) wearing a hat and suit stands on his toes at the booth but the old man won't let him in. There are pictures of very fifties-looking pinup girls on the walls. Their legs are crossed and opaque rectangles hide their breasts. There's a picture of Madonna among them, but it shows no more than her face. The rest of the video consists in a succession of short scenes: the boy outside, Madonna in the peep-show, the "audience," the boy again, etc. Regularly a curtain rises or comes down behind a glass partition, allowing the viewer to suppose that the "spectator" has just put another coin in the slot. Madonna begins her show with a raven black wig (similar to her natural hair color), but she rapidly takes it off to reveal her (bleached) platinum blond hair, thus deconstructing the artifice of striptease,[85] as well as those of her own creation, on multiple levels.

In one of the booths, two gorgeous twins, navy officers, sit quietly, locked in a tender embrace; there is an ordinary middle-aged man in a suit in the second booth; and in the third booth there is an overweight man with huge cheeks and a moustache, wearing a particularly vulgar print jacket. In the fourth booth, a young laughing man in a cowboy shirt and ridiculous bracelets takes pictures of Madonna with a cheap camera. In the fifth booth, a young dreadlocked man in a white shirt and waistcoat shakes his head; in the sixth a man in a striped shirt observes Madonna and takes notes. He may be a journalist, but is more probably an academic. In the seventh booth, an old alcoholic with a ravaged face, wearing a loud checked jacket, drops his denture in a glass. In the eighth booth there is a long-haired man with mismatched gloves who protects his face with his arms. In the ninth booth, there is a short-haired woman, clearly coded as lesbian, who's wearing a jacket with embroidered lapels, a white shirt, and a tie.

There are four other men, elegant, in booths too, but they are made of wood (reproductions of paintings by Tamara de Lempicka). Whereas Madonna, in a bustier, spike heels and fishnets dances around a chair à la Marlene Dietrich in *The Blue Angel* via Liza Minnelli in *Cabaret* (Bob Fosse, 1972) under the gaze of those fourteen "voyeurs," the boy closely examines the pictures outside. Madonna's breasts are adorned with classic stripper props: tassels[86] that whirl around.[87]

Toward the end of the video, Madonna takes off her two long gloves, evoking Rita Hayworth in *Gilda* (Charles Vidor, 1946), and points at one of the painted men, as if her finger were a gun; the painting collapses and she blows on her finger. The old boss sleeps in his booth whereas the little boy looks at himself in the mirror and dances. He rolls up one of the legs of his pants to exhibit a white calf, imitating a stripper. At the end, one of the men straightens up his tie (as if he had just put his clothes back on), the man with the huge cheeks twists the handkerchief he had used to wipe his glasses (then presumably his sweat or sperm), the old man with the denture knocks on the window; and the woman rests, leaning sideways against the glass screen, smoking a cigarette. Madonna comes out; she has traded her costume for a suit identical to the boy's; her hair under her hat is wet and disheveled, contrasting with the very soigné hairdo of the preceding pictures (she has supposedly showered). She looks like a (young) boy, indeed she looks like the little boy who has been waiting for her and whom she kisses on the lips. They then stroll off in the sunrise, reminiscent of Charlie Chaplin and Jack Coogan in *The Kid* (Charlie Chaplin, 1921), as the old boss chases them, shouting (the words are written on the screen): "*Ritorna ... Ritorna ... Madonna ... Abbiamo ancora bisogno di te.*" Of course this is a pun, "Madonna" can stand for the name of the quitting stripper or for the Virgin Mary, in the traditional Italian interjection.[88]

Open Your Heart is the first Madonna video that features gay imagery. The two sailors signify gay *and* incestuous relations, finding either an alibi or added spice to their own erotic games in the peepshow; as for the lesbian, "in male drag," to quote Rettenmund,[89] she has clearly found satisfaction in the spectacle, smoking a traditional after-sex cigarette, even if the sex act has been mostly visual. Steven Drukman speaks of a "lesbian gaze seemingly sated."[90]

What seems to have shocked people most, however, is the ambiguity of "Madonna's" relationship with the "underage" boy. The kiss seems rather chaste to me, even if it is "full on the mouth." It is a kiss that a mother and son could exchange, or a sister and brother. Lisa A. Lewis speaks of the innocence of the boy, and tends to see his interest in the show as "pre-sexual." Alternatively it is possible to consider this love between two young people as a very innocent kind of puppy love, contrasting with the libidinous preoccupations of the peep-show voyeurs. Whatever the case may be, this video raises more issues about sex between adults of all genders and pornography than about pedophilia. Camille Paglia calls it a "brilliantly mimed psychodrama of the interconnections between art and pornography, love and lust."[91]

The visuals of *Open Your Heart* generated many comments among musical critics and feminists. The musicologist Susan McClary writes:

> The leering patrons are rendered pathetic and grotesque [...], the usual power relationship between the voyeuristic male gaze and object is destabilized [...]. The video is risky, because for all those who have reduced [Madonna] to a "porn queen in heat,"[92] there she is: embodying that image to the max.[93]

For her part, the feminist Shelagh Young deems that Madonna teaches women in "this parody of a classic pornographic peepshow" that their sexuality need not be passive and powerless:

> When Madonna confidently returns the fetishist's gaze while wearing his favorite sexual accessories, she reveals herself to be in the possession of knowledge: she knows because she has looked and is now looking back.[94]

Lisa A. Lewis dwells on the resemblance between "Madonna" and the little boy whom she finds is inscribed in a questioning of female spectacle rather than male spectacle.[95] In the same line of thought, Rettenmund has probably best perceived the true implications of the peep-show and the relationship between the boy and the stripper:

> The boy falls in love with the apparent glamour of the stripper's life [...]. Though there were indignant whispers that the video pushed pedophilia at the time, it's pretty clear that the boy-child is heroine-worshipping the stripper—coveting her feminine allure, even—a phase common in boys. That the stripper's "real" persona is that of an androgyny rather than a siren only underscores the false allure of the strip show and the artifice of performance as opposed to the genuine feelings of the boy.[96]

Open Your Heart means to question the stereotypes that proliferate in American society as far as pornography, homosexuality and gender are concerned. It raises many different issues—detailed later—that have to do with Madonna's postmodern feminism (which is often mistaken for non-feminism, or worse, antifeminism).

Justify My Love. As for the *Justify My Love* video, also shot by Jean-Baptiste Mondino, banned on MTV and sold as a video single (the first in history), I'll merely describe it.[97] We'll see that its many obvious implications confirm a great deal of the aspects of Madonna's practices that are discussed throughout this book.

In this succession of strong black and white images, sexual scenes alternate with shots of a very camp African American dancer. He is wearing numerous earrings, and his nails are prolonged by blunt blades that evoke a witch as much as an Asian folk dancer. He performs a kind of slow and very stylized voguing (further addressed in chapter 4) that seems to comment on the action of the video. In the beginning, a very blond Madonna walks down a corridor (Royal Monceau hotel in Paris) in a raincoat and spike heels, carrying a suitcase. She brings her hand to her forehead. Has she got a headache? Does she want to shield her face from the light? She sashays past a few open doors, allowing us to see, in succession:

- A dark-haired bare-chested woman wearing necklaces and gloves, standing at the entrance of a room.
- A very young man, extremely thin, bare-chested, long-haired, wearing a crucifix around his neck, sitting on a bed. The suspenders of his pants are down on his hips.
- A man wearing a shirt and black vinyl pants behind a woman in a black leather corset and stockings. He seems to be busy tightening his companion's corset, pulling on the laces.
- A woman in a black bustier. Her face and lower legs cannot be seen. Her hips are gyrating.
- Madonna stops walking, leans against the corridor wall and starts singing. A man in a black suit comes out of a room and walks toward her. It's Tony Ward again. Madonna squats and shows off her underwear underneath her raincoat, then her shoulders. She strokes her thighs as the man draws near. He stands in front of her; she gets up, caressing him, and kisses him.
- Then they are filmed in a room (or maybe a succession of rooms, it is hard to tell), along with other characters. Madonna indulges in several erotic games with Tony Ward, barely avoiding the X-rating guillotine. She also disports herself with a heavily made-up and slightly androgynous woman who kisses her on the lips as Ward watches. His muscular torso is highlighted with tattoos, jewels and crucifixes. All sorts of other individuals (men and women in and out of drag) can be seen engaging in erotic exchanges along different patterns. A creature who has hailed straight out of *Nightporter* (Liliana Cavani, 1974), evocative of Charlotte Rampling, with short hair, cap and suspenders on naked breasts, takes on Tony Ward, who has donned a harness which is typical of sadomasochistic imagery. Madonna, wearing fewer and fewer clothes, ends up straddling

Ward (she's on top). The fun is interrupted (at least for the viewer) by a close shot of a Christ hanging on the wall.

• Toward the end, a woman with a painted moustache paints one on another woman. Behind them, Madonna bursts out laughing. Tony Ward, exhausted, crashed in a sofa, holds out his hand as if he were saying to her: "Don't go." She finishes getting dressed in the corridor and starts running joyfully. She laughs and gestures in a way that can only be interpreted as meaning something like: "Oh my God, I am so naughty!" On the screen appear the words: "Poor is the man whose pleasures depend on the permission of another."

Videos are not Madonna's only TV appearances, however, there are also interviews and talk-shows. It is said that on such occasions, so as to fully master her image, she insists on checking the position of each camera, and tyrannizes the makeup people; but she does her lips herself, it would seem.

Photographs. Madonna's visual rhetoric is also deployed in photographs. She is one of the five most photographed women in the world. The possibilities offered by the global village have never been so astutely exploited. When she poses for a photographer, she knows that the pictures will rapidly be circulated all over the planet, from one magazine to another, from one press agency to another, sometimes pirated. Then of course Internet fan sites will offer scans. It is frustrating for the fan or researcher, who avidly acquires German, Italian, Spanish, American, French, Australian or British magazines, lured by the covers, only to realize that he is only buying the same images, reproduced *ad infinitum*, along a totally Warholian postmodern mode. Disappointed, he then reads the accompanying article or interview, but it is merely the nth translation of an original American text. When Madonna grants a press conference, hundreds of journalists publish the same questions and answers as if each of them were their author.

Paparazzi photographs also circulate around the world. They are less numerous than those approved by Madonna, a rather rare occurrence in show business (at least they were until 1999, for 2000 and 2001 saw a tremendous clutter of paparazzi Madonna pictures in the tabloids). In 1996, the most expensive paparazzi efforts were shots of supermodels, the Monaco Grimaldi family, Michael Jackson, Princess Diana, and Madonna. In 1997, pictures of Lourdes Maria were even more expensive than pictures of her mother, breaking records.

Like some bygone stars, Madonna has ambiguous relationships with paparazzi. As Vinnie Zuffante, one of the most eager representatives of the profession, inelegantly puts it, "she's a publicity whore."[98] Mark Bego explains Madonna's ambivalent attitude in this respect. He shows that she views them as a necessary evil, but finds they can be a pain in the neck in certain circumstances.[99] During her marriage to Sean Penn the paparazzi who hounded her were often assaulted by the angry actor. For her part, she freely admits that she has tried to establish some sort of profitable arrangement with paparazzi. They are part of the general Madonnology, they bring a parallel visual discourse that complements the one Madonna spreads. Their snapshots are sold to tabloids, whose readers dream of the lives of the rich and famous. In this respect, a double identification process is at work. Consuming glamorous pictures at the movies and in *Vanity Fair*, they can fantasize that they are equally glamorous. But they also need the pictures of the *National Enquirer*, which show stars in unflattering postures, ludicrous getups or extremely banal domestic situations: the stars are mere human beings after all, just like them, and not gods.

This process functions particularly well when it comes to Madonna, who as we have seen is not very beautiful *au naturel*. When Princess Diana died in 1997, the world realized just which peaks of indignity could be reached when paparazzi compete in pugnacity, and Madonna was among the first who reacted publicly against Diana's persecution.

Many commentators say that the way paparazzi humanize stars (albeit against their will) is characteristic of post golden age Hollywood.[100] In fact the same sort of thing took place in the old days, but the identification process did not deploy itself in quite the same way, and the worship is more ambiguous today.

The photographs I discuss below are not the work of paparazzi, they are conceived by Madonna as an integral part of her work, and they are often touched up. They are due to celebrated photographers such as Bert Stern, Matthew Rolston, Mario Testino, Helmut Newton, Francesco Scavullo, and especially Jean-Baptiste Mondino, Bruce Weber, Steven Meisel and Herb Ritts.

When a Madonna record or movie comes out, or when a Madonna tour begins, photographs bloom in magazines (no publication is ruled out); this is a typical promotional move. What is less typical, however, is that each of the pictures can function as a product *per se*, as each of the pictures is loaded with signs that beg for analysis. Every pose, every item of clothing, every accessory is planned by Madonna to signify.

The Mirror. Bruce Weber's picture of Madonna kissing her reflection in a dressing-room mirror exposes the narcissism of stars in general and of Madonna in particular, as well as the platinum blondness of the seductress. But it also operates a reversal of a typical situation. The classic sexual object becomes feminist subject. This questioning of the heterosexual male gaze[101] is a habit of Madonna's. In this picture she seems not to care about the gaze-desire of the man; she has of course been looking at herself for a while before kissing the mirror, she is the subject of the gaze, the object of her own gaze, a female gaze. She is also subject and object of her narcissistic desire.

Yet, if she does offer an identification model or a support for lesbian desire to the female readers of the magazine in which the photo is published, she will also be looked at by heterosexual men, who may "consume" her as a dual object: Madonna and her double. It is common knowledge that one of the favorite erotic spectacles of heterosexual men who buy pornography is that of two women engaged in intercourse. As for gays (see chapter 3), they can only rejoice at the sight of such a *mise en scène* of the star, the gay icon admiring herself the way gays admire her, piling up artifices in front of her mirror before kissing her own lips, pleased with the result of her preparation. Drag queens (see chapter 4), for their part, will enjoy seeing the star in the process of self-creation: Madonna has just made her face up, all the cosmetics over which she's leaning prove it. In other words, she has just painted over her face the features of the persona she's about to incarnate, reminding us that all gender is constructed, that the signs of her femininity are but a sum of manufactured spare parts that drag queens may use just as profitably. Madonna is in a dressing room, so she is coded as showwoman, and not *realitatis femina*. Spreading this picture around the globe, Madonna flaunts her postmodern practices.

All Access. Steven Meisel's photograph *All Access* was used to promote different Madonna products and was reproduced frequently over a period of two years in literally hundreds of magazines. Madonna is standing, seen from the back, in a Greek statue pose. She's wearing a pink curtain-like skirt. The zipper is down, showing off the top of her buttocks. She's holding up her platinum blond hair. On her naked back, a trap door has been drawn, tattoo style; it has a little handle and bears the inscription ALL ACCESS. Madonna's shadow on the pink wall is very marked. The photo looks a bit like a René Magritte painting.

In the context of the promotion of the movie *Truth or Dare* on video, this photo seems to indicate that Madonna allows total access to the viewers.[102] But access to what? Does this trap on her back lead to her heart? Are the viewers invited to examine her feelings? Or her body? There is no trap on her skull permitting an observation of her most intimate thoughts. If her body is what's at stake here, she does show (dis-play) a lot of it in the movie. We'll see that as she unveils herself she dissimulates more than ever, and that the movie is but another Madonna fiction. *That* Madonna is in no way more "real" than her shadow, which for all you know might be more "material" than she ever was. Doesn't the postmodern constantly remind us that everything is but representation? That it is naïve to suppose that we may reach the profound nature of things?

In the context of the promotion of the book *Sex*, the picture clearly points out that the reader will have access not only to the body of Madonna (or to its image, at any rate), but also to all her fantasies, as this is the way the book was peddled. The French magazine *Lui* (similar to *Playboy*) chose this picture for its April 1992 cover. Next to the half-naked body were the catching words "Madonna X-rated."

Exhibiting this trap door on her back, Madonna also evokes an android, a replicate, or simulacrum, to use Philip K. Dick's terminology.[103] Such androids might be extremely sophisticated, but they remain imitations. The joke allows Madonna to point to the artifices of her postmodern creation, her pastiche work and simulacra.

In keeping with the traditions of science fiction, the engineers have built the android with a trap in her back so as to allow access to her essential functions. Behind that trap, there are bound to be an on-off switch and the memory banks supposed to rule her behavior. But we are all familiar with the disgraceful tendency of androids to rebel, so Madonna may be signaling her own rebelliousness again.

In Ira Levin's novel *The Stepford Wives* (1972), the eponymous wives have been replaced with theoretically obedient androids. The novel is based on the fantasy of your average macho, sexist, white American male to *own* a submissive woman. And of course, women who let themselves be totally dominated are comparable to androids. Madonna does not let anyone dominate her. What she's doing here is exhibiting a fake trap door on her back so as to better assert her independence. This trap is the door to the fantasies of the Madonna consumer; it functions in various ways: fans dying for details about the intimate life of their idol[104] dream of being granted some revelation; people who desire her dream of accessing the totality of her body, or better yet, to control her, thanks to strategically placed switches. The message of the trap is reinforced by the opening skirt that looks as if it were about to slip down her hips, and by the promising upper buttocks. The whole thing is bathed in shades of pink that can be linked to a certain kind of tacky eroticism, and to the fake freshness of a falsely innocent pretend little girl (*Like a Virgin*).

But of course, this is just a game. Like the film *Truth or Dare*, it is show business, as the curtain-like fabric of the skirt reminds us; curtain means theater means play means fiction. If you separate this picture from its promotional context (go see my movie, go buy my book), it still remains a support for fantasy. In any case, Madonna signifies a fantasy of penetration. Like many Madonna products, this strong image shows Madonna's postmodern feminism. Pretending to submit to the male gaze, she parodies its might, while irritating the radical feminists who are hostile to any display of feminine flesh in the media, even tongue-in-cheek display. Madonna gives herself over, the better to begrudge herself, rewriting the classic striptease and arousing the desire (to buy) of the future readers of *Sex*. The apparitions of the Madonna, considered by so many Catholics as so many revelations, do nothing but thicken the mystery; the apparitions (appearances) of Madonna such as this one reinforce the ambiguity and have to do with surfaces. By definition, no-one can have all access to myth.

Model for Gianni Versace. Madonna is also a model, although that activity is the least lucrative of her multiple endeavors. She has sashayed down a catwalk for Jean-Paul Gaultier, notably in a world-famous outfit that framed her naked breasts like a work of art. After the age of thirty-five, she operated a publicized personal and professional *rapprochement* with the more subdued Gianni Versace, but then she went back to Gaultier, patronized the Belgian Olivier Thieskens, then moved over to Dolce & Gabbana and back to Gaultier again. In between, she went through a brief sartorial *embourgeoisement*, sporting Christian Dior outfits (at the time of her "peronization"). Versace asked her to pose for extremely glamorous promotional shots. Madonna wore tremendous dresses that promoted herself as much as Versace. Indeed her name sometimes appears at the bottom of the photos, which is a rare occurrence even when the model is a supermodel of the old eighties Linda Evangelista or Naomi Campbell stature. Sometimes it even goes further, and you can read "Versace presents Madonna photographed by Steven Meisel." Versace had understood Madonna completely. In an *Interview* supplement entitled *The Art of Being You*, he entitled a Madonna picture *Invent yourself*.[105] As a matter of fact, Madonna has a place of honor in his book *Rock and Royalty*, which appropriately features her with a crown on her head.[106]

Sex, the Book. Though *Sex* failed to delight a majority of critics, it was one of the most spectacular publishing successes ever, since a million copies were immediately printed and quickly sold. Only dictionaries reach such records.[107] It came out simultaneously in numerous countries on October 21, 1992. Its release was publicized just about everywhere, with more or less daring excerpts or making-of pictures. Some of the numerous photos from *Sex* are discussed elsewhere in this book, so I'll only examine a few at this point.

Madonna, as is her habit, conceived this book with humor, which was not—far from it—always perceived. She sums this up herself in an important interview, analyzing the reasons why many critics rejected the book:

> [*Sex*] was meant to be funny, mostly, but everyone took it very seriously—which just showed me what little sense of humor most of us

have when it comes to sex [...]. A woman who is rich and famous and intelligent and naked is a very daunting thing for most people [...]. You're allowed to be naked if you're stupid, or if you're perceived to be a victim, or something that can be objectified.[108]

To begin with, let's examine the way Madonna exploits Vanilla Ice's fall from grace. To those who suppose that they had an affair, she answers: "I am not romantically involved with Vanilla Ice, I just like to befriend the underdog."[109] Indeed after his fall, when his "honorary African American" status burst like a balloon, Madonna posed with him in forty pictures between pages 96 and 103 of *Sex*.

Vanilla Ice may be described as good-looking; he has had millions of teenage fans, but this does not account for Madonna's choice. She can afford any gorgeous male supermodel. In some of the pictures, Madonna is naked, in others she is covered by a pair of shorts or frilly knickers; Vanilla Ice, on the other hand, is never naked. As opposed to other scenes of *Sex* where Madonna disports herself with more or less clothed men,[110] it is practically impossible in spite of the varied *mises en scène* to think when looking at this series of photographs that a sex act is taking place or is about to take place. No amount of willing suspension of disbelief will do the trick. The zipper of Vanilla Ice's jeans or Bermuda shorts may be open, showing off a pair of boxer shorts, but the reader still cannot imagine him taking them off. From this point of view, this series is the least convincing in the book; but this is certainly the result of a deliberate Madonna strategy.

Indeed, what does Vanilla Ice stand for? He's a fallen celebrity whose success was grounded on a vast mystification enterprise. He was no real "wigger." Madonna, for her part, was never really chastised for her borrowings from African American culture or her autobiographical exaggerations. Vanilla Ice accumulated the macho sartorial signs and gestures of the rappers; whereas Madonna derides them regularly. What she accomplishes in those photographs is an ironic deconstruction of Vanilla Ice the persona, decoding the hypercoded and signifying her own success and longevity through the mocking of the discomfiture of the disgraced rapper. Ice doesn't take his clothes off because he is fundamentally harmless: the phallus is on Madonna's side.

On page 13, Madonna is sitting on a sofa between two lesbians— hypercoded as butch dykes: Allistair Fate and Julie Tolentino, two lesbians who are well-known "on the scene." Their skulls are almost totally shaven and they are abundantly tattooed and pierced. They are almost entirely naked, whereas Madonna is wearing a white lace nightdress that uncovers half a nipple. The laughing lesbians are watching Madonna but

she is not looking at them, she's looking to the right. Her face expresses—
with the emphasis of a silent movie actress—stupefaction and amused
horror. You feel that you can see the cry "Oh my God!" forming on her
lips.

What is she looking at? The preceding pages of the book where she
masturbated? Those where tied up to a chair she kissed one of the dykes,
threatened by a flick knife, as the other dyke sucked at her breast? Or
maybe the page where she hinted at a "golden shower" with a third? Maybe
she's simply watching television, pausing before another heavy S&M session. In fact, this photo constitutes one of the best examples of the essential ambiguities of Madonna's work. As is often the case, several radically
different interpretations are possible. Amazingly, Madonna's resolutely
pro-gay attitude is sometimes mistaken for homophobia. Might she have
sinned out of awkwardness? bell hooks reviews the series of photos that
involve the two aforementioned dykes, and deems that Madonna constructs them as freaks,[111] reinforcing the clichéd view of gay people as
predators. hooks thinks Madonna incarnates the ideal woman (according
to heterosexual norms), posing as a voyeur; whereas the two lesbians are
marginalized:

> Madonna is the symbol of innocence. Unlike her, they do not have firm
> hard bodies, or wear on their faces the freshly made-up, well-fed all-
> American look. One of the most powerful non-erotic or pornographic
> images in this sequence shows Madonna at a distance from the two
> women, looking anguished as though she does not belong. [Madonna's]
> presence invites status quo readers to imagine that they too can consume
> images of difference, participate in the sexual practices depicted, and yet
> remain untouched — unchanged.[112]

That picture where, according to hooks, Madonna looks anguished
can only be the photo page 19 where she has been untied from her chair.
You can see the traces of the rope on her forearms and wrists; she's holding her head with her right hand and closing her eyes. A few inches behind
her (what hooks calls "at a distance"), the two lesbians are busy; they
might conceivably be picking up the accessories. That photo happens to
be featured on the booklet of the *Erotica* CD, an album that is entirely
devoted to the glory of carnal pleasure in all its forms. So it is difficult to
imagine that Madonna may have wished to look "anguished" in it...

Without going so far as to accuse Madonna of homophobia in her
essay, hooks reproaches her with her participation in a society that is globally homophobic; she even deplores Madonna's forgetting feminism, as if
Sex had marked the end of a period. I cannot possibly agree with hooks
on this. Besides, she forgets that on those incriminated pictures Madonna

is alone, whereas there are two butch dykes. However representative of the heterosexual norm, *she* is the minority in those pictures. What is more, it is natural that *she* be in the center, since that book is supposed to illustrate *her* fantasies (see chapter 5). *Sex* is a temple that was purposefully built as a place of Madonna worship.

Finally, to see in these images Madonna as the incarnation of innocence threatened by perversity shows a certain lack of realism; surely that is a reproach she very rarely gets. She can very easily be seen as lesbian fem(me) to the two butch lesbians, anyway.

Many feminists (like Andrea Dworkin[113]) imagine that eroticism-pornography always goes hand in hand with misogyny and machismo, whereas the postmodern feminist work of Madonna in *Sex* proves the opposite. Against many commentators I persist in seeing nothing patriarchal in *Sex*, which is completely controlled by Madonna. She turns the habitual clichés of eroticism-pornography upside down, addressing female readers perhaps even more than male readers. She empowers women, signifying that they are as much entitled as men to consume erotic-pornographic images, and that it is simplistic and passé to think that such images necessarily entail the degradation of women and their reduction to the position of victim.

Madonna is not (re)presented as a victim in *Sex*. When she acts out an S&M scenario and plays the bottom, it is another way to remind the reader that she is the one who is pulling the strings, even though she may be the one whose limbs are tied up. Indeed, she has been criticized for this—in the same book where hooks writes the above.

In any case it would be naïve to suppose that in sadomasochistic relationships, the one who ties up and "tortures" is necessarily the one who retains the power, just as it would be naïve to disapprove of sado-masochistic practices in the name of some generic condemnation of violence. Such practices, between consenting adults, have to do with play, and when Madonna stages them, she is only playing a persona who is playing a game. I agree with Anne McClintock, who deems that *Sex*'s only "crime" is to expose the theatricality of S&M.[114] To evoke the particular brand of sadomasochism that Madonna stages, José María de Juana uses the delightful term "sadomadonnism."[115]

In *Sex*, Madonna encourages readers to broaden their horizons, develop their open-mindedness, and — why not — attempt new sexual experiences. Let's not neglect the influence of Madonna on her fans. It is clear that in the years 1985-1987 she helped the first generation of wannabes to emancipate themselves, to control their own lives as responsible and free women able to make their own sartorial, sexual, and professional choices. Why should it be assumed that she doesn't continue exercising that kind of influence (it is one of the avowed aims of *Sex*)? Her better-disposed readers will think that if Madonna lets herself be photographed in the company of tattooed bondage lesbians, it is because they have little to do with freaks worthy of ostracism, because on the contrary their sexuality is just as "normal" as that of anyone else.

Could Madonna possibly be watching on that page 13 photo the reaction of radical feminist critics? Then the "Oh my God!" forming on her lips would signify something like: "Do you realize what these women are capable of writing?" Already the *Open Your Heart* video featured a critic busy taking notes during the peep-show. Madonna enjoys cutting the grass under the feet of criticism.

Actually, she has probably filmed her lovemaking with the two women, and is now watching the tape, marveling at her acrobatics. Extra *mise en abyme*: not only does she practice voyeurism and exhort the reader-spectator to follow in her footsteps, but she is her own object, adding the joys of narcissism to those of lesbianism. As for the picture on page 19 that bothered hooks, it presumably signifies that Madonna is exhausted due to the aforementioned acrobatics and ready to take a well-deserved nap; for she will later visit an S&M club (The Vault in New York) to whip one or two "victims" before settling in a "sling" (pages 21 and 22).

Madonna's narcissism is concretely exploited in *Sex*, as its fundamentally libidinous nature is comically established in various ways. The photographs of *Sex* principally mean to annihilate guilt. Catholicism, Madonna often says, causes major damage, including a permanent association between sex or masturbation and guilt. She suffered a lot from this as a girl and continues to exorcise her childish anxieties throughout her work, twisting Catholic images.

There is no point in lingering on the photos of *Sex* at this stage, other than to indicate that on page 50, Madonna shaves a man's pubis, playing with her reputation as a castrating woman; or that on page 25, a man on a "sling" in full S&M gear drinks out of Madonna's spike-heeled shoe. Seeing the context, he can only be drinking urine. It is tempting to see this as a corruption of the stereotype of the chivalrous gentleman drinking champagne out of a shoe to pay a tribute to the femme fatale who has conquered him. But is it really a corruption? Isn't it simply a more down-to-earth *mise en scène* of the same situations, implying the same sentimental and libidinal politics? That photo echoes the photo on page 36, where the joys of "uro" are even more obvious (a pierced man receives a stream directly in his mouth). It also echoes the photo on page 71, where Madonna sits astride a fish statue that spits water in a pool.

On page 59, to conclude, Madonna treats zoophiliac practices in a humorous mode: she stands on all fours above a dog in the grass. The dog's head is directly under the star's genitals that are covered by a G string. To complete her outfit Madonna wears long satin gloves and spike-heeled shoes. But she's laughing wholeheartedly, and on the back of her G string a rabbit tail has been sewn. This is her way of spoofing Hugh Hefner and his bunny girls, and everyone remembers how many times she has parodied playmates. She is laughing to show that she is playing with the dog, as if she were a pet rabbit, and that the reader should not imagine she is seriously advocating bestiality. She is thus comically answering the rules imposed by the publishers, who had ruled out pedophilia and zoophilia.

In the same order of ideas, some pictures of the series do not appear in *Sex* but were published in *Vanity Fair* and *Glamour*: they depict Madonna as a Lolita. In those bucolic photos she seems to be age twelve and plays with teddy bears or swings on a swing, dressed in pink. Of course, when the magazines came out she was accused of glorifying pedophilia.

This is what the psychoanalyst Gérard Miller says about this aspect of Madonna's work:

> Madonna perfectly personifies what from Freud to Lacan psychoanalysis has always called the *black continent*. In other words the very enigma of female sexuality.[116]

If that is the case, how could you be surprised by the quantity of comments Madonna's pictures occasion?

Movies. Madonna is on top when it comes to records, videos and photographs, but she hasn't quite managed yet to convince everyone that she is to be taken seriously as a movie actress; even some of her most devoted fans remain skeptical. Most of her movies have been commercial failures, systematically attributed to her presence: "Everyone behaves as if I were the only one to blame, as if I had written, directed, produced it, and acted all the parts."[117] That is the unsurprising price to pay for such a level of stardom, but also for the powerful woman image she embodies.

Dangerous Game. Dangerous Game is one of her most striking failures, in the U.S. at any rate. Yet that movie is far from devoid of qualities. If it doesn't thrill as much as *Bad Lieutenant* (Abel Ferrara, 1992), it doesn't bore as *The Addiction* does (Abel Ferrara, 1996). Though Madonna's acting in that film was severely disparaged, it persuaded Alan Parker to entrust her with the part of Evita a few years later. *Dangerous Game* may have failed because Madonna's fans and Ferrara's are rarely the same. Moreover, Madonna's look in that film, singularly unglamorous, was not appreciated. Her movie fiascos also result from a specific phenomenon that is never as virulent when other stars are concerned: the spectator is more concerned with her look(s) than with her acting. She is of course largely responsible for this state of affairs, notably because she spends so much energy recycling dead Hollywood stars (see chapter 4).[118]

Desperately Seeking Susan. In 1985, Madonna's look significantly contributed to her popularity; in *Desperately Seeking Susan*, her first (non-underground) movie, Madonna as Susan wears a lot of black, which has connoted for young Americans since the forties some kind of cool detachment, chic refusal of the mainstream, vaguely left-wing semi-intellectualism, and the like. She dresses exclusively in vintage clothes that she accessorizes with cheap jewels, scarves, fingerless gloves and rags in her hair. Her hairdo is approximate, her black locks streaked with dirty blond highlights. It is a look that fascinated teenage girls. Interestingly, *Desperately Seeking Susan* is the only movie in which Madonna doesn't allude to bygone Hollywood stars.

Who's That Girl?. In 1987, Madonna stars in *Who's That Girl?* (James Foley, 1987). During most of the movie, she flaunts an uninspiring look that presumably contributed to put off a certain number of spectators: a black leather cap with a silver chain (boringly connoting fifties bikers and sadomasochists), ruffled hair bleached practically white, thick coal black eyebrows (badly plucked), a very old-fashioned studded black leather jacket (vaguely punk and vaguely sadomasochist), as well as a tacky ragged sweater which looks like something you might use to wipe the floor with. To complete the outfit, she wore a Latina little girl's black and red miniskirt, fishnet tights with standard fetishist connotations, and a New Wave pair of shoes with numerous buckles that only Michael Jackson still wore in those days, long after they had deserted gothic nightclubs. Her complexion itself is abominable. So her look in *Who's That Girl?* is a bit of a failure, slightly compensated by a short scene in which she glamorizes herself (see chapter 4).[119]

Bloodhounds of Broadway. In *Bloodhounds of Broadway* (Howard Brookner, 1988), Madonna gratifies the spectator with a fascinating look, mostly made up of allusions to Josephine Baker, Louise Brooks and Theda Bara; she plays Hortense Hathaway, a showgirl who gets dozens of diamonds from her beau, but who really only wants to get married, have babies and raise chickens. The story takes place in 1929, and her specialization in Hollywood palimpsest is getting clearer; as Hortense she already announces the Breathless Mahoney of *Dick Tracy*. The public did not rush to see *Bloodhounds of Broadway*, but this had more to do with its mediocre scenario than with Madonna's acting — which admittedly is not excellent in this movie.

Dick Tracy. In *Dick Tracy*, Madonna's extremely glamorous look is primordial. The essential interest of the movie is its particularly elaborate aesthetics; Warren Beatty's work, notably as far as the colors are concerned, does hold water. Nothing has been left to chance. Yet Beatty has given almost totally free rein to the palimpsestuous tendencies of Madonna (as Gérard Genette would put it), who efficiently slips into the skin of a golden age actress in order to confer a generic Hollywood flavor to the character of Breathless Mahoney.[120] Amazingly, Madonna reminds the public in this movie of everyone and of no one in particular; leading critics establish various comparisons with this or that bygone star, according to their sensibility: Jean Harlow, Carole Lombard, Carroll Baker, Madeleine Carroll, Joan Bennett, or even Bette Davis. As Evelyne Caron-Lowins says: "In *Dick Tracy*, she appears as the reincarnation of all the vamps."[121] The Breathless Mahoney comic book character — dating back to 1931 — seems to have been created for Madonna, but can you really marvel at the fact that she incarnates another archetypal blonde femme fatale so convincingly? She says it clearly herself at the beginning: "I'm Breathless".

Blue in the Face. In *Blue in the Face* (Wayne Wang & Paul Auster, 1995), Madonna's striking cameo allows her to parody some of her past personae with a hilarious sense of self-derision: she plays a telegram girl who arrives in Brooklyn perched on spike heels to sing a telegram in a way that redefines the meaning of the word "sexy." Wearing a bright red minidress with shoulder pads, a little groom's hat and white gloves, she provides the introductory music with her lips (chi chi chi), sings the message, including the "stops," and bends down to conclude, showing off her buttocks to Harvey Keitel before singing "pa da boom." She is heavily made-up, very blond, very vulgar. Her getup and behavior are playful allusions to former personae of hers. Immediately after she leaves, RuPaul, the most famous drag queen of the nineties, makes an appearance, logically brought forth, as it were, by Madonna's fugitive performance.[122]

An Organized Cult: The Wizard and Gays

Jean Domarchi writes about yesteryear's stars:

> Tyrants and slaves at the same time, stars owe to this dual condition a legend that only great historic figures enjoy. What makes them heroes for our time is precisely that contradiction in which American capitalist society imprisons them. At once substitutes of the gods in whom people have ceased to believe and privileged propitiatory victims of all scandals [...], they constitute [...] the source of our daily mythology. They have their rightful place next to the gods and goddesses, the kings and queens.[123]

Madonna strove to organize her own cult like those ancient goddesses who came down to earth to instruct humans: temples were to be built according to precise instruction. In the process, Madonna particularly targeted gays, for multiple reasons; their number is not negligible: between 4 percent and 10 percent of the American population.[124]

This is important in electoral terms, and it is important in terms of marketing too. You often hear that gays are an interesting market, and that they tend to spend more on cultural products. Besides, they are traditionally more inclined to indulge in personality cults, especially when divas (in the widest sense) are concerned. Several factors account for this, which Queer Theorists like Burston, Richardson, or Higgins analyze in their works. Madonna offered her own explanation:

> I feel one of the reasons gay culture more readily accepts strong females and divas, or likes women in general, is that the sexual tension is removed [...], so they just deal with women on an intellectual and emotional level. And straight men only think about how they may dominate them in some way or make them shrivel up or something.[125]

She forgets the aesthetic aspect. As a diva and powerful woman, she is heiress to a tradition of gay icons, coming after Greta Garbo, Marlene Dietrich, Mae West, and others. She is now an indispensable part of the gay cultural landscape, and gay magazines regularly use her to boost their sales, even when no particular breaking news justifies it. In the same order of things, she is featured on the cover of Alan Sinfield's book *Cultural Politics — Queer Reading,*[126] whereas Sinfield did not write a single line about her in the book.

Michael Musto writes: "We [gays] don't even know this girl, but we spend more time talking about her than about our real friends, devote more hours to analyzing every cut of her gowns than to our own personal problems."[127] In the film *Love! Valor! Compassion!* (Joe Mantello, 1997), adopted from Terence McNally's play, the character named Buzz complains that everyone is always asking him, "who's Ethel Merman?" or "who's Julie Andrews?" I'll leave you to your Madonna, he more or less says to the new generation gays, before adding: "I long for the day when people say, 'who's Madonna?'"

This book is not the place for a complete survey of all the precise elements that come into the constitution of a gay icon, so I'll merely say that the only element all theorists agree upon is that a female gay icon is always "larger than life." This certainly fits Madonna.[128]

Truth or Dare and *The Wizard of Oz.* The word "glamour" comes from "*gramarye*," "grammar," and it is related to "*grimoire*." Glamour is magic, and so Madonna's glamour, her charm (in its etymological sense), and her seduction (also in its etymological sense) are magic. Her particular artistic grammar is the weapon she uses to bewitch, to enchant, as *Truth or Dare* singularly exemplifies. And talking about magic, is there not a filiation between *The Wizard of Oz* and *Truth or Dare*? Didn't Madonna play in a school production of *The Wizard of Oz* as a girl? Isn't she the new Dorothy?

Obviously *The Wonderful Wizard of Oz* is a text that has influenced countless American artists.[129] *Truth or Dare* clearly operates a work of quotation that is inscribed in that omnipresent intertextuality. That tale (supposedly for children) by L. Frank Baum, published in 1900, is right there next to Shakespeare and the Bible. But this is equally true (if not more) of its oh-so-famous movie adaptation *The Wizard of Oz* (Victor Fleming, 1939), with the young Judy Garland.[130] Not counting the sequels and rewrites— including a cartoon featuring Judy Garland's daughter Liza Minnelli's voice and a wretched remake with Michael Jackson, *The Wiz* (Sidney Lumet, 1978)— it would be interesting to draw up a list of the impressive number of novels, movies and songs that refer to *The (Wonderful) Wizard of Oz*.[131] Europeans don't always identify the references, because the mythic *Wizard* doesn't count among the compulsory stages of the formation of their imagination, as it does for most Americans. Europeans do not automatically recognize Elton John's Yellow Brick Road as that of Oz, nor do they necessarily identify the reference when a gremlin yells "I'm melting."

According to a survey conducted by John F. Kennedy Jr.'s magazine *George*, a colossal 93 percent of Americans have seen the film.[132] The year 1939 is an important one for the movies, as it is the year when Technicolor developed, notably with *Gone With the Wind*, equally directed by Victor Fleming. Fleming chose to film most of *The Wizard of Oz* in color (Technicolor), but he shot the initial scenes in black and white.[133] Nowadays recourse to a combination of the two processes is current, but Fleming then pioneered it.[134] Little Dorothy lives on her farm in the heart of Kansas with her aunt Em and her uncle Henry, in black and white, singing and wondering what lies *Over the Rainbow*,[135] until one day a tornado (a dream?) takes her to the wonderful land of Oz with her dog Toto; there she goes through all sorts of adventures in color, following the famous Yellow Brick Road to the Wizard's domain. We know that the Wizard of Oz turns out to be a disappointment: he is nothing but an illusionist, a technician, a crook (a trickster?), so Dorothy can only rely on her own resources, like Madonna.

Dorothy and her friends travel through the wonderful land of Oz because a quest animates them: the Tin Man is looking for a heart, the Cowardly Lion seeks courage, the Scarecrow a brain, and Dorothy the way home. In fact, the object of their quest is the acceptance of difference. Dorothy will help her friends realize that they need not envy other men: the Tin Man already has a heart, the Cowardly Lion is already courageous, and the Scarecrow is obviously not brainless, in spite of appearances.

It's easy to see the young girl's new life as more exciting than the dreary existence she led in her native Kansas, in spite of or thanks to the many dangers it involves, and find her quest far less thrilling than her companions'. That aspect is reinforced in Fleming's film by the use of Technicolor. So what accounts for that wish to return to "reality"? Is she like a reformed junkie determined to flee artificial paradises and bravely face daily routine? Is she so conventional after all that she is desperate to get away from that colored strange world of Oz and find shelter in the reassuring grayness of her family's farm? Is it simply the affection that she feels for her aunt and uncle that motivates her? Unless we are faced with a rule that has to be respected, perhaps, a WASP order of things: the only acceptable role of dream would be to modulate reality, but not to allow us to escape it; perhaps such worlds are allowed to exist only as long as the hero returns...

Truth or Dare purports to be a documentary movie. It is in fact nothing but (postmodern) fictions. *Truth or Dare* is a game. Alek Keshishian follows Madonna's *Blond Ambition* tour. His cameramen shadow Madonna everywhere, night and day, except when she has sex ("They weren't in the room when I was fucking!"[136]), business talks ("Get out, I'm having a business talk!") or when she goes to the bathroom.

In *Truth or Dare*, which many members of her intimate circle begged her not to release, Madonna is filmed in black and white (16mm) backstage, in hotels, with her family, her friends, and so forth, but she is filmed in color (35 mm) on stage. Are we then to understand that the scenic space where she performs constitutes her own wonderful land of Oz? Or is it the audience's? Or both? Christopher Andersen, one of her unauthorized biographers (they all are, up to now) writes in *Madonna Unauthorized*:

> [*Truth or Dare* is] a feature film focusing on the backstage drama as it unfolded during the course of the entire three-month tour. For contrast, behind-the-scenes footage would be shot in black and white, the concert scenes in color.[137]

We are indeed dealing with "backstage drama," in the proper sense of the word "drama," but the alternation between black and white and color goes far beyond mere contrast ("backstage drama" is obviously oxymoronic, hence the interest of Andersen's phrase). Dorothy, a charismatic creature, leads her odd friends to the emerald city like a real leader, helping them along the way to accept their true nature. This is exactly what Madonna does with her staff (in black and white) and her public (in color). She said about *Truth or Dare*: "This really will definitely be one of those all time classics, like *The Wizard of Oz*."[138] Dorothy's companions , the Tin Man, the Cowardly Lion, the Scarecrow (and the dog Toto) are all male, but male with a "structuring difference." They are *eccentric* creatures, in the original sense of the word. Salman Rushdie reminds us that the actors who played those three characters were not allowed in the MGM studio canteen, because their appearance caused a malaise.[139] He speaks of "full metallic drag" when referring to the Tin Man.[140]

All this can function efficiently as the following metaphor: accepting yourself as a homosexual in a homophobic world is difficult, but with the help of an optimistic gal pal who has no prejudices and a lot of energy ("fag hag"? "fruit fly"?), the homosexual can bravely face adversity. Indeed, the now outdated phrase "a friend of Dorothy's" commonly designated a homosexual, until the generalization in the sixties of more liberated and less cryptic words like "gay." Didn't Baudelaire write in *Fusées* that liking intelligent women was a queer's pleasure?

Madonna has always had many gay friends. According to gossip, she even has gay lovers. One of her most often quoted declarations goes: "I'm very aroused by two men kissing, I think every straight man should have another man's tongue in his mouth at least once."[141] She expanded upon this in her book *Sex*, explaining how most men have at least fantasized at one point or another in their life about going to bed with a man. The men who have treated her best, she seems to be saying, are those who had slept with men before, or at least kissed men.[142]

Madonna never stops promoting gay lifestyles. She even got an award in 1991 from the Gay and Lesbian Alliance Against Defamation (GLAAD), for her contribution to the development of "gay awareness." Puritans hate her for this. When Madonna has an affair with a model (Tony Ward), he turns out to be bisexual and well-known as an old favorite of erotic gay magazines. In 1996 he starred in *Hustler White*, a more or less underground and very gay film by Rick Castro and Bruce LaBruce.[143] When Madonna has an affair with Dennis Rodman, whose heterosexuality seems exclusive, people still comment upon the fact that this basketball champion is a cross-dresser. He wears pink feather boas and enjoys multicolored hair dyes. She has made the most of her (ambiguous?) friendship with British out gay actor-writer-model-singer Rupert Everett, her partner in *The Next Best Thing* (John Schlesinger, 2000); in that uninspiring movie she plays a heterosexual woman who has a child with a gay man. She has also publicized her closeness to comedian Sandra Bernhard and encouraged rumors about the nature of their relationship. But as she says herself:

"Whether I'm bisexual or not is of no interest. My position on sexuality is that it is not necessary to have a position, whatever that may be, but it is necessary to be free to do what you want."[144] Her friendship with Bernhard meant a lot of free publicity for both women. More recently Madonna did little to discourage rumors, as her first pregnancy was nearing its conclusion, that she was having an affair with a singer she produced, Me'Shell NdegéOcello.[145] She posed in lesbian contexts in her book *Sex*, which also features male homosexuals, and repeated in interviews that her best friends are gay. She even outed her brother Christopher during an interview for the gay magazine *The Advocate*.[146] As recently as August 2000, she disported herself with sexy girls in the *Music* video (directed by Jonas Akerlund), going as far as to hire a female stripper for a lap-dance.

In *Truth or Dare*, Madonna leads her troupe like Dorothy. She is surrounded by two chorus girls, and several "very gay" dancers (one exception). She mothers them all a great deal, and seems to really enjoy this role, with its tender aspects and its repressive aspects ("Let Mama get her makeup done"). Isn't the very essence of a Madonna maternity? In 1991, she declared in several interviews that the premature death of her mother accounted for her maternal attitude toward her staff. The birth of her daughter Lourdes fulfilled an overwhelming maternal instinct, she repeatedly said in 1996. In 1998, she seemed determined to become "the mother of the world" (see chapter 4) and in 2000 she gave birth to Rocco.

There are not many quest narratives that center around a female character surrounded by men (gay or not). A few can be found in heroic fantasy, sword and sorcery or science fiction novels like those of Elizabeth A. Lynn and Ursula Le Guin, which upset the established conventions of the genre.

It would be naïve to think that things stop at the equation color equals dream for the fan-spectator, since the latter dreams of the black and white life of the star as much as he dreams of her color tour. But maybe Madonna has playfully or hypocritically chosen to warn her fans. Watch out, she seems to be saying, do not get mixed up, the dramatis personae are in color whereas the realitatis femina is in black and white, to help you tell them apart!

Or is it that like Dorothy she expresses herself in color, because that is her art, she needs it to better cope with her life in black and white? Her quest is *mise en scène*. The wonderful land of Madonna's show is in no way more pleasant than the world backstage, and vice versa, they are complementary.

In fact, the realitatis femina is nothing here but a fiction, as oxymoronic as this may sound, for Madonna can in no way forget the presence of cameras, were it for one second. It would be more appropriate to speak of two different kinds *mises en scène* in *Truth or Dare*: the star is putting on a show in color and another show in black and white. What she lets us see in black and white is the construction of a "reality" that is as fictional as her stage show.

Trish Deitch Rohrer writes: "The ambitious blonde bares all — and nothing at all — in a raunchy new documentary, *Truth or Dare*."[147] Black and white has often been used, depending on periods, to depict the fantastic, the surreal or the unreal, as in *Deadman*, by Jim Jarmusch, for instance. Could we not see in *Truth or Dare* an inversion of the narrative process at work in *The Wizard of Oz*? Francis Bordat writes:

> [Color] remained restricted to great historical films in the thirties, and, in the forties, to the great vehicles of dream and mythology: musicals (about 50percent of all color films in the forties) and Western films (about 15percent).[148]

The year of the turning point was 1939. *The Wizard of Oz* (a musical) was indeed the support of dream and mythology, it generated myth, and it has vastly informed American popular culture, for decades. *Truth or Dare* (another musical, after all, but here the word has new meaning) functions in the same way, and you are led to wonder whether here the black and white passages do not convey more dream and more mythology than the color scenes, even though Madonna seems to present her movie as revolving along the principle apparently at work in *The Wizard of Oz*.

Salman Rushdie notes that the Kansas filmed in *The Wizard of Oz* is just as unreal as Oz: it is painted on MGM studio walls. Rushdie rightly finds the "slogan" of the film unconvincing, "there's no place like home." He sees *The Wizard of Oz* more like a movie (notably because of the song *Over the Rainbow*) about "the human dream of leaving, a dream at least as powerful as its countervailing dream of roots."[149] Like *Truth or Dare*?

Alek Keshishian was interviewed for a "metadocumentary" on MTV with Madonna.[150] He pretends that Madonna enforced no censorship, which I for one very much doubt. He says his crew shot 250 hours of Madonna[151] and she never demanded in the editing room that any scene be cut off. He forgets to recall that, as I said before, there were some activities she simply did not allow him to immortalize. And she got her entire tour staff to sign a confidentiality contract, which is revealing.[152]

But the most revealing element of that interview comes when Keshishian tries to explain the shifts from black and white to color passages: Madonna interrupts him, oh-so-charmingly but in an authoritarian way at the same time, multiplying jokes, and in fact does not let him finish. Revealing absence of revelation…

Judy Garland and Madonna equally qualify as pop icons and gay icons.[153] Judy Garland died in June 1969 and many see in her demise the spark that lit the Stonewall riots. As is well-known, those riots are traditionally seen as the beginning of gay militancy. During three days the lesbian and gay patrons of the Stonewall Inn and other nearby establishments fought the police, beginning on the evening of Judy Garland's funeral. Roger Baker writes that "it was drag queens who were among the fiercest fighters during New York's Stonewall Riots."[154] Their sadness triggered their anger. They had had enough police harassment.[155]

The similarities between Judy Garland and Madonna are too numerous to list. They both wear drag queens' ruby slippers and both enjoy cross-dressing. In *Girl Crazy* (Norman Taurog, 1943), Garland sings Gershwin's song *I Got Rhythm*, subtly parodied by Steven Sondheim for Madonna in the *Dick Tracy* song *More*. Garland repeatedly demonstrated an undeniable talent for Camp that prefigured Madonna's. Gay icons usually belong to one or the other of two types of female stars: either the very vulnerable and suicidal star, or the strong idol whom nobody or nothing resists, like Madonna. Sometimes a star belongs to the two types, notably when her private life contradicts her public persona. In 1950, Garland cut her throat with a piece of glass. As she was in bed convalescing, she never lost her sense of humor, cracking morbid jokes. Isn't humor — and camp humor in particular — the politeness of despair? [156]

I cannot for one second imagine Madonna committing suicide. She will not join the Pantheon of the stars who died young, stirred by self-destructive passions, like James Dean, Marilyn Monroe, Janis Joplin, Jim Morrison, Kurt Cobain, or Michael Hutchence.

Madonna, however, as a deliberate gay icon, is not only inspired by glamorous icons of the Garland type. She also feeds on the work of gay icons that fit in a more "intellectual" culture, painters and filmmakers like Andy Warhol or Luchino Visconti.

As Pamela Robertson writes: "Although Andy Warhol influenced Bowie and Reed, his true heir is Madonna. She captures the full force of Warhol's ironic redefinition of fame and celebrity."[157] In *Sex*, there is a photo romance supplement that is a tribute to Andy Warhol and to his film *The Chelsea Girls* (1966). Long before Madonna, Warhol enjoyed upsetting preconceived notions of gender and sexuality. Warhol, Pope of Pop Art,[158] king of the postmodern, virtual father of Madonna, is the champion of intertextuality, whether it be in terms of lifestyle or artistic production (it is actually the same thing when it comes to Warhol). He blew up the frontiers between high art and low art, between art and journalism, between social and sex life, between supermarkets and museums.

You may also compare the scenes that Keshishian shot in 16mm for

Truth or Dare with Warhol's first films ("home movies"), and you may establish links between Warhol's use of S&M imagery (notably in the ideas he shared with The Velvet Underground) and Madonna's (especially in *Sex*, during the *Girlie Show* tour and in the *Justify My Love* video).

In the *Deeper and Deeper* video, directed by Bobby Woods, Madonna simultaneously pays tribute to Warhol and Visconti. She moves from the twenties and thirties to the sixties and seventies and back again. She evokes Isadora Duncan, Dita Parlo, and Ingrid Thulin in *La Caduta degli dei (The Damned,* Luchino Visconti, 1969). She recreates the atmosphere of the underground films of Warhol and Morrissey, particularly *Flesh* (1968) and *Trash* (1970). She echoes John Travolta in *Saturday Night Fever* (John Badham, 1977). The mirror balls in the disco show evoke the thirties and the seventies. The better to round off this double palimpsest, Madonna gratifies the viewer with a scene where she peels bananas on a sofa with Warholian creatures. Who can forget the mythic banana sleeve of *The Velvet Underground and Nico* (1967), designed by Warhol? Madonna and her companions watch a man in seventies underwear who exhibits himself on a mattress thrown on the floor. He looks like a cross between Andy Warhol's fetish actor Joe Dallesandro and Iggy Pop.[159]

For that video, Madonna hired the actor Udo Kier. He wears a leopard skin jacket and is there as a character, but even more so as himself. His presence signifies: remember me, I'm that oh-so-Warholian creature, that German guy with the very distinctive face who only ever played perverts, notably in *Flesh For Frankenstein* (1973); Madonna has already employed me, I was holding gorgeous naked boys on leashes in her book *Sex*, and already I was evoking the spirit of the Factory. See, I'm organizing strange rites that have to do with black magic or the mystical preoccupations of the hippy period.[160]

The images of *Deeper and Deeper*, associating drag, modeling, narcissism and lesbianism, provide a typical commentary on the construction of Madonna's success. The viewer is obviously meant to gather she has signed some kind of Faustian pact with the diabolical Udo Kier. But on second thought you don't know exactly who possesses whom, for before the music begins, Udo Kier is seen uttering German words that are subtitled in English: "Beware! Our idols and demons will pursue us. Until we learn to let them go!" Quite. This camp warning is followed by a launch of spermatozoa-shaped balloons. All this can but comfort Madonna's gay icon status, especially when you spot on the disco dance floor the voluminous drag queen Chi Chi LaRue, famous singer and director of gay pornographic movies. A few measures of *Vogue* have been sampled to enhance the ending of the song, in an ultimate postmodern twist.

Parallels can also be established between Madonna's fascination for stars and Warhol's, noting however Madonna's preference for dead stars (she knows she has no living competition). In *Truth or Dare*, she displays a hilarious lack of respect for box-office big names, trashing Kevin Costner for calling her show "neat," for example.

Some of the pictures of Madonna in a Mercedes are a direct echo of Visconti's work. She likes Visconti so much (even more than Fellini) that it is possible to wonder whether her tributes to Marlene Dietrich are not occasionally filtered through the memorable scene of *La Caduta degli dei*, when Helmut Berger impersonates Dietrich.

Donna Summer and Barbra Streisand have preceded Madonna in the gay icons' pantheon. In a way, those two women accompanied the transition Before Stonewall and After Stonewall. Back in 1973 already, with her planetary hit *Love to Love You Baby*, Summer personified seventies disco better than anyone. But in the eighties, she became a born-again Christian and started uttering homophobic pronouncements. So she was deserted by a considerable part of her gay public. In 1994, Paul Burston spoke to Summer: "She seems to occupy the same space that you once did. Madonna is very much the gay diva of the moment, the Nineties Bad Girl to your Seventies Bad Girl." Donna Summer answered: "I don't really think about it."[161] She is probably bitter. A former gay icon, she has now lost her fairy powers.

In *The Wizard of Oz*, Dorothy is surrounded by good witches, wicked witches, and a phony wizard, but *she* is the real magician. In *Truth or Dare*, Madonna is the magician (trickster?).

Madonnophobes would probably say that if there had to be a *rapprochement* between *Truth or Dare* and *The Wizard of Oz*, Madonna would be the Wicked Witch of the West (i.e., the Western world) rather than Dorothy. A single phoneme separates witch from bitch, and you may wonder about the different degrees of bitchiness and magic powers of the ones and the others. Dorothy is clearly a good witch. But as a spell-casting femme fatale, Madonna can be assimilated to a witch, concocting her charms in a Hollywood laboratory.

Four Rooms. In *Four Rooms* (Allison Anders, Alexandre Rockwell, Robert Rodriguez, Quentin Tarantino, 1995), Madonna plays precisely ... a witch. This movie is composed of four sketches.[162] The sketch Madonna stars in, *The Missing Ingredient*, was written and directed by Allison Anders. Several witches meet in the bridal suite of a hotel. Their aim is to resuscitate the goddess Diana. Elspeth, blond witch (Madonna), arrives at the hotel accompanied by a rebellious teenager. She wears a tight black vinyl low-cut dress, sunshades and black spike heels. According to traditional sartorial codes, such a getup connotes the femme fatale or at least the sexy woman. She expresses herself in a dry, biting way, reinforcing her double inscription in the bitch and witch categories. A woman of power, she is totally in control. Indeed she bitchily blames one of her "sisters" for having "an amazing lack of control." However, a very Madonnesque blurring of codes manifests itself when Elspeth turns out to be a lesbian. And the teenager might be her daughter *and* lover. Just in case the male viewer — desperately clinging to her appearance for reassurance — should be tempted to continue reading her as available for heterosexual sex, the dialogue shows that Elspeth is exclusively lesbian, and a virgin heterosexually speaking.

Haven't witches always been merely feminists (sometimes lesbians) far too ahead of their time? Independent women who refused to let any man dictate their conduct? Liberated women who meant to choose their lovers and bear children only when they decided they were ready? They were burnt at the stake, just as Madonna is sometimes burnt at media stakes. Isn't Diana, the goddess who is worshipped in *Four Rooms* the patron of lonely huntresses, amazons and other marginalized women who will not put up with masculine domination?

But Madonna claims the bitch label more than she claims the witch label (for instance, the jokes she cracks between songs on stage when she tours the globe, sometimes similar to those of Bette Midler). In *Erotic*, she sings that she is not a witch, but "a love technician."

Kurt Cobain's widow Courtney Love is one of Madonna's supposed rivals. She seems for her part to accept the implications of the witch label. She has been photographed with "witch" in big red letters on her left arm, and "bitch" on her right arm. Though the similarities between the two women are only superficial, the press has often exploited them. Love is post-punk and grungy, not particularly postmodern. In 1997, she embarked upon a movie career and tried to come up with a chic look, but she merely succeeded in looking disguised for a fancy dress party. She is no expert practitioner of tongue-in-cheek art like Madonna, and her vulgarity is not the characteristic of a dramatis persona. For Madonna, who knows she is not threatened, their pseudo-rivalry is yet another game, whereas according to Larry Flynt, Courtney Love "has a real fixation with Madonna."[163]

Madonna sheds neither habitual sangfroid nor customary humor when she deigns address this:

> I think [Courtney Love] is supremely talented [...]. But I think that drugs have destroyed her brain, or they are slowly destroying her. I am fascinated by her, but in the same way I am by somebody who's got Tourette's Syndrome [...]. I know that if she reads this, she'll be slagging me off on the Net for the next eight months. I do think she knows not what she says. It's true for all people who go around spewing venom,

that deep down inside they're hurt, they're sad, lonely, whatever [...].
Years ago, she probably admired me and looked up to me, and now I'm
like a parent to her or something, and she wants to destroy me.[164]

Who else would thus allow herself to mix biblical allusions, and psy-
chiatric and psychoanalytic discourses in an example of bitchiness masquerading as charitable considerations? Who's the worst bitch-witch of
the two?

Madonna went as far as to imitate the appearance of Courtney Love
for one photo session, as if to signify that she was not only able to pastiche stars of the past, but could also derisively ape contemporary pseudo-
rivals.

So *Truth or Dare* is nothing but a game. To further examine the use
of black and white, you must take into account that it is not infallibly
restricted in *Truth or Dare* to backstage passages; certain scenes question — as was to be expected — apparent rules.

In one of those scenes, in black and white, Madonna gets her father
to join her on stage (in Detroit) and asks the audience to sing *Happy
Birthday* to him with her. That is a remarkably "wicked" game on her part.
She seems to be warning the viewer that this moment constitutes a sud-
den intrusion of her private life in her professional life, whereas obviously what she is doing is integrating her father in the show — not even
as a guest star, merely as a prop. Madonna generates a feeling of intimacy
that is totally fabricated, of course, since she fundamentally remains inaccessible. The joy of the delirious spectators reaches a paroxysm when she
makes them partake in what would normally not exceed the boundaries
of the family circle: this birthday song, which is obviously reminiscent of
Marilyn Monroe's *Happy Birthday, Mr. President*.

That scene is akin to a religious service. Madonna kneels and bows
low to her father. Who else would dare? And it comes after various offstage
insincere-sounding comments on the chances that her father might be
shocked by the "racy" contents of the show....

Her relationship with her father and with father figures in general
plays a capital role in her career, notably because of her mother's premature death. She has integrated it in her show: another way to show everything the better to show nothing. The most frequent interpretation of her
bowing low to her father is that having reached such a level of power, stardom, autonomy and wealth, she may now make official the end of her ado-
lescent rebellion. Yet all her biographers insist on the "fact" that when she
visits her father Silvio (known as Tony), she sleeps in a sleeping bag on
the living room floor. After all, even mythological Greek gods have parents. If Madonna is a goddess, Tony Ciccone is supposedly some sort of

god himself,[165] so it is logical that she should bow low at his feet. But as she has spent years displaying signs of rebellion against paternal figures, you can't help wondering if her father is not the unconscious victim of a vast disrespectful joke.

Madonna had already used her progenitor in the 1985 *Like a Virgin* tour, when his voice was heard in the speakers: "Madonna, get down off that stage this instant!" To which Madonna answered: "Daddy, do I have to?" The evening of the concert in Detroit, Tony Ciccone appeared on stage to drag her backstage.

E. Deirdre Pribram calls *Truth or Dare* a docudrama and explains how the film finds categories such as "truth" and "artifice" ultimately irrelevant.[166] In a much-discussed black and white scene of *Truth or Dare*, Warren Beatty sums up Madonna's *mises en scène* (he was her "exploited" boyfriend in those days): he says she cannot exist without cameras. In that scene he addresses her as much as he addresses the viewers. His words are part incredulous statement, part bitter reproach, and part mockery. As it happens, he did his best during the shooting to avoid Alek Keshishian's team's cameras.

The remark is legitimate: would the existence of Madonna the exhibitionist still make sense if cameras stopped following her? If her public deserted her one day?[167] She refuses to question the docile participation of her entourage in *Truth or Dare*, as Warren Beatty exhorts her to do, because she is being filmed. It does not mean at all that she doesn't measure its implications. Many commentators have neglected a capital element: Madonna had absolute power over *Truth or Dare* the finished product, obviously, whatever may have been said to the contrary. But she chose not to censor that scene. Consequently it is ludicrous to use it "against her," as if she had been caught red-handed. *She* is the one — totally postmodern — telling us through Warren Beatty that she cannot live off camera.

There is presumably no actual confusion on the part of the star between her public and private lives. Madonna pretends to get mixed up the better to promote confusion in the viewer. Thus she allows among other things the viewer to fantasize about his own possible celebrity, playing with one of America's principal obsessions. Didn't Andy Warhol say: "One day, everybody will be famous for fifteen minutes"? And hasn't the notion become as commonplace and as American as apple pie?

The whole movie is a huge game of truth or dare, but she literally plays that game with her troupe in one memorable scene of the movie. Rather than answer a question, she very graciously demonstrates her talents for fellatio on a Vichy bottle. This constitutes without a doubt the most efficient (free?) advertising campaign ever conceived for Vichy.

As it happens, Madonna once declared that she did not care much for fellatio, whereas she demanded from her lovers the practice of cunnilingus. She amply promotes the merits of cunnilingus in *Sex* through her alter ego Dita Parlo. Her old boyfriend Dennis Rodman tells in his book that she tried to force him to perform. This belongs to the political side of Madonna, who claims the right to pleasure for women. That Vichy bottle echoes the beer bottle she holds in her mouth on a very evocative photograph by Herb Ritts which predates the movie. Madonna returned to the theme for a photo in *Sex*. One page 104 she is squatting in the grass, naked. Between her legs stands a bottle of mineral water (Vichy?). She concluded one concert of the *Girlie Show* tour splashing her breasts with mineral water (Vichy?), causing the audience to yell with joy…

To conclude, the viewer is free to sterilely speculate about the quantity of truth in *Truth or Dare*. He is also free to appreciate the numerous instances of Madonna's daring in that movie.

Madonna the Producer

Madonna, like any self-respecting businesswoman, has created many different companies throughout the years, covering her tracks with an array of various-sized and interestingly named firms: Madonna Incorporated, Boy Toy, Slutco, Siren, Maverick, all those subsidiaries being more or less linked to AOL-Time-Warner.

The fact that she produces herself is not surprising in the least; it is but a logical step in the career of a woman who has such thirst for power and defines herself as a control freak.

Madonna has yet to proclaim herself a movie director or photographer, but because she produces herself she is totally free to carefully handpick her collaborators so each of her products can be considered *her* work, even if it is not exactly correct from a purely technical or legal point of view. Indeed, most people don't care much about the name of her associates. They are mostly employees in the vast Madonna cult enterprise.

For the time being, only her movies (with the exception of *Truth or Dare*) sometimes escape her control. This explains the relative failure of some of them: many fans clearly prefer consuming more specifically Madonnesque products. But perhaps this will not last, now that she is married to a filmmaker.

Madonna doesn't mean to clutter the market with a collection of sub-Madonnas, on the contrary. Let us look at a few examples.[168] She first produced Nick Kamen, one of the gorgeous models made famous by Levi-Strauss commercials (Nick Kamen is to laundromats what Jane Russell was to barns[169]). She allowed him to record an album, supervising it down to the most minute details. The single, released in 1986, was entitled *Each Time (You Break my Heart)*. Madonna had written the lyrics. Everyone has forgotten it today, as well as the albums which followed and rapidly found themselves on discount shelves. Nothing distinguished Nick Kamen's syrupy melodies from those of any other teenage heartthrob. In 1991, Madonna renewed the operation with another model and actor named Nick Scotti with the (song *Get Over*).

More recently, Madonna produced the American singer Me'Shell NdegéOcello, who is black, chubby, and an out lesbian. Her music is less commercial than Madonna's, more "authentic," but it may please average (white) Americans, just as it may please the most politically aware of African Americans.

In 1995, Madonna and her company Maverick started producing Alanis Morissette, a white North American singer whose music might be said to belong more to the rock world than Madonna's. Morissette's songs can please Madonna-immune rock purists and can be played on deep America's FM stations. *You Oughta Know* was a worldwide hit. Alanis Morissette's look is very different from that of her producer and she now sells quite a lot of records.

The record *The Fat of the Land* by the British band Prodigy was number one in more than twenty countries in 1997. So it earned Madonna a lot of money, as she distributed it in the U.S., in spite of her reported bones of contention with the band: their lyrics were deemed too offensive in the U.S. and it is said Madonna would have liked to impose some sort of censorship on them, as amazing as this may sound. Apparently Madonna toyed with the idea of asking Prodigy's Liam Howlett to arrange *Ray of Light*.

Madonna has also produced the British band Erasure, though they became famous before she took an interest in them. The composer, Vince Clarke, had been in Depeche Mode and Yazoo. Erasure is a slightly militant gay duo. Its music, rather electronic, is generally seen as dance music.

Those are only a handful of examples. Madonna has also produced the band Muse, the Deftones, Cleopatra, and many others. To sum up, she seems to choose to produce either artists who are no more than good-looking boys and can in no way compete with her, or musicians who are so different from her that they couldn't steal her fans, but who share her feminist, antiracist and anti-homophobic ideas.

Beside making money, Madonna means to act as a real patron, in the old tradition, generously helping some artists out of anonymity, or at any rate helping famous Asians or Europeans to become famous in the States too. She made it possible for the Chinese film *Farewell, My Concubine*

(Chen Kaige, 1993) to reach a relatively large American public. Madonna wishes to help finance more films, whether she is in them or not. In the meantime, she produces soundtracks. Obviously she means to release on Maverick Records the soundtrack of every movie she'll be connected with in the future.

Madonna's most significant patronage seems to me to be that of the photographer and now filmmaker Cindy Sherman. Sherman's work is totally postmodern, her conceptions and Madonna's are similar in a number of ways, even if Sherman's are expressed in a more intellectual way. Everything Sherman undertakes is done tongue-in-cheek; she is a feminist, and for many years she kept taking pictures of herself as actresses of the past, with a preference for B movies. In June 1997 Madonna was the only sponsor of Sherman's exhibition *Untitled Film Stills* at the Museum of Modern Art in New York. The *Time* critic wrote: "Between them, these two women have executed more image makeovers than any other beauticians will in a lifetime. All on themselves—and all in the name of art, of course."[170] Laura Mulvey has noted that Sherman and Madonna find a great part of their inspiration in the fifties, like Debbie Harry before them.[171]

Recuperation

The 1992 Quentin Tarantino film *Reservoir Dogs* begins with a breakfast scene in a café. Eight gangsters about to holdup a jewelers' are making small talk. The gangster nicknamed Mr. Brown (Quentin Tarantino) suddenly embarks on a very personal interpretation of Madonna's *Like a Virgin*,[172] disagreeing with Mr. White (Harvey Keitel). To him, it's a song about a woman who is keen on large penises—as opposed to a song about a fragile girl who's been hurt in the past and has found love. The song "narrator," says Mr. Brown, tells about a very sexually potent man, of the John Holmes variety, who hurts her with his huge organ (the word "dick" is repeated dozens of times), "it hurts just like it did the first time," hence *Like a Virgin*.

The fact that Madonna didn't write the lyrics of *Like a Virgin* herself matters little. It is a Madonna product. She claims for her part that the size of her lover's dick in the song is irrelevant. But in the exact same way it has become difficult to read, say, Edgar Allan Poe's "The Purloined Letter" without thinking of what Lacan has written about it,[173] Mr. Brown's reading of *Like a Virgin* will forever remain linked to the song. Jami Bernard writes that when Tarantino finally met Madonna, she "gave him a copy of her album and inscribed it with 'to Quentin — it's about love, not dick.'"[174]

There are too many connections between Madonna and Quentin Tarantino for me to try and list them here. Jami Bernard quotes one of the filmmaker's old friends: "[Quentin Tarantino is] busy reinventing himself, much like Madonna."[175]

Jami Bernard also quotes Oliver Stone, who filmed a Tarantino script, *Natural Born Killers* (1994):

> The question is, can [Quentin Tarantino] expand his worldview beyond that genre, the combination of violence and humor? Pop-culture icons, references to Madonna and Michael Jackson — it's fun. But that's not what you can live on. You can't dine out on it for the rest of your life, in my opinion. You can make fun movies, or pulpy movies, but I don't know, is there really something being said?[176]

Oliver Stone's words are terribly reductive. Tarantino does say something, and it will undoubtedly remain possible to base an existence or at least an artistic (or academic) production on references to pop icons like Madonna. Tarantino and Madonna have absorbed American popular culture, filtered it through their postmodern idiosyncrasies and now restitute it to the public. They are the magnifying mirrors of America.

Having perceived the cultural links between Madonna and himself as well as the cultural importance of Madonna, Tarantino pays her a tribute that may seem disrespectful but will remain a milestone in movie history. Of course, it serves Madonna's career; any pop celebrity whose work is thus analyzed for 2.37 minutes in a cult film that runs 99 minutes can only rejoice.

In *Dick Tracy*, Madonna plays Breathless Mahoney. It is said that Madonna found the first name of the detective very appropriate when she was offered the part. Indeed Breathless expresses the same sentiment in various double-entendres in the film, and particularly in the song *Now I'm Following You*, which mentions "ninety million dicks" and begins with the idea that an unscrutinized existence is not worth the trouble, which Madonna can only endorse.

The *Reservoir Dogs* Madonna scene shows that the eight gangsters present, from the youngest to the oldest, all know Madonna. She belongs to the American cultural landscape just like the McDonald's quarter-pounders with cheese of *Pulp Fiction*. She belongs in Mr. Brown's tirade alongside Charles Bronson and Charlie Chan.

Tarantino and Madonna both enjoy pastiching film noir and French New Wave works. Madonna pays a tribute to film noir in the movie *Body of Evidence* (Uli Edel, 1993), in the song *White Heat*— a homage to the James Cagney movie (Raoul Walsh, 1949).[177] During the *Who's That Girl?* tour, filmed in Italy and released on videotape as *Ciao Italia*, Madonna sings that song in front of a large board of Cagney with a machine gun. She plays with a revolver and there are gunfire noises.[178]

Given Madonna's habitual personae, Mr. Brown's interpretation is amply justified. A song like *Like a Virgin* could only have been created by an artist known for her many lovers, an artist with a man-eater image. It is imperative for the lyrics to be efficient that the interpreter give the impression of having left her virginity far behind in a distant past. The forty-first line, about sensations "inside," obviously polysemic, did little to deter Mr. Brown.

Before coming up with his interpretation of the song, Mr. Brown obviously watched the Mary Lambert *Like a Virgin* video. It shows Madonna strutting in the Venice of honeymooners, changing from a sluttish getup into a virginal wedding dress. She moves like a stripper and undulates sinuously. She uncovers the furniture of a Venetian palace the way others would uncover flesh. There are all sorts of games with carnival masks, men, lions and "werelions," allusions to eighteenth-century practices and Saint Mark, and it's all extremely sexy. In the different *mises en scène* (*mises en abyme*) of the song that followed, on stage or on TV, Madonna did nothing but develop that tendency, rolling about on the floor in her white dress in a way that shocked all the family associations of America. It is easy to understand how such a piece of clothing, so symbolic, so Catholic, so non-feminist, may make her feel like committing sacrilege.

When on the day of her twenty-seventh birthday Madonna married Sean Penn, she wore a white dress, but she also wore a gender-bending bowler hat, similar to that of Liza Minnelli in *Cabaret*. She couldn't possibly wear a virginal wedding dress without some tongue-in-cheek element in her behavior or outfit signaling some ironic distance. It is more difficult to comment upon the dress she wore for her second wedding at the age of forty-two: it was the subject of intense speculation on the part of tabloid and mainstream press alike but was never actually shown.

What is more, Mr. Brown's reading is subsequent to the *Blond Ambition* tour. The *mise en scène* of *Like a Virgin* for this tour differs significantly from that of the video. The arrangements are different, the rhythms are Hispanic-Arabic; the choreography evokes voguing, but also Thai dancing, or even the arm movements of Sahara squatting dancers. Sitting on a red and gold queen size bed, Madonna simulates masturbation, whereas standing at her side, two male dancers move lasciviously, caressing different parts of their own bodies; they lightly caress Madonna for a while, only to encourage her auto-erotic practices. They are wearing legendary Jean-Paul Gaultier cone-bras, similar to Madonna's but even longer, more phallic. Need I say more?

Beverley Skeggs analyzes the way Madonna represents men in her videos:

> In some videos, these men are set up as powerful, only to be ultimately under her control. In others she de-sexualizes them, as in the use of hermaphrodite costumes on the Blond Ambition Tour (1990). In others, such as the "Burning Up" video, they become irrelevant. She plays with and destabilizes the fixing and categorization of male sexuality in much the same way as she does with female sexuality.[179]

I don't believe Madonna de-sexualizes men during the *Blond Ambition* tour, except perhaps when she sings *Cherish* and her dancers play mermen, with half their bodies imprisoned in a fishtail. It is true, however, that Madonna plays with every possible preconceived idea of masculine sexuality. Like Dorothy, Madonna is surrounded by men, but their chief preoccupation is to masturbate their cone-bras, further contributing to Madonna's reshuffling of cards. At the end of the song, Madonna lies on her stomach and rubs her pudendum against the bed; the rhythm accelerates, imitating the rise of pleasure, and then the music stops brutally, once the simulated orgasm has been reached. In this Madonnesque symbolic new order (this new disorder?), the phallus is everywhere and nowhere.[180] The dick evoked by Mr. Brown is desired and possessed by Madonna as well as by her dancers, and *Like a Virgin* enlarges its semiotic field. We are not merely dealing with penis envy (*Penisneid*) here, but also with breast envy (*Busenneid?*), which is certainly more rare. Unless it is the same thing, as those Gaultier cone-bras seem to suggest, borrowing as they do from the traditional imagery of heroic fantasy's or sword and sorcery, in which metallic bras with lethal points abound.

In *Sex*, Madonna (Dita) writes that she would have little use for a penis, having a "dick in [her] brain."[181] Doesn't she say elsewhere in *Truth or Dare*, when two of her gay dancers are kissing, that it gives her "a hard-on"? This also alludes to the clichéd vision of her as a "gay man trapped in a woman's body."

In 1990 Madonna exploits that Dick Tracy "dick story" to the full in postmodern stage moves, for *Sooner or Later*, or for *Hanky Panky*— a comic hymn to spanking. At some point "Dick Tracy" arrives on stage, played by a dancer who's wearing the famous yellow raincoat and matching hat. While she goes on singing, Madonna-Breathless starts flirting with him, then shows her buttocks to him and calls him: "Hi Dick, come over here!" Then she turns to the Spanish public[182] and declares, grabbing the dancer's genitals: "*Esta es mi polla. Mi polla es muy bonita. Si. Mi polla está dura. Por qué?* Wouldn't you like to know?" The word "*Polla*" is of course the Spanish equivalent of "dick." It is as if Madonna were staging her revenge, or at any rate the revenge of Breathless, who has just died for Dick at the movies. In the cinematic diegesis, she fails to lure Dick away from the "right path," i.e., Tess Trueheart. In this new diegesis, he is hers entirely, he is reduced to his function as pleasure instrument, which his name indicated all along.

Further playing with the notion of dick, Madonna later takes hold of Dick's revolver, shoots in the air, and blows on the barrel. She thus parodies the artificial virility of Western movie cowboys, so intimately linked to their guns,[183] as well as the profession of Dick Tracy. This is when six other Dick Tracy dancers come in. Madonna and Dick disappear offstage, indicating that they are about to have sex (with Madonna on top). Like flashers, the six dancers then open their raincoats: they are wearing little. Then they start dancing in pairs, adding to the general (organized) confusion with this very gay and narcissistic *mise en scène*.

To get back to *Reservoir Dogs*, it shows only two women (briefly), nameless and ill-treated.

On the other hand, Madonna occupies center stage, without being filmed by Tarantino. She is The Woman. The Woman according to Tarantino might very well be the free woman, and not that creature reduced to the primeval sexuality men are willing to grant her — the only type the gangsters in the movie can imagine. The breakfast scene is constructed around the idea of a woman who is entirely dependent on her man's dick to reach orgasm, a purely vaginal woman (when he has enough brain cells to worry about female orgasm, the average male chauvinist cannot imagine another kind of woman). The absent star of the film, Madonna never ceases to contradict this stereotype.

The French psychoanalyst Lidia Franquet analyzes the film. She writes about the allusions to The Fantastic Four (comic book superheroes), and notes that there is no female character. When male and female relationships are evoked, she notes, it is always negatively.[184] But the feminine does find its place in an unconscious way in the three "couples" that will be formed among the male characters. Franquet revealingly writes that *Like a Virgin* "tells the story of a woman who," etc. It does not tell such a story; that is Mr. Brown's interpretation.

Franquet is right, however, to point out that female characters are not to be seen in *Reservoir Dogs*. Women are indeed invisible. Except Madonna. "The Invisible Bitch," as she is called in the film, member of The Fantastic Four, has acquired along the years not only extra superpowers, but also an ever increasing autonomy and spectacular capacities for initiative.[185] Her invisibility gift is precisely what makes her powerful (surely there is some dubious moral to this story), since it is linked to the possibility she has of creating a defensive force field that can turn into an offensive weapon. As Madonna in *Reservoir Dogs* she is invisible but terribly present, *"elle brille par son absence."* Do stars stop shining during the day just because we do not see them?

When discussing Madonna (super)power, we ought to recall the words of Mr. White, who says he has "Madonna's big dick coming outta [his] left ear." Beyond the attribution of a phallus to Madonna, if the phallus comes out of Mr. White's ear, it follows that it has penetrated it first. Does this not work as another comment on Madonna's power, that manifests itself notably through her *discourse*, her voice, that of the singer, the actress, the public figure, that reaches the ears of millions of individuals around the globe, to poison them, perhaps, like Hamlet's father? This reminds me of a passage in postmodern novelist Donald Barthelme's *Snow White*, when a Mr. Quitsgaard is threatened by a Jane in a letter:

> [...] at any moment I can pierce your plenum with a single telephone call, simply by dialing 989-7777. You are correct, Mr. Quitsgaard, in seeing this as a threatening situation.

Abel Ferrara, who directed Madonna in *Dangerous Game*, has observed the constant Madonna-sex association in the public's mind and shows it in *The Blackout* (1997). The actor played by Matthew Modine comes back to Florida after a prolonged absence; his friends welcome him at the hotel, and one of them says: "Hey, Madonna was here, she was looking for you. She's finished with the basketball player. She says, Matty, he's got a big, you know." And this is where we find Mr. Brown's dick again (if I may say so); which is no coincidence. Ferrara alludes here to Madonna's habitual persona, to Tarantino's film, and to Madonna's persona in *Dangerous Game*.

Extraordinarily enough, this Tarantinian dick scene has become so integrated in the minds of moviegoers that many commentators now mistake Tarantino's interpretation for the undisputable meaning of *Like a Virgin*.[186] If I were Tarantino, I don't know if I would be pleased or angry.

That scene in *The Blackout*, incidentally, also alludes to the *Truth or Dare* scene, when Madonna arrives in Madrid and meets the actor Antonio Banderas (then practically unknown in the States), as she has arranged, because she finds him extremely sexy. In those days, Banderas was married to a Spanish woman. Several years later, he became a Hollywood box-office name, Melanie Griffith's husband, and shot *Evita* next to Madonna. During the shooting, the tabloids never tired of recalling that *Truth or Dare* scene.

Another American postmodern film director, Jim Jarmusch, also used Madonna's image in one of his films, *Mystery Train* (1989), thus bringing his contribution to the general Madonnology.

Madonnology

Alain Morel writes: "Do you remember the first time you saw Madonna? This question has become the 'Where were you when Kennedy was shot?' of a different generation."[187]

Indeed, in the U.S., in Australia, in Japan, in the whole of Western Europe and a good section of the rest of the globe, Madonnology is omnipresent. Madonna is in the majority of encyclopedias, whether they be generalist or specialized (music and cinema). In the French *Quid* of 2001, for instance, one of her Parisian concerts (August 29, 1987, Parc of Sceaux, 120,000 spectators) is used to illustrate record amounts of decibels that a concert may generate. That concert, if you are to believe the specialists of *Rock & Folk* magazine, counts among the 101 most memorable dates in the history of rock.[188]

Madonna is interestingly defined in the *New York Public Library Book of Popular Americana*, between the legendary Welsh prince Madoc and the Mafia. But my favorite example is that of the 1995 *Cambridge International Dictionary of English*. Here is its definition of the word "virgin":

> **Virgin.** n. Someone who has never had sex. *She remained a virgin till she was over thirty. D'you think he's still a virgin?* "Like a Virgin" (title of a song by Madonna, 1984).

A dictionary that is published in Cambridge, a place with so many connotations of cultural respectability, has chosen Madonna's song to illustrate the word "virgin." When you think of the millions of other possible examples, from the Bible, Shakespeare, Milton or Keats, you can only be impressed.

Between May and December 1996, I conducted a makeshift survey. I asked 1,227 people what they thought of Madonna. They belonged to every social, professional, and age group, and they lived in France (70 percent), in Australia (20 percent), in England (5 percent) and in the U.S. (5 percent). My findings were very interesting: every single person knew who Madonna was and had heard at least one Madonna song. Every single person had an opinion on Madonna. Half of the people I polled found her "good-looking," the other half said she was "ugly" ("indifferent looks" was not an option). Four people ticked "good-looking" *and* "ugly." Also, 523 considered her subversive, 1,098 sexy, and 331 irritating. Several surveys of that kind have been conducted in the U.S.

The academics who analyze Madonna certainly don't harm her career. They all deem her representative of U.S. and world popular culture or mass culture, and almost all see her as postmodern, like Christgau, who writes: "Madonna has rendered me a postmodernist in spite of myself, one of the burgeoning claque of marginal, generally left-leaning intellectuals for whom she has come to embody nothing less than mass culture itself."[189] E. Ann Kaplan looks at Madonnology today and speaks of an "exaggerated metacritical level":

> Thus, Madonna discourses proliferate in an unprecedented series of contexts, warranting a different critical approach that would address the discourses along with specific texts. One main argument for seeing the Madonna Phenomenon[190] as subversive has been advanced by scholars working within a strand of British cultural studies that relies on audience research.[191]

I try for my part not to limit myself to narrow angles. Douglas Crimp asked a very pertinent question:

> My hesitancy to participate in the "Madonna studies" phenomenon is that I generally think and write about things that really do matter to me, and Madonna doesn't matter to me that much. But it's a problem even to say that, because it sounds like denial or snobbishness or elitism. At some point you have to ask, How can anything that's captured so many people's imaginations, that's generated so many millions of dollars, how can it fail to interest you?[192]

In the press, the most insignificant journalist behaves without scruple like a seasoned Madonnologist. It is to be expected, as by definition myth belongs to everyone. Even a daily newspaper as "serious" as the London *Times* sometimes exploits Madonna's name when nothing in her news justifies it. Thus on July 30, 1997, its headline went "Madeleine Albright Plays Madonna," and was accompanied by a recent photo of the then Secretary of State paired with a 1986 picture of the star. When you read the article page 15, you realize the title is a gross exaggeration: Madeleine Albright merely sang *Don't Cry For Me Argentina* at a summit in Malaysia.

Madonna did not release any particular product between *Evita* in 1996 and the single *Frozen* in 1998, aside from one or two dance remixes, but countless tabloids frequently mentioned her, as if to maintain in her "absence" the flame of worldwide Madonnology.

In another vein, some journalists enjoy being particularly venomous when writing about Madonna, revealing more about themselves than anything else. Taki, for instance, who wrote the "Atticus" column in the London *Sunday Times*, regularly trashed her for years, quite gratuitously, calling her a slob, for instance.[193]

The tremendous majority of articles about Sean Penn, Tony Ward or Warren Beatty in magazines other than *Les Cahiers du Cinéma* or *Sight and Sound* mention Madonna. Beatty was already famous three years after Madonna was born and had affairs with countless gorgeous stars, but he now has to put up with the mention "Madonna ex" in the list of his credentials. As for her new husband, Guy Ritchie, the press generally refers to him more as "Madonna's husband" than as "British filmmaker."

David Tetzlaff decided to study the relationship between the press and Madonna. He explains that when he began to get interested in her social impact, he naturally envisaged to examine in detail the available tabloid articles about her. But he was compelled to give up, seeing the enormity of the task. As that *Time* journalist he quotes says: "Cut Madonna, and ink comes out." Madonna is a "metatextual girl," says Tetzlaff. "She is ubiquitous at the newsstand [...], unavoidable for anyone but cultural hermits, this alone makes Madonna a phenomenon worthy of analysis."[194]

E. Ann Kaplan writes: "The anti–Madonna media discourse serves those threatened by her challenges to patriarchal heterosexual norms."[195] But the discourse of Madonnophobes contributes no less to the star's celebrity than that of the Madonnophiles. Besides, Madonna reaps the benefits of the competition that rages between different media, as analyzed by Pierre Bourdieu.[196]

It has become hard to open a book that has to do with U.S. popular culture without encountering some mention of Madonna, even if it is a book by authors who think about the Beatles when they hear the word pop. In the same way, it is now common to hear her name in sitcoms, or in movies (*The Ref, True Lies, Four Weddings and a Funeral, French Kiss, The Real Blonde, Simple Men,* to name but six) or to read it in comics and novels.[197]

When Random House decided to publish a collection of quotations entitled *Word of Love*, they subtitled it *Romantic Quotations from Plato to Madonna*.[198] When New York State University published a book of philosophy about "commodity fetishism," one of the three chapters was devoted to Madonna Studies.[199] Of course, the association of her name with that of philosophers like Plato and Hegel is intrinsically postmodern.

Producers and distributors also use Madonna's image to serve their interests. When the movie *A League of Their Own* was released in France, Columbia gave away with the magazine *Hollywood Avenue* an audio cassette that helped promote the movie, which had not garnered that much money in the States. The tape sold sex and Madonna's stardom. It exploited Madonna's sexual image, praising the product like a stallholder at the market, especially when you consider that hers is not the main part in the movie. Her name was repeated a dozen times, and the pitch was her vamp's seduction and her tendency to be linked to scandals.

So the myth feeds on that constant evocation. The words of journalists, of fans, of Madonnologists and of Madonna herself — Madonnologist if ever there was any — echo each other, contradict each other, and mix until they form a huge information maelstrom which, while developing confusion, promotes the celebrity of the star.

I'll conclude with Cosmo Landesman, who writes: "Everyone, from middle-aged academics to teenage wannabes, [is] utterly fascinated by the minutiae of the Madonna Phenomenon. And none more so than the media."[200] But other celebrities are also keenly aware of Madonna's impact.

Bad As I Wanna Be, the autobiography of the basketball champion Dennis Rodman (a Madonna ex) was number one in the U.S. during eight whole weeks in the nonfiction best-selling list. That 1996 book partakes of the general Madonnology, but with the following particularity: Rodman claims to establish a clear distinction between private Madonna and public Madonna. He devotes one chapter out of thirteen to Madonna, detailing her sex life, and mentions her abundantly throughout the book. When you consider his age and career, and the fact that his affair with Madonna lasted "a wild six months" in 1994,[201] that is blatantly disproportional. It either shows Rodman's greed, or an implicit avowal on his part: Madonna is one of the most important things that ever happened to him. Or both.

Rodman asserts that Madonna crawled at his feet, wanting to marry him and bear his children.[202] He is the one who broke up, he writes, but a simple phone call would have her come back crawling. Now here is a remarkable jab at the widespread image of Madonna-the-woman-of-power.

At any rate, it is clear that Rodman took lessons in stardom from Madonna, and determined to keep on building his own celebrity on the very model of Madonnesque mythology. As he writes unflattering things about Madonna he reinforces her stardom and adds to the myth, notably when he exemplifies the idea that Madonna's stardom is not dissociable from her name: indeed at some point in the book Rodman finds himself incapable of calling Madonna by her name. Can't you just picture a human elected by Aphrodite feeling the same difficulty and picking a sweet nickname? So he decides to call her Tita (symbolic deicide) and doesn't seem to realize where this came from. Well, Tita seems to me remarkably close to Dita, Madonna's alter-ego in *Sex*. *Sex*'s Dita probably dug her bed in his unconscious, just as she did in the collective unconscious of America.[203]

He repeatedly confirms the absolute stardom and the sexual power of Madonna, indicating in various ways that she can go to bed with anyone she chooses. Then he goes for truism: "Madonna's fame is based on sex."[204] You don't say.

In an interview, Julie Salamon confesses to Madonna that the only passage she ever read in Rodman's book was the "Madonna chapter". This is Madonna's reaction:

> I'm sure that's all anyone's reading […]. It's not the first time I feel he's exploited his *very brief* relationship with me […]. It really wasn't much of a relationship, which is why it astonishes me that he's gotten so much mileage out of it […]. I can only imagine they urged him to be as imaginative and juicy as possible, and to make things up, and maybe offered him more money if he would talk about me […]. Much as I should hate him, I actually feel compassion for him.[205]

Here's divine stardom at work: Madonna the merciful can afford to forgive, she has nothing to fear anyway. The myth absorbs everything.

In his novel *The Black Album* (1995), the writer Hanif Kureishi mentions Madonna six times. One of the two main characters, Deedee Osgood, lectures at the university. Kureishi describes her office: "Her office was only three times the size of a telephone booth. Pinned above the desk were pictures of Prince, Madonna and Oscar Wilde, with a quote beneath it, 'All limitations are prisons'."[206] Deedee Osgood is interested in popular culture as much as she is interested in literature: "She and other post-modern types encouraged their students to study anything that took their interest, from Madonna's hair to a history of the leather jacket."[207]

Further down, Kureishi deals with a little bit of gender-bending *à la* Madonna: Deedee has an affair with a Pakistani student named Shahid. One evening she decides to make him up, to the sound of *Vogue*, of course.[208] Only one other song could have been used adequately in that scene, *Makeup* by Lou Reed,[209] but it wouldn't have been quite as good. Maybe Kureishi has read *Sex*, in which Madonna paints the lips of a very young boy (page 46). Kureishi somewhat mocks that new species of teacher but he understands Madonna's impact and knows why she is studied in universities.

In his science fiction novel *Vurt*, Jeff Noon describes Manchester (England) in the near future, peopled with "shadowcops" and rebellious drug-addicts who hang curious posters on their walls: "Beetle shooting apple cum. It splattered over my poster of Interactive Madonna at Woodstock Seven […]. The blood was spraying over Interactive Madonna, mixing with the spunk already plastered there. I guess that dead star was really interacting now."[210] Virtual Marilyn Monroes intervene in many science fiction novels;[211] now it is Madonna's turn, and we know already that she will remain famous decades after her demise, like Elvis Presley.

The singer Sade is supposed to have said: "Madonna is like a McDonald's hamburger. When you ask for a big Mac, you know exactly what you're getting. It's enjoyable, but it satisfies only for the moment."[212] As the proverb says, "*Se non è vero, è molto bene trovato.*" As it happens, Madonna's aim is not to create immortal music that will be taught alongside Mozart in conservatories. In a postmodern context, the analogy with McDonald's is very revealing, and not as derogatory as you might think. There seems to be some sort of equation between the "McDonaldization" of America and its "Madonnization," which can both be celebrated by postmodern critics.[213]

The singer-actress Debbie Harry (Blondie), who notoriously influenced Madonna,[214] was quoted everywhere when she declared that she was delighted to hear Madonna acknowledge her debt, but that she would have preferred a check.

The best-selling Canadian singer Céline Dion said that she decided early in the day to become as famous as Madonna. Spreading the image of a proper clean-cut vice-free young woman, she has often been hailed as the anti–Madonna.

Show business types like Meryl Streep, Gwen Stefani, Arsenio Hall, Bette Midler and even her ex-husband Sean Penn have been known to bad-mouth Madonna in the press.

Tony Ward tells how Madonna was totally metamorphosed on the set of a video: "She'd be just a natural, real person. Then the music went on and instantly she'd turn into 'Madonna'. You could see her turn the power on." This does nothing to invalidate my views. Ward evokes their affair and breakup and explains: "She's a great heartbreaker and a great man-crusher[...]. How the hell could you compete with her?" He then reminisces about his past drug addiction and tells us that Madonna generously paid for the bill at his rehab clinic, even though they had parted.[215]

Some celebrities seeking publicity do not hesitate to use Madonna's name (sometimes quite inventively). Generally they count on the sulfurous bad girl reputation of she whose stardom presumably represents an ideal they wish they could attain. The actress Pamela Anderson, made famous by her lifeguard part in *Baywatch*, worked hard to try and rival Madonna as sex symbol. She once stated on TV that never having had homosexual sex, she dreamed of trying with Madonna, adding that her husband rocker Tommy Lee agreed to participate.[216]

The French Spanish–TV host Marlène Mourreau (who is to Madonna what K-Mart is to Bloomingdale's) declared that she was just like Madonna, because she too had a Cuban in her life. When will we hear someone claim to be just like Madonna because she too has two arms and two legs?

In the same way, the press never stops comparing female singers to Madonna, attempting to create or spur more or less plausible rivalries.

Madonna does play the same game, to a certain extent, in a funny exchange system. The most obvious illustration of the process is the very hyped Cyndi Lauper "issue," but there is also Kylie Minogue, and more recently Britney Spears. In November and December 2000, Madonna found the perfect answer, wearing glitter T-shirts that screamed "Kylie Minogue" or "Britney Spears" to the world. The message was clear enough, it seems to me. And the joke postmodern. For all you know, she might actually like Minogue and Spears. She has said so.

The power of Madonna resides very largely in that planetary Madonnology: everyone has an opinion on Madonna. Her likeness (e.g. by Peter Blake or Antonio of Felipe) is now exhibited in museums, along with John Fitzgerald Kennedy's, Elvis Presley's or James Dean's. Madonna has become the ultimate reference in several domains. Some mention her as a paragon of beauty, like the Peruvian writer Jaime Bayly in *No se le digas a nadie*.[217] Some use her as a paragon of fashion, like the Spanish writer Vicente Molina Foix in *La mujer sin cabeza*, where women *and* men imitate her.[218] In her novel *Run Catch Kiss*, Amy Sohn uses Madonna as a paragon of provocation and reinvention.

One of the most significant examples of the privileged position Madonna occupies is the record by the famous American DJ Junior Vasquez, *If Madonna Calls* (1996). You can hear her voice, in a message on an answering machine, and various playfully offending comments spoken and sung by Franklin Fuentes. On the sleeve, you can read "Vocals by Who's That Girl" (possibly a professional Madonna impersonator). When pop artists practiced sampling in the past, they chose Winston Churchill (Supertramp), Sean Connery (Dr. No) or Peter Sellers (MacSample); today, they sample Madonna, or a Madonna impersonator. Of course, sampling is intrinsically postmodern.

It is true, as Tetzlaff says, that the power of the omnipresent Madonna has to do with hyperreality, and that she somehow embodies the hyperreality of Debord's *société du spectacle*;[219] what is named "Madonna" being nothing but an infinite accumulation of simulacra, an overabundance of information.

It is easy to see Madonna as a heavyweight participant in the vast information-producing machine (the media); she keeps indulging in Baudrillardesque *mises en scène* of communication and meaning. And isn't she, moreover, one of the most striking manifestations of McLuhan's global village, because of her ubiquity?

But it is possible even if you are a "regular" person, *pace* Tetzlaff,[220] to examine the postmodern spectacle of the star in a way that is not entirely passive. You may worship her as a divinity, you may consume her. You may also dream of becoming the next Madonna, supposing such a thing were possible, or, why not, get busy to do as well financially, it is one version of the American Dream.

Paraphrasing Baudrillard again, I might say that Madonna's originality lies in her status as a new, postmodern type of star: you can believe in her as you believe in an idol (in the original sense), i.e., without really believing, and while keeping your distance. You may love her without being obliged to believe in her.[221]

More than any other star in history, Madonna approaches that total omnipresence which characterizes the divine in the majority of widespread religions. Having perceived with implacable lucidity the nature of the society she lives in, a society in which information is everything (and nothing at the same time), she is determined to master it. Like a sort of Big Sister, she invades our screens, our hi-fi equipment, our magazines, and our books. She is a radically postmodern phenomenon which feeds upon itself, self-reproducing. More than ten thousand Internet sites speak of her, more than a hundred are entirely devoted to her.

To reach such results, Madonna has shown limitless ambition. She has organized her own cult and its derivative products; octopus-like, she has expanded her power around, so as to be literally everywhere, or at least spread her image everywhere. In the postmodern Madonnesque hyperreality, trying to locate any *realitatis femina* Madonna is absurd; what matters is the multiplication of reproductions, of simulacra and simulations, clones and clones of clones, which include the numerous singers who imitate Madonna.

In our image civilization, the Holocaust is dealt with in primetime soaps, and frequently interrupted by commercials. When there is no more informational hierarchy, Madonna acquires as much (or as little) importance as the Gulf War or African ethnic massacres.[222] Back in the fifties, Rev. Billy Graham already deplored that America knew the measurements of Jayne Mansfield much better than the text of the Second Commandment. Today, America knows more about Madonna than about any passage of the Bible.

What makes Madonna such a rich object of study is that as a postmodern star and number one Madonnologist, she provides an ever-running commentary upon stardom. Annalee Newitz claims that *Sex* marks the moment in her career when Madonna "ceased to be a hot commodity and became instead a comment upon herself as a star."[223] But hasn't Madonna always been both the one and the other?

In 1990, politics in the restricted sense of the word were as yet the only domain Madonna hadn't touched upon, although she had been seen as wielding political power since 1985. She remedied this by agreeing to take part in the Rock the Vote campaign. In her Rock the Vote TV ad, she totally flattens history, inscribing figures like Thomas Jefferson and Martin Luther King in pop culture. Apparently she started voting in the nineties.[224] During Monicagate, Madonna publicly declared that whatever had transpired between Clinton and Lewinsky, it did not make him a bad president.[225]

Having obtained her desperately sought stardom, Madonna can now do just about anything, as long as she continues playing, and occupying the media landscape.

THREE

The Fundamental Contradiction

Is she a nun or a whore, a dominatrix or a victim?
According to her mood, Madonna contradicts herself.
— Thomas Job[1]

"Virgin," "vamp," "mother," "saint," "nun," "prostitute:" the apparent simplicity of those words is deceitful. Applied to Madonna, they have
multiple connotations this chapter proposes to analyze. The different sup-
ports of Madonna's extreme stardom are linked to a fundamental contradiction that was already present in the work of the mythic stars who
preceded her. In this respect too, she embodies the postmodern of the end
of the twentieth century and the beginning of the twenty-first, manipulating efficiently and with humor the allusions to the dichotomy that fed
golden age Hollywood. Having devoted long hours to the observation of
her dead predecessors, Madonna did not merely pay tributes to their hair-
dos or getups, she paid tributes to their gestures and diction (see chapter
4), and absorbed the subtlest mechanisms of their seduction, including
the contradiction(s).

A few nuns shared with silver screen femmes fatales the favors of Madonna the schoolgirl. They left traces. Eva Perón also counts among Madonna's idols, and her impact will be taken into consideration.

Is Madonna a good girl, a bad girl, or a good-bad girl? This is one of the questions her work poses. The birth of her daughter Lourdes opened new horizons, later more or less confirmed by the birth of her son Rocco, that must also be taken into account.

The Virgin and the Vamp

Madonna's resentment toward Catholicism is proportional to the marks it left on her, which of course isn't particularly original; many Catholic artists and writers built entire careers on such ambivalent feelings.[2]

At Catholic school, Madonna often fell for nuns, which did not stop her from misbehaving. She nevertheless still admires the devotion and selflessness of nuns. For her confirmation, she chose to add Veronica to her two Christian names Madonna Louise, as a tribute to Saint Veronica. She was no doubt seduced by the way the saint had reproduced a famous face. Madonna would be busy doing exactly the same thing in later years, using her own face in lieu of white veil to appose the features of a celebrity. As a future postmodern icon, she could not have chosen a more appropriate name (it probably means "*vera icon*," i.e., true image). What is more, Saint Veronica isn't mentioned in Rome's martyrology; she is a contested saint. It is easy to suppose, of course, that Madonna also thought of Veronica Lake when she chose her confirmation name. During the 1998 *Ray of Light*, she was often nicknamed Veronica Electronica.[3]

As a child, Madonna liked Nancy Sinatra for her glamour. Blonde, sexy, gifted with an interesting voice, she mostly influenced her because of the all time classic *These Boots Are Made for Walking*. Isn't that song one of the very first S&M (feminist?) songs in pop history?

The Madonna of the beginning exploits the notion of virginity much more than the post 1989 Madonna. Her first four albums play with the two images of the Virgin and the Whore: *Madonna, Like a Virgin, Like a Prayer* and *The Immaculate Collection*. I am not entirely sure that Madonna is now over that age old dichotomy. Aren't her drag and exhibitionistic practices a continuation of that ambiguous relation to religion and Marian cults?

The *Take a Bow* video is packed with pious images and dubious representations of the Virgin (the Andalusian context justifies it); Madonna plays an aristocratic lady in love with a Spanish torero. They can be seen consummating their love, but more often than not they make love via TV pictures (postmodern post–AIDS love), as if the purity of the one or the other had to be preserved. At the end of the video, you can see an imposing sculpture of the Virgin Mary on the wall: she has Madonna's face.[4] The least that can be said is that Madonna sometimes carries her identification with the Virgin very far.

Another woman, another myth, was accused of every sin under the sun, and called a whore: Eva Perón. Whereas some revered her, others vilified her, it is a situation Madonna knows well. Playing Evita on the screen, Madonna wished to develop once more the sinner-saint dichotomy, remembering notably the generosity of Evita toward the underdogs. Eva Perón, while keeping many enemies, managed to impose herself as a national heroine. She was as strongly worshipped as the Virgin Mary. It is hard to imagine Madonna being unanimously worshipped after her death, but she is already adored like a saint by her fans. In *Survival*, she sings that she will never be an angel, nor a saint. She simply does what she must to survive.

The cult of Eva Perón is vivacious, and the cult of Madonna mirrors it: this is the leitmotiv of the world press between October 1996 and January 1997, when all sorts of special screenings of *Evita* took place all over the globe.

Let's not forget Evita was nicknamed *La Madona de los descamisados* (the Madonna of the poor, of the shirtless). Madonna admirably played up the similarities between Evita and herself. Where others would have waited for the release of the movie to read the reviews and check if her acting had been favorably reviewed, Madonna decided to warn the world beforehand. Be prepared, she more or less said, you will see how far the identification process went, you will see that I am Evita. And she told the press: "[In Argentina] I kept getting told how much I looked like her, or moved like her."[5] It was a remarkable campaign, barely disguised as emotional and artistic comments on the part of the star. More postmodern than ever, she did everything she could to make *Evita* a cult film even before it came out. The preceding sentence only sounds oxymoronic in a non-postmodern perspective; it is on that sort of paradox that a postmodern stardom thrives. Madonna elaborated for *Evita* an absolute and hyper-controlled palimpsest.

The film got mixed reviews. The song *You Must Love Me* got an Oscar. The Evita part was Madonna's *schibboleth*, but she did not get the best actress Oscar. She wasn't even nominated, but she did get the Golden Globe. As for the single *Don't Cry For Me Argentina*, it was number one in the charts of a great many countries.

For *Evita* Madonna moved from pop sex bomb to serious music diva and serious actress capable of sobriety (ultimate postmodern twist: the incarnation of anti-sobriety turning sober). The 1998 *Ray of Light* Madonna would still be relatively sober. But she'd go back to more "kinky" stuff in 2000.

She had tried sobriety before, playing a missionary in *Shanghai Surprise*; but the movie, a veritable financial disaster, had been unanimously decried by the critics. Evita herself tried to be taken seriously as an actress, even though her acting was bad. She finally obtained the greatest part of all, and played it to perfection, the dream part of Evita, president's wife, most famous woman in her country (like Madonna), but also most loved.

The best illustrations of the vast media sweeping operation Madonna orchestrated are to be found in the magazines *Vogue* and *Vanity Fair*—which she has often used to promote her metamorphoses.

Madonna published in *Vanity Fair* the *Private Diary* she kept during the shooting in Argentina. Those pages—with pictures—constitute another tremendous fiction, a *tour de force* worthy of *Truth or Dare*. She comes across as a manipulator, and the diary contains the implicit avowal of her manipulating.

Initially, the authorization to film Madonna at the Casa Rosada balcony in Buenos Aires had not been granted to Alan Parker. Madonna had decided to meet President Carlos Menem so as to make him change his mind.

In her diary she claims that she means to "explore and investigate the myth of Eva Perón." She wants to meet people who were close to her, and charm them. She is determined, she writes, to sing *Don't Cry For Me Argentina* on the Casa Rosada balcony, and not in some studio. On January 30 she meets the manager of a library, with whom she discusses Pablo Neruda, Gabriel García Márquez, Jean Renoir, Jean-Luc Godard, Luis Buñuel, Pier Paolo Pasolini, Jean Cocteau, Roberto Rossellini, and Luchino Visconti. On January 31 she meets the chief of police, who very conveniently volunteers that some "people were angry with Evita in her day for the same reason they are angry with [her] today". They talk about reincarnation and the chief of police quotes Oscar Wilde: "Something about Art imitating Life."

The next day she confides that she resents the fact that President Menem has entertained other celebrities, but avoids her. This just goes to show, she deems, that "if you have an opinion or stand for something in this world you are considered a threat. Something to be feared." On February 6 she grants a press conference that makes her feel good, because a number of beautiful young men "[sit] in the front row blowing [her] kisses and mouthing the words I love you." On February 8, she finally meets President Menem, who tells her she looks just like Evita.

> I caught Menem looking at my bra strap, which was showing ever so slightly. He continued doing this throughout the evening with his piercing eyes, and when I caught him staring, his eyes stayed with mine[...]. We talked about everything from Mao Tse-Tung to mambo.

On February 12, she is happy to note a procession of fans in her honor. They chant "Eva, Madonna" under her balcony and practically move her to tears. On March 10 she writes:

> Last night I walked out on the balcony of the Casa Rosada in front of thousands of people and sang "Don't Cry for Me Argentina." In the exact place where she had stood so many times before, I raised my arms and looked into the hungry eyes of humanity, and at that moment I felt her enter my body like a heat missile, starting with my feet, traveling up my spine, and flying out my fingertips, into the air, out to the people, and back up to Heaven [...]. When you want something bad enough the whole earth conspires to help you get it.[6]

Not only the whole earth conspires to help Madonna, it would seem, but even spirits from the other world. Her numerous literary allusions are deliberately vague, so as not to demonstrate too blatantly the point they make about this new Madonna: a cultured but still sexy woman, who spends evenings with presidents and has intellectual conversations. I myself feel tempted to vaguely quote Oscar Wilde in connection with Madonna; what he said to André Gide about putting genius in his life and merely talent in his work, for example. Is it not wonderful that she did not have to make this or that point, that helpful chiefs of police or presidents should oblige?

To complete that *Private Diary*, Madonna unsurprisingly granted a handful of interviews, always going extremely far to promote the equation Evita equals Madonna.

And indeed, there are many true similarities. Like Madonna, Evita came from nowhere. Like Madonna, she was accused of practicing the casting couch and of being manipulative. Like Madonna she bleached her hair and radically changed wardrobes. Evita and Madonna share the same thirst for power. Like Madonna, Evita reinvented herself entirely, beauty included. So you may find it logical that Madonna embodies her at the movies. The Evita project was passed around Hollywood for years, from producer to directors to actresses. Finally Madonna won the day. How? By besieging all the interested parties throughout the years, eliminating her rivals (Meryl Streep, Michelle Pfeiffer, Barbra Streisand, and the like), and fighting like a woman used to winning her fights. There is for instance that mythic letter she wrote to the director who finally directed the movie. Sometimes Alan Parker himself mentioned that letter; most of the time,

Madonna took care to promote it, the better to promote the movie and herself, talking about her being practically possessed by Evita...

For that movie, Madonna reached shape-shifting powers which were unheard of. She is the spitting image of Eva Perón. She had looked like other icons before, but never to this extent. The nineties icon is a very convincing double of the forties icon. I find her work as an actress in *Evita* quite worthy of praise. Beatriz Salazar, Argentine, Professor at Rouen University, met Evita when she was a child. She told me that she had been impressed by Madonna's interpretation, and thought that Madonna — on top of the physical appearance — had uncannily reproduced Evita's gestures. From a historical point of view, it is clear that the movie is only slightly more acceptable than the stage musical. But who cares if such works are faithful to history?

See the Way She Walks

The influence of the band The Velvet Underground on rock-pop culture and on Madonna can never be exaggerated. In their classic *Femme Fatale*, Nico sings about a woman who breaks the heart of the clownish men who succumb to her charms. The line "She's a femme fatale" is sung in fact by the rest of the band, who act as a Greek chorus, commenting upon the tragedy happening, the fall of the individual who loses all dignity as he submits to the femme fatale. Let us remember poor Professor Unrat (Professor Rath), who in Heinrich Mann's eponymous novel (1905) is literally reduced to the sad clown state by the cruel Lola.[7] That is the destiny of the man who falls for a femme fatale. When the seduction logic is pushed to its limits, nothing can result but ruin, humiliation, and death, often by suicide. This is not remarkably original, of course. Mythologies abound in femmes and goddesses fatales, who caused the end of men, not to mention Eve the sinner...

It is difficult to establish with precision the nuances between "vamp" and "femme fatale." Many dictionaries (in all sorts of languages) give them out as synonyms. However, you may see the femme fatale as cursed, and observe that she frequently if not systematically ends up being fatal(e) to herself, whereas the vamp seems fatal(e) only to men. Let's note that "vamp" was originally used exclusively in the context of movies. It is of course the abbreviation of "vampire," and seems to have surfaced in 1911, after the release of a Danish film, *Vampirish Dance*, before spreading considerably after *A Fool There Was* (subtitled *Kiss Me, My Fool!*). The star of that film of 1915 (or 1916, depending on sources) is Theda Bara, who is seen by many film historians as the very first vamp. Madonna presumably enjoys the legend that was built around Theda Bara, and the findings of the publicists who spread the notion that the pseudonym Theda Bara was the anagram of "Arab death." *A Fool There Was* was adapted from Rudyard Kipling's 1897 poem *The Vampire*.[8] In the twenties, the character of the vamp was abundantly exploited on the screen, one of the most interesting examples being Greta Garbo's *The Temptress* (Fred Niblo, 1926).

Theda Bara, the ur-vamp, based her entire career on vamp parts. It would be superfluous to develop the sexual connotations of vampirism here, they have been amply documented elsewhere, and intelligently exploited in Anne Rice's novels. Don't forget the old blood and sperm analogy (vital liquids). Didn't Mae West once pose with vampire wings on her back?[9]

If on the album *The Velvet Underground and Nico*, the song *Venus in Furs* comes immediately after *Femme Fatale*, it is because the association with masochism is obvious. Femmes fatales owe their existence to the fact that there are men who are sufficiently masochistic to complacently fall into their clutches. There is but a small step from the standard spike-heeled femme fatale to the leather and steel dominatrix. The celebrated fifties Betty Page had understood this, as Lou Reed and Madonna remember. Years before Madonna, Amanda Lear exploited sexual ambiguity. Model, early friend of David Bowie, actress, friend and inspirer of Salvador Dali, writer, painter, TV presenter and Euro-disco singer, Lear is rumored to have been a man, and once sang *These Boots Are Made for Walking*. A sort of Madonna precursor, she used S&M imagery abundantly in the late seventies.

The movie or pop vamp owes little of her power to nature. She deploys elaborate strategies to seduce a public that isn't limited to one man but is composed of millions of individuals. In the case of Madonna, that seduction is invariably practiced with irony. It constitutes a playful tribute to yesteryear's vamps, as well as a deconstruction of the vamp myth, with all the antifeminist connotations it carries. Yet, at the very same time she indulges in that postmodern game, Madonna does seduce; she really does become a sex symbol that millions of women and men desire, as surveys have shown. In other words she wins on every level.

Apropos of the femme fatale, Mary Ann Doane notes:

> The femme fatale is the figure of a certain discursive unease, a potential epistemological trauma. For her most striking characteristic, perhaps, is the fact that she never really is what she seems to be. She harbors a threat which is not entirely legible, predictable, or manageable.[10]

Isn't that a fitting description of Madonna?

In *Sooner or Later*, Madonna states that she always gets her man. The woman who always gets what she wants is the femme fatale. Note the use of the adjective "lethal" and the adverb "lethally" in many descriptions of the art of Madonna, in their complimentary meanings, obviously. Lethal means fatal(e).[11] To get also means to kill, in some contexts, and why not eat, like a praying mantis? The phrase "man-eater" is common. So the vamp–femme fatale is vampirish, or even something of a succubus; old clichés, of course, but still valid, otherwise Madonna wouldn't have made such a career out of them. I am thinking notably of the ancient Lilith myth (I see Lilith as the first feminist). When you speak of Madonna, you're never very far from the nun, and the praying mantis. And isn't the Madonna traditionally represented as a nun? Caillois evokes the myth of the *vagina dentate*, and the castration complex as studied by psychoanalysis.[12] If Madonna sometimes arouses hatred, even mock-hatred, to the point that there exists a book called *The I Hate Madonna Handbook*, it is because she embodies the vamp myth so convincingly, complete with castration anxieties— plus she is a feminist vamp.

But isn't the vamp feminist by definition, terrifying for those who believe in the superiority of males, whatever their own gender? Lilith, in the eyes of some, is also the first whore.

The Mother and the Whore[13]

Mae West used to say: "When I'm good, I'm very good, but when I'm bad I'm better."[14] While Michael Jackson screams "I'm bad" till he drops with exhaustion, having failed to convince anyone, Madonna is commonly seen as a bad girl, in more ways than one. Her language, to begin with, never stops shocking.[15]

The most famous of Madonna's language excesses is her performance on the David Letterman show in 1994. She said "fuck" thirteen times, beating the record of beeps ever imposed by censorship on an American talk-show. The way she treated Letterman definitely categorized her: she's a bad girl. Among other provocations, she gave him a pair of her panties and insisted that he should sniff them. It must be said that Letterman had mentioned her a lot in previous shows, constantly alluding to her sex life.

During her early shows, she would sometimes throw her panties to the audience. That was abundantly commented upon in the press, especially in Italy and France. Many jokes circulated around the connection between now President Jacques Chirac and Madonna's underwear. His daughter had announced her keen interest in the star, and he himself declared that he was not quite immune to her charm after he attended her concert. Rumor says he actually kept the panties that fell on his lap when

Madonna threw them.[16] Madonna and the future French President even appeared together on TV, with the singer Line Renaud. A bad girl, then, even if one who mixes with heads of states (like Carlos Menem in Argentina), notably because she exhibits her body. She is regarded in American conservative circles as a stripper who made it.

Woody Allen knows what he's doing: he chose Madonna to play the cameo part of the circus trapeze woman in *Shadows and Fog* (Woody Allen, 1992). Very much reminiscent of Mae West in *I'm No Angel* (Wesley Ruggles, 1933), she is heavily made-up, clearly coded as an easy lay and a bad girl, since she debauches the John Malkovich character, hurting the initially virtuous Mia Farrow character.

According to the same principle, Spike Lee hired Madonna to play the owner of a phone sex company. Even though her lines are extremely few, one of her scenes was understandably used for the trailer of *Girl 6* (1996). In a close shot, she announces: "No inhibitions, no restrictions, total freedom, no taboos." Lisa Kennedy writes: "Spike Lee and the Material Girl encouraged us to reconsider our most important categories: race and sex and, when it was bound up with color, class."[17]

Considering the frequency of a celebrity's appearances in popular jokes is a good way to judge the level of his stardom. In the sixties, for instance, many jokes circulated (especially in Europe) about Brigitte Bardot, which were all linked to her legendary powers of seduction. Madonna is also entitled to her own Madonna jokes now. Indeed you hear about Madonna jokes as you'd hear about lightbulb jokes or baby jokes or Irish jokes. And they all have to do with her reputation as a sex fiend. There is, as I said, an *I Hate Madonna* Handbook, but there is also an *I Hate Madonna Jokebook* and a book called *The Sexiest Jokes about Madonna*, which is edifying.[18]

You may have heard the following jokes: "McDonna, over one billion served," or "McDonna, people line up but never stay long." You may even have heard one of the very vulgar jokes linked to the birth of Lourdes Maria: "The first words of the little girl when she was born were: 'Now I hope I'll be visited less frequently'."[19]

So Madonna is a bad girl, an exhibitionistic stripper. Roland Barthes writes: "Striptease[...] is based on a contradiction: it is about de-sexualizing woman at the same time as she is undressed [...]. So there will be in striptease a whole series of covers gradually laid on the woman's body as she pretends to denude herself."[20]

Without getting into the question of masks at this stage, let us note that such words echo Madonna effortlessly. Like myth, like Madonna, striptease is based on a contradiction. Madonna pretends to denude herself, but uses props that "mask" her nudity or get attention away from it, while valorizing it. Her nudity, besides, is extremely coded, and almost always echoes identifiable erotic traditions. Madonna is also a bad girl because this way she deliberately frustrates the public. Almost all the photographs in *Sex*, for example, are quotations or allusions of sorts. When they are not framed by invisible quotation marks, they are framed by invisible inverted commas, signaling tongue-in-cheek. She even borrows from traditional striptease imagery.[21]

Madonna undulates like a stripper in the *Like a Virgin* video. Madonna takes off her clothes in public (for example in her book *Sex* or in the *Open Your Heart* video) only to better clothe herself. This cannot but enrage those who hope that the naked Madonnesque truth will be revealed, those who wait for the apparition of the Madonna, for an epiphany of sorts. *Truth or Dare* disappoints them for the same reasons. Here lies the central Madonnesque paradox: Madonna is everywhere to be seen, Madonna bares her flesh, but she does not unveil herself. She is more preoccupied with the parody of the voyeuristic male gaze.[22] She is a parody, an embodiment of the classic sex object and porn Queen;[23] she is a bad girl, but no more or less than Rita Hayworth in *Gilda*. And of course, when someone like Jordi Bianciotto writes a book called *Sexe et Rock 'n' Roll*, who should be on the cover but Madonna, in a typical bad girl pose?[24] A bad girl too, because she never conforms to what Madonnologists, Madonnophiles or Madonnophobes expect; a bad girl, because she knows what she wants, she takes what she needs where she knows she can find it; a bad girl finally because like old time Hollywood stars she ravages men's hearts. But doesn't she also renew the tradition of the good-bad-girl?

Madonna is a bad girl because in a macho world, women of power are disturbing. The most effective scenes of *Dick Tracy* are those when Madonna shows up as Breathless Mahoney. The dialogue is full of sexual puns that make you wonder who's speaking, Breathless Mahoney or Madonna. The confusion is calculated. That is how stardom can be reinforced. Madonna plays on all levels. She parodies yesterday's femme fatale and appropriates her at the same time. She is a comic book vamp in a stylized, self-conscious comic book adaptation. The Stephen Sondheim parodic torch song *Sooner or Later* develops the argument: sooner or later, Madonna-Breathless always gets the man she wants. Has ever a song functioned so much as a commentary on its interpreter's work?

The tabloids love reporting, however, that if she always gets her man, she does not necessarily keep him as long as she would wish. When Madonna got married to Guy Ritchie in December 2000, British bookmakers made fortunes taking all sorts of bets related to the wedding and the marriage; the bets were based on questions ranging from "what is Guy

Ritchie going to wear under his kilt?" to "how long is the marriage going to last?"

In an America that is still very phallocentric, a woman who won't let men step over her will be called a bitch by those who feel threatened, and a woman who flaunts an uninhibited sexuality will be called a slut by the same men. So Madonna the bad girl is often seen as a prostitute. She is the Great Prostitute of the myth, the Whore of Babylon, the sacred prostitute of the temple. In *Sex*, her alter-ego Dita sees a doctor. He asks her if she has ever been mistaken for a prostitute, and Dita answers: "Every time anyone reviews anything I do, I'm mistaken for a prostitute."[25]

The bed is the workplace of the whore. In *El País*, Fatima Ramirez writes: "The singer and actress Madonna, the most desired woman in the world according to a recent survey, turned the bed into a workplace — at least visually."[26]

As its title indicates, the bed is indeed at the center of *Bedtime Stories*. Of course, that title is a pun. Madonna is referring at once to (possibly erotic) stories told at bedtime, and to (erotic) stories that take place at bedtime (in bed); often fairy tales (pun intended). In a way, that album really is a book of stories you can tell your kids at bedtime. It may help them dream of being Madonna, or of having her. For *Bedtime Stories* is also sexuality explained to children: Madonna has always thought that children should be better informed in that respect.

The titles of the songs *I'd Rather Be Your Lover*, *Don't Stop*, *Inside of Me*, and *Forbidden Love*, evoke sexual activities. Yet when you listen to the tracks you find that they are mostly about love, and in a very sentimental vein — as often happens with Madonna. She sprinkled them with borrowings from Walt Whitman and other literary allusions, so clichéd that those of her enemies who like claiming that she has never read a book in her life won't change their mind.

The bed is very conspicuous during the *Blond Ambition* tour, and Madonna famously simulates masturbation on it. Beds are also to be found in *Sex*. And *Truth or Dare* allows us to actually find ourselves *In Bed with Madonna*. The bed is also central in the videos of *Take a Bow* and *Justify My Love*. Samuel Blumenfeld writes: "Everybody's heard about Madonna's bed. But one question remains unanswered: was it really necessary to go and visit it?"[27]

Let's see, however, if a good girl isn't hiding behind the bad girl. Curiously, when Madonna sings *Bad Girl*,[28] the single never goes very high up the charts. What is the explanation? The music is neither better nor worse than that of her other singles. The video, shot by David-*Seven*-Fincher, is a masterpiece of the genre. Could that relative failure be due to the subject matter? Or perhaps just bad timing?

The song is about a bad girl who drinks and smokes too much and generally misbehaves. Her boyfriend is leaving her, she feels terrible because she still loves him. It's another sentimental song that really depicts a good girl, capable of contrition. Maybe that's what was disliked by her public: the persona was not ambiguous enough. As for the video, it shows a woman who's not so young anymore, bent on self-destruction. Being flanked by a *Wings of Desire* guardian angel (Christopher Walken) doesn't stop her from being assassinated by a one-night-stand. You could hardly convey a more conventional moral message.[29]

In *Body of Evidence* Madonna plays an irredeemably bad girl, and that might be one of the reasons for the movie's commercial failure. In the appalling *Shanghai Surprise*, Madonna is nothing but a good girl. She plays a missionary, who was deemed not credible by many spectators. Admittedly, you need to greatly suspend your disbelief to even vaguely enjoy the movie. Gloria Tatlock does offer her body to the tie salesman played by an uninspired Sean Penn, but only so as to obtain his help in a charitable enterprise.

That movie only delighted diehard fans. The producer (the late George Harrison) lost enormous sums of money. Playing a total good girl, Madonna is boring. Not everyone can be Audrey Hepburn.

Diana, the Princess of Wales, had become a myth and a gay icon[30] even before her death in August 1997. The tabloids frequently compared Madonna and Diana in the nineties. They were both very image-conscious and hunted by paparazzi and stalkers, they both had many gay friends (and supported AIDS associations). Apparently they liked each other. They say Madonna was not very pleased with Prince Charles's behavior toward Diana, but finally forgave him, and even went to dine at his country house.[31]

When Princess Diana died in Paris the word "stalkerazzi" was popularized, soon followed by "videorazzi." If Diana, a good girl with one or two light bad girl aspects, did not use the same strategies, she certainly shared with Madonna the power of making people dream.[32] In many ways they were invested with the same societal function. Here's an excerpt from a December 2000 *New Yorker* article:

> Something funny is going on between Madonna and the inhabitants of the United Kingdom. Since taking up with an Englishman, the film director Guy Ritchie (*Lock, Stock and Two Smoking Barrels*), bearing his son (Rocco), and announcing her intention to live in London full time, Madonna has replaced the late Diana, Princess of Wales, as Fleet Street's favorite mother.[33]

As (or like) a good girl, Madonna does not drink, nor does she do drugs. This is what she frequently declares, at any rate, which is what matters here. As an idol, she might worry the parents of her young fans: they already deplore the sulfurous image of the star, the explicit lyrics of her songs, they might feel sorry that she is so gay- and lesbian-friendly, as well as very liberal in terms of interracial relations; but they love that she doesn't drink and is into sports and health food. This of course did not stop Tipper Gore's Parents Music Resource Center from counting Madonna in its fifteen most undesirable people list.

A parallel can be established at this point with the (mostly European and now moribund) boy band phenomenon. Most boy bands have a very gay look,[34] but their fans' parents don't seem to realize; they delight in the sober anti-drug athletic images of those "wholesome" boys. The comparison stops here, obviously, boy bands being to Madonna what *The Little House on the Prairie* is to *Gravity's Rainbow*.

An important nuance: Madonna claims that she doesn't do drugs *any longer*, whereas clean-cut boy bands say they never did. She has been known to lack consistency on this score, though. She wouldn't sell so well in certain quarters if you couldn't at least credit her with a heavy and raunchy sinful past.

> I haven't done [ecstasy] in years [...]. You just love everybody. I mean, you could walk up to Bob Dole and have a conversation and find something to like about him. It's pathetic [...]. I found when I did it I would see people in clubs that I couldn't stand and I'd find myself being nice to them. It's not a very good drug. I mean, there are no good drugs, but it made me as sick as a dog.[35]

The second "I mean" is sufficiently ambiguous to reassure some (drugs are bad) and comfort others (certain drugs did give me pleasure). At any rate, Madonna being determined to remain in control at all times, it is difficult to imagine her indulging in substances that would make her lose control altogether.

But doesn't Madonna also renew the Hollywood tradition of the good-bad girl, the delight of European critics? Francis Bordat rightly states: "There is no real great female star who isn't a good-bad girl."[36] Edgar Morin defined her:

> A sort of synthesis of the vamp, the lover and the virgin is at work in glamour to give birth to the good-bad girl. The good-bad-girl [...] appears as the impure woman: naughty outfits, daring attitudes, heavy with innuendo, equivocal job, dubious company. But the end of the film will reveal that she had been hiding all the virtues of the virgin: pure soul, innate goodness, generous heart.[37]

This text dates back to 1957, and refers to the forties, but if you don't linger on the prefeminist adjectives, you see Madonna is not far. If her appearance is that of the impure woman, her name itself refers incessantly to the Virgin. Her goodness and generosity have manifested themselves, notably through her constant involvement against AIDS and homophobia, unless this is just another *mise en scène*,[38] which is unlikely. Questioning Madonna's "sincerity" makes little sense. What is important is the effect.

Her star personae are almost all informed by this good-bad-girlism. And I believe that aspect of her career hasn't been discussed enough: admittedly, she provokes, but she sings of love. She is a love goddess, as Morin would say. She sings good girl sentimental lyrics that are deconstructed or contradicted by her videos. With Madonna, you don't need to wait for the end of the movie to see the good girl behind the bad girl or vice versa, they are simultaneously on show.[39]

In *Dick Tracy*, Madonna directly revives the Hollywood tradition of the good-bad-girl, as Breathless the bombshell sacrifices herself. In *Who's That Girl?* she plays a fundamentally good character half-hidden behind delinquent looks, exactly as she does in *Desperately Seeking Susan*. In *Dangerous Game*, Madonna plays Sarah Jennings who plays Claire who wants to become a good girl after years of bad-girlism. The movie *A League of Their Own* offers a rare spectacle: women on a baseball field. How could Madonna not be interested in the part of All-the-Way-Mae[40] when you hear a radio anchor woman speak of the "masculinization of women" and then declare that those feminine teams constitute "the most disgusting example of this sexual confusion?"

All-the-Way-Mae allows the spectator to distinguish the image of Madonna the bad girl behind the baseball bat. When the players are asked to wear ridiculous minidresses, she complains that there are no pockets for her cigarettes. Then when the girls are told that the team policy is "no smoking, no drinking, no men," Mae rises, ready to abandon baseball forever there and then. When the coach, drunk, urinates in full view of the players, Mae is the only one who isn't afraid of looking at his penis; she even decides to time his micturition.

When Mae goes to confession, the horrified priest drops his Bible twice. So Mae-Madonna is a bad girl. But the simple fact that she goes to confession and prays on her knees makes her a good girl, even though she did poison (not lethally) the team chaperon so that they could go out dancing. Besides, she teaches the team's illiterate girl to read with a lot of devotion. However, the book she has chosen is an erotic novel. Madonna never forgets that, as Yvonne Tasker puts it, "any film redefines and works over star images."[41]

When Madonna gave birth to her daughter Lourdes, the press popularized the notion of a sobered-up and wise Madonna, a low-key family woman and dedicated mom. As usual, journalists chose to be accomplices in her supposed transformation. They rarely admit that she merely drops one persona for another because their papers sell better if they don't. Hence the caricatured good girl image promoted by the media at the beginning of 1997. Some journalists went as far as to report that she washed the dishes.

When Lourdes Maria's father, Carlos León, was "given the sack," the tabloids changed their minds. In 1997 they described Madonna as an abominable creature who had exploited León and kept some of his sperm frozen for future use.

The papers which had predicted the marriage of Madonna and Carlos León made up for it by publishing the names of the alleged successors in the diva's bed: Chris Paciello, Ingrid Casarès, Andrew Bird, and others. However, when the album *Ray of Light* was released in February-March 1998, many articles insisted again on Madonna's ideal mom image, forgetting the single mom stigma, and pretending again to believe that the latest persona of the star was the "real thing."

Lourdes Maria (or the Marian cult)

In a *USA Today* article, Karen Thomas advises Madonna on child-rearing. This no doubt stems from good intentions, but it mainly indicates the space Madonna fills in American daily life. The journalist consulted child psychology experts, who were only too willing to provide well-meaning guidance, in an open letter to the star that also contains a prognostic, since the reader is clearly meant to suppose that poor Lourdes Maria will suffer — as all children of stars suffer, poor things.

On October 14, 1996, Lourdes Maria Ciccone León was born and Madonna became the world's most famous mother.[42] She was the most famous woman before. In August 2000 she became the world's most famous twice mother.

So that October 1996 night, the French AFP (halfway between Reuters and the Associated Press) was on strike. The computers were desperately mute all night, except for *one* piece of news, that of the birth of Lourdes Maria. I could not have hoped for a better illustration of my view of Madonna. Does it not spectacularly prove her never-before-achieved degree of stardom? I almost feel sorry Madonna did not time her baby better and become impregnated on April 25. Here were journalists on strike, busy defending their interests, categorically refusing to transmit news (there were civil wars in various parts of the globe), who when they received word of the coming of the divine child simply could not help themselves. They just had to communicate the event.

Le Monde, Libération and other French newspapers reported the shocking fact that this piece of news alone filtered through the blackout imposed by the strike. All the media in the whole world reported on the birth of Lourdes Maria. When her second child, Rocco, was born on August 11, 2000, the media did not report on it quite so spectacularly, but only because she'd had a child before. However, Rocco's christening in Scotland on December 21, 2000, was very heavily covered by the international media, as was his mother's wedding to his father, Guy Ritchie, the next day. The Internet spoke of little else for two days. On this occasion another postmodern summit was attained, since the wedding was completely private (in stark contrast with Madonna's first helicopter-ridden wedding), and absolutely nothing was shown — which did not stop the world's TV crews from filming it.

In early 1997 there was a common joke that went: "I thought she could not have babies, she's got everything." It echoed a very general feeling. According to a certain "order of things" a femme fatale–vamp is not supposed to have babies. As Mary Ann Doane writes: "The femme fatale is represented as the antithesis of the maternal."[43] But of course, Madonna should not be pigeon-holed.

Many journalists joked about typical Madonna and Child representations when Lourdes was born.[44] During Madonna's pregnancy, apart from two series of paparazzi snapshots (published everywhere), the glamorous photographs that were published show a Madonna-Evita who is more gorgeous than ever, however pregnant. She very much influenced world fashion during that period.[45] A pregnancy and a movie of that magnitude at the same time constituted efficient publicity. During the last few weeks of shooting, the technical crews had to work overtime to hide the protruding belly of the star. But there is nothing that cannot be done in movies nowadays, especially when you have a body like Madonna's.[46]

The Estée Lauder company took advantage of all the premieres of the movie in various capitals to launch a gamut of cosmetics called Evita, signing a deal with Madonna to use her face. Few women are hired by cosmetics companies at such an advanced age. Madonna did even better, of course, when she landed a contract with Max Factor at the age of forty,[47] an age when most models are sacked.[48]

It all began a few years ago when Madonna started to express in the media a longing for motherhood, notably in connection to her ex-husband Sean Penn. She did so in sufficiently ambiguous ways, as usual, to be able to reinterpret her own words later as suited her needs, faithful to her number one Madonnologist's tricks. Then in 1995 she cracked the following joke in several interviews: her desire for a child had become more urgent, she was looking for the perfect progenitor, and considered placing an ad in the papers.

Madonna is far too shrewd not to have anticipated that this joke would last and be transformed by sensation-seeking media into a serious quest for inseminators. Indeed, this gave rise when her pregnancy was announced to amusing speculation about Carlos León's DNA. She subsequently complained about this on various occasions, but I tend to think that it was all part of a vast plan. When you are the most desired woman in the world as well as the most media-covered, if you joke about placing an ad, i.e., *using the media* to find a progenitor, you show a great talent for publicity and a particularly postmodern sense of humor.

In her Evita *Private Diary*, on April 17, she purports to be shocked and offended by the media's behavior when the whole world speaks of her pregnancy. Her surprise doesn't sound very convincing at all. She cites the examples of the *Washington Post*, or CNN, and it makes you feel that she is actually pleased, since it all confers a certain prestige to her pregnancy; few maternities enjoy such coverage. After so many years of stardom, Madonna may be blasé, but she has worked so hard to promote that stardom that she is quite entitled to derive a legitimate pleasure from it, in spite of fleeting feelings of persecution. "I feel like my insides had been ripped open," she says, as if she actually felt the gaze of the world on her womb, aware of the fact that many magazines would not hesitate to publish the ultrasound pictures of her fetus if they could get hold of them. She alludes to the journalists who suggested that she got pregnant "for shock value," telling how only men could come up with such comments; but I myself overheard a *woman* in a restaurant say: "I am convinced that her baby is just part of a publicity campaign."[49] Without going quite so far, we will note that she was able to profit —career wise —from that new stage in her eventful life. In the same way, the 2000 release of *Music* was in no way harmed by the practically simultaneous birth of Rocco.

When pregnant, Madonna let the world know that she would call her daughter Lola. She later claimed that she was in no way responsible for that "rumor." Yet it really did *not* look like a journalistic invention. Lola seemed a perfectly Madonnesque first name. Lola is Dolores, Lola is Lolita, of course, with all its connotations: Lolita the creation of Vladimir Nabokov (one of the fathers of postmodern writing), Lolita the sexy nymphet,[50] Lolita the name of Marilyn Monroe's persona in the song *My Heart Belongs to Daddy* (*Let's Make Love*) (1960).

Finally, the baby was born. On French TV, even Jean-Paul Gaultier, who is close to Madonna, "mistakenly" spoke of "little Lola." The minute Lourdes was born, Madonna (understandably) started circulating a pre-

cision as far as the pronunciation was concerned, with approximate pho-
netics, so as to let the whole world know that her child's name was not to
be pronounced "Lurds" but "Lour-dess."

Thousands of presents were sent to her home through the post, no
doubt by disappointed fans, engraved in the name Lola. The whole world
indeed asked the question, why Lourdes, such a difficult name to bear?

About the choice of Maria,[51] let's simply remember that Madonna
signifies Mary / Maria / Maria / Marie, and that Eva Perón was also
called Mary / Maria, like Marlene Dietrich, Mae West or Marilyn Monroe. As for the choice of Lourdes, many explanations can be offered:
Madonna's mother (named Madonna) was a French-Canadian devout
Catholic who dreamed of going to Lourdes on a pilgrimage; Lourdes had
a Cuban father and an Italian-American mother; Lourdes's birth was
something of a miracle (daughter of a goddess equals half goddess).

Even more remarkable: in her book *Sex*, Madonna named one of her
erotic short fiction characters Lourdes (page 113). Her friends call her Luli
(one letter away from Loli, another form of Dolores-Lolita), and a man
is subjugated by "that Lolita."

Postmodern metafictional intertextuality, always, right down to the
name of her daughter... Whether she creates a movie, a song, a book, or
a child, Madonna's creation is hyper-referenced. The mother role she took
up in 1996 and perfected in 2000 was but another persona, and it would
be simplistic to believe that she stopped playing after her first delivery.

As for the child, already the object of a Marian cult, like her mother
the Madonna, she remained, of course, Lola, according to postmodern
logic. Even before she was born she was caught in a game of codes, a game
of Madonnesque deceitful semiotics. And in the same way that it is always
possible to perceive under any Madonnesque persona all the preceding
avatars, it will always be possible to read Lola under the letters
L.O.U.R.D.E.S. Indeed, if you like anagrams, you can read D.O.L.U.R.E.S.,
just one letter away from Dolores.[52]

Naturally, Madonna is aware of this. In 1996, I was prepared to bet
Madonna would not actually call her daughter Lourdes, in everyday life,
maybe she would call her Maria, or Luli, unless she in fact called her Lola.
Well, in February 1998, when the single *Frozen* came out, journalists
around the globe suddenly reported that Lola is what Madonna called her
daughter at home.[53] At the end of the month, Madonna herself confirmed.
In the same way, David Bowie never really called his son Zowie, and finally
said, twenty years after he was born, that he was called Joe, or Joey, or
Duncan. The latter studied philosophy, maybe Lourdes will follow suit.[54]

Anyway, Lourdes and Dolores both belong to a Latin tradition of very
Catholic names, like the name Madonna. Dolores is Our (My) Lady (Ma-

donna) of the Seven Pains, she is the pains of S&M practices that Madonna always stages. Lola is also Lola Montés, it is Dietrich's name in *The Blue Angel*,[55] it is Anouk Aimée in Jacques Demy's film *Lola* (1960). There is also Lola the Blonde, played by Zsa Zsa Gabor in *Il Nemico pubblico numero uno* (Henri Verneuil, 1953). None of that takes us very far from the mother-whore dichotomy. Maybe Madonna also remembered the movie *Damn Yankees* (George Abbott, 1958), in which Gwen Verdon plays a very Madonnesque diabolical camp witch who rewrites striptease politics and does a historic number, *Whatever Lola Wants (Lola Gets)*. She adopts a Hispanic persona and wears a Carmen Miranda costume.[56] Madonna loves pastiching Carmen Miranda.

When Madonna was pregnant with Rocco, she wasn't able to stop the worldwide publication of unglamorous pictures of her with a gigantic belly, bathing in Italian mud with the family.

Madonna's second child also bears a postmodern first name: it echoes Luchino Visconti's film *Rocco e i suoi fratelli* (*Rocco and His Brothers*, 1960). Alain Delon plays the gorgeous lead, and Madonna once again signals her rather intellectual European cinematic tastes, at the precise moment when she is in love with … a European film director, Guy Ritchie, Rocco's father, maker of such excellent films as *Lock, Stock, and Two Smoking Barrels* (1998) and *Snatch* (2000).[57] But "Rocco" also inevitably makes you think of the porn star Rocco Siffredi, who is to the nineties what John Holmes was to the seventies. So it is also an allusion to Mr. Brown's speech in Tarantino's *Reservoir Dogs*. Besides, Rocco is an Italian name, in keeping with Madonna's origins. We can only hope that Lourdes will be just as glamorous and interesting as her namesakes, and that Rocco will be just as well-endowed and good-looking as his namesakes.[58]

▨ ▨ ▨

The Madonna myth is built around a contradiction that is inherent to her status, like the Hollywood myths that inform my next chapter. This allows her to preserve some indispensable elements of mystery. As Jean-Pierre Lavoignat writes: "[Madonna is] ready to give herself while begrudging herself, so that at the very moment when you think you have learned a lot, you realize she has just fed the mystery that surrounds her. In that respect too, she is a real star."[59] Mysterious, at once virgin and vamp, saint and femme fatale, good girl and bad girl, mother and whore, Madonna shifts from one persona to another with disconcerting ease. It is one of the paradoxes of the myth that if humanity recurs to it to (apparently) solve contradictions, it carries contradiction(s) itself. Most religions rest on founding myths that can hardly resist rational analysis. Naturally, those contradictory foundations are precisely those that faith depends on. In the same way, Madonna's fans worship her in her entirety, including the contradictions. If they realize, what is more, that all is but games to her, they are all the less perturbed. As Patrick Bollon says, "Madonna always offers the commentary on her act at the same time as the act itself."[60]

Doesn't that sound like a definition of the postmodern? Of course, those contradictions I've examined rest on dubious social constructs: if there are such dichotomies as virgin and vamp, mother and whore, it is because the sexist dominant culture has invented them, the better to dominate women. They are but subcategories of the category woman, as it has been constructed in the context of the dictatorship of gender roles. After the pressures that little girls undergo, when they have to conform to the mould of the gender they have been assigned, they have to put up with new pressures as they grow up, forcing them to conform to one subcategory or another, to be a good girl or a bad girl. Is it any wonder Madonna upsets such appalling structures?

In the next chapter, I show the way Madonna is determined to dynamite all the preconceptions that rule everyone's gender, and illustrate that Madonna is to pop what Judith Butler is to gender studies.

F O U R

Drag

[Madonna] can play [...] in a Protean way, incarnate all
the possibilities of difference or sexual deviancy [...];
either [...] she has a fantastic identity, an authenticity
that can resist anything, or she has none at all. Obviously, my opinion would be that she has none at all,
but needless to say it's a weapon, she has no identity at
all and she plays with that absence of identity. We have
all more or less reached this stage today, and maybe
that is indeed the post-modern universe.[1] Or maybe it
is both, maybe she has at the same time a solid nucleus
and the possibility to dislocate,[2] in every sense.
— Jean Baudrillard[3]

Like David Bowie, Madonna is a cultural sponge: "I am not a scholar.
I'm a sponge. I just soak things up."[4] She absorbs fashions, trends, others
people's artistic successes — past and present. As a postmodern icon, she
seems constituted of successive layers of signifiers, gathered according to
a very precise Madonnesque logic. What is then named "Madonna" is a
collection of masks, of personae. To do drag is to wear the clothes and
signifiers of the Other, to do drag is to transpose a personality.

So in this chapter I wish to delve into two essential sources for

111

Madonna, drag queens and bygone Hollywood stars (themselves having so often done a drag queen's job), and I try to evaluate the effects (nostalgia and subversion) of that cultural appropriation. I examine the Madonnesque redefinition of Camp and I indulge in one or two semantic precisions.

The Expression Under the Mask

Camille Paglia writes: "Feminism says, 'no more masks'; Madonna says we are nothing but masks."[5] Peter Wilkinson writes: "Peel away one of Madonna's masks, and you'll usually find another."[6] As Baudrillard has it, Madonna is Protean. The only one who competes with her (and inspires her) in that respect is David Bowie. But of course, Bowie seems to carry the schizophrenic process much further. Proteus is not only gifted with the power to shape-shift, but also with that of divination. That particular talent has often been attributed to Madonna and David Bowie, who recurrently seem to foresee the new trends in terms of sartorial fashion and music. Proteus gets back to his original form if those who come to see him aren't impressed by his transformations; then he speaks to them, revealing "truths." Well, Madonna regularly *pretends to pretend* to her public that she is taking off the mask and showing her true face, when all she's doing is moving from one disguise to the next.

Baudrillard evokes above Madonna's gift to "incarnate all the possibilities of difference or sexual deviancy." Let us keep in mind the original sense of the verb "to incarnate," which designates a divine talent. Along her permanent *mises en scène*, Madonna changes identities, genders and sexual orientations, just like Bowie in the old days. I'd go as far as to say they are the two most important gender-benders in the history of popular culture. But didn't the old gods indulge in the same kind of antics, in their own way?[7]

Whether Madonna has an identity or not is actually an irrelevant question in a work that examines—precisely—the multiplicity and multiplication of Madonnesque identities.[8] Didn't Oscar Wilde say that what some call lack of sincerity is nothing but a means to multiply personalities?[9] When Baudrillard speaks of a "fantastic identity," he uses the adjective in its common meaning, referring to something that is strange, unusual, extravagant, eccentric (Webster's); but it wouldn't be altogether wrong to understand it in its first meaning, as characterizing something that exists only in the imagination (Webster's). Baudrillard also draws attention to the way Madonna uses her body like a weapon. The star answers: "I think anyone's body has the potential to be a weapon, yeah.

But ultimately, it's your mind that tells your body what to do so it really is your mind that's the weapon."[10] That is all the truer since she forged an entirely new body for herself through long hours of daily sports (jogging, body-building, etc.).

The playful recourse to masks is also one of Madonna's weapons. She is travestied in every sense. The first picture of *Sex* shows her as if in a shadow show, and the picture is printed as a negative. On the second one, she's wearing a mask that conjures up Venetian Mardi Gras balls as well as sadomasochism. That mask can be seen in the *Like a Virgin* video, in the *Girlie Show* tour, and in the *Erotica* video. The point is to draw attention to the disguise, the mechanisms, the artifice on which an artistic production rests. In the *Rain* video, a short-black-haired Madonna kisses a boy. But even as she offers her lips to him, an extradiegetic hand with a brush enters the frame to touch up her foundation. Better still, the *Beautiful Stranger* video (1999) begins with Austin Powers (Mike Myers) in a car getting a video call from his boss (Michael York) who warns him against a dangerous spy who is "a master of disguise." His face on the car video screen is replaced by a succession of five totally different Madonna looks, ranging from the mid-eighties to 1999.

Madonna holds her public captive by constantly changing masks. Like TV soap fans, Madonna fans find themselves wondering whatever it's going to be next time. Who could have predicted, for instance, that she would suddenly emerge as a cowgirl in August 2000?[11]

Talking about Marilyn Monroe, John Kobal proposes the following definition of stars: "You're a star when you stop looking like all the others and they're all trying to look like you."[12] What does he mean by "all the others"? Ordinary women, non-stars? If that's the case, the definition suits Monroe as it does Madonna. If "all the others" designates other stars, his definition is doubtful. Didn't Marilyn try to look like Jean Harlow? And doesn't Madonna look precisely *like all the others*?

Of course, the wannabes do try to look like her, but she — the original wannabe — never stops looking like other stars, including Monroe. Stardom as defined by Kobal belongs to the modern, whereas stardom as defined by Madonna belongs to the postmodern. Madonna rewrites stars of the past such as Marlene Dietrich and Mae West, and warns us that this is what she is doing. Sometimes she poses with a beret *à la* Garbo in a position *à la* Garbo. Sometimes she poses with a beret *à la* Dietrich in a position *à la* Dietrich. Roland Barthes commented upon Garbo's face in *Queen Christina* (Rouben Mamoulian, 1933):

> The makeup has the snowy thickness of a mask [...]. Even in its extreme beauty, this face that is sculpted in smooth and brittle materials rather

than drawn, i.e. simultaneously perfect and ephemeral, echoes the chalky face of Charlie Chaplin's Tramp [...].[13]

The use of makeup as a means to gain access to stardom has been frequently analyzed in the past seven decades or so. Of course, that thick movie makeup is basically the same, whether you're looking at glamorous icons or slapstick comedians;[14] it is equally reminiscent of European theater before the perfection of modern lighting systems, of Japanese theater, of geishas,[15] and so forth. And it is especially akin to that of drag queens. Jean-Pierre Coursodon says:

> Of that old Hollywood makeup, one can first say that it is almost as artificial and exaggerated as stage makeup, without being equally justified. The camera magnifies [...], and so the makeup could have been discreet, invisible. Yet the opposite happens, at least as far as feminine makeup is concerned [...]. That operation is obviously not innocent.[16]

It is in that tradition that Madonna's makeup and metamorphoses are inscribed. Depending on pictures, her face can be amazingly unattractive, or uncannily beautiful. It can be sculpted, perfect and ephemeral; perfect because it is the result of a very self-conscious and totally controlled artistic production, ephemeral because it is only one of the ever-changing faces she shows to the public.

Barthes also writes:

> [Garbo's face was] an archetypal human face. Garbo gave off a sort of Platonic idea of the creature, and this is what accounts for the fact that her face is almost sexless, without being dubious for that matter [...]. Garbo does not [...] accomplish any drag act.[17]

I don't subscribe to that so easily. "Androgynous face" would be more appropriate than "sexless face," and the use of the adjective dubious is dubious. Unlike Barthes I believe that Garbo, like Madonna, does accomplish a "drag act," in every sense of the word. In a way, Garbo was in drag in every one of her films, just like Madonna in everything she does. Garbo and Dietrich paved the way for her. As modern gender-benders, they announce the postmodern gender-bending of Madonna. Knowing perfectly well that books *are* judged by their cover, they went for male drag or female drag according to their needs or whims. In either case, all they did was wear a sum of signs connoted "man" or "woman," which would then additionally allow them to signal some sexual preference (real or fanciful). Choosing this or that element of makeup or clothing, Garbo reinforced her phantasmal creature qualities. Garbo was a dream woman,[18] Madonna dreamed herself up, with postmodern cosmetic writing.

The use of makeup, for a genetic woman, may signal submission to macho codes, and many feminists denounce it. Most cosmetics commercials do comfort the dominant culture in its patriarchal worst: the point is to encourage women to conform to stereotypes, to the mold conceived by men, to accept themselves as objects, of the desire and gaze of men. But if the makeup is integrated in a philosophy that is quite liberated from the yokes of our macho society, if it is done totally tongue-in-cheek, then it becomes something else altogether. See the commercials for M.A.C.'s Viva Glam products with K.D. Lang and RuPaul for example. RuPaul wrote an autobiography which contains a rather Madonnesque passage:

> If you knew all the references, you could deconstruct one of my performances and place every look, every word, and every move. I do. I know all the references, and watching myself on tape I love to sit with friends and unstitch (to their amazement) the patchwork of my performance, identifying this bit from here and this bit from there. I really see myself as a sampling machine.[19]

This is how the movie producer Julia Phillips describes her first meeting with Madonna and Sean Penn:

> She is dyed platinum and dressed from head to toe in black leather. She looks adorable. I like that she is into her image and is dressed in Madonna gear. He is in jeans and leather jacket, what a surprise. He is a dim bulb in her supernova aura.[20]

She is pinpointing one of the reasons for Madonna's breakup with Sean Penn. He is but a dim bulb, whereas she shines like a supernova. This of course has nothing whatever to do with their respective acting talents. The sentence highlights Madonna's gift for permanent representation. Madonna is "into her image," which delights Phillips, whose job among other things consists in identifying true star quality when she sees it. The familiar phrase "to be into something" might be taken literally here: isn't Madonna constantly *inside* her image, i.e., buried under signifiers? Phillips confirms: Madonna is wearing "Madonna gear." She might as well have written "Madonna drag." In the same way, Elvis wore Elvis drag, especially at the end of his life. There are thousands of Elvis impersonators throughout the world who do a drag act exactly as a female impersonator might do one.[21] According to a similar process, thousands of wannabes and hundreds of drag queens imitate Madonna. What could be more logical, when you consider that the "original" itself is but a person wearing the appropriate gear?[22] As Leigh Raymond says: "Drag fits the postmodern like a long evening glove."[23]

Drag Culture

In her essay "It's Never Too Late to Switch," Alisa Solomon evokes Eve Merriam's play, *The Club*, whose seven male parts were played on Broadway in 1976 by seven women. She wonders:

> It's hard to say whether *The Club* would be as effective now, more than fifteen years later — now, that is, in this age of Madonna, when the play's ironic stance toward gender has become so taken for granted.[24]

Isn't it remarkable that Madonna has come to be used thus in such phrases? Will we one day refer currently to the age of Madonna as we speak for instance today of the age of silent movies? Doesn't *Le Monde* write that the "irruption of Madonna [at the Cannes film festival] signifies a change of epoch"?[25] So Madonna is linked in Solomon's mind to drag, as well as to an ironic distance toward gender roles.

The time has come for a slight lexical pause. The word "drag queen" fits an observation of Madonna better than the words "transvestite" or "female impersonator." I mean "drag queen" as defined by the English-speaking world between the twenties and the eighties, roughly. When it comes to defining the phrase, dictionaries are unhelpful and politically incorrect. I am referring to the world of glamorous artistic performances. The drag queen I'm thinking of is a man who dresses up and makes up his face so as to resemble a woman,[26] in order to put on a show. I use "drag queen" as in "drag act," and associate it to cabaret. Such drag queens tend to be in drag only at night. Forget the connotations that the phrase fleetingly carried in the nineties in New York and Paris (extra-terrestrial-looking parodies of drag queens).

It is commonly admitted that you say "queen" in "drag queen" as you say "Queen Elizabeth," and indeed this does seem somehow adequate. A queen is rarely dressed simply, a queen is constantly on show, and a queen wears jewelry that signifies as much as a drag queen's. But it is not the case. "Drag queen" does stem from "queen," in the old sense of effeminate[27] homosexual. Does that mean a drag queen is nothing more than a queen in drag? Things are not so simple. In fact, the word "queen" does not derive from the word that designates a monarch, its etymology is different. The word has been subjected to a very interesting spelling twist, and was originally a homophone. "Queen" in the sense I am discussing was once spelt "quean." And you have to go back to the Goths to find a common origin to the two words.

This might seem to lead us astray from Madonna, but it does not. The word "queen" is associated to "wife," whereas "quean" is associated to "woman." Here we are already on the right track. A quean, according to the 1975 *Concise Oxford Dictionary*, is "an impudent or ill-behaved girl, a jade, a hussy." It warns us that the word is archaic. For the 1917 *Blackie's Standard Dictionary*, it is not yet archaic, and designates "a worthless woman." Soon afterward, in the twenties, drag queens became commonly referred to as such. A queen or a drag queen may behave today as a monarch, but she is etymologically a hussy. And here we are back to Madonna.

I do not resist the temptation of seeing in that semantic shift a political act orchestrated by the queens in question. Gays are masterly in the art of upsetting signifiers, to claim an identity that is contested or stifled. The adoption of the word "gay" itself is a case in point. Indeed it is increasingly abandoned by the politically-conscious in favor of the word "queer," which obeys a different logic. When an insult is recuperated by the offended party and *systematically* used (cf. Queer Theory), it obviously becomes political. Let us not forget that the word "gay" itself evokes more than joyful people in a good mood. In the fifties it was still used in the sense of "debauched," notably in Britain. Gay houses were brothels.[28]

But whether they be monarchs or hussies or both, precisely, drag queens have contributed to forging the stardom of women like Mae West, Marlene Dietrich, or Madonna. I am evoking here an androgyny that might seem superficial to some, one that might not be as efficient as that of the ancient Supreme Beings (akin to hermaphroditism), but one that is just as inspiring for a great number of people, notably fans of the supreme being called Madonna, and just as mythic.

So I use "gay" throughout, as Madonna does, unlike many academic Madonnologists who favor "queer." "Queer" might have been more appropriate for this book. Constructionist postmodern critics favor it. But if Madonna can be identified as constructionist,[29] if she can easily be said to adopt gay politics, I am not sure she can be said to belong on the "queer" side without getting into serious semantic and political debate.

As for the origin of "drag" in "drag queen," it seems that it designated originally some kind of petticoat or underwear that women used to wear. Madonna for her part prefers wearing it on top of her clothes (*Express Yourself*).

Madonna's mythic drag allows her to be father and mother to the world at the same time, and shows her wish to dominate.[30]

Harry Blake says of Mae West:

> She looks at the Other as only Man must [...]. Mae West's technique irresistibly evokes that of the drag queen who blurs the discourse/sexual difference link [...]. Mae West [...] has even been accused of being

a drag queen. For it is inconceivable that a woman should thus exhibit herself; in the mind of critics, Mae West could only be a man.[31]

Cathy Schwichtenberg writes that Madonna doubles the inversion, "she becomes king as she behaves as a queen; she is a woman playing a man playing a woman."[32] Madonna does do double inversions, in more ways than one. Greg Seigworth,[33] Andrew Ross,[34] Marjorie Garber[35] and David Tetzlaff[36] have all noted similarities between Elvis and Madonna. In his way, Elvis himself already questioned one or two preconceptions in terms of race and gender. Let us not forget his borrowings from African American music, his celebrated pelvis movements and his shiny costumes *à la* Liberace. But Madonna is no victim. Elvis Presley was, just like James Dean or Marilyn Monroe. Those three stars—whose popularity is comparable to Madonna's—are undoubtedly those whose faces adorn the greatest number of gadgets worldwide. But they were fragile. They were broken by their celebrity and very probably their sexuality, whereas Madonna remains strong: constructed, reconstructed and deconstructed in the general *plaisir du texte*, but never destroyed.

The successful, non-burlesque, and glamorous drag queens who inform my research and Madonna's work are first and foremost actors and semioticians. I might even go as far as to say that a man who is too effeminate[37] to begin with makes a bad drag queen, because he is handicapped by caricatured body language.

By overcoding her creation, by investing it with all the cliché-signifiers of "femininity," a drag queen embodies the Ideal Woman, she who by definition does not exist. As she constructs an identity from scratch, the drag queen deconstructs the dictatorship of gender. By definition, the drag queen is rebellious; she frightens and destabilizes people when she points out the artificiality of the very concept of femininity in our society.

The examples are numerous and I'll only mention the classic instance of hairs: to look like a "woman," the drag queen shaves her legs, and armpits, and plucks her eyebrows. But women are equipped with hairs too, and may have thick eyebrows, as some radical feminists remember, who make a point of remaining hairy. As for outside signifiers such as clothing and makeup, surely it would be pointless to dwell on their arbitrary and historical aspects.

The ideal drag queen has a smooth physiognomy, with no excess of character. She paints on this base the features of her choice. People don't always realize to which extent the eyebrows account for the way a person will be perceived; they are key individual characteristics. The drag queen sometimes plucks them, but sometimes she shaves them off altogether, or glues them to her skin with wig glue before hiding them under a layer of pancake, so that she can then paint completely new ones, with the shape and height best suited to the persona she will animate. Dietrich had shaved them off. Her eyebrows are never the same shape or the same height in her films. Madonna plucks them differently according to her avatars. David Bowie had shaved them off during his Ziggy Stardust period.[38]

Thus, Madonna, under her drag queen's mask, may lose her facial expression, but gains in artistic expression, and her subversion comes through. She learned a lot from New York drag queens, including an acute sense of Camp. Her "femininity," as hypercoded as that of drag queens, is a mask. But of course, drag queens themselves are inspired by such stars and gay icons, in a remarkable system of exchange. The novelist Robert Rodi, author of *Drag Queen*, writes about a drag queen who knows she is a semiotician (whereas most, like M. Jourdain, do semiotics unknowingly). Kitten Kaboodle discusses her role models, namely Bette Davis, Joan Crawford, Marlene Dietrich, Katharine Hepburn, Diana Ross, but also Elizabeth I and Marie-Antoinette. There are not enough female icons in the distant past, she says, apart from "the Virtuous Wife and the Whore. Octavia and Cleopatra. Agrippina and Messalina. The Virgin Mother and the Magdalene. Kind of limiting, ain't it?" Elizabeth I, Kaboodle recalls, had an entire country as fan club. "I even did my senior thesis on *The Faerie Queene*," she narrates, "then I got my diploma and became one."[39]

One can hardly get more Madonnesque. This also echoes Warhol's factory, the Velvet Underground, and Lou Reed's song *Walk on the Wild Side*, on the Bowie-produced album entitled *Transformer* (1973).[40]

Madonna and drag queens never let you forget that all is performance. Madonna signals this through all sorts of ironic hints in her videos. Drag queens systematically present one element that "betrays" the genetic sex of the performer. That element, perfectly controlled, is part and parcel of the show. The size of the feet, suddenly highlighted, sometimes fills that role.

It is no coincidence that postmodern novelists, notably Spanish-speaking ones, often use drag queens in their fiction. Those *"femmes d'emprunt,"* as the Franco-Spanish writer Agustin Gomez-Arcos calls them, allow them to signify the impossibility of considering anything at all at face value. Their epistemological processes are reinforced by this device. To be convinced, you only need to peek at *Stella Manhattan* (1985) by the Brazilian Silviano Santiago, or *¿De dónde son los cantantes?* (1967), *Cobra* (1972) and *Colibri* (1982) by the Cuban Severo Sarduy, or even *Una mala noche la tiene cualquiera* (1988), by the Spaniard Eduardo Mendicutti.

Marjorie Garber writes:

> This emphasis on reading and being read, and on the deconstructive
> nature of the transvestite performance, always undoing itself as part of
> its process of self-enactment, is what makes transvestism theoretically
> as well as politically and erotically interesting — at least to me.[41]

In the seventies, the song *This Is My Life* was one of the most popular numbers among European drag queens. It often ended their show, for
obvious reasons: the point was to lip-synch to Shirley Bassey while gradually getting rid of all the signifiers that had been used to construct the
female persona: dress, spike heels, wig, eyelashes[42] and makeup. The number ended almost in the nude, so as to display clear evidence of the fact
that the drag queen belonged to the genetic category "man."[43] Drag functions better as "theoretical and deconstructive social practice"[44] if the audience knows it is facing a man.

In the same way, Madonna's deconstruction can be appreciated better if you don't forget that she is playing, in every sense of the verb. Look,
she's saying, see the way I'm parodying the result of years of brainwash-
ing with Barbie dolls. Barbie dolls and their Barbie universe are increasingly studied by academics.[45] Connections with Madonna are, needless to
say, hundreds. Barbie is admittedly one of the worst examples of fascistic
propaganda for racist, sexist, weightist, and lookist values. She is also a
tremendous inspiration for many a drag queen.

In the video of *Express Yourself*,[46] Madonna reveals her multiple
strategies as drag expert. The song itself is generally seen as a hymn to
freedom, an encouragement for all women and all oppressed minorities
to resist, to express their ideas and their strength faced with tyranny. It
expresses especially a revolt against one particular aspect of the dictatorship of gender: the fact that boys are encouraged to keep their feelings
secret whereas girls are taught to express them. Indeed, the lyrics also
make it a simple love song, again.

Once more, however, the images complicate the Madonnesque discourse. The grand décor of the hugely expensive video has been mostly
borrowed from the film *Metropolis* (Fritz Lang, 1926), and the images presented by Madonna refer to expressionist German cinema and to the
"decadence" of twenties Germany in general. Moreover, Madonna echoes
with the artificial colors she has chosen the colorized version of *Metropolis*, with its New Wave and technopop soundtrack.[47]

Madonna alternately plays the android of *Metropolis*, or its model
Maria (yet another Maria). Then she plays a heterosexual leader, and then
a lesbian leader wearing a man's suit and a monocle. She leads a company,
a country, the world. Later she is an idle and glamorous lady, or a chained
masochist. The muscular men who can be seen in the video are slaves,

workers and musicians. One of them, played by the supermodel Cameron, is noticed by "Madonna," who picks him to serve as a stud.

Before launching in the hermeneutics of *Express Yourself*,[48] Melanie Morton abundantly analyzes the film *Metropolis*. Then she defines the similarities between the film and the video, judging that Madonna's work is "informed by a keen insight into the connection between subjectivity, power, and ideology."[49] Using Foucault and Baudrillard, she explains that *Express Yourself* does not look like *Metropolis* but simulates it.

Apropos of the "sweaty, sexy men enslaved to fearsome machines" who are located in the bowels of Metropolis; she reminds us that Madonna's work largely depends on the vagueness of the limits between identification and desire.[50] This sort of thing is best exemplified by Schwarzenegger-type celebrities, whose popularity is linked to the fact that their male public may desire them — more or less consciously — while also wanting to be or look like them.

As most critics have noted, ambiguity remains; it is true that Madonna plays with fascist signifiers in the video, which may not necessarily be decoded by the general public. It is also true that the images of *Express Yourself* in no way constitute a precise critique of fascism or even capitalism. Should this be seen as a problem? Madonna has shown her possibly clichéd vision of twenties and thirties Germany, expressionism and drag, without worrying too much about the possible Nazi connotations. Bowie once did the same, in his own way.[51] Madonna may have been thinking more of films by Visconti, Cavanni, and Fosse, then of history. Indeed, her vision of twenties and thirties Germany always seems very seventies; a question of generation, no doubt.

Anyway, *Express Yourself* shows once more how indebted to drag queens many Madonnesque products are. According to Karlene Faith: "In the more glamorous routines, she appears as if in drag, which is a part of her appeal to camp culture in the tradition of Judy Garland and Bette Midler. By imitating drag queens, who are "masters of gender deceit [...], Madonna imitates the master imitators."[52]

Dictionaries are quite useless when it comes to defining Camp. Along with many commentators I do believe Madonna is camp. I cannot try and circumscribe Camp here, for lack of space,[53] but let me just write a few paragraphs, beginning with the fact that I believe the substantive "Camp," with a capital C, should be distinguished from the adjective "camp," with a small C. I also believe the adjective "campy" and the noun "campness" are quite useless. The verb "to camp (up)" might on the other hand come in useful. Camp may be a form of self expression, artistic, political, or other; it can be a movement, a trend, a state of mind, a line of thought. The adjective "camp" designates a creation in which Camp is apparent (to those who can discern it), whether it was deliberately put there or not. The adjective can also be used to qualify a practitioner of Camp. But it is also still unfortunately used, especially in Britain, as a synonym of "effeminate."[54]

Some theorists, like Moe Meyer or David Bergman, see in Camp an exercise which is exclusively reserved for homosexuals. That is very debatable indeed. What is the point of acting as a historian, I wonder, identifying the sources of Camp in the seventeenth and eighteenth centuries, to then restrict it to some more or less politicized gay site of resistance? This aspect is undeniable, of course, but Camp goes beyond that.

Susan Sontag is burdened with the heavy responsibility of a 1964 definition that was long seen as authoritative[55] and yet leaves much to be desired — although she can only be saluted for doing it before anyone else. People like Meyer or Bergman are unhappy because she de-homosexualized Camp, as they say.

David van Leer proposes a definition that highlights the affinities between Camp and the postmodern:

> A complex of loosely defined theatricalisms, Camp imitates the hyperbole of musicals and popular movies as well as other visual extravagances like overstated decor and fashion, and especially cross-dressing. In its verbal forms, it favors quotation, mimicry, lip-synching, gender inversion, trenchant put-downs, and bad puns.[56]

Those words could refer to the art of Madonna and to that of many a postmodern creator. There is no coincidence in the fact that the adversaries of the postmodern are often also those of Camp. Some refuse to see a real artistic endeavor in Camp. Yet, as Anna Graham and Rhonda Plume write: "To dismiss Camp as a rummage through white trash culture or a celebration of retro is to misread it as reactive rather than generative."[57]

Camp is often linked to kitsch, but they mustn't be seen as synonyms. Things get even more complicated when you remember that some objects are kitsch only because of their association with others. As for the art of the connoisseur of Camp, it also consists in spotting among kitsch objects those that may count as camp. The décor inside the bus of The Adventures of Priscilla, Queen of the Desert (Stephan Elliott, 1995) provides an excellent example.

A woman can perfectly be camp. The list is long, in Hollywood or elsewhere: Liza Minnelli, Greta Garbo, Marlene Dietrich, Mae West, Tallulah Bankhead, Joan Crawford, Elizabeth Taylor, Joan Rivers, Eartha Kitt or Joan Collins are camp; but not Doris Day, Debbie Reynolds or Grace Kelly. What is more, Camp when practiced by a woman frequently constitutes a form of feminism, as Pamela Robertson shows. "We can [...]

reclaim Camp as a political tool and rearticulate it within the theoretical framework of feminism."[58]

Chuck Kleinhans writes: "To some extent, Camp originates in a gay male perception that gender is, if not quite arbitrary, certainly not biologically determined or natural, but rather that gender is socially constructed, artificial, and performed."[59]

Curiously, Camp is a very Anglo-Saxon art. There are exceptions though, like Pedro Almodóvar, Sylvie Vartan, Dalida, Mina or Milva.

Now surely the lines above are enough to call Madonna camp. Her camp sensibility is expressed in so many different videos, such as those of the songs *Cherish*, *Express Yourself*, and especially *Vogue*; let alone her concerts, when she has male dancers writhing together in erotic ecstasy before dressing them up as extras in *My Fair Lady* (George Cukor, 1964[60]). Madonna's Camp sometimes echoes the Camp you may find in Bette Midler, in Oscar Wilde, in Noël Coward, in the series *Bewitched*,[61] in the sixties series *Batman*, in the British series *Absolutely Fabulous*, in Little Richard, Liberace, and the like.

Wayne R. Dynes sums up: Camp consists in "taking serious things frivolously and frivolous things seriously."[62] Isn't this exactly what Madonna does in *Truth or Dare*?[63] In many instances, Camp is practically synonymous with postmodern (de)construction(ism) *à la* Madonna.

To practice Camp is also to turn hilarious bitchiness into an art form. It can be applied to others and to yourself. Madonna, self-proclaimed Material Bitch, likes mocking her colleagues (such as in *Truth or Dare* and her interviews), but she shows that she is an expert at self-mockery, gifted with a strong camp sense of humor. She provided a choice example in 1985, when she agreed to mock her own wedding (Sean Penn) on *Saturday Night Live*, described by Andy Warhol in his *Diaries*.[64] The party was spoilt by the deafening roar of 13 helicopters, reminiscent of *Apocalypse Now* (Francis Ford Coppola, 1979). Madonna complained about that journalistic invasion, but reaped the fruit of the free publicity. It can't have been very pleasant, anyway, and Madonna made sure to conduct her next wedding (to Guy Ritchie) in complete privacy.

In *Saturday Night Live*, Madonna also unsurprisingly played Princess Diana, Marilyn Monroe, and a Joan Collins clone, all in a very camp way. As John Dean writes: "U.S. rock has a ruling camp queen with Madonna."[65]

Voguing Along

Madonna was not content with mere borrowings from drag culture in general. In *Vogue*, she refers to a very particular type of drag queen.

Few Madonna songs have given rise to as much writing as *Vogue*, for various reasons I'll explain.

Madonna wrote the lyrics herself. For the profane (in the strongest sense) this song probably does not call to mind anything further than an exhortation to join the dance floor in a club and dance, interrupted by a list of celebrities. Of course, things are not so simple. Those utterly familiar with voguing may skip the next two paragraphs.

Voguing (some spell it "vogueing") is a state of mind, a political statement, and a dance. It dates back according to sources to the sixties or the seventies,[66] and developed in the Houses of Harlem, those shelters for gay street gangs.

They are remarkably documented in the film *Paris Is Burning* by Jennie Livingston, who filmed them between 1985 and 1989. The most famous are the *House of Labeija*, the *House of Xtravaganza* and the *House of Ninja*. They are managed by Mothers (older drag queens) whose Children are drag queens who regularly take part in competitive drag balls. Those Children are all African American or Hispanic American, economically disadvantaged, they live in the ghetto and hold records of exclusion from American society: they are rejected by WASPs because of their race, their social background and their sexuality, but they are also rejected by their own community, because of their sexuality. Naturally, a drag queen constitutes the ultimate outrage, the most violently perceived transgression; a "discreet" gay man "passes" much more easily.

The aim of these drag balls is to allow the Children to invent a glamorous identity for themselves, during a parody of access to the American Dream. Judges evaluate contestants who rival in inventiveness, gorgeous clothes and gorgeous makeup. They pick the one who has created the most striking persona, who has elaborated the most impressive poses; hence voguing: to vogue is to dance in a way that is inspired by the poses of models in the pages of *Vogue*, especially the *Vogue* of the twenties, thirties, forties, and fifties. In the sixties models began to adopt more natural poses (as oxymoronic as this may sound), less glamorous and less evocative of stardom. During a drag ball, the (drag) queen becomes a star, for one night, dancing with ample and extremely stylized leg and mostly arm movements. Voguing, which also incorporates Afro-Caribbean kick-dancing, means to revive bygone Hollywood stars, whose poses on professional pictures were anticipatory instances of voguing (such as Marlene Dietrich), all this, need I add, is done tongue-in-cheek, halfway between pastiche and parody.

In fact, in the lyrics of *Vogue* Madonna narrates (among other things) the voguing of the Houses of Harlem, and in the video she dances with humor, voguing with multiethnic camp dancers. Her face is sublime, lit as of by Josef von Sternberg. Her work in this video is more hypertextual than ever, for her rewrites of yesteryear's stars is filtered through the rewrites of those stars by African American and Hispanic American drag queens (that's what the postmodern is).

Yes, voguing is political; Livingston's documentary celebrates this. Cindy Patton writes:

> Where some critics have viewed *Vogue* and Madonna's work in general as parasitic on, variously, black and gay culture and even on feminism, I will suggest that she reroutes through mass culture quotidian critiques of dominant cultures (in this case, voguing's critique of whiteness and of gender), making them more available as places of resistance, although this may come at some cost.[67]

My sentiment exactly. So what if Madonna ransacks various subcultures, as long as she signals their existence to the tenants of the dominant culture? So what if she makes a lot of money functioning as a parasite on places of resistance, as long as she provides food for thought? Critics often reproach her with the way (according to them) she makes trite and commonplace cultural elements that were initially subversive. She transforms them into mass consumption products, they say, but to my mind she can be praised for it — precisely. Is she not working for the development of open-mindedness in the world? Why should this appropriation, defined by commentators as the essence of the postmodern, whose meaning carries derogatory or laudatory connotations according to the speaker, not be capable of accomplishing a good (social) deed?

For of course, Madonna's voguing becomes particularly relevant when it crosses over — as everything she does — into the dominant culture. There is something irresistibly ironic in the sight of a white heterosexual male voguing in a discotheque. Usually quite unaware of what he is doing, he is mimicking movements imagined by the Other (the Low-Other, Schulze *et al.* say, the Subaltern, Patton says), whom possibly he hates, fears, and considers inferior.[68] By its very essence voguing deconstructs gender, and it belongs to a culture that is hypercoded as non-white — even and because the models voguing pastiches are white. So when a white heterosexual male vogues, is he showing that the subversion has been stifled, and it's all Madonna's fault again, or on the contrary that subversion has won? As Patton writes:

> Voguing simultaneously enacts and deconstructs race and gender, it might be that in crossing over, the white, middle-class, heterosexual club dancers are being signified on as they reenact the homoerotic and Afro-Latin resolutions of voguing. That is, they are performing, however noncognitively, the kinesthesia that embodies the problematics of race and gender from the perspective of subalterns.[69]

That sort of phenomenon is in no way new. You can go very far back in time, but even if you merely examine the recent cultural history of the U.S., you'll find that it is full of instances of minority artistic creations, the works of groups such as African Americans, Hispanic Americans, or gays, which have crossed over into the mainstream. To name but three at random: jazz, the disco band Village People, or the fashion for bandannas, those different color scarves stuck in jeans pockets that in the seventies constituted a precise code signaling in detail sexual preferences among gays.[70] They were soon adopted by hordes of youths who knew no better. These youths perverted signifiers, adopting as they did an elaborate gay semiotic system that they mistook for mere fashion. This is neither the first time nor the last this sort of thing has happened. The debate is not recent, and will divide the minorities that are thus aped for many years: when black is taken over by white, is it automatically whitened (if not altogether whitewashed), or does it darken white, if only slightly? The central question that *Vogue* poses, is whether it is profitable for groups who live in the margin to find themselves absorbed by the dominant culture, or if on the contrary this is to be seen strictly as recuperation, in the worst possible sense of the word, a recuperation that chokes identities which have sometimes been built in suffering. Voguing may seem almost as ridiculous when it is danced by white gays from middle-class or upper-class neighborhoods.

From the Margin to the Dominant Culture

Madonna is a myth, and as such might feed more on the desires and frustrations of the lower orders of a given society than on those of the dominant ranks. This is part of the game.

Andrew Blake writes:

> [The lyrics are focused] on the absence of personal identity and the time-bending reality of "stardom." *Vogue*'s lyric helps to sum up the point: the elements of contemporary and traditional in Madonna's work are not merely juxtaposed: they are also posed, re-interpreted under the control of that focused strength of desire which marks all Madonna's work.[71]

I thoroughly agree with Blake's second sentence, but why are so many Madonnologists and anti-postmodern academics so preoccupied with the notion of loss or absence of identity? Is it their own identity they are afraid of losing? Does this reflect their own anxiety? When Madonna sings about the listener longing to be something better, does she necessarily imply that what he is today does not exist? That he *is not*? Of course not. When she

tells the listener that he is a superstar, what she is conveying is the power
of dream and imagination, which she has mentioned before in the song.
I am always extremely suspicious of people who tend to pose as responsible adults with an extremely developed political conscience and seem to
believe that this somehow entitles them to think for others, to stand up
for the oppressed, sometimes in spite of the oppressed who have not asked
them for anything. So many critics have reviled Madonna as an evil supporter of racism, homophobia, and capitalism, writing as self-appointed
guardians of ghetto underdogs, although they rarely stray away from their
campus. I wonder what such moralizers made of the persistent rumors that
said Madonna (up to her Evita phase) drove along Latino quarters at night
and picked up very young strapping Latino boys. Did they see that as sex-
ploitation?

The two lines from *Vogue* that have been most frequently quoted
have to do with race and gender not making the slightest difference. Cindy
Patton reports that "these lines are politically unsettling to feminists, gay
activists, and black activists because it dismisses the 'real' to which identity politics pretend an allegiance."[72] She is generalizing; she should write
that this is true for some, but not all, surely. The reactions these two lines
have raised show that in some circles, Madonna can never win. I myself
choose to see in them her usual antiracist, anti-homophobic, anti-sexist,
and dare I say anti-dragqueenophobic message. Call me naïve. I am certain of one thing: such lyrics are much more clearly understood by those
most endangered by the prevailing ideology than by many identity politics theorists.[73]

So according to Madonna (or at any rate her voguing persona), when
the music pumps energy into you, it allows you to become Other for the
night (without necessarily losing your identity), to become a superstar (in
the Warholian sense of the word I evoked earlier on, maybe), while the
dance lasts. What is there here that is politically blamable? The fact that
dancing/dreaming/listening to Madonna stops people from taking arms
and starting a revolution? So Madonnamania, that new religion, is the
new opium of the people?

I am prepared to bet that when African American or Hispanic American drag queens listen to these lines, they see them as more or less descriptive of their activities in the Houses; when they are heard by white gays
or young women of any race stuck in a daily life that is no bed of roses
they help, providing solace through a little bit of harmless escapism. Is
that not the definition of entertainment? Madonna has rarely claimed to
be much more than an entertainer. If as she entertains she delivers one or
two messages that promote open-mindedness, then it is all the better.

Some lines in the song, to do with beauty, are polysemic. They echo the American obsession with working out, Madonna's own strenuous efforts to construct her beauty along the years, they conjure up visions of plastic surgeons equipped with scalpels, but they also recall that beauty is in the eye of the beholder.[74] When you examine photographs of Madonna throughout the ages, you can only be convinced: she is sometimes almost repulsive, sometimes gorgeous, according to shots and clichés and angles and observers, unlike most other stars who look the same in every picture.

Life, to Madonna the voguer, is a ball. That is an optimistic message which beyond the set phrase refers of course to the drag balls of the Houses. The list of stars that she speaks in the song is somewhat puzzling. This enumeration has been frequently taken apart by researchers. The outsider, first, Joe DiMaggio, may seem incongruous here. The only sportsman in a list of actors, he may have been married to Marilyn Monroe, but I do not really understand what he's doing here, unless Madonna wanted to signify that she knew baseball players (and basketball players and football players) are just as starified as actors in the U.S. In that case she should have included names of non-acting singers as well, shouldn't she? Whatever the case, the other names, all pure Hollywood, provide more than enough information as to the point she is making.

To begin with, those stars' names signal her fascination (for those who might not have observed it yet) for pre–1962 Hollywood icons. That's nostalgia at work, but active nostalgia, as it were, one of the frequent aspects of the postmodern. Secondly, this list establishes a link between Madonna, today's principal gay icon, with gay icons of the past. The women she cites were for the most part either cross-dressers, regularly seen in men's attire, or inspired by drag queens, or even ideal models for drag queens. They were frequently powerful women like herself, inside or outside the studios. Gene Kelly and Fred Astaire danced according to a choreography that would have got them arrested had they done so in real streets as opposed to the reconstituted safe streets of the studios, because they were so camp. James Dean, a very unbalanced, very unhappy man, extremely sensual but as fragile as a child, made his female fans but a great number of his male fans also feel like protecting him; we now know that he was gay. As for Marlon Brando (the Marlon Brando of the forties and fifties, naturally), he built his career on an overflowing sensuality that affected men and women alike. Of course, Madonna chose people who inspired her personally, but people the general public can recognize immediately, and enjoy as much as gays might, she is showing here again that she means to assemble the largest possible audience and sell a great deal of records. Some reproach her with this, which is silly.

In the middle of her list, Madonna evokes the actress's preoccupation with showing herself to her best advantage, to catch the light as aesthetically as possible: this is Dietrich in front of von Sternberg's cameras, Madonna in front of Herb Ritts's, this is what she mimes in the *Vogue* video, when she frames her face with her hands, like Harlem drag queens.

Patton reacts to the lines that follow in the song:

> Because Madonna reinscribes both "bitch" and "drag" as the province of female masquerade, the beauty of *Vogue* risks repudiating the difference constituted through the performance of femininity by homosexual men. The song blurts out its own confusion when it reverses the regendered "perversions" that voguing constituted: "Ladies with an attitude, fellas that were in the mood," neatly inverts the claims that voguing wished to make about male bitchiness ("attitude") and female desire ("in the mood"). Indeed, this misrecognition of the gender critique of voguing inadvertently restabilizes gender by returning us to what we thought we knew: that women are bitches and that men always "want it."[75]

There are limits, surely, and Madonna shouldn't be blamed for being a genetic woman, and white. Or perhaps she should apologize. We have to be weary of that old moral judgment passed on many artists the minute they appropriate elements of a culture that is not initially theirs. This type of discourse negates multiculturalism; many academics who elsewhere champion cultural exchanges sharpen their claws as soon as a white artist ventures out of the narrow bounds of the culture he stemmed from. Multiculturalism does not only mean white teenagers buying rap records...

Patton uses the words "bitch" and "bitchiness" in restricted senses, when in fact the bitchiness of the House drag queens is polymorphous and polysemic; she does the same with the phrases "attitude" and "in the mood." "Ladies with an attitude" may define women who will not let anyone dictate their conduct, women as strong as any man, possibly lesbians, or even drag queens precisely (playing a lady with or without attitude is one of their favorite occupations[76]). Remember the way the radical rappers Niggers With an Attitude (NWAA) use the word. And we must be careful as far as the association of the phrase "in the mood" is concerned: it evokes the stereotyped refusal of the wife on Saturday night, "not tonight darling, I'm not in the mood," similar to (but franker than) "not tonight darling, I have a headache." So a woman who is in the mood is a woman who accepts the male desire, so the expression applied to a "fella" could designate a man who accepts male desire, couldn't it?

Before the musical introduction of *Vogue* begins, a voice asks: "What are you looking at?" This voice could be Madonna's, it could also be that of one of her chorus girls. The words are uttered in a "street" accent, that might conceivably evoke a white person, but more probably an African American or a Hispanic American woman or drag queen. What matters even more than the accent is the tone. "What are you looking at?" means here, "Hey you, stop looking at me like this or you're gonna get into trouble." It is threatening. So who is this "you"? The listener? A voyeur? The reader of a *Vogue* type magazine lost in contemplation of the photographs? Could it be simply a WASP who is looking at a drag queen engaged in the act of voguing, i.e. constructing a site of resistance? In which case the listener can conjure up the picture of the disapproving gaze on the part of the WASP, and hear "what are you looking at?" as a strong political statement.

Clearly enough, everything that precedes in no way stops those two lines from being descriptive of the aforementioned stars, nor prevents the word "attitude" from referring to the attitudes and poses struck by Hollywood ladies; nor does it encourage me to neglect the allusion to the song *In the Mood*, so characteristic of the period Madonna is exploring, reinforced by the Tamara de Lempicka paintings on show in the video.

Moreover, every time Madonna utters in the *Vogue* video the name of a female star she is filmed in such a way as to give the viewer the impression that the star in question suddenly appears, her features superimposed on Madonna's, and this without recurring to special effects. But that is not all: when appearing on MTV for an awards show, she sang *Vogue* in an eighteenth-century dress, with a Marie-Antoinette wig, surrounded by her dancers in matching costumes. On that occasion the choreography was even more stylized (I wouldn't have thought this possible), the movements were slower and even more emphatic — yet economized. This was a *mise en scène* that plunged as deep as her cleavage, it echoed films like *Barry Lyndon* (Stanley Kubrick, 1975),[77] the French restoration, *marivaudage* and *libertinage*, it was a definitive finger at those who accuse Madonna of inauthenticity, of lacking in rock spirit, as if that could worry her. She was saying that day, yes, I am all mask, and I love it. She later confirmed that attitude when during *The Girlie Show*, she sang *Vogue* wearing a heavy Asian headset and voguing in a way that had as much to do with Indian and Thai folk dancing as with Harlem drag queens. May we then assume that Madonna is *au fait* of the discourse of postmodern theorists and the way they set off the postmodern against the *Siècle des Lumières*?

We have not heard the last of *Vogue*. Indeed in the song *Deeper and Deeper* (deeper and deeper in metapop) Madonna quotes (samples?) one or two lines of *Vogue*. Another moment of *The Girlie Show* allows Madonna to reach summits of stylization she rarely reached before: for the song *Justify My Love*, she recreates an ambiance *à la* Sir Cecil Beaton which evokes as much Truman Capote's famous Black and white Ball (at the Plaza Hotel in 1966) as the work of Beaton for *My Fair Lady*. Dressed like her dancers in lace, waistcoat, chemise à jabot, foulard, redingote, hat and gloves, Madonna does an elegant dance that evolved from voguing. Camping it up as if her life depended on it, she plays with her chorus girls and her dancers: a bunch of ladies and gentlemen of a sort you're more used to seeing in period Hollywood movies.

Hollywood Palimpsests: Greta, Rita, Dita and Others

The myth of the good-bad-girl and the drag queen mythographers I mentioned earlier led me to identify some of the glamorous actresses who inform Madonnesque (camp and nostalgic) texts.[78] Madonna has been notably inspired by Josephine Baker, Theda Bara, Greta Garbo, Marlene Dietrich, Carmen Miranda, Judy Garland, Lana Turner, Marilyn Monroe, Diana Dors, Mamie van Doren, Angie Dickinson and Liza Minnelli. In some photos, she resuscitates Louise Brooks, Jean Harlow, Dorothy Lamour, Carole Lombard or Carroll Baker.[79] In some videos she revives other stars, like Veronica Lake (*Vogue*).

In order to grow, the Madonnesque myth borrows from older myths, according to processes that are similar to the passage from the Greek myth of Aphrodite to the post–italic myth of Venus, for instance. And when Madonna isn't alluding to a star of the past through her own appearance, she is busy conveying more veiled but just as significant allusions. In *Sex*, she indulges in lesbian pastimes with a very *garçonne* Isabella Rossellini. As a supermodel, Rossellini adds to the glamour of the enterprise, just like Naomi Campbell, but her presence is also destined to remind the spectator of her mother, Ingrid Bergman.

Tallulah Bankhead has her part in the Madonnesque construction. She was well-known for her wild lifestyle and risqué *bons mots*. Madonna has no doubt read all the naughty anecdotes about her. Bankhead said: "Daddy always warned me about men and alcohol, but he never said a thing about women and cocaine."

Greta Garbo also had a sulfurous reputation as a rebel and a bisexual. Rejecting dominant sartorial codes, she wore trousers. Generally speaking, she never submitted to anyone, like Madonna. The big difference between them lies in the discretion of Garbo, as far as her private life was concerned. Like Dietrich and Madonna, Garbo began as a fan, devouring female stars' biographies to find inspiration. Unlike Madonna, Garbo had a Pygmalion, Mauritz Stiller. If the latter did not have much time to perfect his task, he at least encouraged her to lose fat (like Dietrich and

Madonna), and mostly he found her name. Garbo designates in Swedish a strange spirit that dances and whirls around on the moon rays. It's a remarkably apt name for a mythic star, for a creature full of mystery who exercised a quasi-divine power that Madonna is emulating.

In her movies, Madonna often resembles or at least recalls thirties and forties movie stars, like Lauren Bacall, Marlene Dietrich, Gene Tierney and Rita Hayworth (*Shanghai Surprise, Who's That Girl?, Dick Tracy*). But she doesn't limit herself to Hollywood stars. She sometimes remembers her origins, and uses Italian actresses. Thus she occasionally evokes Italian bombshells of the Sophia Loren or Gina Lollobrigida variety.[80] In the video of *Justify My Love*, she pays an impressive tribute to the Jeanne Moreau of *La Baie des anges* (Jacques Demy, 1962).

Sometimes Madonna mixes Hollywood and European references, as in the very cinematic *Bad Girl* video. As I've mentioned earlier, it is inspired both by *Looking for Mr. Goodbar* (Richard Brooks, 1977) and *Der Himmel uber Berlin / The Wings of Desire* (Wim Wenders, 1988). I have already evoked the European Dita Parlo persona that Madonna adopts in her book *Sex* and in her album *Erotica*.[81] "Erotica" must be understood in its English sense, but also in its Italian or Spanish sense: it is the adjective "erotic" in the feminine gender. It is the adjective that Madonna–Dita proudly uses to qualify herself.

The process is characteristic of Madonna: she chose Dita Parlo, a woman who existed (real name Gerthe Kornstadt, 1906–1971), a German actress with a strange and mostly French career, "an anarchist, who didn't care what people thought."[82] The faces of the two women do look a bit similar, but what matters more is that inspired pseudonym recycled by Madonna. "*Dita*" means "fingers" in Italian (those that seize the power?), "*Parlo*" means "I speak"; Madonna expresses herself, Madonna has been speaking since 1983, and people listen to her. Dita is also short for Perdita. It has more to do here with the Shakespearean name from *The Winter's Tale* meaning "lost" in Latin, than with the Italian meaning of "loss." It is a name that is rare but still used in the English-speaking world today. Surely "lost" is to be understood in a moral sense.

Using Dita Parlo's name, Madonna appropriates her life and a career she admires; making her a high priestess of sex, she rewrites her to suit her fancy.[83]

Madonna's March 1991 Academy Awards performance is packed with cinematic references, a choice that befits the context. She wears a long, tight, white dress covered in sequins and pearls that is sufficiently generic to conjure up the evening dresses of many stars of the twenties, thirties, forties, fifties and early sixties. On her naked shoulders rests an ostrich feather boa. Her hair is platinum blond and styled halfway between Jayne

Mansfield's and Marilyn Monroe's. She wears a lot of real diamonds (insured for millions of dollars), high white gloves reaching above her elbows, and of course white spike heels. Her face recalls Ava Gardner, Jayne Mansfield, Marilyn Monroe, and Marlene Dietrich, but also Lauren Bacall (the look).[84]

She sings Stephen Sondheim's *Sooner or Later*, her good-bad-girl Breathless song from *Dick Tracy*. Douglas Thompson writes:

> The veterans ogled and said she had brought the glamour back to Hollywood and the annual cavalcade of self-acclaim — with a bang.[85]

That night Madonna sings in a new voice (no more Minnie-Mouse-on-helium), a mature voice, more suited to the powerful woman who always gets what she wants, a voice that shows she has taken singing lessons, but at the same time a pastiche voice that matches Sondheim's pastiche of himself. Madonna moves her hips like Marilyn Monroe in *Some like It Hot* (Billy Wilder, 1959), she teases like Jayne Mansfield in *The Girl Can't Help It* (Frank Tashlin, 1956); but most of all, she rewrites the striptease scene in *Gilda*, (Charles Vidor, 1946), adding her inverted commas to Rita Hayworth's. When the orchestra plays the first notes of *Sooner or Later* she walks down the stage a bit like Lana Turner, like no one has walked since the fifties (except possibly Joan Collins), takes off her first glove and throws it to the ground. Her shoulders are bare as Rita Hayworth's. She sways about, showing her face, then turns round, strokes her buttocks (the modern Hayworth cannot stroke her buttocks, the postmodern Hayworth can), then she raises her arms in a pyramid and holds her hair up exactly like Hayworth (or should I write Gilda?). To conclude with an apotheosis, she takes off her second glove at the end of the song, like Gilda's original pin-up girl, and definitively appropriates that historic scene, so frequently discussed by so many critics, that scene which confirms Barthes's aforementioned words on striptease. Finally, she plays with her stole of white fur like Rita Hayworth in the promotion studio shots. It is a cliché: Rita Hayworth and Madonna do not show anything here, and they arouse infinitely more desire than if they took all their clothes off.[86]

What Madonna is saying that night is "I always get what I want," and you should start taking me seriously as an actress. She associates her name to the Gulf War in a *Gentlemen Prefer Blondes* and *Diamonds Are a Girl's Best Friend* send-up, shouting "Talk to me General Schwarzkoff, tell me all about it." GIs of old would pin up Rita Hayworth's photograph on the door of their cupboard, and I rather enjoy the idea of Gulf War soldiers pinning up Madonna's on theirs.

With that tongue-in-cheek nostalgic camp old Hollywood rewrite, Madonna addresses the few survivors of that bygone era in the auditorium, but also addresses people like her and like me who have fed on old Hollywood images decades after the event.

But two actresses in particular are inscribed in Madonna, visible by transparency, as it were: Mae West and Marlene Dietrich. A third woman, Marilyn Monroe, is constantly linked to her — or at least was in the eighties and early nineties. Madonna was repeatedly inspired by her, but we shall see that she doesn't rewrite her in the same way she rewrites Mae West and Marlene Dietrich.

Mae West

Mae West was born in 1892 in Brooklyn, and after an extraordinary stage career in New York went to Hollywood in 1932. When she arrived she said: "I'm not a little girl from a little town makin' good in a big town. I'm a big girl from a big town makin' good in a little town."[87] She saved Paramount with her movie *She Done Him Wrong* (Lowell Sherman,1933).

Mae West was a powerful woman, like Madonna. She kept control, whatever the circumstances (at least in her heyday). She wrote her own plays and scenarios, always mastering her own image. "It's not what you do, it's how you do it," she used to say. The said image, like that of Madonna, was sulfurous. Mae West exuded sex, in a totally tongue-in-cheek way, and was hated by conservatives, notably Catholics, like Madonna.[88] Madonna is the author of a picture book called *Sex*, Mae West wrote decades before a play called *Sex*, which got her locked up for a week. "I was the first one to ever say 'sex' on stage," she recalled in 1976.[89]

Mae West is an authentic star, Mae West is a myth. Her most famous film, *I'm No Angel* (Wesley Ruggles, 1933), can be seen as the beginning of her famous war with censorship. In fact, the Hays Office code largely owes its development to Mae West. The people of the Hays Office went as far as to send an employee onto the sets to watch Mae West and her language.

Madonna would no doubt have no objection to titles such as *I'm No Angel* and *It Ain't No Sin*, nor to the immensely famous "Is that a gun in your pocket, or are you just glad to see me?" and other such lines. She is more than aware of her heritage, which she exploits adroitly.

Madonna is a West-like sex symbol, she practices irony and naughty puns in a Mae West way. She is motivated by a kindred sense of provocation.[90] She is a camp gay icon like West, and a "fag hag" like West. She has recruited lovers among Hollywood actors, like Dietrich, but also among muscular sportsmen, like Mae West and Jayne Mansfield. Bodybuilders were seen as freaks not so long ago, and only women like Mae West and Jayne Mansfield — a bit freakish themselves — found them desirable lovers. This says a lot about the sexuality of those women.

Finally, what links Mae West and Madonna is the absence of obvious predisposition to stardom, as far as their initial physical appearance was concerned. J.M. Lo Duca writes about Mae West: "Thanks to which magical trick did a 5'2" and 115 pound woman turn out to be the appetizing queen of sex-appeal?"[91]

Mae West and Madonna constantly elaborate *mises en scène* of (their) sexuality. They have both mixed with a lot of drag queens, and learned a great deal from them. Mae West wrote a play entitled *The Drag*, banned on Broadway because it openly dealt with homosexuality, as well as *The Pleasure Man*, which features five women and five drag queens.[92] Both women know that there is no sexuality nor gender that is not hypercoded, they have listed the usual signifiers and accumulate them to extremes, so as to better provoke and induce reflection. Harry Blake writes that Mae West "is not an actress of the Marilyn type, embodying the masculine myth of Woman, but, and it is a rare occurrence, a woman who dared make hers that discourse."[93] That is indeed rare, maybe it is alas a star's privilege. Madonna too dares tackle the prevalent discourse on sexuality in our still patriarchal and sexist society. A man who multiplies feminine conquests is at worst admired, at best indulgingly called Casanova or Don Juan, whereas a woman who accumulates lovers is vilified and called a slut. It is against that type of fundamental inequity that Madonna's discourse can be efficient. Mae West was nicknamed The Madonna of Queers; I could not have hoped for a better coincidence. Like Madonna decades later she defended the gay cause in public, at a time when it was practically unheard of.

It might be argued that Madonna's use of nudity and Mae West's extreme reluctance to resort to it set them radically apart; Mae West's discourse on sexuality was expressed strictly through words and gestures. But would she do as much (or as little) today? Is not the overwhelming presence of nudity in advertising and the media today partly responsible for Madonna's own contribution? If naked flesh were not so ubiquitous, perhaps she would not have written *Sex*, or at any rate not as such. At a (postmodern?) time when even yogurt is promoted on television with erotic images and intensely suggestive voice-overs, who can be surprised by Madonna's attitude? When Madonna is inspired by a Mae West dress, she conceives a version that shows more flesh. As a matter of fact, Mae West may very well have been a puritan deep down. But what is at stake, of course, for West and Madonna, is power, rather than sex. And Madonna never shows *everything*. Norman Mailer writes:

There is not a single photograph ever published of Madonna with her legs spread. Ah! She draws the line. We may have to redefine our media universe. Is this the last barricade left in our leached-out TV society? Can celebrities get away with everything except giving the public a look at their genitals? Yes, is the answer: gods always keep one last refuge.[94]

Besides, the Madonnesque text is just as constantly ironic as the Westian text, although it is not so much based on classic humor, as in gag humor. Harry Blake writes:

The idea is not to impose a love scene on the audience, but to make the audience fantasize. One must insist particularly on that aspect of Mae West's gags, for they include the audience in the semiotic process of their mechanisms. The laughs they cause imply for the audience a certain complicity when it comes to the sexual practices that are always the referent of Mae West's repartee: and it is not only the representation of Mae West's sexuality that is at stake, but also the audience's own sexuality.[95]

Here are some of the elements that will inform Madonna's work a few decades later, evidently. In *Sex*, for example, she is busy making the reader laugh and fantasize at the same time, while developing their complicity.

Madonna, who has sometimes been called the punk Mae West, and who according to Jerome Charyn looks like a "streamlined Mae West,"[96] enjoys greater freedom, even if she arouses just as much hatred, and even if numerous puritans from miscellaneous factions would dearly like to silence her.

Unfortunately, Mae West never totally got the meaning of the word "camp," unlike Madonna, although she incarnated it so well for decades. At the end of her career she became rather pathetic, in a way surely Madonna will never reproduce.

Because of her usual persona, Mae West was seen as more "into sex" than Marlene Dietrich, but if you believe her biographers it was exactly the opposite. Dressing room neighbors at Paramount, they got on very well, says Maria Riva.[97]

Marlene Dietrich

Dietrich was *Blonde Venus* (Josef von Sternberg, 1932), Madonna is *Blond Ambition*. The essential difference between the two Venuses is Josef von Sternberg. Madonna is her own von Sternberg. Feminism has no use for Pygmalions. This in no way means that Dietrich, vamp among vamps, was an easy-to-manipulate bimbo. On the contrary, she broke more than one taboo of her very patriarchal era, and she herself manipulated others abundantly.[98] Dietrich was a tough woman, maybe even more tyrannical than Madonna.

Regrettably, she did not enjoy Madonna's constant tributes to her at all. Her biographer, Steven Bach, tells how when she heard about the remake of *The Blue Angel* that was being planned by Madonna,[99] Dietrich angrily yelled: "*I* acted the vulgarity, Madonna *is* vulgar."[100]

Dietrich and Madonna both changed appearances during their starification process. Their bodies went from plump and soft to lean and hard, their hair from brown to platinum. Paramount had insured Dietrich's legs for a million dollars in 1931, and Madonna is said to have signed a twelve million dollar contract with Lloyd's at the time of *Dick Tracy*, to insure her breasts.[101]

Their faces have been subjected to similar metamorphoses. There are persistent rumors to the effect that Dietrich had her wisdom teeth or even back molars pulled out in order to make her cheeks hollower. Madonna had recourse to collagen once or twice (see the sleeve of *Justify My Love*). I won't dwell upon such considerations; suffice it to observe the uncanny changes, from one series of photographs to another, from one movie to the next.

The two stars share a clever use of lighting. Sternberg's films owe a great deal to lighting, obviously. Without competing with Sternberg's genius, the work of the directors and photographers that Madonna employs is comparable. Moreover, numerous photos of Dietrich and Madonna are touched up. That is the stuff myths are made of.

In *Witness for the Prosecution* (Billy Wilder, 1957), Dietrich plays a character who invents a second identity to deceive justice. The metamorphosis is fascinating, and certainly fascinated Madonna: dark wig, makeup and different accent, Dietrich is quite unrecognizable.

Dietrich, archetypal woman fatale, is without doubt an authentic mythic star; she meets the most demanding criteria. Like Madonna, she had a rather severe education. She often played good-bad girls, and of course she transgressed every taboo in terms of gender and sexuality. W.K. Martin writes about her reputation as a bisexual, and mentions her supposed mistresses in Berlin and Hollywood. He reminds us of the way she used lesbian signifiers like violets and monocles.[102]

The first part Dietrich ever played, at school in 1917, was a drag role: in *Die Gouvernante*, by a writer called Kohner, she played a man. *Morocco* counts among Madonna's permanent references. Dietrich in that film probably shocked viewers more than Madonna as sadomasochistic lesbian in *Sex*. Not only did she wear men's clothes and kiss a woman on the lips, she also adopted in the first few scenes gestures that were seen in 1930 as strictly masculine, encompassing Gary Cooper (playing a legionnaire) in her subversion of established codes.

The movie *Who's That Girl?*, in spite of its numerous flaws, renews the Dietrich tradition. Madonna plays a good-bad girl, and spectacularly transforms. From street girl with dubious methods, she becomes in the hothouse scene a glamorous femme fatale in a dress worthy of a screen goddess, holding a wild cat on a leash, as befits a feline star. Indeed, some scenes echo *Bringing Up Baby* (Howard Hawks, 1938).

However, Madonna speaks throughout the movie in an appalling nasal twanged high-pitched voice. Admittedly, the part more or less justifies it, and you may decide you're prepared to forgive her for doing a badly imitated Bronx drawl while under the impression that she's doing a lowlife Philadelphia accent. Still, you can only be reassured when you hear her speak more acceptably in *Body of Evidence* a few years later. What is more, her singing voice has never stopped evolving with the years. It was sufficiently mature in 1996 for her to sing *Evita*; then it was even more mature in 1998, so that she felt confident enough to experiment with it for *Ray of Light*. In 2000, she could afford processing it through a Vocoder for *Music*, as if to say, "you see, I have shown I can actually sing, now I can allow myself to play around again."

Dietrich's voice also evolved considerably, all along her career. The songs Madonna listens to today[103] are interpreted in a very low voice, which became her trademark. But in *The Blue Angel*, some of those oh-so-well-known numbers, like *Ich Bin Von Kopf Bis Fuss Auf Liebe Eingestellt,* are sung over two registers, including one that's high and unprepossessing, as everyone agrees.

The voice of David Bowie, the other chameleon star of the pop world, has also changed with time: high-pitched and Brixton-accented when he started, then low and mid–Atlantic, it has always been universally praised, as opposed to those of Dietrich or Madonna.

In *The Girlie Show*, Madonna wears a blond Afro wig identical to the one Dietrich sports in *Blonde Venus*. It allows her to parody the seventies, wearing bell bottoms and a bolero, in shades of hippie mauve; but it remains another tribute to Dietrich. Marjorie Garber enlighteningly described some of the elements that Madonna owes Dietrich in *Open Your Heart, Express Yourself* or *Vogue*.[104]

At such times, Madonna's hypertextual writing is unrivaled. In the same way John Barth or Thomas Pynchon may write *à la manière de* this or that eighteenth-century author, Madonna "writes" *à la manière de* Dietrich. The pencil of the former is the makeup brush of the latter. The resemblance between the two stars is sometimes so uncanny that my niece Mathilde, eleven, seeing a portrait of Dietrich in my study in November 1996, asked: "Is this Madonna?"

It is in the *Like a Virgin* number of *The Girlie Show* that Madonna paid her most stupendous tribute to Dietrich, via *Cabaret* (Bob Fosse, 1972). *Cabaret* is of course a cult film that is already overripe with intertextuality. It begins with Christopher Isherwood's 1939 *Goodbye to Berlin*, inspired by real people. Then, there is John van Druten's 1951 theatrical adaptation, *I Am a Camera*, then a film with the same title (Henry Cornelius, 1955[105]), in its turn transformed into a Broadway musical in 1966 by Joe Masteroff.[106] Finally, there's *Cabaret* in 1972, with Liza Minnelli, which got eight Oscars. Since then, the rewrites of the Sally Bowles character have been countless.[107]

The choreography, the décors, the costumes and the songs of *Cabaret* are very much inspired by *The Blue Angel*, *Morocco* and *Blonde Venus*, most notably the girl-gorilla number, *If You Could See Her (through my eyes)*. Although she no doubt enjoys the political implications of such numbers, Madonna has yet to adopt Dietrich's gorilla suit — but Grace Jones has done it before.[108] *Cabaret* is a monument of Camp, thanks to the composition of Liza Minnelli.[109] As expected, the film has become the number one inspiration for Western drag queens, followed closely by *The Rocky Horror Picture Show* (Jim Sharman, 1975).[110]

In *The Girlie Show*, the palimpsestuous process is extreme. For *Like a Virgin* Madonna plays a drag queen who plays Liza Minnelli who plays a drag queen who plays Marlene Dietrich who plays a drag queen. Can you get more mythic and postmodern? Madonna uses Dietrich tunes and performs an astonishing androgyny exercise, made-up and dressed so as to recall Dietrich in various films, but also Liza Minnelli *and* Joel Grey in *Cabaret*. At the beginning of the number she is sitting on a trunk that echoes Dietrich's barrow in *The Blue Angel*, as well as the stereotypical trunk of artists on the road.[111]

Singing very slowly, she imitates simultaneously Dietrich's low voice and — in a very funny way — Joel Grey's fake German accent. She laughs in a manner as "perverse" as Joel Grey's, and plays with her walking-stick like him, raising it between her legs to evoke an erection, for example. In that number Madonna's face changes every second, so that you could almost end up wondering briefly if anti-postmodern Madonnophobes aren't just a little bit on the right track when they say that Madonna is deprived of identity.

At other moments in *The Girlie Show*, Madonna even succeeds in conjuring up shades of *A Clockwork Orange* (Stanley Kubrick, 1971) and *Singin' in the Rain* (Gene Kelly & Stanley Donen, 1952),[112] while never ceasing to pastiche Dietrich, Grey and Minnelli.

In an interview that Madonna granted the scriptwriter, novelist and actress Carrie Fisher, the daughter of Debbie Reynolds and Eddie Fisher,[113] the subject of Marlene Dietrich came up:

— In terms of your career, won't you have to stop being as sexual at a certain point before it becomes weird?

— Why?

— That's the law [...].

— Sexy in what way? Marlene Dietrich is still sexy.

— My father slept with her.

— Really? I wish I had slept with her.

— With her?

— Yeah, she's gorgeous. She had a very masculine thing about her, but I think she maintained a sexual allure.[114]

Why does Madonna pretend to confuse "sexual" and "sexy"? To avoid answering Fisher's question? After less sexual personae in the late nineties, she was a bombshell again in 1999 for the *Beautiful Stranger* video, then again in the *American Pie* video (if somewhat grungy), and a more tongue-in-cheek than ever sex-spot during the promotion of *Music* in 2000 and the *Drowned World* tour in 2001.

You may also wonder if the word "but" in her last line isn't a transcription mistake, because she showed repeatedly that having "a very masculine thing" could help "maintain a sexual allure." That confession of desire for Dietrich (more symbolic and political than anything else), and that mixture of present tenses and preterits are particularly revealing.

One of the most stupendous Dietrich rewrites by Madonna is that passage of *Vogue* when her face is framed by her hands (limp wrists) and irresistibly echoes those studio shots of Dietrich by Don English. In the same order of thing, for a Matthew Rolston photo, Madonna offers a paroxysmal Dietrich simulacrum and the *mise en abyme* goes very far indeed: she simultaneously pastiches a Dietrich shot by E.R. Richee and another by Don English, while alluding to Josef von Sternberg's *Morocco*. Wearing a man's suit, a man's shirt with cufflinks and a tie, she poses facing a mirror, holding a cigarette the way Dietrich did. She has the same hairdo that Dietrich has on E.R. Richee's shot, but because Rolston shot her in a mirror, the blond lock is "on the other side," as if it were Dietrich looking at herself through the decades in a magic mirror.[115]

Madonna is sitting like Dietrich in Don English's picture in a star's armchair, one hand on the back. You can read the end of the word "Dietrich" on one chair, and the end of the word "Madonna" on the other. The mirrors of the two dressing-rooms are framed by similar lightbulbs. Madonna's game with Rolston prolongs that of Dietrich and English; in the two cases, a spectacle-illusion code is at work. English appears on Dietrich's picture, whereas Rolston preferred a diegetic suggestion written in lipstick (the pen of the star *par excellence*) on the mirror: "I changed my mind. Good luck." This is lifted from *Morocco*.[116] To add a comic element, Madonna thought of placing a no-smoking sign behind her.

What About Marilyn, Then?

I have chosen to show that Madonna does not rewrite Marilyn Monroe, whereas she rewrites Marlene Dietrich and Mae West, among other stars, but I could just as easily have formulated my idea by claiming exactly the opposite; it is a matter of vocabulary. The distinction I am establishing is that where Madonna accomplishes an actual work of palimpsest as far as Dietrich and West are concerned (I have specified that you can "read" them through the Madonna text, there is a transparency at play), she but uses the image of Marilyn Monroe in a game of reflections rather than superimpositions.

The reference is constant, it is undeniable, Madonna has repeated for years that she was greatly attracted to Marilyn, which numerous journalists have wrongly interpreted as idolatry (Madonna is self-deified, and as such has but one idol, herself); she then declared that she was tired of reading articles that relentlessly compared her to Marilyn, which naturally gave rise to understandable mockery.

In more ways than one, Madonna only usurps Marilyn's stardom. She *wears* it, the way you wear a plastic raincoat that you can't wait to put away in the closet when the rain has stopped.

This explains why she finally grew weary of Marilyn, whereas she will never tire of rewriting Dietrich. This phenomenon has its counterparts in other domains, notably in literature. Sometimes it is not postmodern, but merely pitiful.

Moreover, the media always show a desperate need to qualify new celebrities as the new somebody or other. In the seventies and eighties, the new Bardot was regularly "discovered" in France. That journalistic tradition weakened in the nineties. In the same way, the comparisons between Marilyn and Madonna became rarer at last after 1995.

The enormous difference between Marilyn and Madonna is that Madonna is not a victim.[117] So she could drape herself only superficially in the deceased star's mantle.

To my mind, Marilyn was not really a femme fatale, nor a good-bad girl, nor someone who satirized her own sexuality or that of others like Mae West and Madonna. She was often unaware of what was happening around her. As David Thomson writes: "Those who discern in Marilyn Monroe either the inclination or the ability to satirize her own sexuality can never have seen the great Mae."[118]

In *Gentlemen Prefer Blondes* (Howard Hawks, 1953), *How to Marry a Millionaire* (Jean Negulesco, 1953), *The Prince and the Showgirl* (Laurence Olivier, 1957) or *Let's Make Love* (George Cukor, 1960), Marilyn charms, evidently; she gets her man, but she is basically no more than a very sexy small-town girl-next-door with a heart of gold. In *The Seven Year Itch* (Billy Wilder, 1955) all she does is cause the main (male) character to fantasize, but he will successfully suppress his fantasies and bring about the triumph of family values. In *Bus Stop* (Joshua Logan, 1956) she is nothing but the eventually willing victim, antifeminist, of an abominably chauvinistic cowboy who claims her as he would the prize of a rodeo competition. In *Some Like It Hot* (Billy Wilder, 1959), which is a masterpiece of gender deconstruction but which in this respect owes Monroe nothing, she yields to the advances of a saxophone player who will not bring her unadulterated happiness, judging by his past. In *The Misfits* (John Huston, 1961), she displays various neuroses, pathetic fragility and sad weaknesses, yielding yet again to the dubious charms of an aging cowboy. Where is the mystery? Where is the vamp? Where is the destructive force of seduction?

It is only in *Niagara* (Henry Hathaway, 1953) that she plays a bad girl, but one who quickly pays for her sins, without ever manifesting much power. In *River of No Return* (Otto Preminger, 1954), she does bow to the good-bad-girl tradition, but the tremendous difference between a Marilyn Monroe and a Marlene Dietrich or a Madonna is apparent in the concluding sequence that plagiarizes the sublime final scene of *Morocco*. Leaving with Robert Mitchum (yet another chauvinistic cowboy), she throws her spike heels in the dust, as Dietrich throws hers in the sand to follow Gary Cooper in the Sahara. But where is the dramatic intensity? Where is the power struggle, the tragic renouncement, the promise of wild sex, the desired slavery of the sadomasochistic relationship? What you get is nothing more than a showgirl who turns into a housewife. Of course, some of Marilyn's movies do not lack in parodic aspects and tongue-in-cheek elements, but those owe more to the scriptwriters and the directors than to her.

Marilyn Monroe was the most desired woman in the world, before Madonna, but she was fundamentally unhappy, and more or less exploited, whereas Madonna is an optimistic and powerful woman who won't let anyone step on her toes ("power is a great aphrodisiac, and I'm a powerful woman"[119]). Marilyn suffered a thousand ills, crawled from therapist to depression and back again, and from booze to barbiturates; Madonna is into sports and yoga, does not drink, and does not take drugs (any longer). Marilyn didn't control much, Madonna controls everything.

Besides, Marilyn rarely showed any sexual ambiguity; she was not particularly subversive (though the CIA, the FBI, the Mafia, the Communists and the Kennedys may have deemed her somewhat dangerous). Madonna is frequently subversive. Marilyn always retained a certain innocence and freshness, Madonna is probably the least innocent performer ever.

That extreme fragility, that heartbreaking vulnerability are precisely what to a large extent explain Marilyn's success; they are what make her so endearing, possibly more than the beauty of her body and face. The success of Madonna, on the other hand, is constructed on her mastery of events.

Once you have observed the essential differences between Marilyn Monroe and Madonna, you won't be any less impressed by the frequent performances of the latter as the former. Madonna has shown her determination by taking the game rather far, and always with humor. In the context of her masterly visual rhetoric, she has repeatedly borrowed poses outfits and looks from Marilyn. For Steven Meisel's cameras, for example, she has playfully posed like Marilyn during her *Last Sitting* for Bert Stein: in the same positions, with the same props, on an identical bed, the movement of the sheet on her hip reproducing exactly that of the sheet on Marilyn's body more than thirty years before.[120]

It is in the *Material Girl* video that Madonna really began to pounce on the Marilyn myth. Of course, she is not content with merely aping her. She establishes a distance, and shows her difference inside the very pastiche. "Details" like different gloves or different ways to use fans signify. In both cases the fan might symbolize royal dignity, as it does in some parts of Africa and Asia, the royal dignity here is that of the star (drag) queen. But it is equally possible to see in Marilyn's the fan of Hindu iconography, Vishnu's attribute, that is used to kindle fires. Here it kindles the fiery desire aroused by Marilyn, but Vishnu's fan is also the symbol of ritual sacrifice, and it eerily foreshadows the sacrifice of the star who died in such sinister conditions in 1962. Madonna's fan, on the other hand, which appears at the end of the performance, may be seen as the Taoist symbol, linked to the bird that liberates forms, to the notion of flight (on ascending winds) toward the land of the Immortals.[121] It is as if Madonna — while paying her dues to the Marilyn legend — were at the same time signaling that she had no intention of dying stupidly, like Marilyn, as a victim, and that she was immortal too, in her way, as a feminist postmodern myth. Let us not forget, incidentally, the other sense of the word fan, nor the Hispanic "language" of the fan.

In *Diamonds Are a Girl's Best Friend*, Marilyn dances surrounded by men, like Madonna, but there are also women, who are used as candelabra (purely decorative); there is no woman in *Material Girl*, which is a way for Madonna to indicate that as a feminist she does not reduce her sisters to such roles, and possibly also a way to show that she will accept no rivalry whatsoever. Besides, the choreography and the facial expressions are, although similar, clearly more sexualized in *Material Girl*.

Marilyn sings about the "kiss on the hand," Madonna sings "some boys kiss me, some boys hug me"; where Marilyn sings about diamonds, which are symbolic, Madonna evokes "cold hard cash."

In *Gentlemen Prefer Blondes*, the tuxedoed dancers around Marilyn are coded as French. In *Material Girl*, they are multiethnic. The conclusions to the songs confirm the essential differences between Marilyn and Madonna. The former foresees her pathetic old age[122], alone but provided for financially speaking, thanks to the diamonds she made sure to get from married men, having clearly filled the role of the mistress, the woman men don't marry, a role which is worse *and* better than that of the wife, according to the angle of observation, but at any rate a role strictly defined by patriarchal society. Madonna, on the other hand, indicates to conclude that she is now an experienced and wealthy woman, and as such she has men running after her.

Norman Mailer credited Marilyn in the part of Lorelei Lee as generator of Camp in *Gentlemen Prefer Blondes*.[123] The movie is camp, and so is Jane Russell; but I'm not so sure about Marilyn. It feels as if Mailer were already waiting for Madonna; he is predicting her, attributing an ironic stance to Marilyn which she does not really muster, in a bout of wishful thinking.

Rewriting *Diamonds Are a Girl's Best Friend*, Madonna appropriates the camp irony of *Gentlemen Prefer Blondes*. The movie's campest moment is the *Ain't There Anyone Here for Love?* number, starring Jane Russell, and not Marilyn Monroe. Several critics, after Mailer, granted Marilyn what rightfully belongs to Jane Russell.[124] David van Leer, for his part, measures the meaning of Russell's performance. He reminds us that at the end of the movie, she pastiches Lorelei / Marilyn:

> The imitability of female performance always, of course, calls attention to the constructed character of gender identity. At the end of Gentlemen Prefer Blondes, for example, Jane Russell can become "Marilyn Monroe" through reprising in a platinum wig Monroe's "Diamonds" number.[125]

That Russell number not only deconstructs "Marilyn Monroe," but also "woman," in the same way a drag number might.[126] Can anyone be surprised that *Diamonds Are a Girl's Best Friend* has become a drag cabaret classic? When Madonna gets hold of *Diamonds Are a Girl's Best Friend* in her turn, she is perfectly aware that she is coming after Jane Russell and several generations of drag queens. Her version is a third rewrite.

Madonna also alludes to Marilyn when she sings *Bye Bye Baby*.[127] Indeed, Marilyn Monroe and Jane Russell sing in *Gentlemen Prefer Blondes* a sentimental song of the same title. But Madonna, for her part, warns us immediately: "This is not a love song."[128] Then she dumps an inadequate egotistic lover. Has Marilyn, on the other hand, ever done anything with her (sentimental) life other than flatter the ego of her husbands and lovers?

Let us compare Marilyn's "Talk to me Harry Winston,[129] tell me all about it," and Madonna's "Talk to me General Schwarzkoff, tell me all about it" on Oscar night, both yelled as a parenthesis between two lines of a song. Madonna is treating the Gulf War as just another fiction — to be appropriated. What can General Schwarzkoff bring Madonna that is comparable to what Harry Winston is capable of bringing Marilyn? Has Madonna observed that the conflict, which I am tempted to call the first postmodern war, looked more like — as seen from every TV lounge in every Western home — a video game than a war, with all those green dots moving about on a black screen? Has she noticed that the Gulf War was as omnipresent and media-covered as she was? After the invasion of Kuwait by Iraq, she agreed to appear on TV to comment upon her *Justify My Love* video.[130] So as the tension was increasing, she provided strong entertainment amd diversion. Schwichtenberg sees that as a "displacement" of the Gulf War.[131] As hundreds of GIs were about to be sent to the Middle East, millions of TV viewers were wondering with Forrest Sawyer if *Justify My Love* should be considered (scandalously) pornographic, feminist, or both.[132]

Marilyn/Lorelei wanted a jeweler to tell her about diamonds, but Madonna situates herself in another sphere of existence: she is as important as the Gulf War, if not more; at the very least she is the equal of the political leaders of this world, and of great generals; she is not a bimbo who expects nothing from life outside expensive presents from men. All this being done, of course, humorously. Incidentally, the jewels she was wearing that night were by Harry Winston.

It seems Madonna took the Marilyn game so far that she had a liaison with John F. Kennedy Jr.[133] The tabloids largely discussed it in 1987, reporting on the alleged anger of Jacqueline Kennedy Onassis, who saw this, they said, as the duplication of the affair between John F. Kennedy and Marilyn. This could show on Madonna's part an extraordinary desire of digging her way into history, in this case by repeating it. That liaison procures a feeling of ineluctable logic: the most attractive Kennedy of the pre–1962 era lets the most compelling sex-symbol of his day seduce him, and the most attractive Kennedy of the post–1962 era lets the most compelling sex-symbol of *his* day seduce him…[134] But of course, Madonna was not victimized by the Kennedy clan the way Marilyn allegedly was.

In an interview granted to Don Shewey,[135] and elsewhere, Madonna confirms my words, declaring that she does not identify with Marilyn Monroe, that Marilyn was just a victim, and explaining that she is playing with the image of the dead actress, but her message is not the same.

■ ■ ■

Madonna expresses herself through masks. This is what an actress does, she exercises her art interpreting dramatis personae (persona equals mask). In this respect, she ought to be considered as an actress who plays and acts constantly, as soon as she offers herself to the public as spectacle, whatever her choice of activity. Madonna is constantly dealing in representation, and as she does so she questions the validity of any representation, while seeming to affirm that there is nothing outside representation. That is what the postmodern is.

So I have observed the tactical multiplication of her identities and their construction, undertaken with an uncommon sense of detail. Madonna joins the drag queens in their drag strategies, and practices Camp on a large scale, irony being systematically present in every single aspect of her artistic output. Like drag queens, Madonna is a semiotician who applies to her creation the result of her observations. As much *au fait* of the artifices on which the traditional gender roles of our society rest as the most cultured gender studies specialist in academe, she is always busy building a *mise en scène* around them, to mock them while utilizing them to further her career. Doing so, she particularly explored the Houses of Harlem where voguing developed, and integrated them in her work. More than ever this caused furor, voguing being by essence political and subversive.

The masks of drag queens and those of golden age Hollywood stars are remarkably alike. Madonna is acutely aware of this, and it is along the same process that she is inspired by the former or by the latter (or the former via the latter). Thus is glamour engendered. So Madonna has rewritten several stars, some for a night or a video, others in more recurrent ways. Her principal targets are Mae West and Marlene Dietrich; it seems that she profoundly assimilated everything that concerns those two stars, to the most minute details of their biographies. On the other hand, she only exploited the image of Marilyn Monroe superficially, for Madonna is no victim: "Rather than Marilyn Monroe, whose secret anguish and vulnerability were showing under the mask, Madonna evokes the ironic Mae West, who is always playing herself. Her provocations are at all times humorous."[136]

Ready to take up whichever metamorphosis it takes to remain the most media-covered of all performers, spreading her image around the globe at regular intervals, she imposes on the avid media a particular look (a mask) with each new album — sometimes more often — like a franchise company that demands to see its logo, its products and its décor reproduced identically by all the franchised establishments (this is the Madonnization of the globe).

Madonna is a fighter, and a winner, the American way, as my last chapter will show.

F I V E

America's Mirror

It is easy to imagine Sicilians or Jews in the late nineteenth century never having heard of William McKin-
ley or Teddy Roosevelt. It is difficult to imagine
Koreans or Jamaicans arriving in Miami or New York
today unable to identify George Bush or Bill Clinton —
or, for that matter, never having heard of Michael Jackson, *Time* magazine and *Reader's Digest*, Madonna and
Eddie Murphy, Woody Allen and Mohammad Ali, and
the Cable News Network.
— Richard Bernstein[1]

Martine Trittoléno writes: "Madonna is more than a witness of her
epoch, she is an active reflection of it, she is an iconoclast, and her aesthetics do not give a damn about 'good taste.' She seizes the trends of the
moment with vampire-like gluttony, recycles them in her very own way
and then throws them in the face of the establishment."[2]

Pamela Robertson, for her part, judges: "The glut of debates revolving around Madonna run the gamut of concerns about the nature of contemporary society itself."[3] As for Steve Anderson, he speaks of "Madonna's
resonance in the minds of the public," a public for whom she has become
"a repository for all our ideas about fame, money, sex, feminism, pop
culture, even death."[4]

148

It is customary to say that art is the reflection of its period. The preceding pages have illustrated this already. In this fifth chapter, I examine the way Madonna's work brings to light some particular characteristics of the U.S. today. How does Madonna fit into the American Dream? What can she teach us about the evolution (or regression) of mores, and about the feminine condition? What are her links with the African American community? Where does she stand in regards to the contradictory discourses that tear the country apart, having to do with AIDS, abortion and religion? In other words, what is she saying about America, its ideals and its contradictions?

Of course, playing the part of the mirror is for Madonna a deliberate strategy, even if she doesn't necessarily plan all the reflections, even if perhaps she is taken over by some of them. "I'll be your mirror / reflect what you are."[5]

The American Dream

The *New York Public Library Book of Popular Americana* defines the American Dream as "the attainment of material and social success"; neglecting the old ideas of liberty (notably religious), of Frontier, etc., it merely recalls formulae like "'upward mobility,' 'rags-to-riches,' 'pulling yourself up by your bootstraps,' 'land of opportunity' and 'self-made man.'"[6]

Books which attempt to show that the American Dream persists — or not — in this or that field are regularly published, and the debate is far from over. The way I see it, the American Dream comes in two different packages today.

The first is the happy middle-class family: two cars, two children, a dog, a house in a "clean" suburb; a small patch of lawn in the front, a substantial backyard on the other side, five TV sets and a basket above the garage door.

The second, which can help you get through the day, daydreaming in the subway or at work, is access to stardom.

It is true that the myth of the self-made man subsists; starting with nothing, the American with an acute business sense can become a billionaire, the Horatio Alger way. Donald Trump and Bill Gates have embodied that.

But I believe such versions of the American Dream generate fewer fantasies than show business, which crystallizes the frustrations of the average American much better than the corporate world. Better than anyone, the mythic pop star or movie star makes Americans dream, closely followed by the sports celebrity.

Let's look at those African American basketball champions, recent illustrations of the new style Dream. Often fresh out of the ghetto, they enjoy considerable wealth and fame, and become the role models of thousands of teenagers. "Basketball has become a dream sport for kids who are desperate to resemble their idols [...]. Though a team sport, basketball is symbolic of individual success, as one single player may make all the difference."[7] That is abundantly documented in Darcy Frey's book *The Last Shot: City Streets, Basketball Dreams*, and elsewhere.[8] In its perverted effect, just so we don't forget that the Dream permanently flirts with the Nightmare, children sometimes kill each other over a pair of sports shoes, because their favorite sportsman promotes the brand. Like Madonna, those famous athletes belong to American pop culture, and may have influence over their fans.[9] Let us note all the same that African American sports celebrities remain victims of insidious forms of racism.[10] They have their exact counterpart in the world of rap. Dennis Rodman speaks of three ways out of poverty: sports, drug-dealing (plus crime in general), and rap.[11]

Dennis Rodman explains that he understands the political ways of some rappers, whose records mean to denounce injustice. But he judges that many rappers only want to make money. Well, isn't that *their* American Dream come true? Originally a site of resistance, combining the power of the African American preacher with that of soul music, attacking the mainstream musically, rap became in the eighties a flourishing and constantly increasing industry. Aware of that progression, Madonna includes bits of rap in her songs, principally in an ironic way (*Did You Do It?*).

The U.S. being what it is, African American celebrities only get to the very top if they are whitewashed (physiologically and culturally), like Michael Jackson. hooks writes: "Like Madonna, they too, have a healthy dose of 'blond ambition.' Clearly their careers have been influenced by Madonna's choices and strategies."[12]

Look at all those interchangeable hip hop girl bands these days, who all dance in exactly the same way and look the same and are filmed in videos that all look the same, with the same white light and the same silly science fiction décor: they are about as threatening for the dominant ideology as Britney Spears.

Tina Turner reached the summits of the charts only after she abandoned soul or rhythm and blues to sing white music, having bleached her hair orange.

When in the late eighties Michael Jackson was busy self-whitewashing, Madonna was appropriating African American culture. They are both keen on metamorphosis. A semiotician's fantasy, Madonna constantly changes looks. "*Ni tout à fait la même, ni tout à fait une autre,*" she moves from Nordic goddess to Mediterranean siren, and back again.

Michael Jackson also transforms, but not as one changes wigs or masks. His metamorphosis is gradual and radical, with no return. His face is a bit more androgynous every day, his skin lighter and lighter,[13] his nose thinner and thinner, to the point of becoming the mere suggestion of a nose, his hair more and more raven blue and straight (Asianized?). He walks straight ahead, ineluctably moving from one stage to the next. Looking at pictures of Michael Jackson taken at intervals during the last twenty-five years is an unsettling experience. In early 2002, the process seemed to have gone terribly wrong, and he was truly frightening to look at.

La Toya Jackson, one of his sisters, followed exactly the same path and carried the process to extremes; she gives the impression that she took pictures of Michael to her surgeon and merely ordered the same face. She even went one step further and became a blonde. However, Michael also had a mostly unacknowledged model: the actress and singer Lena Horne, first African American woman who ever got a long-term contract with a big studio. She did suffer from racism, but she was quite whitewashed. The resemblance is all the more disturbing. Lena Horne played with Jackson in *The Wiz*, and so did Diana Ross, who provided another model, much more frequently commented upon.

Michael Jackson's sci-fi transformation could be seen as fascinating in the beginning, but it finally makes you queasy, even if you do not take into account its political implications for the African American community.

Garber notes the way Madonna sometimes grabs her crotch on stage, à la Michael Jackson:

> Madonna, squeezing what she hadn't got (or *had* she?), emblematized the Lacanian triad of having, being, and seeming [...]. Madonna is a famous star who is impersonating a famous male star who is celebrated for his androgynous looks and his dancing style. Why is it shocking when she grabs her crotch, repeating as she does a gesture familiar to anyone who has watched a two-year-old male child reassuring himself of his intactness?[14]

A fan explains the hatred that Madonna arouses: "I think some men hate Madonna because she has 'balls.' Some women also hate women who are powerful. Many women hate themselves and worship men."[15]

What Madonna is saying when she grabs her crotch during a concert is that her pants are better-filled than those of Michael Jackson. You can't tell exactly if she is paying him a tribute, satirizing him, or both. She is saying that two can play the number one stardom game. Didn't she cover the song *Billie Jean* on stage in 1987, going as far as to imitate Michael Jackson's famous moonwalk? When he grabs his crotch, Jackson doesn't frighten anyone, except perhaps those who believe he's an active pedophile. When Madonna imitates him, she becomes threatening. Her gender-bending terrorizes people, Jackson's antics amuse them, or make them feel pity.

Janelle L. Wilson speaks of the masks that Madonna and Michael Jackson wear:

> How are selves developed (or constructed) in the postmodern condition? The image we get is that of a mask — or rather, a set of masks — which operate as selves in a complex society. We Xers have come of age in an era which has been dominated by two popular culture icons: Madonna and Michael Jackson. Both of these icons are wearers and expert users of masks.[16]

Madonna does use masks with dexterity, but I'm not so sure about Jackson.

The pop culture version of the American Dream is illustrated by performers who have often grown up in small-town America and now live in sumptuous Californian villas.

Baudrillard writes in *America*:

> [Stars] don't make one dream, they *are* the dream, the characteristics of which they all display: they produce a strong effect of condensation (of crystallization), of contiguity (they are immediately contagious), and especially: they have that character of instantaneous visual materialization (*Anschaulichkeit*) of desire which is also that of the dream.[17]

Madonna constitutes a particular case. Her ascension is the most vertiginous of all, although it isn't exactly a Cinderella rags-to-riches story. Madonna as an independent feminist is her own fairy godmother, and in no way depends upon some Prince Charming to succeed. America is obsessed by celebrity, Madonna reflects that obsession. "If one wants to get postmodern about it, she's mirroring the culture's own fixation with celebrity," writes Ingrid Sischy.[18]

Martin Amis writes that "Madonna tells America that fame comes from wanting it badly enough."[19]

The cover of *Fortune* on December 31, 1990, proclaims: "Pop Culture: America's Hottest Export Goes Boom!" There are ten drawings on that cover: Madonna, Coca-Cola, Arnold Schwarzenegger, Mickey Mouse, MTV, The Teenage Mutant Ninja Turtles, Levi-Strauss jeans, Julia Roberts, McDonald's, and Sylvester Stallone.

In the program *Between the Sheets with Madonna* on MTV, you can hear during the beginning titles Madonna say (voiceover):

People think that being a star is about being fabulous, being in the spotlight, having your picture taken all the time and having everyone worship you and adore you, being rich rich rich, having it all. And you know what? They're absolutely right![20]

So Madonna is aware of her power as incarnation of the American Dream, but of course she keeps her distances and her sense of humor. In the same order of things, you can hear her sum up her biography at the beginning of a handful of videotapes, including the *Like a Virgin* show (voiceover):

I went to New York, I had a dream. I wanted to be a big star, I didn't know anybody, I wanted to dance, I wanted to sing, I wanted to do all those things, I wanted to make people happy, I wanted to be famous, I wanted everybody to love me, I wanted to be a star. I worked really hard, and my dream came true.[21]

On occasions, she seems to seriously defend some values linked to the American Dream. When in 1990 the Vatican tried to get her show banned in Italy, she gave a mini press conference at Rome airport and declared — apparently not tongue-in-cheek:

I'm an Italian-American and I'm proud of it. Proud of being an American, because it is the country I grew up in, the country that gave me the opportunity to be who I am today, and a country that believes in freedom of speech and artistic expression.

On February 18, 1998, when her single *Frozen* came out, she declared with an ambiguous smile on France 2 television: "I think I'm the shining example of the American Dream." As Neil Campbell and Alasdair Kean note: "The idea of self-creation [is] a core myth of American identity."[22]

Icon, the magazine of her official fan club, regularly publishes interviews of "mega-fans." Here's an excerpt that speaks volumes:

Madonna has taught me so much about life. Life is what you make for yourself. She helps me stay strong and never give up. I may not ever achieve what Madonna has, but I have goals and dreams of my own that I want to work hard at and Madonna has helped me gain the confidence, strength and power that I need.[23]

Madonna embodies dream so well that there is a book called *I Dream of Madonna: Women's Dreams of the Goddess of Pop*.[24] Kay Turner gathered the dreams of a great variety of women of all ages, for whom Madonna is alternately friend, confidante, lover, mother, daughter, sister, and so forth. As far as I know, no other such book exists.

Even *Truth or Dare*, seen as mostly about sex, is perhaps more concerned with hard work the American way, as Roger Ebert has noted.[25] Madonna is a no-time-to-waste businesswoman. The homepage of her official fan club Internet site proclaimed in 2000: "icon, diva, mogul, provocateur," not necessarily in that order. She leads several companies and keeps enriching the AOL-Time-Warner group. *Forbes* and *Fortune* have reported on the financial joys of Madonna. Those magazines take her as seriously as more classic millionaires.[26]

Madonna is a totally self-made woman (self-made star). She proves at least one thing: that power is accessible to all, including women — provided they know what they want.[27]

But being Madonna, she also had to illustrate the other side of the coin: in *Dangerous Game*, she plays Sarah Jennings who plays Claire. Madonna, Sarah and Claire participate in Ferrara's scathing deconstruction of the consumerist form of the American Dream. When Claire realizes that she has been swindled by the mall version American Dream, she gets into sexual promiscuity and drugs. And Sarah Jennings ("a bleached blond Hollywood bitch") is also the victim of a Californian version of the American Dream: she's one of those LA TV actresses who ape Barbie in endless soaps waiting for a movie break. They reflect the lookism that causes so much damage in the U.S., and the dictatorship of aesthetic criteria invented and imposed by men, behind the whole showbiz industry and media machine. Somebody in the film asks what Sarah looks like. Does she rely heavily on makeup and hair dye? "It's a lot of money," is the answer.

For one moderately successful blonde like Sarah, how many middle-class frustrated Claires can you find? How many unemployed mothers and supermarket attendants with hair that has been ruined by cheap bleach? And for one unprecedented blond success like Madonna, emblem of the American Dream, how many pathetic losers?

Melting Pot or Salad Bowl?

Reinforcing the multiethnic connotations of the American Dream, Madonna appropriates the different cultures that coexist in the States, as if she were trying to single-handedly form a melting pot. But of course the melting pot never really existed. It's a Hollywood fiction, a myth. It only ever made sense in an 1893 text, *The Significance of the Frontier in American History*.[28] A number of Americans favor "salad bowl" over "melting pot"; between the two, "transmuting pot," "hybridity," "mosaic" and "pizzaland" made timid attempts. The point of this relatively new

expression (more politically correct) is the wish to spare the susceptibil-
ities of everyone. The different ethnic groups on American soil should be
able to live in the same container, without being compelled to melt
together as in a crucible, losing their individual identity. Even notions
like multiculturalism, cultural pluralism or pluriculturalism are hotly
debated.[29]

Indeed, the different ethnic groups in the U.S. today do not mix very
much. The cabbage rubs elbows with the carrot, maybe it crushes it, the
lettuce hides the potato or disappears under the tomato, but they never
stick together as pieces of fabric in a patchwork.

For some, such metaphors only cover up attempts at a general
waspification masquerading as Americanization. Questioning all this, once
more, and reflecting the different ingredients of the salad bowl, Madonna
recruits a pluriethnic staff,[30] multiplies African American or Hispanic
American roommates and lovers, and often insists on her father's Italian
origins. At other times, she advertises the French Canadian origins of her
mother. She embodies Hispanic personae more and more frequently, as
she monitors the progress of the Spanish language on American soil and
knows on which side her bread is buttered. Whether out of commercial
calculation or political preoccupation (or both), she does reflect the evolution of the demography — all the better if she unsettles those of her com-
patriots who worry about the old Anglo hegemony.

In fact, the only community Madonna never clearly addressed is the
Native Americans; even in this she reflects America, because they are still
frequently forgotten. As the Spokane-raised novelist Sherman Alexie says:
"In most people's minds, American Indians only exist in the nineteenth
century."[31]

But does "salad bowl" really constitute an appropriate metaphor?
Not to me. I suggest we try "TV dinner." All the elements isolated in their
own plastic cavities, on the same TV tray; but all watching the same shows,
even if they are broadcast in different languages, and of course, all badly
defrosted in an aging microwave oven. In a TV dinner, there is no sauce,
as there might be in a salad bowl, to give a superficially similar taste to
the various ingredients.

Madonna is on every channel, and she eats from each cavity on the
tray. Some congratulate her on this achievement, seeing her as the future
of a successful pluriculturalism; she reflects their hopes — or their illu-
sions. Others call her a hypocritical opportunist and an identity thief;
maybe she reflects their bitterness. Art is the reflection of a period, and
so is myth. The American Dream and the melting pot are myths, reflected
by Madonna the myth.[32]

I have examined the Madonnesque appropriations of gay culture and drag culture, notably African American and Hispanic American drag culture. Let us now look at Madonna and heterosexual African American culture. She has said in interviews that some black men have treated her particularly badly; she has tried to understand, she has formed all sorts of practically sociological opinions about it, taking economics into account, but her conclusion remains the same:

> I think that black men, certainly in America, are probably more nar-
> row-minded than any other group I can think of. They're incredibly
> narrow-minded, homophobic and sexist.[33]

Some say she sets out to broadcast the image of a woman totally devoid of racism, sexism, and homophobia, whereas she is a vile supporter of the establishment and as such really racist, misogynistic, homophobic, heterosexist and heterocentric. I find this hard to credit.

In *Did You Do It?*,[34] Madonna parodies the machismo of rappers. Many American rappers famously convey homophobic and sexist messages, when they are not busy conveying racist and anti–Semitic ideas.[35]

The rapper of *Did You Do It?* boasts that he has "done it," and you can hear Madonna repeat "I'm waiting." She thus quotes herself (it might even be sampling), since the line comes from *Justify My Love*. Anyone who knows the song *Justify My Love* knows that Madonna is waiting for her man to justify her love. So the song conjures up a sexually inadequate black partner. But the song can also target African Americans (rappers or not) who pretend that they had sex with Madonna.[36]

I don't mean to generalize unduly or dwell on the machismo of African American men (there are statistics),[37] so I'll merely note that Madonna at least tries to find an explanation. Let us not forget that women were not exactly welcome at Louis Farrakhan's Washington march of October 16, 1995. What should also be pointed out is that before determining they tended to ill-treat their female partners, Madonna did have African American lovers. There is an African American *Cosby Show* bourgeoisie in the States, but Madonna as it happens has mixed more with ghetto African Americans, notably to recruit authentic Harlem voguers.

bell hooks writes that Madonna appropriates certain aspects of African American culture and transforms them into commercial products. This is indisputable. Madonna does it with gay culture too, or any other subculture that might be integrated into her postmodern spectacle. hooks sees there the manifestation of a "fascination and envy of blackness,"[38] which is debatable, seeing that it's difficult to determine what actually fascinates Madonna, apart from old Hollywood. It doesn't really matter, in fact. What Madonna borrows from African Americans should be seen as manifestations of her antiracism, rather than interpreted as insulting.[39] When bell hooks speaks of the "air of sham and falseness" of white cultural productions "inspired" by African American traditions, I'm not sure she understands Madonna's postmodern work.

Of course, Madonna knows only too well that she could never have reached mythic status in the U.S. if she hadn't been white. But her employment policy goes beyond Affirmative Action, as the majority of her employees on tour are African American or Hispanic American and/or gay, the rest being lesbian or straight women and Asians of both genders, gay or not. Her "Validator" Liz Rosenberg is Jewish.

Madonna's first single (*Everybody*) came out without her picture on the sleeve, so that many buyers thought the singer was African American. The sound of that record was indeed very close to that of the disco hits (sung by African American females) of the day. It was even featured in African American charts. This has famously been achieved by two other Caucasians, with their picture on the sleeve, David Bowie and George Michael. After *Everybody*, some African American singers deliberately set out to sound like Madonna.

Several commentators have deplored Madonna's "facile" use of Blacks in *Sex*, like the rapper Big Daddy Kane and the supermodel Naomi Campbell. Criticism is easy in this domain. You can see Naomi Campbell as generally whitewashed: she's British, she wears green contact lenses in most of her fashion photographs, she mixes mostly with Whites, she often covers her body with light foundation, and she spends a lot of her time in Monaco (the whitest, least politically correct country in the world). As for Big Daddy Kane, he keeps his trunks on (dissimulation of the penis equals occultation of the phallic threat of the black male, contribution to the mythology of the black male as superior lover?), and he seems bored to tears. There are only two Blacks in the book, whereas there are quantities of Whites. Madonna in a photograph in *Sex*, stands naked above Naomi Campbell who is lying down on the sand on a beach, and makes a bottle of something white and creamy (sun lotion?) spurt on the supermodel.[40] Some have seen that parody of ejaculation as humiliating for the African American community. Why is it not the other way around, they ask. The answer seems obvious to me. *Sex* is a book that celebrates Madonna and her power. And she happens to be white.

Sex and Puritanism

It is by definition dangerous to reach celebrity, especially in the U.S., and especially if your career is linked to sex. Madonna accumulates risks. Her fake candor in *Truth or Dare* suffices to convince some unbalanced people that they know her intimately, with all the consequences this might entail. Indeed, she makes the naïve viewer believe that she hides none of her most personal feelings. With *Sex*, she has "tempted the Devil" more than ever. That *pronunciamiento* book seems to advocate a kind of anything-goes universal sexuality and has upset a fair share of people.

Madonna is often "accused" of polymorphous perversity. But in *Madonnarama*, bell hooks, Douglas Crimp and Michael Warner[41] (among others) criticize her for not giving enough space to lesbians and gays in *Sex*, and for presenting those she does show in a non–PC way. She gets trashed for similar reasons when it comes to her S&M *mises en scène*. But isn't it irrelevant to regret that the sadomasochism of *Sex* isn't "authentic" enough — that it looks more like fashion photography than anything else? In her song *Hanky Panky*,[42] Madonna isn't any more determined to present an accurate description of S&M relations, and her evocation of spanking is clearly ironic, a bit like that of the postmodern writer Robert Coover in *Spanking the Maid* (1981).

Pat Califia wonders if *Sex* can stimulate sexually, and who it can stimulate.[43] Carol A. Queen tells how she masturbated reading it.[44] According to John Champagne, it is possible to suppose that *Sex* is mostly "designed to evoke the impossibility of sex in an age haunted by the threat of HIV disease."[45] In the eighties, the American press never stopped proclaiming that AIDS had put an end to the sexual revolution[46]; so, could *Sex* be the incarnation of the new kind of sex for a new era? But, anyway, as Sue Wiseman recalls: "Where such images might indeed be used for masturbatory fantasy, the star presence is always the central issue."[47] Indeed.

Objectively, the presence of lesbians and gays, of S&M and interracial relations, and of women who are not treated as objects are at least enough to shock puritans, promote open-mindedness and encourage reflection — whatever some self-righteous feminist or gay militant "Stalinist" censors may say to the contrary.

One of the risks of extreme stardom is that you cannot walk down the street without causing a riot. The hysterical herds that assail celebrities can easily become aggressive, as they feel celebrities *belong* to them: after all, they are the buying public. In some extreme cases, fans mutate into stalkers, and no star is safe.[48] But before Madonna, no star ever made people fantasize quite so much. She has assembled all the prerequisites to attract the mentally unbalanced.

"Fame does a funny thing to you," says Madonna, "everyone thinks that they know you. Perfect strangers coming up to you and asking very personal things and touching you and taking liberties."[49] In 1995, a stalker from Oregon named Robert Dewey Hoskins managed to enter Madonna's California house twice. He claimed that she had secretly married him. Another stalker had done this before. Hoskins was sentenced to jail. The myth also feeds on that sort of incident. After the trial, the London *Times* quoted a member of the jury: "She was very *real*, very *believable*. We all walked away feeling she was frightened."[50] Quite. That jury was composed carefully, to the point that one of the originally envisaged members was eliminated because he owned a copy of *Sex*!

Symptomatic of American society and of Madonna's place in it, Hoskins's lawyer, John Meyers, chose to kindle confusion between Madonna, the *realitatis femina*, and Rebecca Carlson, her *Body of Evidence* dramatis persona (a perjured witness). Systematically referring to her as "the actress," Meyers presented her as a chronic liar.

Wherever they live, stars of that stature must be surrounded by bodyguards, like politicians, the phrase *body*guard being particularly apt when speaking of Madonna. It is not surprising that the press, when it echoes such risks and the job of bodyguards, almost always mentions Madonna's case. Along with a picture of her, the article is bound to get that little extra attention from the readers.[51]

Star status is necessarily linked to a minimum of exhibitionism. If you believe the tabloids, Madonna made it her trademark. *Body of Evidence* was trashed by just about every critic in the Western world. It was a terrible movie, everyone wrote, and Madonna was too much of an exhibitionist in it.

I myself use the word "exhibitionism" without the least pejorative nuance. According to most dictionaries it is a morbid obsession that leads some people to exhibit their genitals; by extension it designates a tendency to show oneself in the nude. In the figurative sense it is used for someone who likes making a show of his feelings, or his private life. Interestingly, only recent dictionaries tend to restrict exhibitionism to the display of genitals. Isn't a writer or an actor or a pop star exhibitionistic by definition?

The exhibitionism of stars is what countless magazines live on, and Madonna's makes the research of Madonnologists progress. In the United States, the exhibitionism of celebrities, as well as that of average Americans who appear on talk shows and reality shows, is what an entire industry lives on.[52]

It is true that *Body of Evidence*— a pun that applies equally well to Madonna and her persona Rebecca Carlson — suffered from the release of *Basic Instinct* (Paul Verhoeven, 1992).

There was a time when journalists loved pitting Sharon Stone against Madonna. The beauty of the former rests less on artifice than that of the latter. Stone has a colder, more Deneuve-like touch. In that respect, *Basic Instinct* does work better than *Body of Evidence*, because it rests on a contrast between the distinguished and superior attitude of Stone and her exacerbated sexuality.

The journalist Henry-Jean Servat once asked Madonna: "Do you mind if I call you an exhibitionist?" She answered: "No, I deserve the term, and I claim full responsibility for it."[53] Some might find it surprising that she still arouses (interest) when exhibiting her body, having shown so much of it over the years. Some might also ask whether her exhibitionism remains subversive — it's so systematic.[54] The psychoanalyst Gérard Miller provides an answer: "That the announcement of a 'naked' or 'forbidden' Madonna still turns on the customer, provokes his emotion and the desire to know more, is an impressive victory of the signifier over the real."[55] Precisely.

Madonna sometimes takes precautions to circumvent censors. The lyrics of the standard version of the song *Erotica*[56] are already very explicit, suggesting S&M affairs, but a more hardcore version, entitled *Erotic*, is provided on a CD single that accompanies the book *Sex*. In *Erotic* Madonna completes *Sex* and *Erotica*, and she also promotes her movie *Body of Evidence*, in which she ties up Willem Dafoe and holds a dripping candle above his chest. There are lines in *Erotic* which are not to be heard in *Erotica*, about rope and cages and candles. The more reactionary parents' associations will not have heard the new version, and Madonna of course laughs all the way to the bank.

Sex and Religion

Madonna, star, queen and divinity, but also sometimes scapegoat, is a privileged source of scandal and of mythology. People don't forgive the Great as easily as they forgive the hoi polloi, especially in the U.S. But she gets by. Goddess and priestess of her own cult, she upsets the adepts of more traditional cults: Christians, Muslims or Jews.

Stardom as tremendous as Madonna's inevitably engenders proportional enmities. The simple fact that there is a book called *The I Hate Madonna Handbook* is representative.

As it happens, the adversaries of Madonna are especially those whose moral convictions are "damaged" by her production. What they don't necessarily suppose is that Madonna uses them adroitly: they provide free exposure. There is no such thing as bad publicity, as they say in Hollywood. With enemies like that, who needs friends?

Let us begin with the negative reactions that she gets abroad, which are of course faithfully reported by the American press. In Argentina, for example, Madonna attracted the hatred of a handful of nostalgic Peronists and some angry graffiti ("Madonna Go Home" or "*Fuera Madonna*") were quoted all over the place. This was good publicity for *Evita*. A couple of people did proffer astonishingly aggressive sentences. A former secretary of Evita's, Clara Marín, almost a hundred years old, declared: "We want Madonna, dead or alive, if she does not leave, I will kill her."[57] The archbishop of Buenos Aires said she was "pornographic, blasphemous, Satan in drag — a real insult to Argentine women and the memory of Eva Perón."[58] What is more, Caresse, one of Madonna's employees, used as a decoy in Buenos Aires, was actually attacked.[59]

In February 1997, when *Evita* came out in Argentina, the Peronist organizations screamed boycott, and even Vice-President Carlos Ruckauf spoke ill of the movie. One or two stampedes, a couple of tear gas bombs, some torn-off posters, none of that deterred the 20,000 viewers who rushed to see *Evita* on the first day.[60]

In France, she is more often appropriated than vilified. Charles Penwarden writes:

> Did not Jacques Chirac [...] attempt to [appeal to young voters] by organizing that Madonna concert in 1988 and hinting that he, too, was sensitive to her charms? To put it in a Jean-Paul Gaultier conical-cupful, Madonna provokes, but plays the game, and the outrage is largely hypocritical.[61]

Even if Madonna repeatedly denied that she deliberately set out to shock people, it is not very risky to think otherwise.

Various attitudes are to be found among journalists, notably that which consists in claiming not to be shocked so as to better trash Madonna. Besides, it is *de bon ton* in some circles, especially in Europe, to claim that nothing can shock you.

In the U.K., Lynn Barber, for example, writes:

> These would-be shockers always operate within the same narrow pornographic gamut. You *know* there will be bondage gear and stiletto boots and the odd dildo or two. Yet, who now is truly shocked by such things? In the 1960s, it was conventional for theatre directors to want to "shock audiences out of their complacency." But what complacency? A complacent belief that Madonna wears white cotton underwear?[62]

Naturally, nothing is as simple as Barber would have us believe. Her badly disguised conservatism cannot harm Madonna, who better than anyone masters the nuances and the art of shock. Her definition of pornography is rightly more restricted than Barber's. She has never been a pornographer. Camille Paglia might disagree, she who considers many Italian Renaissance paintings as pornographic, and sings their praise. Even if you approve of the manufacture and commercialization of pornography, as Paglia does, you have to be careful with your definitions.

Sex sells, it's a truism, notably because it still offends conservatives. The question is whether this or that creator is ready to use it. Whatever Barber may think, no one has ever seen Madonna use a dildo on stage or on TV. There is a frontier between eroticism and pornography.

In Spain and Italy, Madonna is very much liked by the public, and by the majority of journalists, but she is intensely disliked by Catholic authorities, who provide lots of free publicity.

Madonna was severely criticized by Pope John-Paul II when she toured Italy in the eighties. He even tried to have her shows banned. Many more or less trustworthy newspapers reported that when she stayed in Rome in 1996, she unsuccessfully solicited a Papal audience. In February 1998 they said she was begrudged the "keys" to the City of Lourdes, in spite of her daughter's name, because of her interest in the Kabala.

Getting back to the U.S., there are resemblances that are more than anecdotal between the reactions to, say, the novels of D.H. Lawrence, Erskine Caldwell, or Vladimir Nabokov in their day, and those that Madonna sets off in the eighties and nineties. Pornography is other people's eroticism.[63] Independently from their literary qualities, *Lady Chatterley's Lover* and *Lolita* would have sold far fewer copies without the scandals they occasioned.

Fran Lloyd notices similarities between Madonna and Jeff Koons.[64] Madonna is often compared to the late photographer Robert Mapplethorpe; yet their *oeuvres* are extremely different. They do share two things: a tendency to embarrass the dominant ideology,[65] and bother booksellers.[66] Those who still care about that type of distinction tend to classify Madonna as low art and Mapplethorpe as high art, even if some Mapplethorpe photos depict extreme sexual practices.[67]

Polls have shown that Madonna recruits her public mostly among Democrats, which partly reflects her political positioning. The Personal is Political. Madonna shows it through her individual, political, and artistic choices. The least conservative voters naturally tend to enjoy Madonna's work more than others, as it is so difficult to dissociate her music from her personae, who almost all showed their attachment to anticonservative values. Bill Clinton once declared that inspiration should be found in the fundamental myths of American culture. People should believe in the capacity of America to reinvent itself, and "begin anew with energy and hope, with faith and discipline."[68] This is exactly what Madonna does, reinventing herself and reinventing America at every moment.[69]

The religious right, as represented by all those fundamentalist groups, those charismatic televangelists, and those very Republican Republicans, has of course been rejecting Madonna throughout the years. The Christian Coalition publicly said so on TV. Such people disapprove of Madonna in the same way they disapprove of gays. The Family Research Council, the Moral Majority, Gary Bauer, or Jerry Falwell are Madonnophobic and have said as much. As for the Baptist Church (something like 30 million souls), it trashes Madonna on air, in the same way it called for a boycott of Disney back in 1997 because the company gave rights to lesbian and gay couples. So Madonna is virulently criticized by various kinds of Protestants as well as Catholics, and also by Jews; in January 1991, Rabbi Abraham Cooper, co-director of the Simon Wiesenthal Center for Holocaust Studies, called Madonna anti–Semitic,[70] for in a remix of *Justify My Love*, she read a passage of the Bible: "I know your tribulation and your poverty and the slander of those who say that they are Jews, but they are not, they are a synagogue of Satan."

This is what puritans of all kinds resent in Madonna: she worries about AIDS too much, about abortion, equality between women and men, homosexuality, African Americans and other minorities. Madonna projects the eternal image of the Babylon prostitute, of the woman who dares say "I" instead of obeying some masculine authority figure, be it a husband, a sheriff, or God the father. Such women frighten puritans. One example will do, that of the journalist Ray Kerrison, who calls Madonna the "degenerate queen of sleaze" and writes in an article entitled "What a Tramp!":

> With a new piece of commercial sleaze to peddle — this time a film entitled *Truth or Dare* — Madonna has embarked on another of her patented excursions into public vulgarity to hype the box office and amuse the jaded. She has given a two-part interview, appropriately, to a homosexual magazine, in which she boasts of early same-sex encounters.[71]

There are more subtle pieces of criticism. The example of the movie *French Kiss* (Lawrence Kasdan, 1995) is revealing. The character played by François Cluzet, a smalltime thief, is filmed at home, *in his underwear*, sitting at his kitchen table, busy flicking through *Sex*. The oh-so-sweet Meg Ryan, anti–Madonna if ever there was one, pure, fresh, innocent, natural, has been victimized by that abominable individual, who lives in a dirty apartment, and who clearly bought *Sex* with dirty money. Of course, only degenerates like him read that kind of book. As for the activity he was about to indulge in before Kevin Kline's irruption in his apartment, it seems obvious enough.[72]

Ilene Rosenzweig tells about religious right leaders who do not refrain from describing Madonna as the Antichrist, finding her truly diabolical.[73] But let us not forget that Madonna declares she is a believer, and that she prays before concerts. Maybe she's not entirely free from the temptation of Puritanism herself. When she agreed to play the missionary Gloria Tatlock in *Shanghai Surprise*, she wished to prove that she could handle a *rôle de composition*. But there might be more to it. That part has to do with traditional Christian values, and it is possible than Madonna did not mean to *exclusively* parody them.

Another example of ambiguity: when she plays Rebecca Carlson in *Body of Evidence*, a bad girl without a hope of redemption, she plays on three levels: she gives the public the spectacle of her talents as an actress, she undoubtedly comforts— knowingly — the conservatives' convictions, by cautioning the moralizing discourse of that finally rather conventional movie, and at the same time she lets her more liberal fans believe that she is once more being tongue-in-cheek, pretending to give weapons to her puritan enemies the better to mock them.

In *Body of Evidence*, Madonna tried to exploit the amalgam between star and persona. Rebecca knows what the members of her jury think: the women detest her and think she's a slut. And the men view her as "a cold heartless bitch."[74] But people are hypocritical. However, Rebecca does turn out to be guilty: so society is right to judge a book by its cover. Puritanism is triumphant, traditional moral values are safeguarded, and the bad girl is punished (she gets shot *and* drowns).[75] The body of evidence is that of Rebecca-Madonna, who like any bad girl, sins with her body. Where is the habitual provocation of Madonna in that enterprise? Maybe she simply made a mistake, thinking she would be able to rewrite the femmes fatales of yesterday, and that the final product would have panache.

This movie is perfectly in line with movies like *Fatal Attraction* (Adrian Lyne, 1987),[76] which allow America to have a clear conscience while allowing it simultaneously to fantasize (to dream of being bad), and feel completely safe, thanks to the moral lesson taught at the end of the movie. The bad girl dies at the end. Surely it is impossible to imagine Madonna willingly participating in that sort of project. Or is it? After all, wasn't the great Mae West herself something of a puritan, deep down, according to many biographers? And didn't Marlene Dietrich turn into a sort of Anita Bryant in her very old age?

When the Mary Lambert video of *Like a Prayer* was shown, few commentators examined the lyrics. They were far too busy discussing the pictures.

In the video, "Madonna" is clearly a woman of the Deep South, maybe of Italian or Mexican origin, with long black curly hair. She "sees" a group of white men (obviously young Southern racist thugs) assault a white woman. An African American is unjustly accused; "Madonna" finally denounces them. She is evidently motivated by a spirit of justice, and scandalized by the fact that the scapegoat is as usual an African American. At some point she takes refuge in an African American church. She is welcomed with open arms and she sings with the gospel singers; that welcome is one of the most important elements in the video. In that church, she "dreams" of the statue of a saint, African American; it comes alive and kisses her (or more, depending on the viewer's sensibility); he is the spitting image of the man who has been wrongly accused. Madonna is seen dancing in front of burning crosses, undoubtedly set on fire by the Ku Klux Klan. She's also seen being afflicted with the stigmata. Thompson sees them as supernatural, whereas other commentators, like Ilene Rosenzweig, say they are self-inflicted. Madonna's videos are often interpreted in different ways.[77]

The video ends with the closing of a red theatrical curtain. The church was a stage, and the Madonnesque diegesis, which already recalled Carson McCullers or Tennessee Williams, ends like a play. Madonna, always true to her postmodern games, continues flaunting her distance and metafictional practices.

As a matter of fact, it is obviously not Madonna the *realitatis femina* who bows to the audience, holding the hands of the gospel singers, but the *dramatis persona* in a flimsy black dress. So the person who witnessed the crime is a third entity: the *dramatis persona* played by the *dramatis persona* played by Madonna. Did she really see the crime or was it some kind of vision? The spectators in the theater allude to Madonna's public, and she reminds us as the curtain falls that her videos differ from those of the competition: they always signify, and they stay away from the face-value commonplace.

I associate in this part interracial relations and Christianity because out of all of Madonna's output, it is this video— where the two themes are treated — that was seen as the most shocking, making hundreds of people fume: different family associations, Christian leagues, witch-hunters of all kinds, including Donald Wildmon. They saw in the video various blasphemes, ultimate sacrilege, Satan's work. Pepsi was supposed to sponsor the 1990 tour of the bombshell and had decided to use the song *Like a Prayer* for a 1989 commercial. Madonna could be seen in a few images from the video, but there was also a child standing for a small Madonna, the idea being that you drink Pepsi all your life, and Pepsi is for every generation. The commercial was not broadcast for long in the States. When it first appeared on TV, a huge scandal broke out, comparable to the reaction to Martin Scorsese's *The Last Temptation of Christ* (1988) and to the fatwa on Salman Rushdie.[78] Wildmon actually wrote in *USA Today*: "For the next year, I will not drink Pepsi. If enough others join me, perhaps respect for religious beliefs of others will be helped tremendously."[79] So Pepsi practiced self-censorship, frightened by the losses that the boycott might entail.

Madonna got tons of free publicity, on top of the five million dollars she earned. That scandal, however, showed that censorship is still thriving. It is a very American type of censorship: self-censorship, in fact, linked to purely financial considerations. Conservatives complain and the makers withdraw the product; it happens with comic books. So much for freedom of speech.

There was something else, besides the reaction to the association of sex and religion: badly dissimulated racism. Religious Puritanism and intolerance, including racial intolerance, make marvelous bedfellows. The fact that the saint to whom Madonna gives the literal kiss of life in the video is certainly Saint Martin of Porres (1579-1639), patron saint of social justice in general — and in the States of interracial justice in particular — was most of the time left undiscussed. Only one Catholic priest, amusingly, Father Andrew Greeley, defended Madonna, deeming the video "charming and chaste."[80]

Madonna shocked puritans more than ever during the *Blond Ambition* tour (1990): when *Like a Virgin* ends, after the simulated orgasm that I discussed above, she cries "God" in the dark, in an interrogative tone of voice, then starts singing *Like a Prayer*, having donned a Mediterranean widow's dress (slightly evocative of a clergyman's robe). Behind her, the bed disappears, and is replaced by hundreds of burning church candles. At the beginning of the song, she even wears a black scarf over her hair. You can hear "Oh my God' several times, cried by the backup singers. Well, anyone who's seen porn or *When Harry Met Sally* (Rob Reiner, 1989) knows that American women tend to scream "oh my God" when they have an orgasm. But the blasphemy is only just beginning. Madonna, wearing an enormous crucifix around her neck, contorts her body on the floor for a moment, then rises and goes on with the song.

The polysemy of *Like a Prayer* is clear: the woman who sings is addressing either God, or her lover. Madonna is also alluding to her own divine status: when whoever calls her name, "Madonna," it is indeed like a prayer — to the Mother of God. Her mention of kneeling evokes either prayer or fellatio: religious or amorous devotion. Behind her, her seven dancers, dressed as priests, dance an extremely camp kind of voguing. One dancer carries her twice, very high in the air, as if to help her get nearer the Lord. Madonna sports a crown embroidered on her back (*Maria Regina*). The music, initially similar to traditional church singing, gradually becomes pure gospel, whereas her chorus singers (as nuns) get really excited, and one of Madonna's dancers rolls on the floor, like someone suddenly struck by divine lightning during the service/show of some Southern itinerant preacher.

Then, the décor looking more and more like a church, Madonna kneels on a prie-dieu, crosses herself, and begins to sing *Live to Tell*.[81] The audience then lights thousands of lighters, like church candles, supplementing the church candles on the stage. The fans pray to her Goddess as she is praying to God. Then she sings *Oh Father*,[82] literally perched this time on the prie-dieu, before sitting on it the way Marlene Dietrich sits on her barrel in *The Blue Angel*. There is only one dancer left behind her, still dressed as a priest, waving an incensory in the air. Having removed her crucifix and her severe dress, Madonna ends this sequence with *Papa Don't Preach*,[83] surrounded by seven priests.

Why do I write "priest"? Because of a cultural reflex. But some have seen in those costumes an allusion, no less provocative, to the garb of Orthodox Jews. According to Roger Baker[84] and Marjorie Garber,[85] there are a million similarities between drag and religious clothes. Boy George illustrated it with his early stage costumes.

On a rare visit to a church, Talullah Bankhead said to the bishop who was waving his incensory: "I love the drag, darling, but do you realize your handbag is on fire?" Madonna no doubt loves that camp *bon mot*. She displays an ambiguous rapport to Catholicism. She honors the memory of her deceased mother like a country Sicilian orphan, hangs a rosary from the rear view mirror in her car, and admires nuns. But she iconoclastically "perverts" Catholic imagery. She went as far as to pose in the nude with a Christ's crown around her forehead, made of barbed wire. During the promotion of *Ray of Light* in March 1998, she sometimes wore a black plastic thorn crown.

Bob Guccione Jr. asked her about it, and she answered that she did not believe in suffering. Catholicism is too masochistic, she declared. She imagined that if her very Catholic mother had not died, she might have ended up living a paltry middle-class life in Michigan instead of being a star. But she wouldn't have been a good nun, as she could not have coped with the chastity vow.[86]

In the final analysis, when Madonna associates sex and Catholicism, she is doing nothing that gothic novels haven't done before. In a way, her candle and stained glass moment in the *Blond Ambition* tour is to pop what M.G. Lewis's *The Monk* (1796) is to literature. No wonder various religious leagues see her as a demon.

Yet, Catholics, according to the *George* survey, constitute a third of her fans. This interesting statistic presumably indicates that many Catholics share with Madonna the desire to question their religious education. Unless they, like her, associate religious ecstasy and sexual ecstasy. All you have to do to see the puzzling similarities between the two is read the writings of Saint Teresa of Avila.

It is clearly Puritans of various kinds that Madonna is addressing in *Human Nature*. She sings about being punished for speaking of her fantasies and disobeying rules, and remarks: "Oops, I didn't know I couldn't talk about sex."[87]

Of course, Madonna was preceded by decades of provocative rock-pop. In the days of Chuck Berry and Jerry Lee Lewis, who were persecuted for their sexual antics, there were already preachers who publicly condemned such performers, like Cardinal Strich.

Abortion is one of the issues that tear America apart. Madonna admitted in various interviews that she has had several abortions. This may "please" a few feminist pro-choice militants; it may also irritate pro-lifers. Those people who chain themselves to abortion clinic doors or terrify teenagers in waiting rooms with plastic fetuses smeared with ketchup obviously do not particularly cherish Madonna's feminist politics. When she was pregnant with Lourdes Maria, beaming with joy, she told Alan Jackson that her abortions had not made her particularly happy. But, she said, "you have to be mentally prepared [for motherhood], if you're not, you're only doing the world a disservice by bringing up a child you don't want.[88]

The impact of Madonna on American society is so great, and her influence on wannabes so deep (in spite of those who pronounce her a has-been between two albums), that such words have undoubtedly influenced the decisions of many young women.

In *Papa Don't Preach*,[89] Madonna sings about the panic of a pregnant teenager who wants to keep her baby, whereas her entourage encourages her to have an abortion, so as not to ruin her chances of an acceptable future. Some moralizing fundamentalist pro-lifers who regard the fetus as sacred[90] applauded, and the majority of feminists hollered. With this song, Madonna made friends and enemies all over the place. Did she think she could get away with such an ambiguous product?

She was seen as irresponsible in many quarters: she was encouraging pregnancy in teenagers, people said. But the record was already number one on the charts.

She did delight thousands of young girls throughout the world whose situation she was faithfully describing. Actually, in that song she does not contradict her "official" pro-choice opinions; she tells a story, more particularly a love story (again), while demonstrating an obvious rejection of patriarchal authority. That papa she's telling not to preach is her dad, he is the Pope, he is God, he's any paternal figure you can think of in our society.

She is telling them all that she is keeping her baby, which means that she's not getting an abortion, but also that she's not breaking up with her boyfriend; the choice belongs to her as an autonomous woman who has the right to do what she wants with her own body, regardless of what any male might think, and regardless of her young age.

The James Foley video shows two alternating Madonnas. The first one is a convincing teenager; she goes to see her sweetheart (Alex McArthur) at the garage where he works. He has a job, he makes a living. In other words, they won't live in luxury, but they'll be all right, and so will the baby. You can read on his face that he will never let her down; his love is sincere and authentic. Then, the teenager confronts her father at home. Let us note that there is no mother figure in the picture. No doubt the girl's mother is dead, like Madonna's. Moreover, the father is played by the Italian-American actor Danny Aiello, who looks a bit like Madonna's father, Tony Ciccone. You can even see a few flashback shots, showing the girl as a small child, i.e., not so long ago. The song is principally addressed to that visibly Italian Papa ("Papa" as opposed to "Daddy").

The second Madonna, as glamorous as can be, looking older, dances in an empty décor. She is "a combination of Marilyn Monroe, Jean Seberg, and Kim Novak."[91]

Could she not know that she was going to cause a huge controversy with this product? It seems hard to believe, even if she repeatedly declared so. With such a song and video, she was throwing in America's face the image of a country ravaged by the abortion debate, which is far from being resolved, as indeed pro-lifers make matters worse every day.

Let us note that during the *Who's That Girl?* Tour of 1987, Madonna sang *Papa Don't Preach* with a huge screen behind her showing the Pope and Ronald Reagan, two paternal and reactionary figures, both opposed to legal abortion.

So basically Madonna is pro-choice in the two meanings of the expression, as it were: I mean she deems that a woman (whatever her age) must choose whether to recur *or not* to abortion without paying any attention to outside pressure. No representative of the feminist lobby or of the patriarchy will dictate her conduct, not even the father of the Church or the father of the state. At the end of the video, the teenager and the father are reconciled, which constitutes a "message of hope," even if the phrase sounds a bit corny in the context of Madonna's work.

Madonna has declared: "Behind everything I do, there's a tongue-in-cheek comment on myself, or a more serious message on the social level."[92] Her most clearly identifiable "more serious message" has to do with AIDS. It can be summed up in three basic ideas: don't reject HIV positive people and people with AIDS, don't stupidly associate AIDS and homosexuality, and practice safer sex. Some Americans, like Rev. Fred Phelps, still seem to think that AIDS is divine retribution for drug-addicts and homosexuals, and attend funerals with signs that say "God Hates Fags."

Without going so far, other leaders of the religious right disapprove of classic prevention campaigns, advocating chastity for all and the renouncing of homosexual practices for gays; for example people like Helen Chenoweth (Family Research Council), Bill Horn (Iowa Family Policy Center), Rev. Lou Sheldon and Andrea Sheldon (Traditional Values Coalition), Ralph Reed (Christian Coalition), or even Bill McCartney (founder of Promise Keepers). It is that same religious right which campaigns in favor of prayer in public schools, of federal subventions for religious schools, and of anti–Darwinian textbooks. Those people don't like Madonna, who sometimes includes AIDS brochures in her CD sleeves. She devotes time and money to AIDS charities, and she often reminds her public during interviews and concerts to use condoms ("Don't be silly, put a rubber on your willy!") During some concerts, she lights up the words SAFE SEX behind her on a screen. She is called an opportunist, but here again, I'd rather think she is doing good, whatever her deep motives. At a time when too many people seem to imagine AIDS is over, her militancy is more relevant than ever.

During *The Girlie Show* tour, as filmed in Sydney (1993), Madonna presented the song *In This Life* as written about two friends of hers who had died of AIDS. "For all of you out there who understand what I'm talking about," she said, "don't give up." The song is sad, makes the spectators weep, and constitutes yet another example of the social impact that Madonna can have.

When David Bowie stopped taking drugs, after his California and Berlin periods (1973-1977), he himself linked numerous personae of his past to schizoid tendencies associated to drug consumption, sometimes comparing himself to his mentally ill brother, who committed suicide. In the case of Madonna, whose personae are numerous but more superficially embodied than Bowie's, a diagnostic of schizophrenia would hardly be credible. Her 2000-2001 avatar had to do with cowboy Western mythology, the one before had to do with New Age preoccupations.

Her frequent "changes of personality" caricature in a way an American phenomenon that is thriving. Multiple personality disorders are fashionable, notably in courts and psychiatry-made-easy books. In fact, they are almost as fashionable as recovered memory, which seems to find new followers every day. So if Madonna has yet to claim she was once sexually abused by a distant uncle and only recently recovered that memory, or that she was once abducted by aliens (like thousands of Americans), she does turn "mystical" at times.

Some New Age gurus make fortunes in the U.S. New Age is about love vibrations, the power of divine creation in each of us, Freudian Christianity, Zen, and witchcraft. It's about reincarnation, astrology, meditation, vegetarianism, holistic medicine, communication with the dead (or with extraterrestrials), telepathy, and that famous "human potential" that so few of us use, which is capable of true miracles.[93] In 1988, according to a Gallup poll, 67 percent of Americans believed in the supernatural.[94]

New Age has won over many university professors and some Wall Street golden boys. Some say the reason many Americans turned to New Age was to recover from the materialistic eighties. And so Madonna, having reflected that materialism (*Material Girl*), logically reflected in the nineties more spiritual quests, as we are about to see. What mostly characterizes New Age, it seems to me, is that astonishing mixture of very different beliefs, a great number of which come from the Orient. In this respect it echoes the hippies, of course, recalling the spiritual groping in the dark of the late sixties, as illustrated by the Beatles. So New Age is postmodern, in its way, it is "mystical-esoteric bricolage proliferating because of the decline of monotheistic religious systems and the crisis of the big utopian ideological systems," writes the political analyst Paul Ariès.[95]

Without going so far as to adopt the most extreme of these beliefs,[96] Madonna, became in 1998, according to *The Times*, an Ethereal Girl,[97] according to *The Advocate*, a Spiritual Girl.[98] "*Le XXIème siècle sera religieux ou ne sera pas.*"

In February and March 1998, Madonna commercialized a single, *Frozen*, followed by an album, *Ray of Light*. More ubiquitous than ever, she embarked on a huge international promotional campaign. She circulated prepackaged versions of herself, as usual, and also appeared in person in many strategic places in the Western world. More than ever, most journalists agreed to play Madonna's game. She had conceived an nth persona for *Ray of Light*, and they practically all pretended to believe this was a real change, announcing the real Madonna, who had allegedly turned her back on stardom, opened her heart, allowed us to get close, etc.[99]

Of course, it was nothing more than yet another avatar, which did not last longer than the previous ones. In 2000 she came back as a Dolce & Gabbana rhinestone cowgirl. Madonna can only make you smile when she declares: "There has never been a moment in my life when I decided: now I'm going to change!"[100]

In the 1998 *Frozen* video, shot by the British director Chris Cunningham in the middle of the Mojave desert, Madonna wears a black saridress and a black cape, both by Jean-Paul Gaultier. She sports a long, raven black wig. Her hands are covered in strange henna signs (*Mehndi*) which, depending on journalists, are Kabala related, or Muslim, or Hindu, or

Buddhist, and so forth. On her left palm there is the Sanskrit letter "of the vibration of the universe, of the beginning and of the end of everything in the universe," that you sing before a yoga session (*OM*).[101] The adjective "gothic" (or "gothic Indian") kept turning up in the reviews, as well as the comparison with Morticia Addams in *The Addams Family*. *Libération* spoke of the look of "a slightly gothic Corsican widow."[102] Madonna repeated everywhere that the song *Frozen* had been largely inspired by the movie *The English Patient* (Anthony Minghella, 1996). In the video, she dances in a very ethereal way, often sitting down, a bit like Sahara women, a bit like Macbeth's witches in a school production. The rest of the time, she turns into a flock of black birds, into a black dog, or is "multiplied." Sometimes she levitates, or absorbs a liquid coming from the earth (unless she is irrigating the ground): the blood of the earth? Some say the video was nearly banned by the BBC because of the witchcraft.[103]

She wore the black wig only in the video. The rest of the time, she was blond. But her blondness had nothing to do with the dirty blondness of the Boy Toy period, nor the peroxide blondness of the *Blond Ambition* period; it was a good girl blond, the successor of her Evita blond, slightly orange (Venetian), which had the "straggly, expensively unwashed look favored by Alanis Morissette."[104] Her hair was curly, sometimes partly braided, her makeup was sober, her eyebrows ordinary. Her famous beauty mark, present in every one of her previous incarnations, had disappeared; so what was it, surgery, thick foundation or a supernatural phenomenon?[105]

Madonna volunteered that her look evoked "the Italian Renaissance, in the days of Raphael." She added: "I want a more peaceful image, that fits my role as a mother."[106] As a matter of fact, that image recalled Botticelli.[107] On TV sets, she demanded blue lighting, for that color matched the atmosphere of the album, she said. However, there were occasional jocular "lapses," like items of clothing that were reminiscent of some of her preceding personae, a bit of breast or navel flashing, or a Christ's crown on her head.

The music of *Ray of Light* divided the press. A majority of critics saw it as a radical change of orientation, others the mere habitual Madonnesque pop, arranged to fit the day's fashion. From that point of view, Madonna reached her objective, since the teenage press—which had somewhat neglected her since 1992—rediscovered her.

Reviewers established comparisons with people like Björk or Portishead. They mentioned trip-hop, drum' n' bass, techno, electronica, space-pop, dub-trance. They spoke of trance guitars and psychedelic guitars.[108] Others evoked cyber-techno mixtures, deep-house, acid-dance killings, and trash-rock tones.[109] Everyone insisted on the very British sound of the album, on the Goa trance influences[110] and on William Orbit's very special arrangements.[111] In other words, once more Madonna knew exactly what was going to sell. "Like [...] Bowie, Madonna is a *passeuse*, picking up tomorrow's norms in the underground," wrote *Les Inrockuptibles*.[112] "It looks suspiciously like a Bowie stroke," said the *Melody Maker*.[113] Most critics worldwide deemed that *Ray of Light* was Madonna's best album since *Like a Prayer* (1989).

As for the lyrics, they too meant to constitute signs of the transformation, of the "new" Madonna, who very much emphasized her status as a loving mother and disconsolate orphan. At times it got almost tacky, it must be said. Madonna's message was that she had grown up terribly, that she had suddenly discovered what a huge heart she had, and that there was a reason for living that was vastly more important than fame, sex or money: Lourdes. Celebrity was only an ersatz meant to compensate for her lack of love, she sang. Many remained unconvinced.[114] Mostly these lyrics expressed a vague ecumenical mysticism that meant to reconcile all possible religions. On some occasions, she almost disavowed *Sex*, reducing it to a last rebellious teenage act.[115]

On the Japanese album, there was an extra song, *Has to Be*, in which she was more religious than ever. Beside the usual commercial calculation — she knew that her more devoted European and American fans would buy the import and the "rare" singles after they had bought the "classic" version — it is possible to wonder if she did not deem the track too "mystical" for the general public in the Western world; it's a question of dosage.

But maybe all those sentimental New Age lyrics were written tongue-in-cheek, like everything else. As it happens, after two months Madonna was dressed like a teenager at a rave party, a denim jacket showing off her midriff; and she danced in the *Ray of Light* video at a vertiginous speed, while behind her urban landscapes and techno club scenes moved about, like a hymn to the joys of ecstasy. Such images clearly targeted a very young public, for the first time since the eighties. However, the lyrics were in keeping with the general New Age tone of the album and the general discourse that accompanied it.

Then came the single and video *Drowned World / Substitute for Love* in August and September 1998. Madonna is shown running away from paparazzi and singing the virtues of true love — as opposed to the adulation of crowds. She was accused by many of shamelessly exploiting Princess Diana's death.

In those days Madonna belonged to an LA Kabala study group, alongside a dozen celebrities. She wore a piece of cheap-looking red string around her wrist that supposedly signaled her devotion to her "instructor." Even when it comes to religion, Madonna is postmodern, practicing as always the art of collage, just as she does with her looks and songs. Negotiating a moderate New Age turning, she took what could be useful to her, she said so herself. That persona was seen by many as perfectly in tune with the zeitgeist, in keeping with the age of the star, and possibly with maternity. She went so far as to pose for *Vanity Fair*[116] with Lourdes, after she had sheltered her from photographers for a long time.[117]

You would have to be particularly naïve to take the song *Shanti/Ashtangi*[118] (chanted in Sanskrit) seriously. But if *Ray of Light* is probably her best album ever (*Music* being close second and *Like a Prayer* third), in terms of voice and musical elaboration, it was but one stage in her career, and it's a bit boringly millennium conscious.

Having played so much with virgin-vamp dichotomies and elaborated a gigantic cult to her own glory, wasn't it inevitable that once a mother (the mother of Lourdes, no less) she should become the mother of the world and the daughter of the Earth, as a priestess-goddess detached from material considerations and determined to preach the good word? But a handful of critics were not fooled: Stéphane Davet, in *The World*, spoke of regrets that had soaked in holy water[119] and wrote that "such serenity can turn to schlock mysticism." He called Madonna the "Rastignac of pop."[120]

Andrew Smith summed up: "As always with Madonna, you either choose to believe her, or you don't. And life is so much more fun if you do."[121]

As it happens, Madonna quickly got tired of that New Age witch–Botticelli Earth Mother phase, even before she had stopped promoting *Ray of Light*. The following singles were sold with extremely different gimmicks, such as the celebrated total geisha black and red look (inspired by Arthur Golden's 1997 novel *Memoirs of a Geisha*) for the song *Nothing Really Matters* (indeed).

Then Madonna changed radically — once more — for the promotion of 1999's *Beautiful Stranger*, from the *Austin Powers: The Spy Who Shagged Me* soundtrack, and then again in 2000 for *American Pie*, from the *The Next Best Thing* soundtrack. But all those metamorphoses were nothing compared to the next huge move: the cowgirl transformation for *Music* in the Fall of 2000. For those who thought she had definitively cleaned up her act, she showed her buttocks in the *American Pie* video, in which she offered a very pluralistic view of America indeed, in ethnic and sexual terms. Then for the *Music* video she alluded to Bowie again (1993 *Miracle Goodnight*,) played a parvenu cowgirl and disported herself with "naughty girls" in the back of a limousine, at a discotheque and at a strip club. She even got the British comic Ali G. to help her mock macho rappers again and recall her icon status.

But to further play with the notions of whore–bad girl vs. mother–good girl, all the time she is "misbehaving" in the *Music* video, Madonna wears a gold necklace that says "Mommy." And to play with the notions of myth, stardom, and hyperreality, she appears as a cartoon character in parts of the video: a superheroine with superpowers, she flies above roofs like Superman, swims underwater like Namor and DJs at some club with half a dozen arms like a Hindu deity. As for the music of that album, ironically entitled *Music*, it has been composed principally by William Orbit again, and by Mirwais Ahmadzaï, an electronic wizard who back in the early eighties—in the wake of German cult band Kraftwerk—already made dance music for funky robots. His mythic French band Taxi Girl practiced gender-bending already, with songs like *Cherchez le garcon*.

A Feminist Credo?

Madonna has often been criticized for being politically incorrect, in many ways, notably when it comes to the representation of women and African Americans, or the treatment of animals. She wore furs in 1996 and gave a rather positive image of bullfighting in the *Take a Bow* video,[122] a sexy video which defied feminists of the Marilyn Frye or Adrienne Rich variety, who see in the video a disgusting example of passé female submissiveness.

She declared in that context: "I don't believe that any organization should dictate to me what I can and cannot do artistically."[123]

It is especially when it comes to sex and feminism (as should be clear by now) that she is savagely criticized. Among the most interesting contradictions of America today, to my mind, are those which divide feminists. And it is *not* only a problem of generation.[124]

Madonna is seen by some as the very antithesis of feminism; yet she is acclaimed by others as one of its more striking and praiseworthy representatives. She reflects the pleasure of some as much as the displeasure of others. She very much reminds everyone that there is no such thing as a single feminist discourse, and that it is in fact difficult to talk about feminism in the singular. The list being endless, I'll have to make do with a few particular examples of feminist Madonnophobes, of feminist Madonnophiles, and of undecided feminists; knowing that the pages which precede should have amply illustrated my conception of Madonna's feminism. Unfortunately, Madonnophobic feminists—although abundantly published in other respects—tend to avoid leaving written records of the horrors they say about the star, for reasons that altogether elude me. They prefer expressing their Madonnophobia orally, during conferences, debates, and other meetings; their words are reported imperfectly and indirectly, and so it is difficult to quote them verbatim.

Madonna, Backer of the Patriarchy?

Women like Betty Crocker and Gloria Steinem, and hard-line feminists who take everything extremely seriously, have often bad-mouthed Madonna. Their discourse is miles away from that of the star, who declared one day: "I want to say to Gloria [Steinem] and the gang, 'Hey, lighten up. Get a sense of humor'."[125] Many feminists never joke about sexual matters, unlike Madonna. Camille Paglia judges: "The old-guard establishment feminists who still loathe Madonna have a sexual ideology problem."[126]

There are those who consider Madonna as a traitor to the cause of women, like many NOW activists, because they refuse to look beyond the bleach and the nudity. Unaware of (or deliberately occulting) Madonna's irony, they don't seem to realize that like Mae West she plays with the male gaze and re-appropriates it. Ruth Conniff deems that the postmodern practices of Madonna are a ball and chain slowing down feminist struggles; the masks of the star hurt Conniff's monolithic conception of Woman.[127]

There are those, among them militant lesbians, who are angry with her for pillaging their culture, whereas others applaud her for the same motives.

Shelagh Young, Madonnophile, perceives a certain puritanism among Madonnophobic feminists, which she links to their anti-capitalist left-wing politics: one of the things they don't like is Madonna's "Thatcherite spirit of free enterprise." [128] In that sense of course, those new puritans differ from yesterday's puritans, who had nothing against money and the spirit of free enterprise (see Max Weber).

Margery Metzstein tells that her daughter was flicking through *Sex* with her friends in her room, when her eleven-year-old son came in. He saw a few pages of the book and burst out crying. He explained: "She doesn't need to show herself like that. She's got lots of money already. She just wants to be popular. She's a sad, sad person." Metzstein comments: "He realized, even if we adults do not — that this book is an insult which degrades Madonna, and humiliates women."[129] Robert Miklitsch finds as I do this scenario entirely ridiculous, and amply laughs at Metzstein.[130] Besides its total lack of verisimilitude, it shows that Metzstein feels the need to hide behind her son (a male), to trash Madonna; the moral of her story being that Madonna belongs to the worst sort of prostitute, for not having the excuse of poverty, she sells her body not because of need, but because she enjoys it. And here's how under cover of feminism you can join the religious right, criticizing *Sex* with arguments that are finally rather similar.

It is possible to perceive more or less "liberal" feminists like Paglia, Califia, Bright, Wolf or Madonna as allies of capitalism. Steven Hill wrote an article entitled "George Bush and Madonna — Hopping into the Same Bed." [131] But so what?

Nadine Strossen, Madonnophile, tells about a feminist conference when Madonna's book "was also ritually torn to shreds [by Mac-Dworkinites]."[132] That convenient neologism, "MacDworkinites," (Andrea Dworkin and Catharine MacKinnon) is used by Paglia, and Madonna. Pornophobic MacDworkinites think that *Sex* encourages the degradation of women, and misogyny. Literally iconoclastic, they ritually tore the images of Madonna the icon; but of course they weren't able to tear the steel cover, in which the title *Sex* is cut out...

Maybe even more than *Sex*, the element of the Madonnesque text that particularly enraged some feminists was the scene from the 1989 *Express Yourself*[133] video where Madonna is in chains. The Mac-Dworkinites saw that as an abject piece of macho propaganda, considering that such images condoned masculine domination — including physical domination.

Madonna's habitual response is that she chained herself, she is chained to her desire, but she is in control, and isn't that what feminism is about?

In the same order of ideas, Madonna posed for a very famous picture (*Esquire* cover in August 1994) in a black leather bikini, with a dog collar and leash. But she is the one who's holding the handle of the leash, the sort of "detail" that MacDworkinites fail to notice.

Camille Paglia doesn't hesitate to say: "Contemporary feminism has simply relapsed into the Puritanism of seventeenth-century New England."[134] MacDworkinites' feminism is also inscribed, and I am aware that this is a paltry cliché, in the supposedly moribund dictatorship of the Politically Correct. Madonna is definitely not PC, and whether you approve of disapprove, everyone agrees on that point.

MacDworkinites accuse Madonna and Camille Paglia of participation in the backlash, but Madonna and Paglia consider them as narrow-minded and censorship-prone as the most extreme religious right-wingers. Madonna bothers feminists like NOW's Kim Gandy, who are capable of burning books, in exactly the same way she bothers fundamentalists. The former denounce the sexual *mises en scène* of Madonna as an attack on the integrity and dignity of women, the latter denounce them as immoral or sinful: the thought processes are the same.[135]

Other Madonna opponents, such as Rosemary Hennessy or Sheila Jeffreys, inscribe their work in modern Lesbian and Gay Studies, rather than in postmodern Queer Theory. Madonna has of course more affinities with the latter. Such feminists, before being enemies of Madonna, are enemies of the postmodern, which they see as "the cultural capital of late patriarchy."[136] Such feminists often remain untouched by constructionist post–Foucaldian[137] theory, and sometimes see not only gender but even sexual orientation as *natural* phenomena, while clinging to identity politics.[138] Rosemary Hennessy considers for her part that Queer Theory and postmodern critique (or art) do nothing but reify capitalist and sexist structures, consolidating a hegemonic culture. She goes as far as to say that Wall Street and Queer Theory share the same ideology.[139] Sheila Jeffreys sees in Queer Theory exclusively masculine preoccupations.[140] As Jagose reports, Jeffreys does not hesitate to state that she thinks gay and heterosexual men belong to the same masculinist confederacy, which means to uphold male supremacy.[141] That type of dated (usually essentialist) lesbian feminism is responsible for the fact that Madonna remains misunderstood in certain quarters. The women of NOW did not hesitate to declare that Madonna "had set women's lib thirty years back," as she herself often reminds journalists. Do they really look at her work, I wonder? Or do they just think that "it is not possible to reclaim or rehabilitate postmodernism for feminist uses"?[142]

The feminist Madonnophile Lonette Stonisch says: "It seems that traditional feminists persistently misread Madonna, either because they feel threatened by her victories, or because they wish she'd keep her clothes on, or because they want a more serious examination and resolution of feminine objectification."[143]

Obviously, the amount of reproaches that Madonna gets is proportional to her popularity, as she is a well-known role model. In some respects she recalls Naomi Wolf, who may be seen as a feminist role model. Her current position, rather Madonnesque, if I am not mistaken, is that the real problem is not whether you wear makeup or not, whether you go on a diet or not, whether you show a bit of leg or not, but whether you decide as a woman to make your *own* aesthetic choices and decisions.

In January 1993 there was a conference at Santa Barbara (University of California), organized by the Women's Center, whose subject was "Madonna: Feminist Icon or Material Girl?" Of course, the title of the conference is dubious, since it is easy to demonstrate that Madonna can be both. But it shows if need be that the question of Madonna's feminism is not easy to decide. Indeed some feminists left the conference declaring that they hadn't been able to make up their minds.

The academic Yvonne Tasker abundantly mentions Madonna in her book *Working Girls,* but she doesn't really choose sides. She writes in her penultimate chapter: "[Madonna] is an interesting figure to the extent that her appropriation does at times work to question assumptions. At other points she constructs hierarchies which seem content with the production of her as embodiment of white womanhood."[144]

Mary Joe Frug can't really take sides either; she is afraid that the work of Madonna might be misinterpreted. She herself believes in some of Madonna's feminist declarations, but, she worries: "There are probably a number of people who won't. Anyone who looks as much as a sex worker as she does couldn't possibly be in charge of herself, they are likely to say."[145]

The Canadian academic Karlene Faith isn't entirely convinced by Madonna's feminism either. She has examined the problems Madonna can represent for old school feminists, and speaks of "Grist for Feminist Thinking." Besides, she rejoices: "The beauty of Madonna is that she couldn't pass any test of political correctness."[146] But Faith is unable to reconcile the S&M *mises in scène* of Madonna with feminist thought. She confesses: "My difficulty in understanding sadomasochism [...] as feminist practice may put me in Paglia's category of the puritanical feminist. I do, in writing about this, feel a bit like Jerry Falwell scolding and wagging my finger at an unrepentant Larry Flynt."[147]

Madonna, Patron Saint of the Feminists?

The academic Pamela Robertson develops over twenty-three pages Madonna's camp feminism.[148] She deems that her postmodern style can mobilize "a historical understanding of gay and feminist Camp both to critique and revitalize feminist politics."[149]

Professor Kay Turner, feminist and singer in an all-girl rock band, demonstrates Madonna's feminism over 127 pages.[150] The feminist academic Lisa A. Lewis is also certain of Madonna's feminism, as she points out repeatedly in *Gender Politics and MTV: Voicing the Differences.*[151]

Camille Paglia has been designated as one of the worst enemies of radical feminists. Her brand of feminism is a bit like that of Caryn James;[152] and it is nothing like that of Susan Faludi,[153] or Barbara Grizutti Harrison.[154] I myself see her as undeniably feminist, even though many see her as antifeminist. She states herself: "I sometimes call my system drag queen feminism."[155] Having written a few short but capital texts about

Madonna, Camille Paglia — sometimes nicknamed the Madonna of academe — counts among those rare women who *think* about Madonna without being blinded by their politics. She declared: "I'm bringing, like Madonna, a sense of beauty and pleasure and sensuality back into feminism."[156] Paglia defends the idea that Madonna provides a positive example; it is in that sense that she has repeatedly hailed her as the future of feminism. Paglia accepts, besides, the notion that a *man* may be a feminist (thank you Camille).

Kate Tentler writes in the *Village Voice*: "I believe in the power of Madonna, that she has the balls to be the patron saint of new feminism."[157]

The history of women's conditions throughout the centuries gives the impression that before the sixties, women only reached orgasm rarely and confidentially. In the sixties and seventies, several women's magazines began claiming the right to orgasm for women. Madonna, thinking the fight isn't over, has undertaken some sort of crusade, notably in favor of cunnilingus. She believes it is necessary to educate men in the matter. Her teachings may be found in her book *Sex* and in songs like the very saucy *Where Life Begins.*[158]

Some feminist commentators enjoy that sort of "militancy," like Cathy Schwichtenberg, Roseann M. Mandziuk, Susan McClary, or Trish Deitch Rohrer.[159]

Obviously, stardom and fortune confer on Madonna a privileged position, but the most striking examples of strong and independent women are not provided, by definition, by anonymous members of the working classes. All the important feminist leaders in America have a university degree and belong to the middle classes. Madonna's great freedom is indeed linked to her particular status, but she has earned that status the hard way.

In *Sex*, Madonna answers the MacDworkinites by anticipation, since she writes that she doesn't see why it would be degrading for women to have a man looking at naked women in magazines. To each his own sexuality, she deems, what matters is the way you behave toward others, and not the fantasies you may have.[160] Of course, this is a far cry from the politics of those who approve of Lorena Bobbitt's gesture. As we have seen, Madonna's adversaries are often adversaries of the postmodern in general. Fortunately, all feminists are not opposed to the postmodern; some are confused, trying to find a way out, like Judith Evans;[161] others like Linda Hutcheon have to recognize that the postmodern and feminism had to intersect at some stage.[162]

I believe like Craig Owens[163] that postmodern feminism and postfeminism can be more or less equivalent, and I see nothing damaging for the cause of women there. I do know that many feminists think like Lisa

Tuttle: "No matter how the term [postfeminist] is redefined or justified, its use is antifeminist, for it works against the continuing feminist struggle by seeking to limit feminism."[164] It seems to me that Madonna's *oeuvre* amply contradicts that.

Let us note to conclude, however, that Betty Friedan, however old-school, author of the classic *The Feminine Mystique* (1963), constitutes an exception, since practically alone among still militant feminists of her generation, she has not trashed Madonna: "Madonna — in contrast to the image of women that you saw on MTV — at least [...] had guts, she had vitality. She was in control of her own sexuality and her life. She was a relatively good role model, compared with what else you saw."[165]

When you're looking for an example of idolatry that may equal or surpass Madonnolatry, you are obliged to refer to male stars, like Frank Sinatra, Elvis Presley, the Beatles, or Michael Jackson. The only woman in the Western world who may be compared to her, in terms of longevity and record sales worldwide (spread over decades) is the deceased Italian-French singer from Egypt Dalida, who indeed beat Frank Sinatra and the Beatles several times, even if she is practically unknown in the States. Madonna has been known to listen to Dalida records.[166]

Now isn't that a victory for women? Isn't Madonna a feminist patron saint, if only because her stardom has *no female precedent*? Madonna is perfectly aware that she is a feminist role model, and is rather pleased with the status. Rather than influencing other pop stars, she'd rather inspire and empower people she doesn't know, young ordinary women with ordinary jobs: "I'd rather feel women out there in the world can draw strength from what I've accomplished in my life than have other pop stars acknowledge their debt."[167]

In *Desperately Seeking Susan*, Madonna composes through the Susan character a particularly feminist role model (see chapter 2). But that is not the only feminist element of the film, evidently. Ginette Vincendeau notes that whereas feminist film theory is largely based on the Mulveyan principle of woman as object of the male gaze, some films involve women gazing at other women, and women as subjects making the narrative progress.[168]

Such films are rare, undeniably. Jackie Stacey explains that she finds many similarities between *Desperately Seeking Susan* and *All About Eve* (Joseph Mankiewicz, 1950). She does not see them as lesbian films, but she uses them to examine certain types of pleasure felt by the female viewers. As in *All About Eve*, Stacey points out, the subject of *Desperately Seeking Susan* is the obsession of a woman for another woman. And of course that woman is coded as sexual spectacle.[169]

There are indeed numerous similarities between those two films; but in *All About Eve*, Eve is presented as a dangerous, sick person. And in the end old moral values and classic heterosexual patterns are respected.

In *Desperately Seeking Susan*, on the other hand, the identification and desire of Roberta toward Susan is the motor of the positive changes of Roberta. Thanks to her "obsession," Roberta is going to bloom, to free herself from her chains, to find a lover who'll pay attention to her needs and wants, and replace her appalling suburban husband. So a woman-as-sexual-spectacle can be the *empowering object* of the female gaze. As Stacey rightly observes, the old distinction in psychoanalytical film criticism between identification and desire has entailed a lot of neglect for the phenomenon of alternation between the two.[170]

The *Hutchinson Softback Encyclopedia* of 1996 defines Madonna thus: "U.S. pop singer and actress who presents herself on stage and in videos with an exaggerated sexuality." Can such a performer be a feminist role model? My answer is yes. The wannabes, as their name indicates, want to be Madonna, but that desire of identification is often accompanied by desire *tout court*; or perhaps in a postfeminist, postmodern era, the distinction is useless.

Thelma and Louise (Ridley Scott, 1991) has often been compared to *Desperately Seeking Susan*. The image that Madonna projects has been linked to female images in Ridley Scott's film. Susanna Danuta Walters writes: "Madonna, Thelma and Louise, Murphy Brown — all are central images in the construction of female identity and ideas about women's lives and women's options."[171] The analogy is interesting. She explains also that *Thelma and Louise* has been seen either as "an angry, violent, 'man-bashing' piece of radical feminist propaganda," or as "a brave film about feminist consciousness and resistance."[172]

Like Madonna, *Thelma and Louise* divides feminists. Is it a feminist film (although made by a man) that denounces phallocracy or just another silly male fantasy of the castrating woman? The debate continues.[173]

In the two films, anyway, a woman finds strength in the frequentation of another woman; in the two films, a woman is freed from a brainless chauvinist pig.

In *A League of Their Own*, filmed by a woman, Penny Marshall, Madonna plays the wartime baseball player All-the-Way-Mae Mordabito. The movie depicts an atmosphere of camaraderie among women that is rarely to be found on screen. As Mike Clark writes: "What other film could offer comedy, feminism, the national pastime, period nostalgia, and Madonna?"[174]

Madonna says of *A League of Their Own*: "It made a really sort of powerful feminist statement." However, she continues: "I'm used to working with men all the time, and it's almost an all-girl cast, and, you know, girls can be really competitive, and catty, impossible."[175] Perpetuating that type of misogynistic cliché is not very feminist. That is precisely the type of attitude that might anger the more militant feminists.

Madonna works to abolish the hegemony of the male gaze. She has illustrated this notably by being repeatedly photographed as the woman who gazes, the naked man being in the position of the object of the gaze and desire. This was understood by her one-time friend James Foley, who directed *The Corruptor* (1999). In one scene, Mark Wahlberg takes all his clothes off to get a massage from a Chinese masseuse. The music is *Candy Perfume Girl*, by Madonna. Not only does this allude to the old systematic association sex / Madonna, it also befits the eroticism of the passage, which has much more to do with Wahlberg's naked buttocks than with the body of the masseuse. This has enabled her, incidentally, to parody the fascination for the penis that many men imagine women feel.

Like Mae West, Madonna proves that even within a system dominated by men, it is not only possible to play with the male gaze (pervert it, trouble it, turn it upon itself, question it), but also to create a site where the female gaze will rightfully exert itself. Madonna is constantly busy redefining the representation *and* the role of women.

In that type of debate, if you handle rhetoric with a minimum of talent, it is easy to defend any idea. In terms of representation of women, the four principal questions are these:

• Can a product elaborated by a man provide a representation of women that in no way degrades them, and in which they may really recognize themselves, as opposed to identifying a distorted reflection?
• To which degree may the homosexuality of the man who elaborates the product facilitate the representation of women?
• For a product to provide a really acceptable representation of women from the point of view of the hardest-to-please feminists, must it necessarily be conceived entirely by women, from beginning to end of the creation chain?
• If such a product exists, but its creator(s) is /are lesbian(s), doesn't that create a situation which is just as problematic ideologically speaking as a male's creation?[176]

But isn't there in the fact of wanting to position yourself as an authority on (or defender of) the "average female viewer" (whoever she is) a condescendence that is as dangerous as the possible condescendence of the male creators of soaps, movies or commercials? Madonna is often at the center of that debate. As Susanna Danuta Walters writes: "Madonna is a likely starting point for a discussion of feminism and cultural theory."[177]

Susan McClary, for her part, deems: "If Madonna does, in fact, 'live to tell'—that is, survive as a viable cultural force—an extraordinary powerful reflex action of patriarchy will have been successfully challenged."[178]

Madonna forces Americans to question all sorts of things. As she herself says: "Somehow I feel that, as much as people complain and moan and groan and criticize me, they're affected by me. I've touched a nerve in them somehow."[179]

So Madonna is a powerful woman, a woman with "a dick in her brain," as she puts it. As a consequence, she worries many people. She once explained why a strong and intelligent woman scared white men even more than African American gangsters with a machine gun. She knows that black people and women are similarly oppressed, the oppressors being white men. If he feels threatened by a black man, the white man can compensate by buying a gun, possibly bigger than that of the black man.[180] But the woman of power frightens in a different way, which no firearm can counterweigh. She exerts her power without recurring to physical strength, she is situated beyond that "primal male thing."[181]

Like *Dynasty*'s Alexis, Madonna takes her destiny in her own hands, and fights to succeed in a man's world. Alexis and Madonna as active and sexual women can both be seen as adequate feminist role models. Of course, what might irritate old school feminists is that on top of the "masculine" weapons of business sharks, Alexis and Madonna use "feminine" weapons: their bodies.

Baudrillard, whose general discourse is not particularly feminist, and who often enjoys (?) provoking feminists,[182] writes in *De la Séduction*:

> [Feminists] are ashamed of artificial *mises en scène* of their body, as something linked to a destiny of vassalage and prostitution. They do not understand that *seduction represents the mastery of the symbolic universe, whereas power represents only the mastery of the real universe.* The sovereignty of seduction is vastly superior to the holding of sexual or political power.[183]

Madonna, for her part, masters *the two universes*. Maybe Baudrillard did not imagine such a thing were possible; as for Madonnophobic feminists, they cannot stand it. I myself think that feminists shouldn't reject Madonna's exemplary thirst for power.

That last chapter should have exemplified the way Madonna reflects America in the last two decades of the twentieth century (and no doubt will continue to reflect America in the twenty-first century). To this aim, comparisons had to be established, with other cultural phenomena, like sports celebrities, rappers, or Michael Jackson. Unavoidably, gender and sexuality have been discussed again.

As a myth, Madonna had to deal with that other myth: the American Dream; *rapprochements* were *de rigueur*. How not to wonder about that new incarnation of the American Dream she constitutes, comparing her to other, more traditional ones? The U.S. is number one in the world in terms of the production of images, Madonna occupies one of the first places in that industry.

America being so clearly divided between different ethnic and religious groups, as well as between different political and social factions, spread from one end of the ideological spectrum to the other, from the most tyrannically PC left-wingers to the most extremely intolerant right-wingers, Madonna had to be situated among her contemporaries.

Madonna having had a rigid Catholic education, I observed its manifestations in the Madonnesque text. That logically led me to examine her positions on AIDS and abortion. To conclude, I have attempted to circumscribe the postmodern feminism of Madonna, opposing Madonnophobic feminists.

In her essay "Power to the Pussy: We Don't Wannabe Dicks in Drag", the critic bell hooks tells about her initial fascination for Madonna, but says that the star's 1992–1993 personae engendered feelings of betrayal and loss: "It appears that Madonna will not fulfill that earlier sense of feminist promise and power."[184] I hope I have successfully shown that such feelings were unjustified.

In the same way as Alisa Solomon corroborated my findings above (chapter 4) using the phrase "the age of Madonna," Judith Egerton gives me one last portentous argument, evoking "post–Madonna feminism"[185]: and she doesn't even elucidate, seemingly convinced that every reader will know immediately what she means...

In the context of that last development about feminism, I have established a link between Madonna and the actress Joan Collins (another gay icon), which allowed me to conclude with the feminist power of Madonna, undoubtedly one of the most important aspects of my corpus.

"There is these days," concludes Madonna herself, "a whole polemic among feminists, and some of them believe I have set the women's movement backward. Others, on the contrary, claim that I have helped its progress. I myself think that intelligent women don't see me as a threat."[186]

Conclusion

Our biggest hero was, of course, Madonna, after she emerged from the Charlene Atlas school of personal reconstruction transformed from tubby pop star into a ... goddess. Suddenly, contradiction was in vogue. Madonna dressed like the star of a soft-porn fantasy, but her biggest fans — and friends — were women. The world's most potent sex object, she was also the mistress of her image and identity whose principal creative pleasure came from re-inventing herself as other icons, from Marilyn Monroe to Mae West. Swearing, sex-crazed, crass, offensive and Catholic, we liked her so much we were prepared to tolerate her poor taste in men.

— Ruth Picardie[1]

America needs myths; those of its innumerable religions and sects, but also those of the American Dream and of the elusive "American way of life." It also needs those of Hollywood and of an entire popular culture. Madonna, the myth, feeds on all those sources.

Alternately good girl, bad girl or good-bad girl, Material Girl or Boy Toy, she tirelessly plays with signifiers. Virgin, saint, mother, vamp or

186

femme fatale, she multiplies personae *ad infinitum*. Nordic goddess or Mediterranean Great Prostitute, S&M priestess, incarnation of Camp, *female* female impersonator and (gay) icon,[2] she forges her own cult. Semiotician, witch, feminist or exhibitionist, she gives new meaning to hypertextual writing. Manipulator, formidable businesswoman, woman of power, Warholian creature, she defines stardom. Constant palimpsest, she never stops giving birth to herself, or being reborn from her ashes, and each of her (re)nascence acts becomes an international event.[3]

Madonna's career is a popular narrative that perpetually evolves, fed by the media and a public who is always ready to fictionalize her fictions, even if they are not really taken seriously. For Madonnesque mythology secretes its own parody. But that doesn't mean the engagement of the star in her job and her times shouldn't be taken seriously.

In some ways, Madonna proposes solutions. She incarnates the grand founding myths of America, and allows its oppressed groups to bear and contest their condition at the same time. More generally, she feeds the reflection of those who wonder about the place of woman in society, about the status of the artist, about relations between the races, about gender, sex, and so forth.

Madonna offers ample material for fantasy and censorship to traditional puritans. In the eyes of the new puritans (radical feminists) she is the enemy. For the press, she constitutes an unending source of information, of comments and commentaries, and successful articles.

If she brings answers to the evils that plague Americans (etiological role of the myth), if she favors the evolution of mores (ethological role of the myth), if moreover she partakes of the establishment of a climate which is propitious to social development (sociogenetic role of the myth), we could not really say that she fills cosmogonic and eschatological functions. She's not far, though, particularly in 1998, when she takes on some of the characteristics of the goddess or the priestess (Madonnolatry is practically a religion), and appropriates numerous myths of the past (Athena, Aphrodite). Besides, there is at least one universe whose origins and ends she is perfectly capable of explaining: hers, that narcissistic Madonnesque show business world of which she is the demiurge, which has become the familiar universe of millions of fans across the world. In a *société du spectacle*, writes Debord, "the merchandise looks at itself in a world that it has created."[4]

So you could say that with her spectacle, Madonna solves some of the contradictions of today's life; without getting rid of her own contradictions, obviously, seeing the postmodern nature of Madonna the myth, who maintains an ironic distance toward everything. So she only *really* reassures those who consume the product at face value, I suppose.

Premodern societies tried to appease with fabulous tales, i.e., pre-modern myths. The modern dreamed of rationalizing the world with universal metanarratives, i.e., modern myths. Madonna, a postmodern myth, deconstructs every certitude, but weaves from one to another a web of metafictions that somehow protects us from the anxiety of that deconstruction.

A problem continues to fuel debates: can the social and political involvement of Madonna be taken seriously? Does not the Madonnesque spectacle encourage a form of irresponsibility, of disengagement? I have tried for my part to show in this book that even if the political aspects of Madonna's discourse remain secondary elements of her creation, her planetary one-woman-show nevertheless transmits clearly progressive values.

André Rouillé writes about postmodern graphic art:

> That postmodernism is inclusive. It doesn't create a new style, it integrates them all. Its paradigm is pastiche. At a time when ideological rigidities are being blurred, when the grand systems are collapsing, when yesterday's antagonisms are being displaced, when identities are increasingly hazy, postmodernism relies in the domain of images on pacific coexistence. Not without ambiguity. For it redoubles the general equivalence, characteristic of capitalism in the days of mass consumption, of the media and of the production of simulacra. When you quote everything indifferently, you generate confusion between high art, kitsch, popular culture and the commercial aesthetics of advertising [...]. Pastiche strips styles of their context and historical meaning. Memory is abolished by color and the mirages of artifice, by excess and overstatement. Analytical and conceptual rigor is sacrificed to the pleasure of the spectacle; reason is sacrificed to sensuality and the satisfaction of the public; and finally, objectivity makes way for beautiful appearances.[5]

He could be talking about Madonna. His comment somehow sums up everything I have been busy describing in her work, notably the way she integrates numerous styles to create her own. Undeniably, Madonna expresses herself principally in the domain of pastiche. She celebrates the collapse of metanarratives (grand systems) and ideological rigidities, as well as the displacement of antagonisms (such as pornophobic feminists). She favors the confusion of identities, propagates and multiplies ambiguities. But if she produces simulacra, if the elaboration of her career rests on mass consumption, if she has no respect for dated distinctions between high art and low art, she does *not* quote indifferently. Her postmodern art is no anarchic accumulation of signifiers. It is more like the literary re-compositions, at the same time sensible, sensitive and critical, of a John Barth.

It is also true that Madonna does not keep away from excess, artifice, overstatement, sensuality and beautiful appearances. She does flatten history and sell mirages; she is preoccupied mostly with the pleasure of the spectacle. But I do not agree with the idea of a sterile ideological blurring — that is all too readily associated to postmodern pastiche. Playful syncretism doesn't necessarily entail abandonment of the world and flight into the virtual. It can be another way to apprehend the complexity of today's world and give yourself new means of action. Bakhtin's dialogism is no synonym of non-involvement; it can be the way to escape the tyranny of a *pensée unique* (monologism).

Madonna's trump card is the fragmentation and complication of codes, but she doesn't use that card to produce a nebulous vortex where thought gets lost; on the contrary, she means to find contact with the concrete world again, and maybe act efficiently, precisely, to help rethink contemporary problems: for example in terms of sexuality and interracial relations. The idea is that today any overly general ideology (too doctrinaire) leads to immobility or fascism. Pierre Bourdieu writes: "You cannot turn on the radio without hearing something about the global village, about worldwide economy, etc. Those are words that don't look insidious, but through which an entire philosophy, a vision of the world is expressed, which engenders fatalism, and submission."[6] That might be true as regards the economy, or politicians' politics, but not necessarily when popular culture is concerned, and certainly not when the village is Madonna's.

Besides, you shouldn't neglect an essential aspect of the Madonna Phenomenon: the uncommon composition of her public. At the beginning of her career, it was mostly constituted of teenage girls, then it gradually spread to a mass public. More recently, however, as academics were getting hold of her work (especially those whose research has to do with gender studies and media studies[7]), Madonna found more and more fans among lesbians and gays. So much so that it was possible to wonder at the beginning of the nineties if her work was still followed (in every sense of the word) by the general public. "Madonna's act has truly crossed over, but she has crossed over from the mainstream to the margin," said Annalee Newitz.[8] However, Madonna did appeal to "everybody" again, in 1998 with *Ray of Light*, then in 2000 with *Music*, and then again with *Greatest Hits II* (GHII) and the *Drowned World* tour and tour DVD in 2001.

Such a phenomenon is seldom observed. In show business, you often find artists who assemble a large audience after they initially seduced a particular fringe. But doing the opposite, from the mainstream to the margin (and back again), that is rare.

In 1997, after the release of the movie *Evita*, the media "forgot" Madonna a little bit, except the tabloids, of course. The mainstream media rediscovered her in 1998 and praised the album *Ray of Light* as much as they had praised the *Vogue* period. Even the *New Musical Express*, the Bible of specialized critics, declared: "The Mother of All Pop is Back—And She's Good Again!"[9] Those who had pronounced her a has-been were then forced to admit their mistake. And then she was *never* out of the media between *Ray of Light* and *Music.*

At the advanced age of forty-four, when "her face is probably more familiar to you than half the members of your own family,"[10] Madonna still inaugurates new Madonnesque fields. She has a new husband, but if you can laugh at her choosing Scotland for her wedding, so she could get a Christian ceremony (the Church of Scotland will marry divorcees), you can also approve of her choice of a *female* parson, the Rev. Susan Brown, who doesn't mince her words and goes around on roller blades. But Madonna doesn't really play so much in the playground of sexual provocation any longer, as she comically signaled in January 2001, wearing a jacket with "Mrs. Ritchie" embroidered on the back, and she has decided to try and develop her many talents outside singing. She once announced: "I don't want to end my career in singing, like a pathetic female Mick Jagger."[11]

In terms of image, she did seem in late 2000, 2001 and 2002 to have opted for a more subdued couple of looks: Evita-like for the christening of little Rocco, sexy cowgirl–parodic country & Western for *Music* (eat your heart out Dolly Parton), and stylish–British–mature mother in beautiful-but-sensible designer duds for her daily life in London.

Those who haven't been convinced by her acting in *Evita* or *The Next Best Thing* should watch her in *Dangerous Game* by Abel Ferrara: you need to greatly master acting to play a bad actress well. I believe we can expect to see more and more of Madonna on the silver screen—notably in her husband's films (see *Swept Away*, 2002)—and to finally hear critics begrudgingly admit that she has praiseworthy acting talents. Her performance in *Up for Grabs* on the London stage in May 2002 was mildly praised.

Besides, she *writes* more and more. It is said she might agree to give her name to a series of products, such as clothing and health foods.[12] She also wants to direct music videos, if not movies.

So there is every chance that Madonna is here to stay. But what can she still wish for, twenty years later, a majority of critics having praised *Ray of Light* and *Music*? Respect, maybe.

Notes

Preface

1. Quoted by Seigworth, 1993, p. 291.
2. As a feminist, I do not think there is anything wrong with the word "actress."
3. I'll come back to the meaning and spelling of "camp."
4. Academics at least agree that she is one of the four or five most famous women in the world; Roy Shuker writes that she is "arguably one of the best-known women in the world."
5. Ranguevaux, 1997. Translation mine, like all the translations from the French, German, Spanish and Italian in this book.
6. "Although she doesn't present herself as an intellectual, I liken substantive aspects of her work to that of a ground-breaking scholar" (Faith, 1997, p. 75).
7. Album *Savage* (Eurythmics), 1986.
8. Many parallels can be drawn between Madonna and the British performer Annie Lennox, but the latter, a notorious cross-dresser and postmodern juggler with signifiers, is classified in the art rock category by U.S. distributors, and too distant to ever become a star in the sense of the word as I use it about Madonna. Besides, Lennox is "naturally" beautiful and androgynous, which does not give exactly the same meaning to her masks.
9. Karlene Faith writes: "Although often irreverent for the cameras, and inarticulate as an interviewee, in other interviews she can be dignified and serious" (Faith, 1997, p. 84). Ingrid Sischy writes: "Talk to her and you'll notice the falling into and out of accents and lingoes: on a busy day, you can hear the sound of Michigan, the in phrases of Manhattan gay boys and street kids, inflections wor-

191

thy of the Queen Mother. Lately, in her elegant mode, she sometimes relies on the kind of Great Lady diction they taught at MGM"(Sischy, 1998).

10. She said in 1991 that she had been seeing an analyst for years, intermittently (Haas, 1991); I dare not deduce anything from the information.

11. She sometimes speaks of Fernand Léger for hours, if you believe the publisher Michel Birnbaum.

12. In an interview she gave Henry-Jean Servat, for example, she mentions Julien Green and Georges Bataille. How many Americans know but their names? She also sometimes speaks of a remake she would like to undertake, of the Agnès Varda 1962 film *Cleo de 5 à 7* (Servat, February 24, 1993). It would seem, besides, that she is a fervent admirer of Marguerite Duras.

13. Oscar Wilde, *The Importance of Being Earnest* (1895), Act I.

14 Tetzlaff, 1993, p. 240.

15. Oscar Wilde, *Lady Windermere's Fan* (1891), Act III.

ONE—*Definitions*

1. Genette, 1982, p. 33.
2. Cuddon, 1979, p. 408.
3. Fowler, 1973, p. 119.
4. Cupitt, 1982, p. 29.
5. Coupe, 1997, p. 6.
6. *Ibid.*, p. 7.
7. Cf. Frye, 1971, *passim*, and Frazer, 1978, *passim*.
8. Eliade, 1963, pp. 16-17.
9. Cf. Bettelheim, 1976, *passim*.
10. Cf. Morin, 1973, *passim*.
11. Cf. Graves, 1960, pp. 9-24.
12. Caillois, 1938, p. 13.
13. Cupitt, 1982, p. 29.
14. Lévi-Strauss, 1964, 1974, 1983, 1985, *passim*.
15. Caillois, 1938, 1970, *passim*.
16. Eliade, 1957, 1962, 1963, 1971, *passim*.
17. Barthes, 1957, p. 143.
18. Cf. Coupe, 1997, p. 9, and Ricœur, 1967, p.5.
19. Lévi-Strauss, 1974, p. 236.
20. *Ibid.*, pp. 236-239.
21. Lévi-Strauss, 1985, p. 22.
22. Jung, 1993, *passim*.
23. Caillois, 1938, p. 19.
24. Baudelaire, 1968, p. 286. Quoted by Carlier & Gritton-Rotterdam, 1994, p. 3.
25. Fuentes, 1990, p. 503.
26. McLuhan, 1962 and 1964, *passim*.
27. Morin, 1972, p.12.
28. *Ibid.*, p. 40.
29. I write "a woman" because it is female stars I am concerned with, or male stars who built their beauty with traditionally "feminine" stratagems, like David Bowie.

30. For example in the States, Theda Bara, first star who was literally made from scratch, by William Fox, as it happens.
31. Cf. Coursodon, 1976.
32. Morin, 1972, p. 47.
33. Segal, 1994, p. 198. Quoted by Ekins, 1997, p. 163.
34. Morin, 1972, p. 8.
35. Morin, 1972, p. 13.
36. Cocteau, 1947, p. 32.
37. Morin, 1972, p. 5.
38. *Ibid.*, p. 8.
39. Morin, p. 38.
40. Cf. Izod, 1993, p. 55.
41. Domarchi, 1976.
42. Dyer, 1998, p. 16.
43. Cf. Bockris, p. 241; cf. also Warhol, 1975, pp. 31-32.
44. Remember in particular Viva, Ingrid Superstar, Joe Dalessandro, Ultra-Violet, Candy Darling, Eddie Sedgwick...
45. Koch, 1973, p. 10.
46. Coupe, 1997, p. 19.
47. Barth, 1995.
48. West, 1991, p. 515.
49. White, 1991, p. 1.
50. Shuker, 1994, p. 28.
51. West, 1991, p. 515.
52. Van Leer, 1995, p. 86.
53. Bignell, 1996, p. 163.
54. Hutcheon, 1989, p. 1.
55. Boisvert, 1996, p. 14.
56. West, 1991, p. 515.
57. Cf. Hudnut, 1966, *passim*. John M. Unsworth recalls that according to Michael Koehler, the term "postmodern" was introduced into English by Arnold Toynbee in the forties. Michael Koehler deems that it is probably Irving Howe who first spoke of postmodern literature, as early as 1959 (Unsworth, 1991). Of course, none of that has anything to do with the Spanish *postmodernismo* in literature as it was still understood by Spanish critics at the beginning of the twentieth century.
58. Cf. Jencks, 1977, 1987, *passim*.
59. *Ibid.*
60. We may add G.W.F. Hegel.
61. White says "technological," but I think the proper word here is "technical."
62. White, 1991, pp. 31-74. Cf. Heidegger, 1958, 1985, 1986, *passim*.
63. Cf. Derrida, 1972, 1978, 1987, *passim*. Cf. also Shapiro, 1989.
64. Cf. Deleuze, 1970, *passim*; Guattari & Deleuze, 1972 and 1975, *passim*.
65. Lyotard, 1979.
66. Cf. Lyotard, 1979, 1988, 1993, *passim*.
67. Cf. Vattimo, 1987, 1990, *passim*.
68. Boisvert, 1996, p. 24.
69. *Ibid.*, p. 47.
70. Cf. Virilio, 1993, *passim*.

71. Cf. Smart, 1993, *passim*.

72. According to the modern, those progresses were supposed to emancipate mankind. The postmodern observe that they only contributed to further alienate mankind.

73. Boisvert, 1996, p. 53.

74. Some wonder if the increasing power of computers and of the Internet does not mark, rather, the beginning of a new era, post-postmodern: the cyber age. But that is another debate.

75. Cf. Raulet, 1988, 1989, *passim*.

76. Cf. Scarpetta, 1985, *passim*.

77. Cf. Debord, 1992.

78. Cf. Baudrillard, 1968, 1972, 1973, 1979, 1981, 1986, 1987, 1990, *passim*.

79. Cf. Paz, 1974, *passim*. Octavio Paz observed that the avant-garde of the sixties did nothing but repeat the patterns of the avant-garde of the nineteen tens; he announced the end of the very concept of "modern art."

80. McHale, 1987, *passim*.

81. Newman, 1985, *passim*.

82. Kermode, 1979, *passim*.

83. Cf. Hassan, 1980, pp. 91-124, and 1987, *passim*.

84. Among those who made (reflection on) the postmodern progress, we can also mention Hans Bertens, Susan Sontag, Leslie Fiedler, William Spanos, and Richard Rorty.

85. Derrida, 1967, *passim*.

86. Foucault, 1966, 1971, 1972, 1975, 1976, 1984, *passim*.

87. Couturier, 1995, p. 5.

88. *Ibid.*, p. 9.

89. *Ibid.*, p. 12.

90. Cf. Habermas, 1988, 1993, *passim*.

91. *Ibid.*

92. Habermas, 1993, pp. 13-14.

93. Boisvert, 1996, pp. 15-16.

94. Cf. Jameson, 1984, 1991, 1993, *passim*.

95. Jameson, 1991, p. 49.

96. Mathieu, 1994, p. 56.

97. Cf. Vattimo, 1987, 1990, *passim*.

98. Owens, 1983, pp. 61-62.

99. Phoca & Wright, 1999.

100. Kroker, 1992, p. 97. We can also mention Stephen K. White, who writes: "Affinities between feminism in general and postmodernism have often been noted, especially in regard to their common questioning of the dominant metanarratives of modern Western Life" (White, 1991, p. 96).

101. Barth, 1997, pp. 62-76. Cf. also *The Literature of Replenishment, Ibid.*, pp. 193-206.

102. Lyotard, 1988, p. 27.

103. Cf. Foucault, 1966, 1971, 1972, 1975, 1976, 1984, 1994, *passim*.

104. Shuker, 1994, p. 28.

105. Genette, 1982, p. 201.

106. 1962: the death of Marilyn Monroe and of the old studio system.

107. Waugh, 1984, p. 2.

108. What is more, I do not believe like Waugh that the lie-reality thing is the *principal* element of metafiction, even if writers such as John Barth, Jorge Luis Borges or Umberto Eco developed it in their metafiction.

109. A distinction that is still very much practiced in Europe.

110. Shuker, 1994, p. 28.

111. Rouillé, 1992.

112. Connor, 1989, p. 186.

113. Jameson, 1984, p. 54.

114. Connor, 1989, pp. 185-193.

115. Hebdige, 1979, pp. 46-71.

116. It is in the wake of New Wave and disco that Madonna began her career, notably inspired by Debbie Harry, the singer of the band Blondie, as she concedes herself: "She did inspire me" (quoted by Jackson, October 19, 1996).

117. Jameson, 1991, *passim*.

118. McRobbie, 1986, p. 57.

119. Vidal, 1993, pp. 121-146. Thomas Pynchon, whom I personally enjoy as much as John Barth, seems "worse" in that domain; none of Barth's books is a "hermetic" as *Gravity's Rainbow*, for example.

120. One of David LaChapelle's photographs shows an old Madonna in a wheelchair, finding a rat in her plate. Next to her stands an old and fat Courtney Love. The models are particularly well-chosen. That is of course an allusion to Bette Davis and Joan Crawford in *Whatever Happened to Baby Jane?* (Robert Aldrich, 1962), and to the actresses' rivalry, comparable to that of Courtney Love and Madonna. In the spring of 1998, Madonna finally posed for him, notably as a Hindu goddess (photos published in *Rolling Stone*, July 9/23, 1998).

121. West, 1991, p. 516.

122. Cf. Seguin, 1994.

123. "Postmodernism is Madonna," writes Daniel Harris ironically (Harris, 1992). I am indebted for this reference to Robert Miklitsch (Miklitsch, 1998, p. 100). Stuart Sims's *Icon Critical Dictionary of Postmodern Thought* mentions Madonna, of course, describing the Madonna Phenomenon over half a page.

124. Connor, 1989, p. 184.

Two—*Desperately Seeking Stardom*

1. Quoted by Thompson, 1991, p. 54.

2. Rosenzweig, 1994, p. 1.

3. Debord, 1967, p. 24.

4. Flynn died of AIDS in 1990; Madonna has frequently evoked the pain this loss caused her.

5. Rettenmund, 1995, p. 85.

6. *A Certain Sacrifice* (Stephen Jon Lewicki, 1980). Victor Lenore describes it as "a psychosexual fantasy, arty and cheap, that mixed thriller suspense, neo-gothic terror and softcore porn" (Lenore, 1996, p. 12).

7. Cf. Shreiber, 1979.

8. Cf. McLaren, 1997, p. 19. The initial title was *Truth or Dare: On the Road, Behind the Scenes and in Bed with Madonna*.

9. Cf. O'Hagan, 1993, p. 33.
10. This sentence is quoted in the majority of Madonna biographies.
11. About the loss of her virginity, cf. among others Thompson, 1991, p. 31; Rosenzweig, 1994, p. 60; Bego, 1992, pp. 35 and 41.
12. Tannenbaum, 1995.
13. Cf. Blake, 1993, pp. 17-28; cf. also Newitz, 1993; Cipriani-Crauste, 1994, pp. 84-98.
14. I'll develop the meaning of the phrase later.
15. Rosenzweig, 1994, p. 6.
16. Cf. Gould, 1967/1990.
17. Phillips, 1987.
18. Bego, 1992, p. 170.
19. Rosenzweig, 1994, p. 36.
20. *Truth or Dare* is a special case; I'll come back to it.
21. Some have seen *Dick Tracy* as a gigantic trailer for her album *I'm Breathless* and her single *Vogue*.
22. Cf. Softley, 1994.
23. Rettenmund, 1995, p. 48.
24. Reproduced in *Microsoft Cinemania 96*.
25. *Ibid.*
26. *Ibid.*
27. Rosenzweig, 1994, p. 23.
28. *Ibid.*, p. 24.
29. Cf. Randall, 1994, p. 53.
30. Those reviews and the following have been reproduced by Andersen, 1991, Randall, 1994, and Rettenmund, 1995.
31. The scriptwriter Leora Barish contributes to this success as much as Susan Seidelman and Madonna.
32. Cf. Randall, 1992, p. 42.
33. Reproduced in *Microsoft Cinemania 1996*.
34. In a postmodern context, it is futile to worry about the fact that a movie looks like a music video.
35. Lesage, 1993, pp. 122-123.
36. *The Cambridge International Dictionary of English* of 1995 defines "Boy Toy" like this: "a sexually attractive young man, esp. one who has relationships with older, powerful, or successful people. Cf. also Toy Boy."
37. Cf. Schulze *et al.*, 1993, p. 26; cf. also Bego, 1992, p. 71.
38. Cf. Rettenmund, 1995, pp. 15 and 180.
39. Charyn, 1988, p. 86.
40. William Blake, *Jerusalem: The Emanation of the Giant Albion* (1804–1820).
41. Frank & Smith, 1993, p. 14.
42. Cf. for instance the very subtle way she pays a tribute to Serge Gainsbourg and Jane Birkin (of *Je t'aime moi non plus* fame) by sampling their daughter Charlotte Gainsbourg in *Music*.
43. Izod, 1993, pp. 49-59.
44. Thanks to John Shirley.
45. Coupe, 1997, *passim*.
46. Izod, 1993, p. 49.
47. *Ibid.*, p. 55.

48. Quoted by Lenore, 1996.
49. Pye, 1994.
50. Wintour, 1996.
51. "She suggested a complete image makeover but found Wacko too stuck in his ways. So instead she said they exchanged powder puffs, powdered each other's noses and compared bank accounts" (Martin, 1998).
52. I'm tempted to write that Ambition is her middle name, but of course Madonna has only one name, like any self-respecting goddess.
53. Album *Like a Prayer*, 1989.
54. Bright, 1995, p. 72. I'll come back to that monocle in chapter 4, when I reminisce about Marlene Dietrich, who wore a monocle in her day.
55. Quoted by Jim Driver, Driver 2001, p. xiii.
56. Kane, 1997. Kane sees Bowie as an avant-garde modern; I see him as postmodern.
57. It is almost regrettable for this book that Madonna did not think about it before Bowie.
58. Smith, 1996.
59. Cf. Kane, 1997.
60. Jackson, October 12, 1996.
61. Some would rather say "Madonnaology," like Roger Ebert, who writes, "Pop sociologists have made a specialty out of Madonnaology" (Ebert, 1990).
62. Sischy, 2000.
63. Bowie also frequently bleached his hair, in the same order of idea. Cf. Charyn, 1986, p. 86.
64. Lloyd, 1993, p. 44.
65. I am indebted to Françoise Giroud for this notion.
66. hooks, 1992, p. 159.
67. O'Hagan, 1993, p. 34.
68. O'Hagan, 1993, p. 30
69. *Ibid.*, p. 31.
70. Quoted by Bego, 1992, p. 91.
71. Cf. Boisvert, 1996, p. 9.
72. E. Ann Kaplan and Fran Lloyd, among others, commented upon that (Kaplan, 1987, pp. 120-123; Lloyd, 1993, p. 37).
73. Reins, 1987.
74. Trittoléno, 1993.
75. In this section I only discuss three videos, since the detailed analysis of many others finds its place elsewhere.
76. Cf. Jameson, 1991, pp. 67-96, among others.
77. Among the details that help build the Madonna myth, we may note that there are two versions of the first meeting of Madonna and Tony Ward: some say they met simply on the set of *Cherish*, others maintain that she saw him at a party and stubbed a cigarette out on his back to get acquainted.
78. Cf. for instance *Divine Madness* (Michael Ritchie, 1980).
79. Quoted by Christoper Andersen, 1991, p. 298.
80. Album *True Blue*, 1986.
81. Cf. Shangai, 1989, pp. 91-98.
82. Madonna has often expressed admiration for Fellini.
83. Andersen, 1991, p. 246.

84. Rosenzweig, 1994, p. 34.
85. Cf. Barthes, 1957, p. 147.
86. She also wears tassels in a great "Egyptian" dance number in *Bloodhounds of Broadway*.
87. Cf. Randall, 1992, p. 75.
88. Cf. Shangai, 1989, p. 97.
89. Rettenmund, 1995, p. 129.
90. Drukman, 1995, p. 90.
91. Paglia, 1992, p. 10. Paglia considers it one of the very best videos ever made.
92. McClary is apparently quoting Tipper Gore.
93. McClary quoted by Randall, 1992, p. 76.
94. *Ibid.*
95. Lewis, 1990, pp. 142-143.
96. Rettenmund, 1995, p. 129-130. Rettenmund develops that line of thought in his novel *Boy Culture* (1995).
97. Robert Miklitsch writes: "Postmodern to the core, *Justify My Love* [crosses] Madonna with Mapplethorpe or [...] Foucault with Butler" (Miklitsch, 1998, p. 115).
98. Quoted by Bego, 1992, p. 172.
99. Bego, 1992, p. 173.
100. According to Edgar Morin, talkies Hollywood stars were already not gods and goddesses any longer, they were already humanized, if only because they were not mute anymore. It's all a question of degree. Cf. interview of Tarantino by Udovitch, 1996.
101. Cf. Laura Mulvey's 1975 classic essay, "Visual Pleasure and Narrative Cinema" (Mulvey 1989, pp. 14-28).
102. Cf. Miklitsch, 1998, p. 134.
103. Cf. notably the novel *Do Androids Dream of Electric Sheep?* (1968).
104. Let us not forget etymology: idol = image = icon.
105. Versace, 1996.
106. Versace, 1997.
107. The Bible does better, but only if you count different editions together.
108. Jackson, October 19, 1996.
109. Quoted in *Smash Hits*, December 1991.
110. Big Daddy Kane is an exception that will be discussed further on.
111. As a matter of fact, even inside the American lesbian community, such women do constitute a small minority. Not all lesbians get their chins and nipples pierced, not all lesbians are tattooed.
112. hooks, 1993, pp. 160-161.
113. Dworkin, 1981, *passim.*
114. McClintock, 1993, p. 207.
115. De Juana, 1998.
116. Miller, 1990.
117. Quoted by McLaren, 1997, p. 239.
118. Cf. Blumenfeld, 1997.
119. Even the years the character has spent in jail cannot account for that appalling look.
120. Breathless Mahoney is a nightclub singer, like Marilyn Monroe and Marlene Dietrich in many of their films.

121. Caron-Lowins, 1995, p. 157.
122. The looks of Madonna in other movies, like *Shanghai Surprise* (Jim Goddard, 1986), will be detailed later.
123. Domarchi, 1976, p. 68-70.
124. Cf. Moisy, 1996, pp. 199-200.
125. Quoted by Guccione, 1996, p. 51.
126. Sinfield, 1994, p. 1.
127. Musto, 1995, p. 428.
128. Cf. Lelait, 1998, pp. 185-193.
129. And many British artists too.
130. The scenario is by Noel Langley.
131. For a general analysis of that movie as myth, see the very documented book by Paul Nathanson (Nathanson, 1991).
132. Issue of December 1995 / January 1996.
133. It is in fact sepia, but I assimilate it to black and white for my demonstration.
134. That combination of the two processes has been through varied periods in the history of cinema, color and black and white having signified alternately dream or unreal according to periods. It will be developed later.
135. One of the most frequently quoted songs in the world, written by Harold Arlen and E.Y. Harburg.
136. Quoted by Deevoy, 1991. Madonna also declared on MTV: "I rarely have sex on tour, because, who can have sex when all those things are happening around you?"
137. Andersen, 1991, 363.
138. MTV, 1991.
139. Rushdie, 1992, p. 9.
140. *Ibid.*, pp. 44-46.
141. Quoted for example by Ragan, 1995. Originally published in *The Advocate* (Shewey, 1991).
142. Cf. Madonna, 1992, p. 65.
143. Cf. Kraft, 1996.
144. Notably quoted by Trittoléno, 1993.
145. Cf. von Scherz, 1996.
146. Shewey, 1991. Basically she outed most of her male dancers in *Truth or Dare*. Cf. Haas, June 1991.
147. Rohrer, 1991.
148. Bordat, 1995, p. 76. Cf. also Nathanson, 1991, pp. 27-28 on color and black and white in *The Wizard of Oz*.
149. *Ibid.*, p. 23.
150. Program "Between the sheets with Madonna," on MTV, 1991.
151. I would love to see the missing 248 — bits of which have been said to be circulating on subterranean markets.
152. Cf. Rettenmund, 1995, p. 142. Only one other movie about that sort of thing can really compare with *Truth or Dare*: *The Great Rock and Roll Swindle* (Malcolm McLaren, 1980), about the Sex Pistols. That movie doesn't hide its aim: exploiting the curiosity of the public and making a lot of money.
153. Cf. Collard, 1994; cf. Dyer, 1987, *passim.*
154. Baker, 1994, p. 239.

155. Cf. Cruikshank, 1982, p. 69; cf. D'Emilio, 1983, p. 232; cf. Jagose, 1996, p. 30; cf. Lige & Jack, 1969; cf. Dick Leitsch, 1969.

156. Cf. Spada, 1983, p. 63.

157. Robertson, 1996, p. 124.

158. Pop art is always postmodern, it seems to me.

159. For the sleeve of *Like a Prayer*, Madonna parodied Andy Warhol's Rolling Stones' *Sticky Fingers* cover: the crotch is female this time.

160. The filmmaker Gus van Sant used Udo Kier in the same spirit in *My Own Private Idaho* (1991).

161. Burston, 1994.

162. Tarantino, who will be discussed at length later, only filmed one of the sketches, but the entire film is Tarantinian.

163. Quoted by John Dugdale, 1997.

164. Guccione, 1996.

165. Unless he is but a mortal who engendered Madonna with the dead goddess, Madonna's mother Madonna.

166. Pribram, 1993, p. 189.

167. I don't think that's possible, for such a myth could not possibly disappear into oblivion, by definition. In spite of what some tabloids say, announcing at intervals the end of Madonna, thus contributing to her promotion (a perverse game?), she always comes back, with new products, new personae, unless like a phoenix she is reborn after each "death"...

168. Madonna is usually rumored to have affairs with the artists (male or female) she produces.

169. Cf. *The Outlaw* (Howard Hughes, 1946).

170. *Time*, June 30, 1997.

171. Mulvey, 1996, p. 75. Cf. also Hutcheon, 1989, p. 156.

172. Miklitsch sees that scene as revealing that "the Madonna Phenomenon went into complete overdrive" (Miklitsch, 1998, p. 108).

173. *Séminaire sur la Lettre volée*, Lacan, 1966.

174. Bernard, 1995, pp. 167-168. The fact that Madonna said her song was more about love than sex doesn't harm Mr. White's interpretation in any way.

175. *Ibid.*, p. 46.

176. *Ibid.*, p. 100.

177. Cagney is actually sampled in the song (lines from *White Heat*).

178. *White Heat* may also conceivably be a tribute to Lou Reed and his song *White Light, White Heat*, which was covered by David Bowie.

179. Skeggs, 1993, p. 70.

180. The band Teenage Fanclub (a particularly apt name) covered *Like a Virgin*, and the male singer didn't change a single line. I don't need to expand on the new significance thus created.

181. Madonna, 1992, p. 42.

182. Madonna chose Barcelona to film her concert.

183. In 2000 she plays again at demystifying the archetypal virility of the cowboy, when promoting *Music* as a cowgirl, dancing with gorgeous muscular cowboys whose heterosexuality she somehow seems to question...

184. Franquet, 1995, pp. 73-74.

185. Like other American superheroines, The Invisible Woman has progressed along lines that are parallel to the progression of feminism in the U.S.

186. Cf. Angevin, 2000.
187. Morel, 1995.
188. Acin & Feller, 1996.
189. Christgau, 1993, p. 201.
190. The Madonna Phenomenon is now a set phrase.
191. Kaplan, 1993, p. 153.
192. Crimp & Warner, 1993, p. 100.
193. Taki, 1996. Cf. also Forestier, 1997.
194. Tetzlaff, 1993, p. 239. Cf. also Bordo, 1993, p. 286.
195. Kaplan, 1993, p. 163.
196. Bourdieu, 1996, p. 24. Cf. also pp. 86-87.
197. Cf. for example Bayly, 1994, Kureishi, 1995, Indiana, 1990, Ellis, 1991, Noon, 1993.
198. Linfield & Krevisky, 1997.
199. Miklitsch, 1998.
200. Landesman, 1995. He also mentions an edifying anecdote: during the *Girlie Show*, the *Daily Mail* declared proudly that it was a "Madonna free zone," which was great publicity for Madonna, obviously.
201. A two month affair according to Madonna, episodic to boot.
202. This was of course before she had a daughter with Carlos León and a son with Guy Ritchie.
203. Rodman, 1996, pp. 187–188
204. *Ibid.*, p. 190.
205. Salamon, 1996.
206. Kureishi, 1995, p. 21.
207. *Ibid.*, p. 22. The hyphen in "post-modern" is Kureishi's.
208. *Ibid.*, pp. 97-98.
209. Album *Transformer*, produced by David Bowie (1972).
210. Noon, 1993, pp. 32-33.
211. Cf. for example *Diamond Nebula* (Jeremy Reed, 1994), which also mentions Madonna. Moreover, Madonna is sometimes recognizable in novels even though she is not named; cf. William Gibson's *Mona Lisa Overdrive* (1988) and other books by Gibson (thank you Robert Miklitsch).
212. Quoted by Rosenzweig, 1994, p. 100.
213. Cf. Ritzer, 1996, 1997, 1998; cf. also Ariès, 1997.
214. In the same way, Madonna was influenced by Grace Slick, Marianne Faithfull, Patti Smith, and Tina Turner.
215. Quoted by David Jays, 1996.
216. Quoted in all the tabloids, like *Ici Paris* 20/08/97 and *Voici* 25/08/97 in France, or *Vale* 23/08/97 in Spain.
217. Bayly, 1994, p. 199. Madonna is used in the same way in the thriller by the German writer Frank Goyke, *Ruf doch mal an* (Schwarzkopf & Schwarzkopf, 1994).
218. Foix, 1997, p. 68.
219. Tetzlaff, 1993, p. 262.
220. Cf. Tetzlaff, *ibid.*
221. Baudrillard, 1981, p. 122.
222. Cf. Baudrillard, 1979, pp. 217-218.
223. Newitz, 1993.

224. Servat, 1997.
225. Cf. American *She* of March 1998.

THREE — *The Fundamental Contradicition*

1. Cf. Dion, pp. 115–118.
2. Cf. Harrison, 2000.
3. Of course that statue is really Madonna leaning against the wall.
4. Jackson, October 19, 1996.
5. This and preceding: Madonna, 1996, pp. 118–170.
6. Lola is of course played by Marlene Dietrich in the adaptation *The Blue Angel.*
7. A companion piece for Pat Campbell's painting as vampire by Edward Burne-Jones.
8. In *Belle of the Nineties* (Leo McCarey, 1934).
9. Doane, 1991, p. 1.
10. In *Tacones Lejanos* by Pedro Almodóvar, the drag queen played by the Judge played by Miguel Bosé is called Letal. That drag queen is informed by many Hollywood stars. Almodóvar has in common with Madonna a great passion for pre–1962 stars.
11. Caillois, 1938, pp. 37–85.
12. Cf. Jean-Paul Sartre's play *La Maman et la putain.*
13. Notably in *I'm No Angel* (Wesley Ruggles, 1933).
14. Cf. the way she speaks off stage in *Truth or Dare.*
15. Cf. Penwarden, 1994, among others. People also say that the panties fell in his hands, or on his face, and many wonder what Jacques Chirac did with them (cf. Chatrier, 1993).
16. Kennedy , 1993.
17. West, 1993, and Syn, 1994.
18. Laurent Ruquier. Program *Changement de direction,* 03/01/97.
19. Barthes, 1957, p.147.
20. Cf. Barthes, 1957, p. 147.
21. Lloyd, p. 13.
22. Ibid., p. 39.
23. Bianciotto, 2000.
24. Madonna, 1992, pp. 122–123. That passage has also been spotted by Margery Metzstein (Metzstein, 1993, p. 97) and Robert Miklitsch (Miklitsch, 1998, p. 132).
25. Ramirez, 1996.
26. Blumenfeld, 1997, Blumenfeld writes that apropos of *Truth or Dare.*
27. Probably among other things an allusion to the hit *Bad Girls* by Donna Summer.
28. Shades of *Looking for Mr. Goodbar* (Richard Brooks, 1977).
29. Cf. Gill, 1997.
30. Cf. "Inside Scoop," *Who Weekly,* 2000.
31. Camille Paglia had imagined in 1993 predictions for 1994: "Madonna and Diana will be revealed to be one person, a hybrid Hindu goddess named Madiana. They will withdraw to a Tibetan monastery, run by Richard Gere, to which

women and hermaphrodites can come for flagellation by Madonna and then nursing and healing by Diana" (Paglia, 1994, p. 422).

32. Cassidy, 2000.
33. Cf. Simpson, 1994, pp. 150–163, & 1996, pp. 69–74.
34. Guccione, 1996.
35. Bordat, 1997, p. 103.
36. Morin, 1957, p. 28.
37. Which would not stop the message from being effective and help to improve the situation. If only one human being decides to use condoms after she or he has heard Madonna recommend it, if she saves but one single life, could anyone deny that this is a good deed, in the simplest sense of the phrase?
38. Cf. Gasca, 1994, p. 104.
39. A name that of course echoes Mae West.
40. Tasker, 1993, p. 234.
41. Cf. Hensley, 1997.
42. Doane, 1991, p. 2.
43. Jackson, *Virgin Birth*, 1996.
44. Cf. Miller, 1996.
45. Cf. interview of Penny Rose (Wark, 1996).
46. Pictures with Italian supermodel and actor Raoul Bova.
47. Cf. what happened to Isabella Rossellini with Lancôme.
48. In the magazine *People (on Line)* on November 18, 1996, you could read: "She's *done* Evita and motherhood." Italics mine.
49. Madonna seemingly told a journalist she had pinned on Lourdes's bedroom wall a poster of Stanley Kubrick's *Lolita* (1962)! (Jaeger, 1998)
50. Maria without an accent, in Italian, not in Spanish.
51. I'm prepared to admit this is slightly far-fetched.
52. Cf. Toucas, 1998, for example.
53. In the meantime, let us note that Madonna writes: "My daughter is going to be the best-dressed girl in the world" (Madonna, 1996). Well, that's something.
54. In the novel by Heinrich Mann, *Professor Unrat*, of 1905, the character is called Lola. Sternberg said he doubled the name so the character would be twice as sexy.
55. Cf. van Leer, 1995, p. 167.
56. In the fall of 2000, Guy Ritchie advertised Madonna's album *Music* on his T-shirts, while Madonna advertised his movie : her T-shirts said "*Snatch*— Coming soon," which of course was a tremendous Madonnesque pun.
57. Let us also hope for the children's sake that they won't be too victimized by the stalkerazzi. At three years old Lourdes was already in the tabloids, wearing a judo outfit, *without* her mother; cf. for instance "Snap," *NW*, July 31, 2000.
58. Lavoignat, 1993.
59. Bollon, 1990.

FOUR—*Drag*

1. Isn't the verb rather strong?
2. Baudrillard, 1994, p. 30.

3. Quoted by Douglas Thompson (Thompson, 1991, p. 199).

4. Paglia, 1992, p. 5.

5. Wilkinson, 1997, p. 146.

6. Cf. Baudrillard, 1986, p. 49.

7. Does the absence of identity Baudrillard speaks of refer to individual or group identity? For in our post-industrial society maybe what can be observed has more to do with a redistribution of identities and communitarian feelings than their disappearance.

8. *The Critic as Artist*, 1890.

9. Morel, 1995.

10. Cf. Rodman, 1996, p. 150.

11. Kobal, 1974, p. 79.

12. Barthes, 1957, p. 70.

13. During the *Who's That Girl?* 1987 tour, Madonna appeared at the beginning of each concert wearing a Charlie Chaplin hat and suit.

14. As Madonna remembered when shooting her *Nothing Really Matters* video...

15. Coursodon, 1976, p. 61.

16. Barthes, 1957, p. 70.

17. Cf. Leprohon, 1967, p. 70.

18. RuPaul, 1995, p. 64.

19. Phillips, 1991, p. 546.

20. Edifyingly, some Elvis impersonators are Asian American, or African American, some are female, see Leigh Crow as Elvis Herselvis.

21. Cf. Garber, 1993, pp. 353–374.

22. Raymond, 1995.

23. Solomon, 1993, p. 148.

24. Blumenfeld, 1997, about 1991.

25. Sometimes to look like one woman in particular, but not necessarily.

26. Whatever that means.

27. For those questions of vocabulary, see Jagose, 1996, *passim*, Dynes, 1990, *passim*, and Lelait, 1998, p.16.

28. Cf. Jagose, 1996, p. 8. Some of us politicized fans trembled with horror when hearing the track *What It Feels Like for a Girl* for the first time in 2000, wondering if Madonna hadn't suddenly turned essentialist on us; but after she's asked if the listener knows what it feels like for a girl, she adds "in this world." What a relief: "world" stands of course for "society," so Madonna is still a constructionist.

29. Cf. hooks, 1992, p. 158.

30. Blake, 1977, p. 9. I have my doubts as to the phrase drag queen here, seeing that I translated this from the French, and Blake uses the word "*travesti*," which he might conceivably mean in the sense of transvestite.

31. Dion, 1994, p. 10. Schwichtenberg is quoting E. Newton, 1972.

32. Seigworth, 1993, pp. 291-313.

33. Ross, 1993, pp. 47–64.

34. Garber, 1993, pp. 353–374.

35. Tetzlaff, 1993, p. 239.

36. Whatever that means.

37. But he did not paint others, so as to better incarnate an androgynous extraterrestrial.

38. Rodi, 1995, p. 205–206.
39. Cf. Ekins, 1997, p. 12.
40. Garber, 1993, p. 149.
41. In the video of *I Want You*, Madonna drops her false eyelashes in a glass, signaling again the artifice of her beauty and "femininity."
42. Cf . the song by Charles Aznavour, *Comme ils disent*.
43. Garber, 1993, p. 151.
44. Cf. in particular Lord, 1995.
45. Album *Like a Prayer*, 1989.
46. Cf. Kaplan, 1993, p. 157; cf. Patton, 1993, p. 95.
47. Morton, 1993, pp. 213–235.
48. *Ibid.*, p. 220.
49. *Ibid.*, p. 223.
50. David Bowie's German period: 1976-1977.
51. Faith, 1997, pp. 65–66.
52. I am currently working on a book on Camp.
53. Whatever that means.
54. Sontag, 1966, pp. 275–287.
55. *Ibid.*, p. 20.
56. Graham & Plume, 1996.
57. Robertson 1996, pp. 6–7.
58. Kleinhans, 1994, p. 188.
59. More on this in the next section of this chapter.
60. Cf. Patricia White's essay on the subject (White, 1995, pp. 91–114).
61. Dynes, 1990, p. 203.
62. Lisa Henderson has developed the links between Judy Garland, Madonna, and Camp (Henderson, 1993, pp. 121-122).
63. Warhol, 1989, p. 670.
64. Dean, 1992, p. 276.
65. Some even say fifties.
66. Patton, 1993, p. 83.
67. Patton, 1993, *passim*.
68. Patton, 1993, p. 86.
69. I hear they are coming back...
70. Blake, 1993, p. 24.
71. Patton, 1993, p. 96.
72. Cf. David Bowie's 1974 song *Rebel Rebel* in which a mother finds it hard to identify the gender of her child. This song was used in 1995 by a French supermarket deodorant called Rebel Rebel. The ice skater Philippe Candéloro starred in the TV commercial; he was clearly constructed as a paragon of heteromasculinity, highly desirable to women (evidenced by his hysterical Japanese fans). How were the viewers supposed to interpret it? Was it a subversive show of humor on the part of gay advertisers? It is hard to imagine that French admen today could be totally hermetic to the English language. But whatever the explanation, there is an amusing parallel to be drawn between buyers of this product (nearly 100 percent heterosexual, I would venture to say) and dancers trying to vogue in a hip discotheque say in Rochester, N.Y., far from the Houses of Harlem. Cf. also Warner, 1993, p. 102.
73. Cf. Lew Wallace and Margaret Wolfe Hungerford.

74. Patton, 1993, p. 92.

75. One might be tempted here to establish connections with people like Dame Edna Average or the tradition of Christmas pantomimes, but the kind of drag queen I have in mind throughout this chapter is the glamorous one, not the burlesque. Besides, the glamorous drag queen tends to be gay and utterly devoid of misogyny, whatever some might say, whereas comic characters in drag in mainstream show business (as opposed to specialized cabaret clubs) tend to be straight and often misogynous in their portrayal of caricatured women as witches.

76. Some call that film postmodern.

77. Cf. Paglia, 1994, p. 371.

78. Cf. Thomson, 1994, p. 793.

79. She said in an interview: "I play [...] with the image of many [...] actresses [...]: Gina Lollobrigida, Greta Garbo, Marlene Dietrich" (Haas, 1991).

80. Cf. Rettenmund, 1995, p. 134.

81. As described by Madonna (Rebichon & Lavoignat, 1993).

82. A similar process has been undertaken by Bibi Andersen, one of postmodern Spanish filmmaker Pedro Almodóvar's favorites. If as they say Bibi Andersen really is a transsexual, taking the name of the Swedish actress Bibi Andersson (changing the spelling, as the latter is still alive) constitutes an ironic homage. Andersen does resemble Andersson, but mostly her pseudonym signals her evolution: from man to woman to actress of European auteur cinema. Remember *Persona* (Ingmar Bergman, 1966), in which Bibi Andersson changes personalities with Liv Ullman? That film influenced Bibi Andersen as the films with Dita Parlo influenced Madonna.

83. Cf. Lauren Bacall's nickname, The Look, that she was given because of the way she looked at people (head down, eyes up).

84. Thompson, 1991, p. 1.

85. Elsewhere, as is well-known, Madonna shows her body entirely naked, and maybe — precisely — arouses less desire. She has "done" Hayworth on many occasions.

86. Quoted by Kenneth Anger, 1975, p. 183.

87. Mae West said: "Between two evils, I always pick the one I never tried before."

88. Huston, 1976.

89. Cf. Halliwell, 1983, p. 825; cf. also the Charlotte Chandler interview (Chandler, 1997).

90. Lo Duca, 1968, p. 100.

91. Cf. Huston, 1976.

92. Blake, 1977, p.46.

93. Mailer, 1994.

94. Blake, 1977, p. 47–48.

95. Charyn, 1988, p. 108.

96. Cf. Riva, 1993, p. 155.

97. Cf. any biography of Dietrich, except her own and her daughter's.

98. Madonna was envisaging that or a biopic of Dietrich. There are countless such projects which never seem to reach their conclusion: Madonna as Dietrich, Madonna as her favorite painter Frida Kahlo, as Tina Modotti, etc. Laura Mulvey operates a *rapprochement* between Kahlo's paintings and the work of Madonna (Mulvey, 1996, p. 75).

99. Bach, 1994, p. 178.
100. Cf. Butticaz, 1997.
101. Martin, 1995, p. 19.
102. Cf. Rebichon & Lavoignat, 1993.
103. Garber, 1992, p. 25.
104. Scriptwriter John Collier.
105. Music by John Kander and lyrics by Fred Ebb.
106. Cf. Mizejewski, 1992, *passim*.
107. Cf. the video *Grace Jones: A One-Man Show*, 1982.
108. Her green nail polish particularly pleases the connoisseurs of Camp.
109. Beyond the fascination of Madonna for Dietrich, there is that nostalgia she shares with drag queens for a period she never knew: the Berlin of the twenties and thirties, said to be "decadent" (cf. the film *Cabaret*). That also inspired David Bowie, and he was in *Just a Gigolo* (David Hemmings, 1979), which offered Dietrich her last role. She commands an army of gigolos (in *Girl 6*, Madonna plays a phone sex company boss).
110. Cf. Judy Garland (Liza Minnelli's mother) and her song *Born in a Trunk*.
111. Kubrick already (precisely) alluded to it in *A Clockwork Orange*.
112. Such details may seem trivial, but they are interesting. Remember that Carrie Fisher's father was lured away by Elizabeth Taylor; myths are also based on that sort of thing.
113. Fisher, 1991.
114. The cigarette is of course "on the other side."
115. In *Morocco*, Gary Cooper is the one who writes that.
116. Madonna has said: "It's funny, some people must mistake me for Marilyn Monroe. They think I have problems, but I'm fine" (Arnaud, 1995).
117. Thomson, 1994, p. 806; cf. also Wood, 1976, p. 113.
118. Deevoy, 1991.
119. Cf. picture book by Bert Stern, *The Last Sitting*, London, Orbis, 1982.
120. I am indebted for the symbols developed here to Jean Chevalier and Alain Gheerbrant.
121. She avoided that by dying young.
122. Cf. Mailer, 1973, p. 106.
123. Cf. Turim, 1990, pp. 101-111, Mulvey, 1996, p. 49, or Arbuthnot & Seneca, 1990, pp. 112-125.
124. van Leer, 1995, p. 169.
125. Please note that Russell wears a wig in that scene, like a drag queen, whereas Marilyn and Madonna have bleached their hair.
126. Album *Erotica*, 1992.
127. *This Is Not a Love Song* is the title of a track by Public Image Limited.
128. Marilyn also sings in *Diamonds Are a Girl's Best Friend* about Cartier and Tiffany's.
129. Program *Nightline* on ABC, December 3, 1990, host Forrest Sawyer.
130. Schwichtenberg, 1993, p. 129.
131. Cf. Smith, 1995, p. 208.
132. Cf. for instance Leigh, 1994, pp. 251-259.
133. Cf. Rettenmund, 1995, pp. 95–96. Cf. also biography of John F. Kennedy, Jr. by Wendy Leigh, who has Madonna say: "Can you imagine how far I've gone, Jackie O wants to know all about me!" (Leigh, 1994, p. 257).

134. Shewey, 1991.
135. Bollon, 1990.

FIVE—*America's Mirror*

1. Bernstein, 1995, p. 19.
2. Trittoléno, 1993.
3. Robertson, 1996, p. 117.
4. Anderson, 1989. I owe this to Pamela Robertson. The last two words, "even death," lead me to quote Jean Baudrillard: "The era of the James Deans, the Marilyn Monroes and the Kennedys, of those who died precisely because they had a mythic dimension [...] is over" (Baudrillard, 1981, pp. 42-43). The mythic postmodern dimension of Madonna doesn't entail death — not hers anyway (cf. chapter 4).
5. Song by Lou Reed, Velvet Underground days, 1967.
6. Tuleja, 1994, p. 9.
7. Combesque & Warde, 1996, p. 38.
8. Frey, 1995, *passim*; Pauwels, 1997, p. 49; Boulet-Gercourt (on Mailer), 1998; Lincoln & Gates, 1996, *passim*.
9. Cf. Rodman, 1996, p. 130.
10. Cf. Rada, 1996.
11. *Ibid.*, pp. 137-138. Cf. also Taub, Taylor, & Dunham, 1987, *passim*.
12. hooks, 1992, p. 163.
13. His skin is much lighter today than that of the majority of Caucasians.
14. Garber, 1993, pp. 126-127.
15. L. Schulze *et al.*, 1993, p. 31.
16. Wilson, 1996.
17. Baudrillard, 1986, p. 57.
18. Sischy, 1998.
19. Quoted by Andrew Blake (Blake, 1993, p. 18).
20. Program *Between the Sheets with Madonna* on MTV, 1991.
21. Video *Madonna Live, the Virgin Tour*, 1985.
22. Campbell & Keane, 1997, p. 24.
23. Interview of Mike Kovalik, 19 years old, *Icon* No. 28, June 1998.
24. Turner, 1993.
25. Cf. Ebert, 1991.
26. Cf. Walker & Sandler, 1994.
27. Cf. Madonna, 1992, p. 123.
28. Cf. Cieutat, 1996, p. 40. Cf. Frederick Jackson Turner and his famous lecture at the *American Historical Association* in Chicago in 1893, entitled *The Significance of the Frontier in American History*. As it happens, the paternity of the idea — if not the phrase — is generally attributed to (Michel-Guillaume-Saint-) Jean of Crèvecœur, who develops it in his *Letters from an American Farmer* (1782). The expression then made its "official" appearance in the title of the play by Israel Zangwill, *The Melting Pot* (1908 or 1909).
29. Combesque & Warde, 1996, pp. 105-107. Cf. also Pierre Mélandri,1997, p. 350 ; Lévy, 1997, p.10-11.

30. Notably Asian American.
31. Quoted by O'Connor, 1998.
32. Cf. Campbell & Kean, pp. 20-43.
33. Jackson, 1996. Cf. also Guccione, 1996.
34. Album *Erotica*, 1992.
35. Cf. Combesque & Warde, 1996, p. 136.
36. Cf. McLaren, 1997, p. 16.
37. Cf. Lévy, 1997, pp. 91-93.
38. hooks, 1992, p. 157.
39. *Ibid.*
40. hooks talks of "golden shower" at this point, an interpretation that is hard to credit (hooks, 1993, pp. 65-80).
41. hooks, 1993, pp. 65-80, and Crimp & Warner, 1993, pp. 93-110.
42. Album *I'm Breathless*, 1990.
43. Califia, 1993, pp. 169-184.
44. Queen, 1993, p. 139.
45. Champagne, 1993, p. 120.
46. Cf. Allen, 1994, p. 146.
47. Wiseman, 1993, p. 108.
48. Cf. Clint Eastwood's *Play Misty for Me* (1971), cf. what happened to the singer Selena.
49. Williams, 1999.
50. Whittell, 1996. Italics mine.
51. Example "The Observers and the Guardians," in *Voyager* of July-August 1996, or "He Will Watch Over You — at a Price" by Bill Frost & Angus Clarke, in *The Times*, 28/02/98.
52. Pamela Robertson notes that outside Madonna, "much of the public discourse on drag, vogueing, and transvestites, as well as other 'gay' topics, has since the 1970s taken place on the daytime talk shows hosted by Phil Donahue, Oprah Winfrey, and others" (Robertson, 1996, p. 121). She might have added Jerry Springer, Rikki Lake, Sally Jesse Raphael, etc. Cf. chapters 3 and 4.
53. Servat, February 24, 1993.
54. Cf. Gordon & Kay, 1993, p. 99.
55. Miller, 1990.
56. Album *Erotica*, 1992.
57. Quoted by Dylan Jones, 1996.
58. Quoted by Goodwin, 1996.
59. Cf. for example magazine *Jane*, March 1998.
60. Quoted by *Nice-Matin*, February 23, 1997, for example, or *L'Express* of February 27, 1997.
61. Penwarden, 1994.
62. Barber, 1993. Curiously, Barber seems to consider stiletto boots as pornographic.
63. Cf. Bandry, 1984; cf. also Bandry, 1997, p. 87; cf. also Couturier, 1996, pp. 147-224.
64. Lloyd, 1993, p. 46.
65. "Picasso, Elvis Presley, John Lennon, Madonna, Robert Mapplethorpe: during the past decade, each of these important artists has been denounced by holier-than-thou groups, from feminists to the Moral Majority" (Paglia, 1994, p. 130).

66. One of Madonna's great victories is the way her book was sold absolutely everywhere (including mall chain bookstores), under its Mylar packaging, that you had to cut or tear to open, like the cellophane wrappings of porn magazines. Then you could use it like a condom to protect the book and its solid but irritatingly prone-to-fall-apart metal cover.

67. Cf. Garber, 1993, p. 161.

68. Campbell & Kean, 1997, p. 28.

69. Funnily enough, Al Gore was compared to Madonna in 2000 as he campaigned, and *accused* of *reinventing* himself all the time.

70. Quoted by Lee Randall (Randall, 1992, p. 148).

71. Kerrison, 1991.

72. Cf. above, the matter of the possible arousal caused by the book.

73. Rosenzweig, 1994, p. 149.

74. Transcription mine.

75. Cf. Williams, 1993.

76. Rebecca Bell-Metereau notes that the scene when Madonna floats in the water, agonizing, is an allusion to that scene of *Fatal Attraction* when Glen Close soaks in a bath full of blood (Bell-Metereau, 1993, p. 264).

77. Thompson, 1991, p. 148.

78. Cf. Lenore, 1996, p. 42.

79. Wildmon, 1999, p. 183.

80. Greeley, 1989.

81. Album *True Blue*, 1986.

82. Album *Like a Prayer*, 1989.

83. Album *True Blue*, 1986.

84. Baker, 1994, *passim*.

85. Garber, 1993, *passim*.

86. Guccione, 1996, p. 54.

87. Album *Bedtime Stories*, 1994.

88. Jackson, October 12, 1996.

89. Album *True Blue*, 1986.

90. Cf. Katha Pollitt's article in *Glamour*, October 1992: "Why Do We Romanticize the Fetus?"

91. Bego, 1992, p. 166-167.

92. Interviewed by Haas, 1991.

93. Cf. *The Crack in the Cosmic Egg* by Joseph Chilton Pearce, New York, The Julian Press, 1971.

94. Cf. Romon, 1988, pp. 21-22.

95. Ariès, 1997, p. 77.

96. Elvis Presley died on Madonna's nineteenth birthday, so there are those who say that his spirit entered her, which accounts for her success (Cf. for example Martin, 1998).

97. Jackson, February 28, 1998.

98. *The Advocate* of March 17 and 31, 1998.

99. Cf. Walters, March 1998; Batey, 1998; Program *Madonna Rising*, April 1998.

100. Quoted by Sisti, 1998.

101. Henna designs by Sumita Batra.

102. Santucci & Renault, 1998.

103. Christophe & Corinne, 1998.
104. Eccleston, 1998.
105. Cf. Thévenin, 1998.
106. Toucas, 1998.
107. In particular *The Birth of Venus*. But the "new" Madonna also evokes Piero della Francesca, or the pre–Raphaelites.
108. Moody, 1998.
109. Boujnah, 1998.
110. Cf. Patterson, 1998, for example.
111. "Ideal to smoke a joint to," writes Isabelle Chelley (Chelley, 1998).
112. Beauvallet, 1998.
113. Roland, 1998.
114. Cf. Farley, 1998.
115. Cf. notably Patterson, 1998.
116. *Vanity Fair*, March 1998.
117. Cf. mocking comments in *Time*, February 9, 1998, Unsigned article. Cf. also readers' mail in *Vanity Fair*, May 1998.
118. We are apparently dealing with an amalgam of two ancient prayers (eighteenth century?), whose first line means something like, "I worship the guru's lotus feet."
119. There is a lot of water imagery in *Ray of Light*.
120. Davet, 1998.
121. Smith, 1998.
122. Madonna is obviously aware of the cult that toreros enjoy, and she is aware of the important similarities between bullfighting cults and pop cults, including hers. But of course, and that is one of the most important aspects of the video, the torero and the star are *both* coded as sexual spectacle.
123. *Music Planet*, Arte, 1997.
124. Cf. Randall, 1992, p. 192.
125. Quoted by Rosenzweig, 1994, p. 114.
126. Paglia, 1992, p. 11.
127. Conniff, 1991.
128. Quoted by Lee Randall (Randall, 1992, p. 192). Linda Leung established in *The Journal of Gender Studies* a judicious comparison between Madonna and Margaret Thatcher (Leung, 1997). Whatever you think of Thatcher, who was never a feminist, you cannot deny her impact on the cause of women, simply due to the fact that she was the first female British Prime Minister. Whatever you think of Thatcher and Madonna from a political and economic viewpoint, and even if you establish *rapprochements* with Ronald Reagan — Madonna's ascension coincides with Reaganomics— you cannot deny a basic truth: they have both reached unprecedented summits as twentieth-century women wielding power.
129. Metzstein, 1993, p. 97.
130. Miklitsch, 1998, p. 133.
131. Hill, 1992. Many texts by Steven Hill (West Coast Director of the Center for Voting and Democracy) are available on the Internet — they all criticize "Madonna feminism" or "MTV feminism" or even "Madonna MTV feminism." Like Susan Faludi, he believes in the backlash.
132. Strossen, 1995, p. 237.
133. Album *Like a Prayer*, 1989.

134. Paglia, 1994, p. 248.
135. Cf. Romon, 1988, pp. 122–145 and Behr, pp. 27–62 and pp. 239–268.
136. Brodribb, 1993, p. xxix, cf. also Brodribb, 1993, *passim*.
137. Some say "Foucauldian," some "Foucaultian," I favor "Foucaldian."
138. Cf. Jagose, 1996, p. 71.
139. Hennessy, 1994, p. 105.
140. Jeffreys, 1994, p. 460.
141. Jagose, 1996, p. 117.
142. Brodribb, 1993, p. 20. According to Susan J. Hekman, feminism finds its roots in modernism, which explains why so many feminists are anti-postmodern (cf. Hekman, 1990). Among those who have particularly decried the postmodern, two women should be mentioned in particular: Nancy Hartsock (cf. Hartsock, 1983) and Linda Alcoff (Alcoff, 1988). Some judge that feminism can use *some* aspects of the postmodern to its advantage, while remaining wary of its "dangers," it is the case of Elizabeth Meese (Meese, 1986), Mary Poovey (Poovey, 1988), or even Leslie Rabine (Rabine, 1988).
143. Quoted by Lee Randall (Randall, 1992, p. 192).
144. Tasker, 1998, p. 184.
145. Frug, 1992, p. 133.
146. Faith, 1997, p. 52.
147. *Ibid.*, p. 59.
148. Robertson, 1996, pp. 115–138.
149. *Ibid.*, p. 152.
150. Turner, 1993, *passim*.
151. Lewis, 1990, cf. especially p. 104.
152. James, 1990, *passim*.
153. Faludi, 1992, *passim*.
154. Harrison, 1991, *passim*.
155. Paglia, 1994, p. 93.
156. *Ibid.*, p. 247.
157. Quoted by bell hooks, 1993, p. 65.
158. Album *Erotica*, 1992.
159. Cf. Rohrer, 1991.
160. Madonna, 1992, p. 18.
161. Cf. Evans, 1995, pp. 125–140.
162. Cf. Hutcheon, 1989, p. 167.
163. Owens, 1993.
164. Tuttle, 1986, p. 256.
165. Quoted by Lee Randall (Randall, 1992, p. 192). Yet Betty Friedan founded NOW in 1966.
166. Cf. Rebichon & Lavoignat, 1993. Many *rapprochements* could be established between the two; though Dalida committed suicide and was depressed half her life.
167. Jackson, October 19, 1996.
168. Stacey, 1993, p. 34.
169. *Ibid.*, pp. 35-37.
170. *Ibid.*, p. 38.
171. Walters, 1995, p. 18.
172. *Ibid.*, p. 4. Other movies are sometimes compared in that vein to *Des-*

perately Seeking Susan or even to Madonna herself: *Alien* (Ridley Scott, 1979, plus sequels), *Terminator II: Judgment Day* (James Cameron, 1991), *Blue Steel* (Kathryn Bigelow, 1990) and *The Silence of the Lambs* (Jonathan Demme, 1991).

173. Cf. Vincendeau & Stacey 1993, *passim*, and Tasker, 1993, p. 92.

174. Journalist of *USA Today*, quoted by Rettenmund, 1995, p. 101.

175. Columbia promotional cassette / *Hollywood Avenue*, 1992.

176. And I'm not even talking about the race, class and age issues that complicate matters...

177. Walters, 1995, p. 1.

178. McClary, 1991, p. 166.

179. Cf. Randall, 1992, p. 5.

180. Cf. Guccione, 1996, p. 51. Henry Southworth Allen writes: "Guns are 'equalizers'. God created man and Samuel Colt made him equal, as the saying went" (Allen, 1994, p. 136).

181. At the end of the long version of *Open Your Heart* (1986), Madonna says, "Well, are you gonna go out with me or not? What's the matter? Scared of me or something?"

182. Cf. Baudrillard, 1986, p. 66; Somer Brodribb writes: "He considers himself outré and daring to criticize feminists but, as anyone who has taken a feminist position knows, misogynous attack is banal and regular" (Brodribb, 1993, p. 16).

183. Baudrillard, 1979, p. 19. Italics his.

184. hooks, 1993, p. 67.

185. Egerton, 1997.

186. Haas, 1991.

Conclusion

1. Picardie, 1995.

2. John Morrish in *The Daily Telegraph* studies the different senses of the word "icon" throughout the ages, notably when it is preceded by an adjective. Then he concludes: "The first person widely hailed as an 'icon', plain and simple, was Madonna" (Morrish, 1998).

3. Cf. Baudrillard, 1979, p. 133.

4. Debord, 1967, p. 47.

5. Rouillé, 1992.

6. Bourdieu, 1998, p. 63.

7. Annalee Newitz writes: "Madonna occupied a definite place in the post–Western Cultures curriculum at universities everywhere — she might be taught alongside Spike Lee and Amy Tan as one 'identity' among many in a multicultural America" (Newitz, 1993).

8. Newitz, 1993.

9. Cover of the *New Musical Express*, March 7, 1998. The preceding issue had proclaimed: "She's back! And it's OK to like her again!"

10. Patterson, 1998.

11. In *VSD*, October 3, 1996, and elsewhere.

12. Cf. The business section of the *Sunday Times*, April 26, 1998.

Madonna's Works: References

Selected Writings

Madonna (photographs by Steven Meisel), *Sex*, New York, Warner Books, 1992 (includes the single *Erotic*).
_____, "Preface," in Glenn O'Brien, *Madonna: The Girlie Show*, New York, Callaway / Boy Toy, 1994.
_____, "If I Were President," *George*, October 1995.
_____, "Private Diary," *Vanity Fair*, November 1996.
_____, "I'm Going to Miss You, Gianni," *Time*, July 28, 1997.
_____, "Introduction," in Alan Parker, *The Making of Evita*, New York, HarperCollins, 1996.

Selective Discography
(official albums)

Madonna (the first album) 1983 Lucky Star/Borderline/Burning Up/I Know It/Holiday/Think of Me/Physical Attraction/Everybody
Like a Virgin 1984–1985 Material Girl/Angel/Like a Virgin/Over and Over/Love Don't Live Here Anymore/Into the Groove/Dress You Up/Shoo-Bee-Doo/Pretender/Stay

True Blue 1986 Papa Don't Preach/Open Your Heart/White Heat/Live to
Tell/Where's the Party?/True Blue/La Isla Bonita/Jimmy Jimmy/Love Makes
the World Go Round

Who's That Girl? (soundtrack of the film) 1987 Who's That Girl?/Causing a Com-
motion/The Look of Love/Can't Stop

You Can Dance 1987 Spotlight/Holiday/Everybody/Physical Attraction/Over and
Over/Into the Groove/Where's the Party?

Like a Prayer 1989 Like a Prayer/Express Yourself/Love Song/Till Death Do Us
Part/Promise to Try/Cherish/Dear Jessie/Oh Father/Keep It Together/Pray for
Spanish Eyes/Act of Contrition

I'm Breathless (Songs from and Inspired by the film *Dick Tracy*) 1990 He's a
Man/Sooner or Later/Hanky Panky/I'm Going Bananas/Cry Baby/Something to
Remember/Back in Business/More/What Can You Lose/Now I'm Following
You/Vogue

The Immaculate Collection 1990 Holiday/Lucky Star/Borderline/Like a Virgin/
Material Girl/Crazy for You/Into the Groove/Live to Tell/Papa Don't Preach/
Open Your Heart/La Isla Bonita/Like a Prayer/Express Yourself/Cherish/
Vogue/Justify My Love/Rescue Me

Erotica 1992 Erotica/Fever/Bye Bye Baby/Deeper and Deeper/Where Life Begins/
Bad Girl/Waiting/Thief of Hearts/Words/Rain/Why It's So Hard/In This Life/
Did You Do It?/Secret Garden

Bedtime Stories 1994 Survival/Secret/I'd Rather Be Your Lover/Don't Stop/Inside
of Me/Human Nature/Forbidden Love/Love Tried to Welcome Me/Sanctu-
ary/Bedtime Story/Take a Bow

Something to Remember 1995 I Want You/I'll Remember/Take a Bow/You'll
See/Crazy for You/This Used to Be My Playground/Live to Tell/Love Don't Live
Here Anymore/Something to Remember/Forbidden Love/One More Chance/
Rain/Oh Father

Evita (soundtrack of the film) 1996 Various artists, including Madonna.

Ray of Light 1998 Drowned World/Swim/Ray of Light/Candy Perfume Girl/Skin/
Nothing Really Matters/Sky Fits Heaven/Shanti-Ashtangi/Frozen/The Power
of Good-Bye/To Have and Not to Hold/Little Star/Mer Girl

Music 2000 Music/Impressive Instant/Runaway Lover/I Deserve It/Amazing/
Nobody's Perfect/Don't Tell Me/What It Feels Like for a Girl/Paradise (Not for
Me)/Gone

GH2 2001 Deeper and Deeper/Erotica/Human Nature/Secret/Don't Cry for Me
Argentina/Bedtime Story/The Power of Goodbye/Beautiful Stranger/Frozen/
Take a Bow/Ray of Light/Don't Tell Me/What It Feels Like for a Girl/Drowned
World/Music

Filmography

A Certain Sacrifice, by Stephen Jon Lewicki, 1980.
Vision Quest (Crazy For You), by Harold Becker, 1983.
Desperately Seeking Susan, by Susan Seidelman, 1985.
Shanghai Surprise, by Jim Goddard, 1986.
Who's That Girl?, by James Foley, 1987.

Bloodhounds of Broadway, by Howard Brookner, 1988.
Dick Tracy, by Warren Beatty, 1990.
Truth or Dare (In Bed with Madonna), by Alek Keshishian, 1991.
A League of Their Own, by Penny Marshall, 1992.
Shadows and Fog, by Woody Allen, 1992.
Body of Evidence, by Uli Edel, 1993.
Dangerous Game, by Abel Ferarra, 1993.
Four Rooms, by Allison Anders, Alexandre Rockwell, Robert Rodriguez & Quentin
  Tarantino, 1995.
Blue in the Face, by Paul Auster & Wayne Wang, 1995.
Girl 6, by Spike Lee, 1996.
Evita, by Alan Parker, 1996.
The Next Best Thing, by John Schlesinger, 2000.
Swept Away, by Guy Ritchie, 2002.

Theater

Goose and Tom-Tom, by David Rabe. Lincoln Center Theater Workshop, 1987.
Speed-the-Plow, by David Mamet, Royale Theater, 1988.
Up for Grabs, by David Williamson, 2002.

Selective Videography

Madonna Live, the Virgin Tour, Warner, 1985.
Ciao Italia: Madonna Live from Italy, Warner, 1988.
The Blonde Ambition Tour (Barcelona), Warner, 1990.
The Immaculate Collection, Warner, 1990.
Justify My Love and *Vogue, MTV Video Music Awards*, Warner, 1990.
La Véritable histoire de Madonna, UGC, 1991.
Rock the Vote video, MTV, 1992.
Madonna Laid Bare, Labyrinth, 1993.
The Girlie Show / Live Down Under (Sydney), Warner, 1993.
Madonna The Unauthorized Biography/We Dare to Tell the Truth, MIA, 1993.
Madonna Vie Privée, UGC, 1993.
Madonna: 93:99, Warner, 1999.
Drowned World Tour 2001, Warner, 2001.

Important TV Programs

Saturday Night Live, NBC, November 1985.
Late Night with David Letterman, NBC, July 1988.
Nightline, ABC, December 1990.
Oscars 1991, Canal +, March 1991.
Between the Sheets with Madonna, MTV, May 1991.
Ciné Stars (Michel Drucker), France 2, September 1991.

7 sur 7 (Anne Sinclair), TF1, October 1992.
Week-end with Madonna, MTV, January 1993.
Spécial Coucou (Christophe Dechavanne), TF1, February 1993.
Journal du Cinéma (Isabelle Giordano), Canal +, March 1993.
Late Night with David Letterman, CBS, March 1994.
Des amours de fans / Les documents de Zone Interdite (Patrick de Carolis), M6, June 1997.
Music Planet (Thomas Job), Arte, May 1997.
Week-end with Madonna, MTV, March 1998.

Bibliography

Books and Collected Essays About Madonna

Abitan, Guy and Danièle, *Lady Madonna*, Paris, Corlet and Encre, 1986.

_____ and _____, *Magique Madonna*, Paris, Edition No. 1, 1987.

Andermahr, Sonya, "A Queer Love Affair? Madonna and Lesbian and Gay Culture," in Diane Hamer and Belinda Budge (ed.), *The Good, the Bad, and the Gorgeous: Popular Culture's Romance with Lesbianism*, London, Pandora, 1994.

Andersen, Christopher, *Madonna Unauthorized*, New York, Simon and Schuster, 1991.

Baudrillard, Jean, *Madonna Deconnection*, in Michel Dion (ed.), *Madonna: érotisme et pouvoir*, Paris, Editions Kimé, 1994.

Bego, Mark, *Madonna!*, New York, Pinnacle, 1985.

_____, *Madonna : Blonde Ambition*, London, Plexus, 1992.

Bianciotto, Jordi, *Madonna*, Paris, La Máscara, 1999.

Black, Susan, *Madonna: Live!*, New York, Omnibus Press, 1987.

Blake, Andrew, "Madonna the Musician," in Fran Lloyd (ed.), *Deconstructing Madonna*, London, B.T. Batsford Ltd. 1993.

Bordo, Susan, "Material Girl: The Effacements of Postmodern Culture," in Cathy Schwichtenberg (ed.), *The Madonna Connection: Representational Politics, Subcultural Identities and Cultural Theory*, Boulder, Westview Press, 1993.

Bright, Susie, "A Pornographic Girl," in Lisa Frank and Paul Smith (ed.), *Madonnarama: Essays on Sex and Popular Culture*, Pittsburgh/San Francisco, Cleis Press, 1993.

Cahill, Marie, *Madonna*, London, Bison Books, 1991.

Califia, Pat, "*Sex* and Madonna, Or, What Did You Expect from a Girl Who Doesn't Put Out on the First Five Dates?," in Lisa Frank and Paul Smith (ed.), *Madonnarama: Essays on Sex and Popular Culture*, Pittsburgh/San Francisco, Cleis Press, 1993.

Celsi, Theresa, *Madonna*, New York, Andrews and McMeel, 1993.

Champagne, John, "Stabat Madonna," in Lisa Frank and Paul Smith (ed.), *Madonnarama: Essays on Sex and Popular Culture*, Pittsburgh/San Francisco, Cleis Press, 1993.

Charest, Danielle, "Madonna ou les boucles," in Michel Dion (ed.), *Madonna: érotisme et pouvoir*, Paris, Editions Kimé, 1994.

Che, Cathay, "Wannabe," in Lisa Frank and Paul Smith (ed.), *Madonnarama: Essays on Sex and Popular Culture*, Pittsburgh/San Francisco, Cleis Press, 1993.

Christgau, Robert, "Madonnathinking Madonnabout Madonnamusic," in Adam Sexton (ed.), *Desperately Seeking Madonna: In Search of the Meaning of the World's Most Famous Woman*, New York, Delta, 1993.

Cipriani-Crauste, Marie, "Les Influences du hard rock sur l'art de Madonna," in Michel Dion (ed.), *Madonna: érotisme et pouvoir*, Paris, Editions Kimé, 1994.

Claro, Nicole, Claro, Bruce, and Gibbons, Leeza, *Madonna* (Pop Culture Legends), Chelsea House Publishers, 1994.

Collin, Françoise, "La Madonna Connection," in Michel Dion (ed.), *Madonna: érotisme et pouvoir*, Paris, Editions Kimé, 1994.

Coward, Rosalind, "Madonna et Marilyn, les sex-symbols ont-ils une date limite de vente?," in Ginette Vincendeau and Bérénice Reynaud (ed.), *20 ans de théories féministes sur le cinéma*, *CinémAction*, No. 67 (1993).

Crimp, Douglas, and Warner, Michael, "No Sex in 'Sex,'" in Lisa Frank and Paul Smith (ed.), *Madonnarama: Essays on Sex and Popular Culture*, Pittsburgh/San Francisco, Cleis Press, 1993.

Curry, Ramona, "Madonna from Marilyn to Marlene — Pastiche and/or Parody," *Journal of Film and Video*, No. 42 (Summer 1990).

Dion, Michel, "Madonna dans la presse française," in Michel Dion (ed.), *Madonna: érotisme et pouvoir*, Paris, Editions Kimé, 1994.

_____, "Madonna et la culture rock," in Dion, Michel (ed.), *Madonna: érotisme et pouvoir*, Paris, Editions Kimé, 1994.

Faith, Karlene, *Madonna, Bawdy and Soul*, Toronto, University of Toronto Press, 1997.

Fleiss, Mike, *Madonna Speaks*, New York, Tribune, 1993.

Frank, Lisa, and Smith, Paul, "How to Use Your New Madonna," in Lisa Frank and Paul Smith (ed.), *Madonnarama: Essays on Sex and Popular Culture*, Pittsburgh/San Francisco, Cleis Press, 1993.

Frith, Simon, "The Sound of *Erotica*: Pain, Power, and Pop," in Lisa Frank and Paul Smith (ed.), *Madonnarama: Essays on Sex and Popular Culture*, Pittsburgh/San Francisco, Cleis Press, 1993.

Greenberg, Keith Elliot, *Madonna* (Entertainment World), New York, Lerner Publications Company, 1986.

Gulick, Rebecca, *Madonna: Portrait of a Material Girl*, New York, Courage Books, 1993.

Haas, Christine, "Interview exclusive Madonna," *Première*, June 1991.

Harris, Thomas Allen, "Phallic Momma Sell My Pussy Make a Dollar," in Lisa

Frank and Paul Smith (ed.), *Madonnarama: Essays on Sex and Popular Culture*, Pittsburgh/San Francisco, Cleis Press, 1993.

Henderson, Lisa, "Justify Our Love: Madonna and the Politics of Queer Sex," in Cathy Schwichtenberg (ed.), *The Madonna Connection:Representational Politics, Subcultural Identities and Cultural Theory*, Boulder, Westview Press, 1993.

Hooks, Bell, "Is Paris Burning?," in bell hooks, *Black Looks: Race and Representation*. Boston, South End Press, 1992.

_____, "Madonna: Plantation Mistress or Soul Sister?," in bell hooks, *Black Looks: Race and Representation*. Boston, South End Press, 1992.

_____, "Power to the Pussy: We Don't Wannabe Dicks in Drag," in Lisa Frank and Paul Smith (ed.), *Madonnarama: Essays on Sex and Popular Culture*, Pittsburgh/San Francisco, Cleis Press, 1993.

Izod, John, "Madonna as Trickster," in Fran Lloyd (ed.), *Deconstructing Madonna*, London, B.T. Batsford Ltd. 1993.

James, David. *Madonna: Her Complete Story, an Unauthorized Biography*, New York, Publications International, 1991.

Kaplan, E. Ann, "Madonna Politics: Perversion, Repression, or Subversion? Or Masks and/as Master-y," in Cathy Schwichtenberg (ed.), *The Madonna Connection: Representational Politics, Subcultural Identities and Cultural Theory*, Boulder, Westview Press, 1993.

King, Norman, *Madonna: The Book*, New York, William Morrow, 1991.

Lagerfeld, Karl, and Dreier, Daniel, *Madonna Superstar* (Schirmer's Visual Library), New York, W.W. Norton, 1991.

Lenore, Victor, *Madonna*, Chartres, La Máscara, 1996.

Lentz, Kristen Marthe, "Chameleon, Vampire, Rich Slut," in Lisa Frank and Paul Smith (ed.), *Madonnarama: Essays on Sex and Popular Culture*, Pittsburgh/San Francisco, Cleis Press, 1993.

Leung, Linda, "The Making of Matriarchy: A Comparison of Madonna and Margaret Thatcher," *Journal of Gender Studies*, Vol. 6, No. 1 (March 1997).

Lloyd, Fran, "The Changing Images of Madonna," in Fran Lloyd (ed.), *Deconstructing Madonna*, London, B.T. Batsford Ltd., 1993.

_____, "Introduction," in Fran Lloyd (ed.), *Deconstructing Madonna*, London, B.T. Batsford Ltd., 1993.

Mandziuk, Roseann, "Feminist Politics and Postmodern Seductions: Madonna and the Struggle for Political Articulation," in Cathy Schwichtenberg (ed.), *The Madonna Connection: Representational Politics, Subcultural Identities and Cultural Theory*, Boulder, Westview Press, 1993.

Marsh, Dave, "Girls Can't Do What the Guys Do: Madonna's Physical Attraction," in *The First Rock and Roll Confidential Report*, New York, Pantheon, 1985.

Matthews, Gordon, *Madonna*, New York, Simon and Schuster, 1985.

Matthew-Walker, Robert, *Madonna, The Biography*, London, Pan Books (revised), 1991.

Matthieu, Nicole-Claude, "Dérive du genre/stabilité des sexes," in Michel Dion (ed.), *Madonna: érotisme et pouvoir*, Paris, Editions Kimé, 1994.

McKenzie, Michael, *Madonna: Lucky Star*, New York, Olympic Marketing Corporation, 1985.

_____, *Madonna: Her Story*, New York, Music Sales Corp., 1991.

McLaren, Lee, *Madonna The Lady*, Paris, Les Editions Contemporaines, 1997.

Metz, Allan, and Benson, Carol (ed.), *The Madonna Companion: Two Decades of Commentary*, New York, Schirmer, 1999.

Metzstein, Margery, "SEX: Signed, Sealed, Delivered," in Fran Lloyd (ed.), *Deconstructing Madonna*, London, B.T. Batsford Ltd. 1993.

Morgan, Richard, "In Being a Good Corporate Citizen," in Adam Sexton (ed.), *Desperately Seeking Madonna: In Search of the Meaning of the World's Most Famous Woman*, New York, Delta, 1993.

Morton, Andrew, *Madonna*, London, Michael O'Mara, 2001.

Morton, Melanie, "Don't Go for Second Sex, Baby!" in Cathy Schwichtenberg (ed.), *The Madonna Connection: Representational Politics, Subcultural Identities and Cultural Theory*, Boulder, Westview Press, 1993.

Musto, Michael, "Immaculate Connection," in Corey K. Creekmur and Alexander Doty (ed.), *Out in Culture: Gay, Lesbian, and Queer Essays on Popular Culture*, London, Cassel, 1995.

Nakayama, Thomas K., "Race, Culture Populaire et Madonna," in Michel Dion (ed.), *Madonna: érotisme et pouvoir*, Paris, Editions Kimé, 1994.

Nash, Bruce, Zullo, Allan and Fleiss, Mike, *Madonna Speaks*, New York, Expression Press, 1993.

O'Brien, Glenn, *Madonna: The Girlie Show*, New York, Callaway / Boy Toy, 1994.

O'Dair, Barbara, and The Editors of Rolling Stones (ed.), *Madonna: The Ultimate Compendium of Interviews, Articles, Facts and Opinions from the Files of Rolling Stone*, New York, Hyperion, 1997.

O'Hagan, Andrew, "Blonde Ambition and the American Way," in Fran Lloyd (ed.), *Deconstructing Madonna*, London, B.T. Batsford Ltd., 1993.

Patton, Cindy, "Embodying Subaltern Memory: Kinesthesia and the Problematics of Gender and Race," in Cathy Schwichtenberg (ed.), *The Madonna Connection: Representational Politics, Subcultural Identities and Cultural Theory*, Boulder, Westview Press, 1993.

Peñaloza, Lisa N., and Nakayama, Thomas K., "Madonna T/Races: Music Videos Through the Prism of Color," in Cathy Schwichtenberg (ed.), *The Madonna Connection: Representational Politics, Subcultural Identities and Cultural Theory*, Boulder, Westview Press, 1993.

Portnoy, Ethel, *Madonna's appel: Over vrouwen en de media*, Amsterdam, Meulenhof, 1992.

Pribram, E. Deirdre, "Seduction, Control, and the Search for Authenticity: Madonna's *Truth or Dare*" in Cathy Schwichtenberg (ed.), *The Madonna Connection: Representational Politics, Subcultural Identities and Cultural Theory*, Boulder, Westview Press, 1993.

Queen, Carol A., "Talking About 'Sex'", in Lisa Frank and Paul Smith (ed.), *Madonnarama: Essays on Sex and Popular Culture*, Pittsburgh/San Francisco, Cleis Press, 1993.

Rajon, Florence, *Madonna de A à Z*, Les Guides MusicBooks, Paris, L'Etudiant, 2001.

Randall, Lee, *The Madonna Scrapbook*, New York, Citadel Press, 1992.

Rettenmund, Matthew, *Encyclopedia Madonnica*, New York, St. Martin's Press, 1995.

Reynolds, Richard, "I always get my Man: Madonna and Dick Tracy," in Fran Lloyd (ed.), *Deconstructing Madonna*, London, B.T. Batsford Ltd., 1993.

Riley, Tim, *Madonna Illustrated*, New York, Hyperion, 1992.

Rooksby, Rikky, *The Complete Guide to the Music of Madonna*, New York, Omnibus Press, 1998.

Rosenzweig, Ilene, *The I Hate Madonna Handbook*, New York, St. Martin's Press, 1994.

Ross, Andrew, "This Bridge Called My Pussy," in Lisa Frank and Paul Smith (ed.), *Madonnarama: Essays on Sex and Popular Culture*, Pittsburgh/San Francisco, Cleis Press, 1993.

Rouchon, Catherine and Michel, *Madonna Séduction*, Dormelles, Editions M. Rouchon, 1994.

St. Michael, Mick, *Madonna: In Her Own Words*, New York, Omnibus Press, 1990.

Schulze, Laurie, White, Anne Barton, and Brown, Jane D., "A Sacred Monster in Her Prime: Audience Construction of Madonna as Low-Other," in Cathy Schwichtenberg (ed.), *The Madonna Connection:Representational Politics, Subcultural Identities and Cultural Theory*, Boulder, Westview Press, 1993.

Schwartz, Deb, "Madonna and Sandra: Like We Care," in Adam Sexton (ed.), *Desperately Seeking Madonna: In Search of the Meaning of the World's Most Famous Woman*, New York, Delta, 1993.

Schwichtenberg, Cathy, "Connections, Intersections," in Cathy Schwichtenberg (ed.), *The Madonna Connection:Representational Politics, Subcultural Identities and Cultural Theory*, Boulder, Westview Press, 1993.

_____, "Madonna's Postmodern Feminism: Bringing the Margins to the Center," in Cathy Schwichtenberg (ed.), *The Madonna Connection:Representational Politics, Subcultural Identities and Cultural Theory*, Boulder, Westview Press, 1993.

_____, "Le pouvoir féminin, les travestis et Madonna," in Michel Dion (ed.), *Madonna: érotisme et pouvoir*, Paris, Editions Kimé, 1994.

Scott, Ronald B., "Images of Race and Religion in Madonna's Video 'Like a Prayer': Prayer and Praise," in Cathy Schwichtenberg (ed.), *The Madonna Connection:Representational Politics, Subcultural Identities and Cultural Theory*, Boulder, Westview Press, 1993.

Seigworth, Greg, "The Distance Between Me and You: Madonna and Celestial Navigation (or You Can Be My 'Lucky Star')," in Cathy Schwichtenberg (ed.), *The Madonna Connection:Representational Politics, Subcultural Identities and Cultural Theory*, Boulder, Westview Press, 1993.

Shangai, Eric, *Madonna*, Paris, Albin Michel, 1989.

Shreiber, Martin Hugo Maximilian, *Madonna Nudes 1979*, Köln, Taschen, 1992.

Skeggs, Beverley, "A Good Time for Women Only," in Fran Lloyd (ed.), *Deconstructing Madonna*, London, B.T. Batsford Ltd., 1993.

Syn, Cardinal, *The Sexiest Jokes about Madonna*, New York, Shapolsky, 1994.

Taraborrelli, J. Randy, *Madonna: An Intimate Biography*, London: Sidgwick and Jackson, 2001.

Tetzlaff, David, "Metatextual Girl: ~ patriarchy ~ postmodernism ~ power ~ money ~ Madonna," in Cathy Schwichtenberg (ed.), *The Madonna Connection:Representational Politics, Subcultural Identities and Cultural Theory*, Boulder, Westview Press, 1993.

Thompson, Douglas, *Madonna: Queen of the World*, London, Blake Publishing Ltd., 2001.

_____, *Madonna Revealed*, London, Warner Books, 1991.

Tredez, Florence, *Madonna*, Paris, Librio, 2000.

Turner, Kay (ed.), *I Dream of Madonna, Women's Dreams of the Goddess of Pop*, San Francisco, HarperCollins, 1993.
Victor, Barbara, *Goddess: Inside Madonna*, New York, Cliff Street Books, 2001.
Voller, Debbi, *Madonna: The New Illustrated Biography*, New York, Beekman, 1990.
_____, *Madonna: The Style Book*, New York, Omnibus, 1992.
Weaver, C. Kay, "Telling Tales: Madonna, *Sex* and the British Press," in Fran Lloyd (ed.), *Deconstructing Madonna*, London, B.T. Batsford Ltd., 1993.
West, Joey, *The I Hate Madonna Jokebook*, New York, Pinnacle, 1993.
Wilkinson, Peter, "Madonna's Favorite Filmmaker is One Smart Alek," in Barbara O'Dair, and The Editors of Rolling Stones (ed.), *Madonna: The Ultimate Compendium of Interviews, Articles, Facts and Opinions from the Files of Rolling Stone*, New York, Hyperion, 1997.
Wiseman, Sue, "Rights and Permission: SEX, the model and the star," in Fran Lloyd (ed.), *Deconstructing Madonna*, London, B.T. Batsford Ltd., 1993.

Books and Essays That Mention Madonna in a Significant Way

Ahmed, Akbar S., *Postmodernism and Islam: Predicament and Promise*, London and New York, Routledge, 1992.
Allen, Henry Southworth, *Going Too Far Enough: American Culture at Century's End*, Washington, Smithsonian Institution Press, 1994.
Ang, Ien, *Desperately Seeking the Audience*, London and New York Routledge, 1991.
_____, *Watching Dallas: Soap Opera and the Melodramatic Imagination*, London, Methuen, 1985.
Bach, Steven, *Marlene Dietrich: Life and Legend*, London, HarperCollins, 1992.
Baker, Roger, *Drag: A History of Female Impersonation in the Performing Arts*, London, Cassell, 1994 (revised).
Bayly, Jaime, *No se lo digas a nadie*, Barcelona, Seix Barral, 1994.
Bell-Metereau, Rebecca, *Hollywood Androgyny*, New York, Columbia University Press, 1993 (second edition).
Bernard, Jami, *Quentin Tarantino, the Man and His Movies*, New York, HarperCollins, 1995.
Bernikow, Louise, *The American Woman's Almanac: An Inspiring and Irreverent Women's History*, New York, Berkley Books, 1997.
Bianciotto, Jordi, *Sexe et Rock 'n' Roll*, Paris, La Mascara, 2000.
Bockris, Victor, *The Life of Death of Andy Warhol*, New York, Bantam Books, 1989.
Bonifer, Mike, *Dick Tracy: The Making of the Movie*, London, Titan Books, 1990.
Bornstein, Kate, *My Gender Workbook*, London and New York, Routledge, 1998.
Boy George, *Take It Like a Man*, London, Sidgwick and Jackson, 1995.
Bret, David, *Marlene Dietrich — My Friend*, London, Robson, 1993.
Bright, Susie, *Sexual State of the Union*, New York, Simon and Schuster, 1997.
_____, *Susie Bright's Sexwise: America's favorite X-rated intellectual does Dan Quayle, Catharine MacKinnon, Stephen King, Camille Paglia, Nicholson Baker, Madonna, the Black Panthers and the GOP...*, Pittsburgh, Cleis Press, 1995.

Browning, Frank, *The Culture of Desire*, New York, Vintage Books, 1993.

Buchbinder, David, *Performance Anxieties: Re-producing Masculinity*, St. Leonards, Allen and Unwin, 1998.

Butler, Judith, *Bodies That Matter: On the Discursive Limits of "Sex"*, London and New York, Routledge, 1993.

Califia, Pat, *Public Sex: The Culture of Radical Sex*, Pittsburghh, Cleis Press, 1994.

Caron-Lowins, Evelyne, *Hollywood Falbalas*, Paris, Pierre Bordas et Fils, 1995.

Charyn, Jerome, *Metropolis: New York as Myth, Marketplace and Magical Land*, London, Sphere Books Ltd, 1988.

Cleto, Fabio (ed.), *Camp: Queer Aesthetics and the Performing Subject, A Reader*, Edinburgh, Edinburgh University Press, 1999.

Cohan, Steven, "Feminizing the Song-and-Dance Man," in Steven Cohan and Ina Rae Hark (ed.), *Screening the Male: Exploring Masculinities in Hollywood Cinema*, London and New York, Routledge, 1993.

Collins, Joan, *Second Act*, London, Boxtree Limited, 1996.

Conniff, Ruth, "Politics in a Post-Feminist Age," *The Progressive*, July 1991.

Cubbit, S., *Timeshift: On Video Culture*, London, Comedia Press, 1991.

Dean, John, *American Popular Culture*, Nancy, Presses Universitaires by Nancy, 1992.

Docker, John, *Postmodernism and Popular Culture: A Cultural History*, Cambridge, Cambridge University Press, 1994.

Doty, Alexander, "There's Something Queer Here," in Corey K. Creekmur and Alexander Doty (ed), *Out in Culture: Gay, Lesbian, and Queer Essays on Popular Culture*, London, Cassel, 1995.

Driver, Jim (ed.), *The Mammoth Book of Sex, Drugs and Rock 'n' Roll*, London, Robinson, 2001.

Drukman, Steven, "The Gay Gaze, or Why I Want My MTV," in Paul Burston and Colin Richardson (ed.), *A Queer Romance: Lesbians, Gay Men and Popular Culture*, London and New York, Routledge, 1995.

Dyer, Richard, *Heavenly Bodies: Film Stars and Society*, New York, St. Martin's Press, 1987.

_____, *White*, New York and London, Routledge, 1997.

Ekins, Richard, *Male Femaling*, London and New York, Routledge, 1997.

Eliot, Marc, *Rockonomics: The Money Behind the Music*, New York, Franklin Watts, 1989.

Ellis, Bret Easton, *American Psycho*, New York, Vintage Books, 1991.

Evans, Caroline, and Gamman, Lorraine, "The Gaze Revisited, or Reviewing Queer Viewing," in Paul Burston and Colin Richardson (ed.), *A Queer Romance: Lesbians, Gay Men and Popular Culture*, London and New York, Routledge, 1995.

Faithfull, Marianne, *Faithfull*, London, Michael Joseph, 1994.

Faludi, Suzanne, *Backlash, The Undeclared War Against American Women*, New York, Anchor Books, 1992.

Fiske, John, *Reading the Popular*, Boston, Unwin Hyman, 1989.

_____, *Understanding Popular Culture*, London and New York, Routledge, 1989.

Franquet, Lidia, "Quentin Tarantino, juste du sang dans les yeux," *Cinéma: une approche jungienne, Cahiers Jungiens de Psychanalyse*, No. 83 (1995).

Frug, Mary Joe, *Postmodern Legal Feminism*, London and New York, Routledge, 1992.

Gaar, Gillian G., *She's a Rebel: The History of Women in Rock and Roll*, Seattle, Seal, 1992.

Gamman, Lorraine, and Marshment, Margaret (ed.), *The Female Gaze: Women as Viewers of Popular Culture*, London, The Women's Press, 1988.

Garber, Marjorie, *Vested Interests, Cross-dressing and Cultural Anxiety*, New York, HarperPerennial, 1993.

_____, *Vice Versa: Bisexuality and the Eroticism of Everyday Life*, London, Penguin, 1997.

Gledhill, Christine (ed.), *Stardom: Industry of Desire*, London and New York, Routledge, 1991.

Goodson, Teri, "A Prostitute Joins NOW," in Jill Nagle (ed.), *Whores and Other Feminists*, London and New York, Routledge, 1997.

Goodwin, Andrew, *Dancing in the Distraction Factory: Music Television and Popular Culture*, Minneapolis, University of Minnesota Press, 1992.

Gordon, Bette, and Kay, Karyn, "Look Back / Talk Back," in Pamela Church Gibson and Rome Gibson (ed.), *Dirty Looks / Women, Pornography, Power*, London, BFI, 1993.

Guilbert, Georges-Claude, "Camille Paglia : féministe ennemie des féministes," *Cercles*, Vol. I, No. 4 (January 2002).

_____, "Chouette planète, on la prend: Tim Burton et la technologie," in Francis Bordat, John Dean, Robert Conrath, Divina Frau-Meigs (ed.), *Médias et technologie : l'exemple des Etats-Unis*, Paris, Ellipses, 2001.

_____, "Justifications d'un genre à part: l'autobiographie d'acteur," *Arobase*, Vol. II, No. 1 (October 1997).

_____, "Mutant Language: The X-Men, Postmodern Super-Heroes," *Arobase*, Vol. I, No. 2 (March 1997).

_____, "Le Voguing, un espace de résistance new-yorkais," in Antoine Capet, Philippe Romanski, Aïssatou Sy-Wonyu (ed.), *Etats de New York*, Publications de l'Université de Rouen, No. 273, 2000.

Hamilton, Marybeth, *When I'm Bad, I'm Better*, New York, HarperCollins, 1995.

Harris, Daniel, "Make My Rainy Day," *The Nation*, January 8, 1992.

Higgins, Patrick (ed.), *A Queer Reader*, London, Fourth Estate, 1993.

Hoesterey, Ingeborg, *Pastiche: Cultural Memory in Art, Film, Literature*, Bloomington and Indianapolis, Indiana University Press, 2001.

Holmlund, Chris, "Masculinity as Multiple Masquerade," in Steven Cohan and Ina Rae Hark (ed.), *Screening the Male: Exploring Masculinities in Hollywood Cinema*, London and New York, Routledge, 1993.

Hooks, Bell, *Feminist Theory: From Margin to Center*, Boston, South End Press, 1984.

_____, *Outlaw Cultures: Resisting Representations*, New York, Routledge, 1994.

_____, *Talking Back: Thinking Feminist, Thinking Black*, Boston, South End Press, 1989.

_____, *Yearning: Race, Gender, and Cultural Politics*, Boston, South End Press, 1990.

Indiana, Gary, *Horse Crazy*, London, Paladin, 1990.

Jagose, Annamarie, *Queer Theory*, Melbourne, Melbourne University Press, 1996.

Kaplan, E. Ann, *Postmodernism and Its Discontents: Theories, Practices*, New York, Verso, 1989.

_____ (ed.), *Rocking Around the Clock: Music Television, Post-modernism and Consumer Culture*, London and New York, Methuen, 1987.

Kellner, Douglas, *Media Culture: Cultural Studies, Identity, and Politics between the Modern and the Postmodern*, New York, Routledge, 1995.

Kitsis, Krystina, "Bound by Our Image," *Fashion, Fetish, Fantasies*, No. 23 (1994).

Kureishi, Hanif, *The Black Album*, London, Faber and Faber, 1995.

LaBruce, Bruce, "The Wild, Wild World of Fanzines: Notes From a Reluctant Pornographer," in Paul Burston and Colin Richardson (ed.), *A Queer Romance: Lesbians, Gay Men and Popular Culture*, London and New York, Routledge, 1995.

Leigh, Wendy, *Prince Charming: The John F. Kennedy, Jr. Story*, New York, Signet, 1994.

Lelait, David, *Gay Culture*, Paris, Anne Carrière, 1998.

Leonard, Linda Schierse, *Meeting the Madwoman*, New York, Bantam Books, 1993.

Linfield, Jordan L., and Krevisky, Joseph, *Words of Love: Romantic Quotations from Plato to Madonna*, New York, Random House, 1997.

Lewis, Lisa, *Gender Politics and MTV: Voicing the Differences*, Philadelphia, Temple University Press, 1990.

MacCabe, Colin (ed.), *High Theory/Low Culture: Analyzing Popular Television and Film*, New York, St. Martin's Press, 1986.

Marcus, Greil, *In the Fascist Bathroom: Punk in Pop Music, 1977-1992*, Cambridge, Harvard University Press, 1993.

Martin, W.K., *Marlene Dietrich*, New York, Chelsea House, 1995.

Mayne, Judith, *The Woman and the Keyhole: Feminism and Women's Cinema*, Bloomington, Indiana University Press, 1990.

McClary, Susan, *Feminine Endings: Music, Gender, and Sexuality*, Minneapolis, University of Minnesota Press, 1991.

McClintock, Anne, "Maid to order / Commercial SM and Gender Power," in Pamela Church Gibson and Rome Gibson (ed.), *Dirty Looks / Women, Pornography, Power*, London, BFI, 1993.

MacCowan, Lyndall, "Organizing in the Massage Parlor: An Interview With Denise Turner," in Jill Nagle (ed.), *Whores and Other Feminists*, London and New York, Routledge, 1997.

McRobbie, Angela, *Feminism and Youth Culture, From Jackie to Just Seventeen*, London, Macmillan, 1991.

_____, *Postmodernism and Popular Culture*, London and New York, Routledge, 1994.

Miklitsch, Robert, *From Hegel to Madonna: Towards a General Economy of Commodity Fetishism* (SUNY Series in Postmodern Culture), Albany, State University of New York Press, 1998.

Molina Foix, Vicente, *La mujer sin cabeza*, Barcelona: Plaza and Janes, 1997.

Mulvey, Laura, *Fetishism and Curiosity*, Bloomington, Indiana University Press / London, BFI, 1996.

Nataf, Z. Isiling, "Black Lesbian Spectatorship and Pleasure in Popular Cinema," in Paul Burston and Colin Richardson (ed.), *A Queer Romance: Lesbians, Gay Men and Popular Culture*, London and New York, Routledge, 1995.

Noon, Jeff, *Vurt*, London, Ringpull, 1993.

Paglia, Camille, *Sex, Art, and American Culture*, New York, Vintage Books, 1992.

_____, *Sexual Personae: Art and Decadence from Nefertiti to Emily Dickinson*, London and New Haven, Yale University Press, 1990.

_____, *Vamps and Tramps*, New York, Vintage Books, 1994.

Parker, Alan, *The Making of Evita*, New York, HarperCollins, 1996.

Phelps, Peter, *Sex Without Madonna*, Sydney, Pan Macmillan Publishers, 1994.

Phillips, Julia, *You'll Never Eat Lunch in This Town Again*, New York, Signet, 1991.

Phoca, Sophia, and Wright, Rebecca, *Introducing Postfeminism*, New York, Totem Books, 1999.

Rettenmund, Matthew, *Boy Culture*, New York, St. Martin's Griffin, 1995.

_____, *Totally Awesome 80s*, New York, St. Martin's Griffin, 1996.

Ritzer, George, *The McDonaldization Thesis*, London, Sage, 1998.

Robertson, Pamela, *Guilty Pleasures: Feminist Camp from Mae West to Madonna*, London, I.B. Tauris, 1996.

Rodi, Robert, *Drag Queen*, New York, Dutton, 1995.

Rodman, Dennis (with Tim Keown), *Bad as I Wanna Be*, New York, Delacorte Press, 1996.

Royot, Daniel, Bourget, Jean-Loup, and Martin, Jean-Pierre , *Histoire de la culture américaine*, Paris, P.U.F., 1993.

RuPaul, Lettin, *It All Hangs Out: An Autobiography*, New York, Hyperion, 1995.

Segal, Lynne, "Sexualities," in Kathryn Woodward (ed.), *Identity and Difference*, London, Sage, 1997.

_____, *Straight Sex: The Politics of Pleasure*, London, Virago Press, 1994.

Shuker, Roy, *Understanding Popular Music*, London and New York, Routledge, 1994.

Sim, Stuart (ed.), *The Icon Critical Dictionary of Postmodern Thought*, Cambridge, Icon Books, 1998.

Simpson, Mark, *It's a Queer World*, London, Vintage, 1996.

_____, *Male Impersonators*, London, Cassell, 1994.

Smith, Anna Marie, "By Women, for Women and About Women Rules OK? The Impossibility of Visual Soliloquy," in Paul Burston and Colin Richardson (ed.), *A Queer Romance: Lesbians, Gay Men and Popular Culture*, London and New York, Routledge, 1995.

Sochen, June, *From Mae West to Madonna: Women Entertainers in Twentieth-Century America*, Lexington, The University Press of Kentucky, 1999.

Sohn, Amy, *Run Catch Kiss*, London, Scribner, 2000.

Solomon, Alisa, "It's Never Too Late to Switch / Crossing toward power," in Leslie Ferris (ed.), *Crossing the Stage, Controversies on Cross-Dressing*, London and New York, Routledge, 1993.

Spargo, Tasmin, *Foucault and Queer Theory*, Postmodern Encounters, New York, Totem Books, 1999.

Stacey, Jackie, "Recherche différence, désespérément," in Ginette Vincendeau and Bérénice Reynaud (ed.), *20 ans de théories féministes sur le cinéma*, CinémAction, No. 67 (2ème trimestre 1993).

Steele, Valerie, *Fetish, Fashion, Sex and Power*, New York, Oxford University Press, 1996.

Stein, Arlene, "All Dressed Up But No Place to Go? Style Wars and the New Lesbianism," in Corey K. Creekmur and Alexander Doty (eds.), *Out in Culture: Gay, Lesbian, and Queer Essays on Popular Culture*, London, Cassel, 1995.

_____, "Crossover Dreams: Lesbianism and Popular Music since the 1970s," in Corey K. Creekmur and Alexander Doty (eds.), *Out in Culture: Gay, Lesbian, and Queer Essays on Popular Culture*, London, Cassel, 1995.

Stern, Howard, *Private Parts*, New York, Simon and Schuster, 1993.

Storey, John (ed.), *Cultural Theory and Popular Culture, A Reader*, Hemel Hempstead, Harvester-Wheatsheaf, 1994.

Strossen, Nadine, *Defending Pornography: Free Speech, Sex, and the Fight for Women's Rights*, New York, Scribner, 1995.

Tarantino, Quentin, *Reservoir Dogs*, London, Faber and Faber, 1994.

Tasker, Yvonne, *Working Girls: Gender and Sexuality in Popular Cinema*, London and New York, Routledge, 1998.

Thompson, Douglas, *Hollywood People*, London, Pan Books, 1995.

_____, *Sharon Stone, Basic Ambition*, New York, Little Brown and Company, 1994.

Versace, Gianni, *Rock and Royalty*, New York, Abbeville Press, 1997.

Walsers, R., and McClary, S., "Start Making Sense! Musicology Wrestles With Rock," in S. Frith and A. Goodwin (ed.), *On Record: Rock, Pop and the Written World*, New York, Pantheon Books, 1990.

Walters, Suzanna Danuta, *Material Girls, Making Sense of Feminist Cultural Theory*, Berkeley/Los Angeles, University of California Press, 1995.

Ward, Peter, *Kitsch in Sync: A Consumer's Guide to Bad Taste*, London, Plexus, 1991.

Warhol, Andy, *Diaries* (edited by Pat Hackett), New York, Warner Books, 1989.

Press Articles and Interviews Devoted to Madonna or That Mention Madonna

(Of course there are hundreds of thousands of articles on Madonna, this is only a significant selection.

A.M., "Madonna: dans son rôle de mère elle étonne Hollywood," *Télé Star*, May 12, 1997.

Acin, Nikola, and Feller, Benoît, "Rock Almanach, 1954-1996," *Rock and Folk*, November 1996.

"Albright Woos Asian Summit with Serenade" (unsigned article), *The Times*, July 30, 1997.

Anderson, Steve, "Forgive Me Father," *Village Voice*, April 4, 1989.

"Andrew Cunanan s'intéressait de près à Stallone et Madonna" (unsigned article), *Nice-Matin*, July 29, 1997.

Armanet, François, "La Dernière tentation de Madonna," *Le Nouvel Observateur*, March 5, 1998.

Arnaud, Henry, "24h avec Madonna," *Max*, November 1995.

Baraké, Irène, "Madonna, celle qui n'a peur de rien," *Fan De*, June 1998.

Barber, Lynn, "Shocking Business," *The Sunday Times*, October 3, 1993.

Batey, Angus, "Immaculate Projection," *Vox*, April 1998.

Beauvallet, J.D., "Dangerous Game," *Les Inrockuptibles*, March 4, 1998.

Blumenfeld, Samuel, "Ave Madonna," *Le Monde*, January 9, 1997.

_____, "Le Taillleur d'Eva Perón sur mesure pour Madonna," *Le Monde*, January 11, 1997.

_____, "13 mai 1991, Madonna, le déclin des stars," *Le Monde*, May 11, 1997.

Bollon, Patrice, "Madonna, ses plus belles photos," *Lui*, July 1990.

Bradfield, Scott, "On the Marilyn-go-round," *The Observer*, December 22, 1996.

Burchill, Julie, "A Stone Gains Weight," *The Sunday Times*, June 5, 1994.

Burston, Paul, "Donna Summer, What's She Like?" *Attitude*, December 1994.

Butticaz, Arnaud, "Madonna ou la paire de seins qui valait douze millions de dollars," *Casting*, June 1997.

Cabrera, Olivier, "Cyndi Lauper se veut unique en son genre," *Télé Star*, March 31, 1997.

Carrière, Christophe, "Vous n'en avez pas marre, Meryl Streep?" *Première*, July 1998.

Cassidy, John, "On Fleet Street: Madonna Mania," *The New Yorker*, December 11, 2000.

Castellano, Koro, "Señora Madonna," *El País Semanal*, November 17, 1996.

Chalumeau, Laurent, "Elle Majuscule," *Rock and Folk*, September 1987.

Chatrier, Jean-Philippe, "Madonna," *Max*, October 1993.

Chelley, Isabelle, "Madonna: Ray of Light," *Rock and Folk*, March 1998.

"El chiste de moda" (unsigned article), *Cambio 16*, May 26, 1997.

Christophe and CORINNE, "Frozen, le nouveau single," *Spotlight (Le Fanzine Français de Madonna)*, February 1998.

Coatanoan, Christophe, "Madonna mise en scène," *Hollywood Avenue*, May 1994 (reprinted as *Star Hits, Spécial Evita*, February 1997).

Dampier, Phil, "Madonna Blunders... Di Blushes," *Woman's Day*, August 19, 1996.

Davet, Stéphane, "Louise Ciccone touchée par une lumière rédemptrice," *Le Monde*, February 28, 1998.

Deevoy, Adrian, "Madonna Talks," *US*, June 13, 1991.

De Juana, José María, "Madonna, la estrella de las mil caras," *Cambio 16*, March 23, 1998.

Delingpole, James, "Madonna: Ray of Light," *The Sunday Telegraph*, March 1, 1998.

Del Vado, Carme, "Lourdes Maria el vivo retrato de Madonna," *Vale*, August 16, 1997.

Dougherty, Steve, "Madonna and Michael," *People Weekly*, April 15, 1991.

Dugdale, John, "Madonna vs. Courtney Love," *The Sunday Times*, January 26, 1997.

Dunn, Jancee, "Boy George," *US*, July 1998.

"Ears We Go! Rocco Sets Up Mum's Big Day in Style" (unsigned article), *The Mirror*, December 22, 2000.

Ebert, Roger, "Dick Tracy," *Chicago Sun-Times*, June 15 1990.

_____, "Truth or Dare," *Chicago Sun-Times*, May 17, 1991.

Eccleston, Danny, "Sexy Mother," *Q*, March 1998.

Egerton, Judith, "Performance Poetry Coming to UK in Physical Spoken Word Tour," *The Courier-Journal*, January 26, 1997.

Farley, Christopher John, "Heading for the Light," *Time*, March 16, 1998.

Ferrara, Denis, "Madonna, sans peur et sans remords," *Cosmopolitan*, May 1996.

Fisher, Carrie, "True Confessions," *Rolling Stone*, June 13, 1991.

Forestier, François, "Sean Penn, le loubard de Hollywood," *Le Nouvel Observateur*, August 21, 1997.

Frattini, Eric, "Madonna: Amo cada canción, cada película, cada día que vivo," *Heraldo by Aragón*, February 22, 1998.

"Free Expression, Well, Almost" (unsigned article), *The Economist*, March 18, 1989.

French, Philip, "Dry-eyed Over Eva," *The Observer*, December 22, 1996.

Galindo, Bruno, "Madurez electronica," *El País Semanal*, February 22, 1998.

Gandee, Charles, "In the Closet with Madonna," *Vogue*, October 1996.

Garber, Marjorie, "Strike a Pose," *Sight and Sound*, September 1992.

Georges, Pierre, "Ave Maria," *Le Monde*, October 16, 1996.

Goodwin, Christopher, "The Argy-Bargy Is Over at Last," *The Sunday Times*, November 17, 1996.

Gorin, François, "Evita," *Télérama*, January 15, 1997.

Grassin, Sophie, "Evitons Evita," *L'Express*, January 9, 1997.

Greeley, Andrew, "Like a Catholic: Madonna's Challenge to Her Church," *America*, May 1989.

Gressard, Gilles, "Che Banderas," *Télé K7*, January 6, 1997.

Guccione, Bob, Jr. "Don't Cry for Me," *Sky*, June 1996.

Haimov, Stéphanie, "Madonna, le rôle qui a changé sa vie," *Télé Magazine*, January 6, 1997.

Harrison, Andrew, "Madonna," *Juice Magazine* (Australia), June 2000.

Harrison, Barbara Grizzuti, "Can Madonna Justify Madonna?" *Mademoiselle*, June 1991.

Hawker, Philippa, "Madonna Gets Down," *Rolling Stone*, October 1993 (Australian edition).

Hensley, Dennis, "Take a Bow," *US*, February 1997.

Hill, Steven, "George Bush and Madonna — Hopping Into the Same Bed," *Seattle Community Catalyst*, December 1992.

Hooks, Bell, "Talk Now, Pay Later," *Sight and Sound*, June 1996.

Huston, Angelica, and Lester, Peter, "Mae West," *Interview*, September 1976.

Iley, Chrissy, "Desperately Seeking Alan," *The Sunday Times*, December 8, 1996.

_____, "Lipstick on Her Collar," *The Sunday Times*, March 20, 1994.

"Inside Scoop" (unsigned article), *Who Weekly* (Australia), August 7, 2000.

Jackson, Alan, "Ethereal Girl," *The Times*, March 28, 1998.

_____, "In Her Own Image," *The Times Magazine*, October 19, 1996.

_____, "Virgin Birth," *The Times Magazine*, October 12, 1996.

Jaeger, Tim, "Madonna: Je ne suis qu'amour," *Glory*, May 1998.

James, Caryn, "Beneath All That Black Lace Beats the Heart of a Bimbo ... and a Feminist," *New York Times*, December 16, 1990.

Jays, David, "Naked Ambition," *Attitude*, July 1996.

Jones, Dylan, "Latin Lovers," *People on Line*, January 27, 1996.

Juana, Jose Maria, "Los Partos de Octubre," *Cambio 16*, October 28, 1996.

Kennedy, Lisa, "Spike Lee," *Sight and Sound*, February 1993.

Keramoal, Alain de, "Le Rêve américain par Monsieur Madonna," *Gala*, May 2, 1996.

Kerr, Sarah, "Working Girl," *The New York Review of Books*, February 20, 1997.

Kerrison, Ray, "What a Tramp!," *New York Post*, May 3, 1991.

Knight, India, "Madonna Moves Up," *The Sunday Times*, December 24, 2000.

Kraft, Ronald Mark, "He's No Angel," *Genre*, September 1996.

Krootchey, Philippe, and Lestrade, Didier, "Junior Vasquez," *Têtu*, February 1998.

Kurz, Martine, "Madonna — Michael Jackson: des parents en or," *Elle*, January 20, 1997.

Lacayo, Richard, "Tagged for Murder," *Time*, July 28, 1997.

Landesman, Cosmo, "Your 15 Minutes Are Up, Dahling," *The Sunday Times*, October 15, 1995.

Lavoignat, Jean-Pierre, and Rebichon, Michel, "Evita Madonna," *Studio*, June 1996.

_____ and _____, "Welcome in My Bordello," *Studio*, March 1993.

Leland, John, "The Selling of Sex," *Newsweek*, November 2, 1992.

Leston, Kimberly, "1992 in Review," *The Face*, Janvier 1993.

Lestrade, Didier, "Madonna," *Têtu*, April 1998.

Levine, Ira, "Fashion and Fetish," *Details*, March 1994.

Lumley, Ricky, "Madonna Facts," Internet, December 1996 (University of Durham).

Lupica, Mike, "Sports Gerbilism," *Esquire*, October 1996.

"Madonna" (unsigned article), *Photo*, November 1992.

"Madonna comme vous ne l'avez jamais vue" (unsigned article), *Le Généreux*, April 1997.

"Madonna Does Medici" (unsigned article), *Time*, June 30, 1997.

Maida, Sabine, "Evita: Le Combat de Madonna," *Casting*, December 1996.

Mailer, Norman, "Norman Mailer on Madonna: Like a Lady," *Esquire*, August 1994.

Martin, Gavin, "Madonna, Mother of Reinvention," *Vox*, April 1998.

Mattera, Adam, "Madonna: Ray of Light," *Attitude*, March 1998.

McLeod, Dan, "Madonna Bares All," *Sky*, August 1991.

Morel, Alain, "Life on Ciccone Island," *Black + White*, August 1995.

Miller, Gérard, "Madonna interdite," *Globe*, December 1990.

Miller, Susan, "Selling Evita to the Masses," *Newsweek*, November 11, 1996.

Moody, Paul, "Tipping the Light Fantastic," *New Musical Express*, February 28, 1998.

Morrish, John, "Frantic Semantics," *The Daily Telegraph*, June 6, 1998.

Mortaigne, Véronique, and Tramier, Sylvaine, "Céline Dion, l'anti-Madonna," *Le Monde*, September 26, 1996.

Myers, Mike, "Chameleon in Motion," *Interview*, June 1993.

Newitz, Annalee, "Madonna's Revenge," *Bad Subjects*, No. 9 (November 1993).

Nicholson, Tim, "The Devil in Jean-Paul," *Attitude*, November 1994.

Palmieri, Michel, "L'amour haute tension (Sean Penn interview)," *Elle*, August 11, 1997.

Patterson, Sylvia, "Living in a Maternal World," *New Musical Express*, March 7, 1998.

Penwarden, Charles, "Seriously Seeking Madonna," *The European*, October 22, 1994.

Phillips, Lynn, "Who's That Girl?," *American Film*, July 1987.

Picardie, Ruth, "Here Comes the New Lass," *Arena*, Summer 1995.

Pollitt, Katha, "Why Do We Romanticize the Fetus?," *Glamour*, October 1992.

"The Post-Graduate" (unsigned article), *People on Line*, November 18, 1996.

Powell, Alison, "Keeping Score on Evita," *Interview*, January 1997.

Pye, Michael, "Madonna Goes Soft," *The Sunday Times*, June 5, 1994.

"Quoi de neuf chez les stars? Crépage de chignon à Hollywood" (unsigned article), *Officiel des Loisirs de Nice*, March 12, 1997.

Ragan, David, "My Favourite Sexual Fantasy," *Cosmopolitan*, April 1995.

Ramirez, Fatima, "Esplendor sobre la cama," *Cambio 16*, June 10, 1996.

Ranguevaux, Félix, "Les petites manies des stars se cachent dans leurs poubelles!" *VSD*, January 9, 1997.

Reborias, Ramon F., "Bisex, ultimo tabu del milenio," *Cambio 16*, April 29, 1996.

_____, "El Girlie Show," *Cambio 16*, October 18, 1993.

Rees, Jasper, "Blondes Are Back," *GQ*, January 1997.
Reins, Sacha, "La Fille en bleu," *Best*, September 1987.
Roberts, Andrew, "Cry For Evita, and a Lustrous Evil," *The Sunday Times*, December 15, 1996.
Robinson, Steven, "Odio Actuar," *Cambio 16*, December 9, 1996.
Rohrer, Trish Deitch, "Madonna Down and Dirty," *GQ*, May 1991.
Roland, Mark, "It Ain't Half Pop, Mum!," *Melody Maker*, February 28, 1998.
Rubenstein, Hal, "Mounting Everett," *Paper*, March 1998.
Salamon, Julie, "Madonna's Moment," *Vogue*, October 1996.
"Sanfte CD von Madonna — passend zum neuen Mama-Image" (unsigned article), *Welt am Sonntag*, March 1, 1998.
Santucci, Françoise-Marie, and Renault, Gilles, "Madonna illuminée," *Libération*, February 27, 1998.
Sarko, Anita, "The Fur Flies," *Paper*, February 1996.
Schifrin, Matthew, "A Brain for Sin and a Body for Business," *Forbes*, October 1, 1990.
Sebastien, "Mais qui est la vraie Madonna?," *Salut*, November 1995.
Segal, Victoria, "Maddy Goes into a New Groove," *Vox*, March 1998.
Servat, Henry-Jean, "Madonna: A Paris, amoureuse mais seule dans son lit," *Paris-Match*, February 4, 1993.
_____, "Madonna: J'ai autant prié pour être Evita que pour être mère. Le ciel m'a donné les deux en même temps," *Paris-Match*, January 16, 1997.
_____, "Madonna: Je suis une exhibitionniste et j'aime ça," *Paris-Match*, February 24, 1993.
Sessums, K., "White Heat: Interview with Madonna," *Vanity Fair*, April 1990.
Sheiffele, Rob, "Sinema," *Genre*, March 1994.
Shewey, Don, "The Gospel According to St. Madonna," *The Advocate*, May 21, 1991.
_____, "The Saint, The Slut, The Sensation ... Madonna," *The Advocate*, May 7, 1991.
Simard, Jean-Pierre, "Stupido," *Rock and Folk*, March 1996.
Sischy, Ingrid, "Madonna and Child," *Vanity Fair*, March 1998.
Sisti, Enrico, "Madonna, la metamorfosi," *La Repubblica*, February 26, 1998.
Slaughter, Todd, "The 80s: Music Video and Madonna," Internet, http://www. engl.virginia.edu/~enwr1016/index.html (University of Virginia), January 1997.
Smith, Andrew, "Material Girl to Earth Mother," *The Sunday Times*, March 1, 1998.
Smith, Richard, "Half a Rebel," *Gay Times*, January 1994.
"Snap" (unsigned article), *NW (Australia)*, July 31, 2000.
Softley, Iain, "Céline and Julie," *Sight and Sound*, September 1994.
Taki, "Material Slob Shows Off Her Stupidity," *The Sunday Times*, October 13, 1996.
Tannenbaum, Rob, "The Mighty Penn," *Details*, November 1995.
Thevenin, Patrick, "La Madone des ragots," *Têtu*, March 1998.
Thomas, Karen, "A Star Is Born. Madonna's Baby Saddled With Fame as Middle Name," *USA Today*, October 17, 1996.
Toucas, Gilles, "Madonna, Diva et mamma," *Télé K7*, February 16, 1998.
Trebbe, Ann, "Stud-u-Like," *Sky*, March 1992.
Trittoleno, Martine, "Madonna: incomprise?," *Vogue*, October 1993.
Turan, Kenneth, "The Art of Revolution: Video Is Taking Over Popular Culture," *Rolling Stone*, December 20, 1984.

Versace, Gianni, "The Art of Being You," *Interview*, December 1996.
Villet, Eric, "A propos, est-il vraiment l'heureux papa?," *Voici*, May 6, 1996.
Von Scherz, Begonia, "Faites donc parler de vous," *Angeline's mag*, Fall 1996.
Walker, Nick, and Sandler, Helen, "Transitions," *Phase*, April 1994.
Walters, Barry, "Beyond the Material," *The Advocate*, March 31, 1998.
_____, "Madonna Chooses Dare," *Spin*, April 1998.
_____, "Sizzling Remixes," *The Advocate*, March 4, 1997.
Wark, Penny, "Transfiguration of Madonna," *The Sunday Times*, December 15, 1996.
Wazir, Burhan, "Mother of All Pop Stars," *The Face*, March 1998.
Whittell, Giles, "Madonna Stalker Convicted," *The Times*, January 10, 1996.
Wildmon, Donald, "This Video Is Offensive to Believers," in Allan Metz and Carol Benson (eds.), *The Madonna Companion: Two Decades of Commentary*, New York, Schirmer, 1999.
Williams, Greg, "And Still I Rise," *Cleo (Australia)*, May 1999.
Williams, Linda Ruth, "Erotic Thrillers and Rude Women," *Sight and Sound*, July 1993.
Wilson, Janelle L., "Postmodernism, Nostalgia, and Generation X," Internet, http://www.d.umn.edu/~socanth/wilson.html (University of Minnesota), December 1996.
Wintour, Anna, "Beyond Khaki," *Vogue*, October 1996.
Zoglin, Richard, "Mad for Evita," *Time*, December 30, 1996.

Secondary Sources: Books and Essays That Do Not Mention Madonna

Ackroyd, Peter, *Dressing Up: Transvestism and Drag, The History of an Obsession*, New York, Simon and Schuster, 1979.
Alcoff, Linda, "Cultural Feminism versus Post-Structuralism: The Identity Crisis in Feminist Theory," *Signs*, No. 13 (1988).
Anzaldua, Gloria, *Borderlands: The New Mestiza = La Frontera*, San Francisco, Aunt Lute, 1987.
Arbuthnot, Lucie, and Seneca, Gail, "Pre-Text and Text in Gentlemen Prefer Blondes," in Patricia Erens (ed.), *Issues in Feminist Film Criticism*, Bloomington, Indiana University Press, 1990.
Ariès, Paul, *Les Fils by McDo: La McDonalisation du Monde*, Paris, L'Harmattan, 1997.
Babuscio, Jack, "Camp and the Gay Sensibility," in Richard Dyer (ed.), *Gays and Film*, London, BFI Publishing, 1977.
Badinter, Elisabeth, *XY, de l'identité masculine*, Paris, Editions Odile Jacob, 1992.
Bandry, Michel, *Erskine Caldwell: Humour et misère*, Paris, Belin, 1997.
_____, "Le pays de Caldwell. Ou des hommes dans des corps d'animaux," in *Revue Française d'Etudes Américaines*, No. 20 (May 1984).
Barth, John, *The Friday Book*, Baltimore, The Johns Hopkins University Press, 1997 (1984).
_____, *Further Fridays*, Boston, Little, Brown and Company, 1995.

Barthelme, Donald, *Snow White*, New York, Atheneum, 1982.

Barthes, Roland, *Le bruissement de la langue*, Paris, Editions du Seuil, 1984.

_____, *Le degré zéro de l'écriture*, Paris, Editions du Seuil, 1953.

_____, *Essais critiques*, Paris, Editions du Seuil, 1964.

_____, *Mythologies*, Paris, Editions du Seuil, 1957.

_____, *Le plaisir du texte*, Paris, Editions du Seuil, 1973.

Baudelaire, Charles, *L'art romantique*, Paris, Garnier-Flammarion, 1968.

Baudrillard, Jean, *Amérique*, Paris, Grasset, 1986.

_____, *Cool Memories I*, Paris, Editions Galilée, 1987.

_____, *Cool Memories II*, Paris, Editions Galilée, 1990.

_____, *De la séduction*, Paris, Editions Galilée, 1979.

_____, *Le miroir de la production*, Paris, Casterman, 1973.

_____, *Pour une critique de l'économie politique du signe*, Paris, Gallimard, 1972.

_____, *Simulacres et Simulations*, Paris, Editions Galilée, 1981.

_____, *La société de consommation, ses mythes, ses structures*, Paris, Denoël, 1970.

_____, *Le Système des objets*, Paris, Gallimard, 1968.

Behr, Edward, *Une Amérique qui fait peur*, Paris, Plon, 1995.

Belmont, J., *Modernes et postmodernes*, Paris, Editions du Moniteur, 1987.

Benhabib, Seyla, and Passerin d'Entreves, Maurizio (eds.), *Habermas and the Unfinished Project of Modernity*, Cambridge, Polity Press, 1996.

Berger, Arthur Asa, *Postmortem for a Postmodernist*, Walnut Creek, AltaMira Press, 1997.

Bergman, David, *Gaiety Transfigured: Gay Self-Representation in American Literature*, Madison, University of Wisconsin Press, 1991.

Bernheim, Nicole, "La drogue, fléau national," in Annie Lennkh and Marie-France Toinet (ed.), *L'État des États-Unis*, Paris, La Découverte, 1990.

Bernstein, Richard, *Dictatorship of Virtue. How the Battle Over Multiculturalism Is Reshaping Our Schools, Our Country, Our Lives*, New York, Vintage Books, 1995.

Bettelheim, Bruno, *The Uses of Enchantment*, New York, Alfred A. Knopf, 1976.

Bewes, Timothy, *Cynicism and Postmodernity*, London, Verso, 1997.

Bidaud, Anne-Marie, *Hollywood et le rêve américain (Cinéma et idéologie)*, Paris, Masson, 1994.

Bignell, Jonathan, "Spectacle and the Postmodern in Contemporary American Cinema," in Gilles Ménégaldo (ed.), *Crises de la représentation dans le cinéma américain*, Poitiers, La Licorne, No. 36 (1996).

Blake, Harry, "Mae West et le regard de l'autre," in *Revue française d'études américaines*, No. 4 (October 1977).

Boisvert, Yves, *Le monde postmoderne, Analyse du discours sur la postmodernité*, Paris, L'Harmattan, 1996.

Bordat, Francis, "Pourquoi il faut aimer Hollywood," in *Américônes, Etudes sur l'image aux Etats-Unis*, Marc Chénetier (ed), Fontenay aux Roses, ENS Editions, 1997.

_____, and Etcheverry, Michel (ed.), *Cent ans d'aller au cinéma*, Rennes, Presses Universitaires de Rennes, 1995.

Boulet-Gercourt, Philippe, "Norman Mailer: Moi, Jésus Christ," *Le Nouvel Observateur*, March 26, 1998.

Bourdieu, Pierre, *Contre-feux*, Paris, Liber-Raisons d'Agir, 1998.

_____, *Sur la télévision*, Paris, Liber-Raisons d'Agir, 1996.

Brodribb, Somer, *Nothing Matters: A Feminist Critique of Postmodernism*, Melbourne, Spinifex, 1993.

Buhle, Mari Jo, *Feminism and Its Discontent: A Century of Struggle with Psychoanalysis*, Cambridge, Harvard University Press, 1998.

Burgess, Françoise, "Race, ethnicité et classe," in Annie Lennkh and Marie-France Toinet (eds.), *L'État des États-Unis*, Paris, La Découverte, 1990.

Burke, Phyllis, *Gender Shock : Exploding the Myths of Male and Female*, New York, Doubleday, 1996.

Butler, Judith, *Excitable Speech: A Politics of the Performative*, London and New York, Routledge, 1997.

_____, *Gender Trouble: Feminism and the Subversion of Identity*, London and New York, Routledge, 1990.

Cahoone, Lawrence (ed.), *From Modernism to Postmodernism, An Anthology*, Cambridge, Blackwell, 1996.

Caillois, Roger, *Approches de l'imaginaire*, Paris, Gallimard, 1970.

_____, *Le mythe et l'homme*, Paris, Gallimard, 1938.

Califia, Pat, "Dildo Envy and Other Phallic Adventures," in Fiona Giles (ed.), *Dick for a Day: What Would You Do If You Had One?*, London, Indigo, 1998.

Campbell, Neil, and Kean, Alasdair, *American Cultural Studies*, London and New York, Routledge, 1997.

Carlier, Christophe, and Griton-Rotterdam, Nathalie, *Des mythes aux mythologies*, Paris, Ellipses, 1994.

Carríon, Ignacio, "Cobayas del Sida," *El País*, February 8, 1998.

Cassirer, Ernst, *Langage et mythe, à propos des noms de dieux*, Paris, Minuit, 1989.

Chambers, Iain. *Urban Rhythms: Pop Music and Popular Culture.* New York, St. Martin's Press, 1985.

Chancey, George Jr., *Gay New York: Gender, Urban Culture, and the Making of the Gay Male World*, New York, HarperCollins, 1994.

Chandler, Charlotte, "Mae West, la dama del sexo," *El País Semanal*, May 25, 1997 (translation of an old and rare interview).

Charensol, G., *Panorama du cinéma*, Paris, Kra, 1930.

Cieutat, Michel, "Les grands mythes fondateurs," *Télérama*, May 8, 1996.

Coates, Jennifer, "Language, Gender, and Career," in Sara Mills (ed.), *Language and Gender*, Harlow, Longman, 1995.

Cocteau, Jean, *Le foyer des artistes*, Paris, Plon, 1947.

Cohen, Ralph, "Do Postmodern Genres Exist?" in Marjorie Perloff (ed.), *Postmodern Genres*, Norman, University of Oklahoma Press, 1995.

Collard, James, "Friends of Dorothy," *Attitude*, December 1994.

Combesque, Marie Agnès, and Warde, Ibrahim, *Mythologies américaines*, Paris, Editions du Félin, 1996.

Connor, Steven, *Postmodernist Culture: An Introduction to Theories of the Contemporary*, Oxford, Blackwell, 1989.

Corman, Louis, *La bisexualité créatrice*, Paris, Jacques Grancher, 1996.

Coupe, Laurence, *Myth*, London and New York, Routledge, 1997.

Coursodon, Jean-Pierre, "Un rituel de la frustration (notes sur la star comme marchandise)," *Cinéma d'aujourd'hui*, No. 8 (May-June 1976).

Couturier, Maurice, *La figure de l'auteur*, Paris, Editions du Seuil, 1995.

_____, *Representation and Performance in Postmodern Fiction*, Montpellier, Université Paul Valery, 1983.

_____, *Roman et censure ou la mauvaise foi d'Eros*, Seyssel, Champ Vallon, 1996.
Coward, David, "Definite Must," *The Times Literary Supplement*, February 7, 1997.
Crenshaw, Kimberlé, "Beyond Racism and Misogyny: Black Feminism and 2 Live Crew," in *Boston Review*, XVI, 6 (December 1991).
_____, "Demarginalizing the Intersection of Race and Sex: A Black Feminist Critique of Antidiscrimination Doctrine, Feminist Theory and Antiracist Politics," in *The University of Chicago Legal Forum*, 1989.
Cruikshank, Margaret (ed.), *Lesbian Studies: Present and Future*, London, The Feminist Press, 1982.
Cupitt, Don, *The World to Come*, London, SCM Press, 1982.
Davidson, James, "It's Only Fashion," *London Review of Books*, November 24, 1994.
Davidson, Michael, "Palimtexts: Postmodern Poetry and the Material Text," in Marjorie Perloff (ed.), *Postmodern Genres*, Norman, University of Oklahoma Press, 1995.
Debord, Guy, *La société du spectacle* (third edition), Paris, Gallimard, 1992.
Delauretis, Teresa, *Alice Doesn't: Feminism, Semiotics, Cinema*, Bloomington, Indiana University Press, 1984.
_____, *Technologies of Gender, Essays on Theory, Film, and Fiction*, Bloomington and Indianapolis, Indiana University Press, 1987.
Deleuze, Gilles, *Cinéma 1, L'Image-mouvement*, Paris, Les Editions de Minuit, 1983.
_____, *Cinéma 2, L'Image-temps*, Paris, Les Editions de Minuit, 1985.
_____, *Marcel Proust et les signes*, Paris, Presses Universitaires by France, 1970.
Delgado, Francisco, Payan, Miguel Juan, and Uceda, Jacinto, *Quentin Tarantino*, Madrid, Ediciones JC, 1995.
D'Emilio, John, *Sexual Politics, Sexual Communities: The Makings of a Homosexual Minority in the United States*, Chicago, University of Chicago Press, 1983.
Demopoulos, Maria, "Thieves Like Us: Directors Under the Influence," *Film Comment*, May/June 1996.
Derrida, Jacques, *De la grammatologie*, Paris, Les Editions by Minuit, 1967.
_____, *De l'esprit. Heidegger et la question*, Paris, Galilée, 1987.
_____, *L'écriture et la différence*, Paris, Editions du Seuil, 1967.
_____, *Eperons. Les styles de Nietzsche*, Paris, Flammarion, 1978.
_____, *Marges — de la philosophie*, Paris, Minuit, 1972.
Dickens, Homer, *What a Drag: Men as Women and Women as Men in the Movies*, London and Sidney, Angus and Robertson, 1982.
Doane, Mary Ann, *Femmes Fatales: Feminism, Film Theory, Psychoanalysis*, London and New York, Routledge, 1991.
Domarchi, Jean, "Des victimes et des dieux/Les stars meurent aussi," in *Cinéma d'aujourd'hui*, No. 8 (May-June 1976).
Dworkin, Andrea, *Pornography: Men Possessing Women*, New York, Perigee Books, 1981.
Dyer, Richard, "Resistance through charisma: Rita Hayworth and Gilda," in E. Ann Kaplan (ed.), *Women in Film Noir*, London, BFI, 1980.
_____, *Stars*, London, British Film Institute Publishing, 1998 (1979).
Eco, Umberto, *La production des signes*, Paris, Le Livre de poche, 1992.
Eliade, Mircea, *Aspects du mythe*, Paris, Gallimard, 1963.
_____, *Méphistophélès et l'androgyne*, Paris, Gallimard, 1962.

_____, *Mythes, rêves et mystères*, Paris, Gallimard, 1957.

_____, *La nostalgie des origines*, Paris, Gallimard, 1971.

Engelhard, Philippe, *L'homme mondial, les sociétés humaines peuvent-elles survivre?* Paris, Arléa, 1996.

Evans, Judith, *Feminist Theory Today*, London, Sage, 1995.

Fausto-Sterling, Anne, *Myths of Gender: Biological Theories About Women and Men*, New York, Basic Books, 1985/1992.

Ferris, Lesley, "Current Crossings," in Leslie Ferris (ed.), *Crossing the Stage, Controversies on Cross-Dressing*, London and New York, Routledge, 1993.

Foster, Hal, *Postmodernism: A Preface*, in Hal Foster (ed.), *Postmodern Culture*, London, Pluto Press, 1993 (First published as *The Anti-Aesthetic: Essays on Postmodern Culture*. Port Townsend, Bay Press, 1983).

_____, *Recodings; Art, Spectacle, Cultural Politics*, Port Townsend, Bay Press, 1985.

Foucault, Michel, *L'Archéologie du savoir*, Paris, Gallimard, 1969.

_____, *Dits et Ecrits*, vol. I, Paris, Gallimard, 1994.

_____, *Histoire de la folie à l'âge classique*, Paris, Gallimard, 1972.

_____, *Histoire de la sexualité, I, La volonté du savoir*, Paris, Gallimard, 1976.

_____, *Histoire de la sexualité, II, L'usage des plaisirs*, Paris, Gallimard, 1984.

_____, *Histoire de la sexualité, III, Le souci de soi*, Paris, Gallimard, 1984.

_____, *Les mots et les choses*, Paris, Gallimard, 1966.

_____, *L'Ordre du discours*, Paris, Gallimard, 1971.

_____, *Surveiller et punir*, Paris, Gallimard, 1975.

Frazer, James George, *The (Illustrated) Golden Bough*, London, Macmillan, 1978.

Frey, Darcy, *The Last Shot: City Streets, Basketball Dreams*, New York, Simon and Schuster, 1995.

Frye, Marilyn, *The Politics of Reality: Essays in Feminist Theory*, Freedom, The Crossing Press, 1983.

Frye, Northrop, *Anatomy of Criticism*, Princeton, Princeton University Press, 1971.

Fuentes, Carlos, *Christophe et son oeuf* (translation Céline Zins), Paris, Gallimard, 1990.

_____, *Le miroir enterré* (translation Jean-Claude Masson), Paris, Gallimard, 1992.

Fuller, Graham, "A Good Music Video is Hard to Find," *Interview*, October 1996.

Gans, Herbert J., *Popular Culture and High Culture — An Analysis and Evaluation of Taste*, New York, Basic Books, 1974.

Garber, Frederick, "Generating the Subject: The Images of Cindy Sherman," in Marjorie Perloff (ed.), *Postmodern Genres*, Norman, University of Oklahoma Press, 1995.

Gasca, Luis, *Chicas malas, mujeres perversas*, Valencia, Editorial La Máscara, 1994.

Genette, Gérard, *Palimpsestes, la littérature au second degré*, Paris, Editions du Seuil, 1982.

Gill, A.A., "Frocks a Guy Could Di For," *The Sunday Times*, February 2, 1997.

Gledhill, Christine, "Klute 1: a contemporary film noir and feminist criticism," in E. Ann Kaplan (ed.), *Women in Film Noir*, London, BFI, 1980.

Gliatto, Tom, and Griffiths, John, "Lady Pluck," *People Weekly*, June 30, 1997.

Goffman, Erving, *Gender Advertisements*, New York, Harper and Row, 1976.

Goodman, Lizbeth, and Smith, Alison, "Literature and Gender," in Lizbeth Goodman (ed.), *Literature and Gender*, London and New York, Routledge, 1996.

Gould, Glen, "The Search for Petula Clark (1967)," in Micheal Ondaatje (ed.), *The Faber Book of Contemporary Canadian Short Stories*, London, Faber and Faber, 1990.

Graham, Anna, and Plume, Rhonda, "The Z to A of Aussie Camp," *Blue*, August 1996.

Graves, Robert, *The Greek Myths: 1*, London, Penguin Books, 1960.

_____, *The Greek Myths: 2*, London, Penguin Books, 1960.

Guattari, Félix, and Deleuze, Gilles, *L'Anti-Oedipe: capitalisme et schizophrénie*, Paris, Editions de Minuit, 1973.

_____ and _____, *Kafka — Pour une littérature mineure*, Paris, Editions de Minuit, 1975.

Guiles, Fred Lawrence, *Loner at the Ball, the Life of Andy Warhol*, London, Bantam Press, 1989.

Guy-Gillet, Geneviève (ed.), *Cahiers Jungiens de Psychanalyse (Le sexe de l'androgyne)*, No. 81 (Winter 1994).

Habermas, Jürgen, *Le discours philosophique de la modernité*, Paris, Gallimard, 1988.

_____, "Modernity — An Incomplete Project," in Hal Foster (ed.), *Postmodern Culture*, London, Pluto Press, 1993 (First published as *The Anti-Aesthetic: Essays on Postmodern Culture*. Port Townsend, Bay Press, 1983).

Hamilton, Marybeth, "'I'm the Queen of the bitches / Female impersonation and Mae West's *Pleasure Man*," in Leslie Ferris (ed.), *Crossing the Stage, Controversies on Cross-Dressing*, London and New York, Routledge, 1993.

Hartsock, Nancy, *Money, Sex and Power*, New York, Longman, 1983.

Harvey, David, *The Condition of Postmodernity*, Oxford, Basil Blackwell, 1989.

Hassan, Ihab, *The Postmodern Turn*, Columbus, Ohio State University Press, 1987.

_____, *The Right Promethean Fire*, Chicago and London, University of Illinois Press, 1980.

Hebdige, Dick, *Subculture: The Meaning of Style*, London, Methuen, 1979.

Heidegger, Martin, *Être et temps* (translation F. Fédier), Paris, Gallimard, 1986.

_____, *Les problèmes fondamentaux de la phénoménologie* (translation J.-F. Courtine), Paris, Gallimard, 1985.

_____, "La Question de la Technique," in *Essais et Conférences* (translation A. Préau), Paris, Gallimard, 1958.

Hekman, Susan J., *Gender and Knowledge: Elements of a Postmodern Feminism*, Boston, Northeastern University Press, 1990.

Hennessy, Rosemary, "Queer Theory: A Review of the Differences Special Issue and Wittig's *The Straight Mind*," *Signs: Journal of Women in Culture and Society*, No. 18 (1993).

Hills, Helen, "Commonplaces: the Woman in the Street: Text and Gender in the Works of Jenny Holzer and Barbara Kruger," in Sara Mills (ed.), *Language and Gender*, Harlow, Longman, 1995.

Hubert, Renée Riese, "Gertrude Stein, Cubism, and the Postmodern Book," in Marjorie Perloff (ed.), *Postmodern Genres*, Norman, University of Oklahoma Press, 1995.

Hudnut, Joseph, *Architecture and the Spirit of Man*, New York, Greenwood Press, 1966.

Huston, Angelica, and Lester, Peter, "Mae West, Interview," *Interview*, September 1976.

Hutcheon, Linda, "The Pastime of Past Time: Fiction, History, Historiographic Metafiction," in Marjorie Perloff (ed.), *Postmodern Genres*, Norman, University of Oklahoma Press, 1995.

_____, *A Poetics of Postmodernism: History, Theory, Fiction*, London and New York, Routledge, 1988.

_____, *The Politics of Postmodernism*, London and New York, Routledge, 1989.

Huyssen, A., *After the Great Divide: Modernism, Mass Culture, Postmodernism*, Bloomington, University of Indiana Press, 1986.

Isherwood, Christopher, *The World in the Evening*, New York, Noonday Press, 1954.

Jameson, Fredric, "Postmodernism and Consumer Society," in Hal Foster (ed.), *Postmodern Culture*, London, Pluto Press, 1993 (published before as "The Anti-Aesthetic: Essays on Postmodern Culture," Port Townsend, Bay Press, 1983).

_____, "Postmodernism, or the Cultural Logic of Late Capitalism," in *New Left Review*, 146, 1984.

_____, *Postmodernism, or the Cultural Logic of Late Capitalism*, Durham, Duke University Press, 1991 (expands on the former).

Jeanne, René, and Ford, Charles, *Les vedettes de l'écran*, Paris, Presses Universitaires de France, 1964.

Jeffreys, Sheila, "The Queer Disappearance of Lesbians: Sexuality in the Academy," *Women's Studies International Forum*, Vol.17, No. 5 (1994).

Jencks, Charles, *The Language of Post-modern Architecture*, New York, Rizzoli, 1977.

_____, *Post-modernism: The New Classicism in Art and Architecture*, New York, Rizzoli, 1987.

Jordan, Glenn, and Weedon, Chris, *Cultural Politics: Class, Gender, Race and the Postmodern World*, Cambridge, Blackwell, 1995.

Kael, Pauline, *For Keeps: 30 Years at the Movies*, New York, Plume, 1996.

Kane, Pat, "The Thin White Duke," *The Times Literary Supplement*, July 18, 1997.

Kaplan, E. Ann, *Postmodernism and Its Discontents; Theories, Practices*, New York, Verso, 1989.

_____, *Psychoanalysis and Cinema*, London and New York, Routledge, 1990.

_____, *Women and Film: Both Sides of the Camera*, New York, Methuen, 1983.

Kappeler, Susanne, *The Pornography of Representation*, Minneapolis, The University of Minnesota Press, 1986.

Kenway, Jane, "Having a Postmodernist Turn or Postmodernist Angst: A Disorder Experience by an Author Who is Not Yet Dead or Even Close to It," in Richard Smith and Philip Wexler, *After Postmodernism: Education, Politics and Identity*, London, The Falmer Press, 1995.

Kermode, Frank, *The Genesis of Secrecy: On the Interpretation of Narrative*, Cambridge and London, Harvard University Press, 1979.

Kleinhans, Chuck, "Taking Out the Trash: Camp and the Politics of Parody," in Moe Meyer (ed.), *The Politics and Poetics of Camp*, London and New York, Routledge, 1994.

Koch, Stephen, *Stargazer: Andy Warhol's World and His Films*, New York, Praeger Publishers, Inc., 1973.

Kristeva, Julia, *Sens et non-sens de la révolte (Pouvoirs et limites de la psychanalyse I)*, Paris, Fayard, 1996.

Kroker, Arthur, *The Possessed Individual*, New York, St. Martin's Press, 1992.

Lacan, Jacques, *Ecrits I*, Paris, Editions du Seuil, 1966.

_____, *Ecrits II*, Paris, Editions du Seuil, 1971.

Lacroix, Jean-Michel, *Histoire des États-Unis*, Paris, Presses Universitaires de France, 1996.

Lacronique, Jean-François, "L'État sanitaire de la nation," in Annie Lennkh and Marie-France Toinet (ed.), *L'État des États-Unis*, Paris, La Découverte, 1990.

Lasch, Christopher, *Women and the Common Life: Love, Marriage, and Feminism*, New York, Norton, 1997.

Lash, Scott, *Sociology of Postmodernism*, London and New York, Routledge, 1990.

Latour, Bruno, *Nous n'avons jamais été modernes: essai d'anthropologie symétrique*, Paris, La Découverte, 1997.

Lebrun, Dominique, *Hollywood*, Paris, Hazan, 1996.

Leitsch, Dick, "Police Raid on N.Y. Club Sets Off First Gay Riot," *The Advocate*, July 1969 (reprinted from the *New York Mattachine Newsletter*).

Lemarchand, Philippe (ed.), *Atlas des États-Unis: Les Paradoxes de la puissance*, Paris, Atlande, 1997.

Leprohon, Pierre, *Le monde du cinéma*, Paris, Hermès, 1967.

Lesage, Julia, "*Céline et Julie vont en bateau*: fantasme subversif," in Ginette Vincendeau and Bérénice Reynaud (ed.), *20 ans de théories féministes sur le cinéma*, *CinémAction*, No. 67 (2ème trimestre 1993).

Lévi-Strauss, Claude, *Anthropologie structurale*, Paris, Plon, 1974.

_____, *Le cru et le cuit*, Paris, Plon, 1964.

_____, *La potière jalouse*, Paris, Plon, 1985.

_____, *Le regard éloigné*, Paris, Plon, 1983.

Lévy, Claude, *Les minorités ethniques aux États-Unis*, Paris, Ellipses, 1997.

Lige and Jack, "N.Y. Gays: Will the Spark Die?," *The Advocate*, July 1969.

Lincoln, Eric C., and Gates, Henry Louis, *Coming Through the Fire: Surviving Race and Place in America*, Durham, Duke University Press, 1996.

Lo Duca, J.M., *Histoire du cinéma*, Paris, Presses Universitaires de France, 1968.

_____, "Technique (non décisive) pour la production d'une star," in *Cinéma d'Aujourd'hui*, No. 8 (May-June 1976).

Lord, M.G., *Forever Barbie, The Unauthorized Biography of a Real Doll*, New York, Avon Books, 1995.

Lyotard, Jean-François, *La condition postmoderne*, Paris, Les Editions by Minuit, 1979.

_____, *Moralités postmodernes*, Paris, Editions Galilée, 1993.

_____, *Le postmoderne expliqué aux enfants*, Paris, Editions Galilée (new Le Livre de Poche edition), 1988.

Mailer, Norman, *Marilyn*, London, Hodder and Stoughton Ltd., 1973.

_____, *Of Women and Their Elegance*, New York, Simon and Schuster, 1980.

Mamet, David, *Speed-the-Plow*, New York, Grove Press, 1988.

Markale, Jean, *L'énigme des vampires*, Paris, Pygmalion, 1990.

_____, *Mélusine*, Paris, Editions Retz, 1983.

McCaffery, Larry, "And Still They Smooch: Erotic Visions and Re-Visions in Postmodern American Fiction," in *Revue Française d'Etudes Américaines*, No. 20 (May 1984).

McHale, Brian, *Postmodernist Fiction*, London and New York, Methuen, 1987.

McLuhan, Marshall, *The Gutenberg Galaxy*, Toronto, University of Toronto Press, 1962.

_____, *The Medium Is the Message*, Harmondsworth, Penguin, 1967.

_____, *Understanding the Media: The Extensions of Man*, New York, McGraw-Hill, 1964.

McNay, Lois, *Foucault and Feminism: Power, Gender and the Self*, Boston, Northeastern University Press, 1992.

McRobbie, Angela, "Postmodernism and Popular Culture," in *Postmodernism: ICA Documents 5*, Lisa Appignanesi (ed.), London, ICA, 1986.

Meese, Elizabeth, *Crossing the Double-Cross: The Practice of Feminist Criticism*, Chapel Hill, University of North Carolina Press, 1986.

Mélandri, Pierre, "Une Crise d'identité? (1974–1997)," in Bernard Vincent (ed.), *Histoire des États-Unis*, Paris, Flammarion, 1997.

Mendes-Leite, Rommel, *Bisexualité, le dernier tabou*, Paris, Calmann-Lévy, 1996.

Meyer, Moe (ed.), *The Politics and Poetics of Camp*, London and New York, Routledge, 1994.

Mizejewski, Linda, *Divine Decadence: Fascism, Female Spectacle, and the Makings of Sally Bowles*, Princeton, Princeton University Press, 1992.

Moellering, Michael, *Les déesses d'Hollywood*, Paris, Atlas, 1990.

Moisy, Claude , *L'Amérique en marche arrière*, Paris, Hachette, 1996.

Montero, Oscar, "Lipstick Vogue: The Politics of Drag," *Radical America*, January 1988.

Moore, Caroline, "Deconstructionism," *The Sunday Times*, May 20, 1993.

Morin, Edgar, *Le paradigme perdu: la nature humaine*, Paris, Editions du Seuil, 1973.

_____, *Les stars*, Paris, Editions du Seuil, 1972.

Mulvey, Laura, *Visual and Other Pleasures*, Bloomington, Indiana University Press, 1989.

Murphy, Nancey, *Anglo-American Postmodernity: Philosophical Perspectives on Science, Religion, and Ethics*, Boulder, Westview Press, 1997.

Nathanson, Paul, *Over the Rainbow: The Wizard of Oz as a Secular Myth of America*, Albany, State University of New York Press, 1991.

Natoli, Joseph, *A Primer to Postmodernity*, Malden, Blackwell, 1997.

Newton, Esther, *Mother Camp: Female Impersonators in America*, Chicago, University of Chicago Press, 1972.

Newman, Charles, *The Post-Modern Aura: The Act of Fiction in an Age of Inflation*, Evanston, Northwestern University Press, 1985.

Nicholls, Peter, "Divergences: Modernism, Postmodernism, Jameson and Lyotard," in *Critical Quarterly* Vol.33, No. 3 (August 1991).

Nicholson, Linda J., and Fraser, Nancy, "Social Criticism Without Philosophy: An Encounter Between Feminism and Postmodernism," in Linda J. Nicholson (ed.), *Feminism/Postmodernism*, London and New York, Routledge, 1990.

Nochimson, Martha, *No End to Her: Soap Opera and the Female Subject*, Berkeley, University of California Press, 1992.

Norris, Christopher, *What's Wrong With Postmodernism: Critical Theory and the Ends of Philosophy*, Baltimore, Johns Hopkins University Press, 1990.

O'Connor, Anne Marie, "Sherman Alexie, Native American Son," *George*, June 1998.

O'Neill, William L., *Feminism in America: A History*, New Brunswick, Transaction Publishers, 1989.

Owens, Craig, "The Discourse of Others: Feminists and Postmodernism," in Hal Foster (ed.), *Postmodern Culture*, London, Pluto Press, 1993 (First published as *The Anti-Aesthetic: Essays on Postmodern Culture*. Port Townsend, Bay Press, 1983).

Patouillard, Victoire, "Antirétroviraux à gober," *Têtu*, January 1998.

Pauwels, Marie-Christine, *Le Rêve américain*, Paris, Hachette, 1997.

Paz, Octavio, *Children of the Mire: Modern Poetry from Romanticism to the Avant-Garde*, Cambridge, Harvard University Press, 1974.

_____, *Deux transparents, Marcel Duchamp et Claude Lévi-Strauss*, Paris, Gallimard, 1971.

Pela, R.L., "Legendary Barbra," *The Advocate*, March 13, 1997.

Perloff, Marjorie, "Introduction," in Marjorie Perloff (ed.), *Postmodern Genres*, Norman, University of Oklahoma Press, 1995.

Phelan, Peggy, "Criss-Crossing Cultures," in Leslie Ferris (ed.), *Crossing the Stage, Controversies on Cross-Dressing*, London and New York, Routledge, 1993.

Place, Janey, "Women in Film Noir," in E. Ann Kaplan (ed.), *Women in Film Noir*, London, BFI, 1980.

Poovey, Mary, "Feminism and Deconstruction," *Feminist Studies*, No. 14 (1988).

Prinz, Jessica, "Always Two Things Switching: Laurie Anderson's Alterity," in Marjorie Perloff (ed.), *Postmodern Genres*, Norman, University of Oklahoma Press, 1995.

Rabatel, Nathalie, Temerson, Catherine, and Warburton, Robin, *Hollywood, petite histoire d'un grand empire*, Paris, Eshel, 1990.

Rabine, Leslie, "A Feminist Politics of Nonidentity," *Feminist Studies*, No. 14 (1988).

Rada, James A., "Color Blind-Sided: Racial Bias in Network Television's Coverage of Professional Football Games," *Howard University's Journal of Communications*, Vol. 7, No. 3 (1996).

Radstone, Susannah (ed.), *Sweet Dreams. Sexuality, Gender, and Popular Fiction*, London, Lawrence and Wishart, 1988.

Rand, Erica, *Barbie's Queer Accessories*, Durham and London, Duke University Press, 1995.

Raulet, Gérard, "L'archipel, réflexions sur la démocratie post-moderne," in *Les cahiers de philosophie*, 6 (1988).

_____, "Stratégies consensuelles et esthétique post-moderne," in *Recherches sociologiques*, XX, 2 (1989).

Raymond, Leigh, "Divided Camps," *Black + White*, August 1995.

Reed, Lou, *Between Thoughts and Expression (Selected Lyrics)*, New York, Hyperion Books, 1991.

Retallack, Joan, "Post-Scriptum-High-Modern," in Marjorie Perloff (ed.), *Postmodern Genres*, Norman, University of Oklahoma Press, 1995.

Rich, Adrienne, *Blood, Bread and Poetry: Selected Prose*, New York, W.W. Norton, 1986.

Richardson, Paul, "Front Idols: Camille Paglia," *Attitude*, July 1996.

Ricœur, Paul, *The Symbolism of Evil*, Boston, Beacon Press, 1967.

Ritzer, George, *The McDonaldization of Society*, Thousand Oaks, Pine Forge Press, 1996 (revised).

_____, *Postmodern Social Theory*, New York, McGraw-Hill, 1997.

Ross, Andrew. *No Respect: Intellectuals and Popular Culture*. London and New York, Routledge, 1989.

Rouille, André, "La question postmoderne," in *La Recherche photographique*, No. 13 (1992).

Royot, Daniel, *Hollywood*, Paris, PUF, 1992.

Rushdie, Salman, *The Wizard of Oz*, London, BFI Publishing, 1992.

Russo, Vito, *The Celluloid Closet: Homosexuality in the Movies* (revised), New York, Harper and Row, 1987.

Scarpetta, Guy, *L'impureté*, Paris, Grasset, 1985.

Schruers, Fred, "From Rags to Bitches," *US*, December 1996.

Sedgwick, Eve Kosofsky, *Epistemology of the Closet*, Berkeley, University of California Press, 1990.

Seguin, J.C., *Pedro Almodóvar, dispositifs de post-modernité*, Saint-Etienne, Editions les-liens-le vide, 1994.

Senelick, Laurence, "Boys and girls together: Subcultural origins of glamour drag and male impersonation on the nineteenth century stage," in Leslie Ferris (ed.), *Crossing the Stage, Controversies on Cross-Dressing*, London and New York, Routledge, 1993.

Shapiro, Michael, "Weighing Anchor: Postmodern Journeys From the Life-World," in Stephen K. White (ed.), *Life-World and Politics: Between Modernity and Postmodernity*, Notre Dame, University of Notre Dame Press, 1989.

Sinfield, Alan, *Cultural Politics — Queer Reading*, Philadelphia, University of Pennsylvania Press, 1994.

_____, *The Wilde Century: Effeminacy, Oscar Wilde and the Queer Moment*, London, Cassell, 1994.

Sischy, Ingrid, "Camille Paglia: Professor of Blonde," *Interview*, December 2000.

Smart, Barry, *Postmodernity*, London and New York, Routledge, 1993.

Smith, Andrew, "Void at Heart," *The Sunday Times*, November 10, 1996.

Sontag, Susan, *Against Interpretation and Other Essays*, New York, Farrar Straus and Giroux, 1966.

_____, *A Susan Sontag Reader*, New York, Vintage Books, 1983.

Stephenson, Ralph, and Debrix, Jean R., *The Cinema as Art*, Harmondsworth, Penguin Books, 1965.

Stewart, Edward C., and Bennett, Milton J., *American Cultural Patterns, a Cross-Cultural Perspective*, Paris, Masson, 1995.

Stoddard, Thomas B., "Gays: des droits conquis de haute lutte," in Annie Lennkh and Marie-France Toinet (ed.), *L'État des États-Unis*, Paris, La Découverte, 1990.

Tabbi, Joseph, *Postmodern Sublime, Technology and American Writing from Mailer to Cyberpunk*, Ithaca and London, Cornell University Press, 1995.

Tasker, Yvonne, "Criminelles: *Thelma et Louise* et autres délinquantes," in Ginette Vincendeau and Bérénice Reynaud (ed.), *20 ans de théories féministes sur le cinéma, CinémAction*, No. 67 (2ème trimestre 1993).

_____, "Dumb movies for dumb people," in Steven Cohan and Ina Rae Hark (ed.), *Screening the Male: Exploring Masculinities in Hollywood Cinema*, New York and London, Routledge, 1993.

Taub, Richard P., and Taylor, D. Garth, and Dunham, Jan D., *Paths of Neighborhood Change: Race and Crime in Urban America*, Chicago, University of Chicago Press, 1987.

Theofilakis, Elie, "Les petits récits de chrysalide / Entretien avec Jean-François Lyotard," in Théofilakis, Elie (ed.), *Modernes et après / Les immatériaux*, Paris, Autrement, 1985.

Turim, Maureen, "Gentlemen Consume Blondes," in Patricia Erens (ed.), *Issues in Feminist Film Criticism*, Bloomington, Indiana University Press, 1990.

Udovitch, Mim, "What Do You Mean, You Liked Showgirls?" (Interview, Quentin Tarantino and Juliet Lewis), *Premiere* (British edition), June 1996.

Ulmer, Gregory L., "The Object of Post-Criticism," in Hal Foster (ed.), *Postmodern Culture*, London, Pluto Press, 1993 (First published as *The Anti-Aesthetic: Essays on Postmodern Culture*, Port Townsend, Bay Press, 1983).

Unsworth, John M., "Practising Post-Modernism, the Example of John Hawkes," *Contemporary Literature*, Vol.32, No. 1 (Spring 1991).

Van Leer, David, *The Queening of America, Gay Culture in Straight Society*, London and New York, Routledge, 1995.

Vattimo, Gianni, *La fin de la modernité: nihilisme et herméneutique dans la culture post-moderne* (translation Charles Alunni), Paris, Seuil, 1987.

_____, *La société transparente* (translation J-P. Pisetta), Paris, Desclée de Brouwer, 1990.

Vaysse, Jean-Marie, and Raulet, Gérard, (ed.), *Communauté et modernité*, Paris, L'Harmattan, 1995.

Vidal, Gore, *United States, Essays 1952-1992*, New York, Random House, 1993.

Virilio, Paul, *L'Art du moteur*, Paris, Galilée, 1993.

Viviani, Christian, "Des stars pour l'éternité," in Francis Bordat (ed.), *L'Amour du cinéma américain*, CinémAction, No. 54 (January 1990).

Warhol, Andy, *From A to B and Back Again, the Philosophy of*, London, Michael Dempsey, 1975.

Waugh, Patricia, *Metafiction, The Theory and Practice of Self-Conscious Fiction*, London, Methuen, 1984.

West, Cornel, "Postmodern Culture," in Emory Elliott (ed.), *The Columbia History of the American Novel*, New York, Columbia University Press, 1991.

White, Patricia, "Supporting Character: The Queer Career of Agnes Moorehead," in Corey K. Creekmur and Alexander Doty (ed), *Out in Culture: Gay, Lesbian, and Queer Essays on Popular Culture*, London, Cassel, 1995.

White, Stephen K., *Political Theory and Postmodernism*, Cambridge, Cambridge University Press, 1991.

White, William, "Camp as Adjective: 1909–1966," *American Speech* No. 41 (1966).

Wieviorka, Michel (ed), *Une société fragmentée, le multiculturalisme en débat*, Paris, Editions La Découverte, 1996.

Wolf, Naomi, *The Beauty Myth*, New York, William Morrow, 1991.

_____, *Fire with Fire: The New Female Power and How to Use It*, New York, Fawcett Columbine, 1993.

Wood, Michael, *America in the Movies or "Santa Maria, It Had Slipped My Mind,"* New York, Columbia University Press, 1989.

_____, "De Rita Hayworth à Marilyn Monroe/Entre la culpabilité et l'innocence," in *Cinéma d'aujourd'hui*, No. 8 (May-June 1976).

Woodiwiss, Anthony, *Postmodernity USA: The Crisis of Social Modernism in Postwar America*, London, Sage, 1993.

Zerzan, John, *The Catastrophe of Postmodernism*, Internet, January 1997.

Secondary Sources: Stars' Biographies and Autobiographies

Affron, Charles, *Divine Garbo*, Paris, Ramsay, 1985.

Anger, Kenneth, *Hollywood Babylon*, London, Dell, 1986.

Bankhead, Tallulah, *Tallulah*, New York, Harper and Brothers, 1952.

Barham, Patte B., and Brow, Peter Harry, *Marilyn, The Last Take*, New York, Dutton, 1992.

Barris, George, (ed), *Marilyn: Her Life in Her Own Words*, London, Headline, 1996.

Bowie, Angela, *Backstage Passes: Life on the Wild Side with David Bowie*, London, Orion, 1993.

Bozon, Louis, *Marlène, la femme de ma vie*, Paris, Michel Lafon, 1992.

Brion, Patrick, *Garbo*, Paris, Editions du Chêne, 1985.

Carpozi, George, *That's Hollywood*, New York, Manor Books, 1978.

Chapier, Henry, *La malédiction des stars*, Paris, Michel Lafon, 1985.

Collins, Joan, *Past Imperfect*, London, W.H. Allen and Co., 1985 (revised).

Conway, Michael, McGregor, Dion, and Ricci, Mark, *Greta Garbo*, New York, Citadel Press, 1976.

DeNavacelle, Thierry, *Sublime Marlene*, Paris, Ramsay, 1982.

Dickens, Homer, *Marlene Dietrich*, New York, Citadel Press, 1974.

Dietrich, Marlene, *Marlene*, New York, Grove Press, 1982.

Ducout, Françoise, *Greta Garbo la somnambule*, Paris, Stock, 1979.

Dujovne Ortiz, Alicia, *Eva Perón, la madone des sans-chemise*, Paris, Grasset, 1995.

Eloy Martinez, Tómas, *Santa Evita*, Paris, Robert Laffont, 1996.

Freeman, Lucy, *Pourquoi Norma Jean a tué Marilyn Monroe*, Paris, Zélie, 1993.

Golden, Eve, *Vamp, the Rise and Fall of Theda Bara*, West Vestal, NY, Emprise, 1997.

Gronowicz, Antoni, *Garbo*, New York, Simon and Schuster, 1990.

Hessel, Franz, *Marlene*, Berlin, Verlag Brinkmann and Bose, 1981.

Higham, Charles, *Marlene, The Life of Marlene Dietrich*, London, Hart-Davis/MacGibbon, 1978.

Irving, Kathleen, *Marilyn Monroe*, Paris, Balland, 1981.

Jay, Bernard, *Not Simply Divine*, London, Virgin Books, 1993.

Kobal, John, and Robinson, David, *Marilyn Monroe*, New York, The Hamlyn Publishing Group Limited, 1974.

Koestenbaum, Wayne, *Jackie Under My Skin, Interpreting an Icon*, London, Fourth Estate, 1995.

Leaming, Barbara, *Rita Hayworth*, Paris, Presses by la Renaissance, 1990.

Livio, Robin, *Greta Garbo*, Paris, Denoël, 1972.

MacPherson, Don, *Grandes dames du cinéma*, Paris, Gründ, 1993.

Mitterrand, Frédéric, "Marlene Dietrich," in *Destins d'Etoiles*, vol. 2, Paris, P.O.L., 1991.

_____, "Eva Perón," in *Destins d'Etoiles*, vol. 3, Paris, P.O.L., 1992.

Nebiolo, Gino, *Le Dernier tango d'Evita*, Paris, J.C. Lattès, 1995.

Nils, Riccardo, *Marlene*, Paris, Bookking International, 1992.

Perisset, Maurice, *Marilyn Monroe, sa vie, ses films, son mystère*, Paris, Editions Garancière, 1985.

Reiner, Silvain, *Evita*, Paris, L'Archipel, 1997.

Riva, Maria, *Marlene Dietrich by her Daughter*, New York, Random House, 1993.
Shulman, Irving, *Harlow, an Intimate Biography*, New York, Dell, 1964.
Slatzer, Robert F., *The Life and Curious Death of Marilyn Monroe*, New York, Pinnacle Books, 1974.
Spada, James, *Judy and Liza*, London, Sidgwick and Jackson, 1983.
Spoto, Donald, *Marilyn Monroe, the Biography*, New York, HarperCollins, 1993.
Strasberg, Susan, *Marilyn and Me, Sisters, Rivals, Friends*, New York, Warner Books, 1992.
Tuska, Jon, *Mae West*, Paris, Henri Veyrier, 1976.
Viva, *Superstar*, New York, Putnam's Sons, 1970.
Walker, Alexander, *Dietrich*, New York, Harper and Row, 1984.
_____, *Garbo*, London, Weidenfeld and Nicholson, 1980.
Zolotow, Maurice, *Marilyn Monroe*, London, W.H. Allen, 1961.

Encyclopedias, Dictionaries and CD-ROM

Baldick, Chris, *The Oxford Concise Dictionary of Literary Terms*, Oxford and New York, Oxford University Press, 1990.
Biographical Dictionary of Women, London, Penguin, 1998.
Brunel, Pierre (ed.), *Dictionnaire des Mythes Littéraires*, Monaco, Editions du Rocher, 1988.
Chevalier, Jean, and Gheerbrant, Alain, *Dictionnaire des symboles*, Paris, Robert Laffont, 1982.
Cinemania 96, Microsoft, USA, 1995.
Coursodon, Jean-Pierre and Tavernier, Bertrand, *Cinquante ans de cinéma américain*, Paris, Nathan, 1991.
Cuddon, J.A., *A Dictionary of Literary Terms*, London, André Deutsch, 1979.
Dictionnaire du Cinéma, Larousse, 1986.
Dynes, Wayne R., *Encyclopedia of Homosexuality*, New York, Garland Publishing, 1990.
Encarta 95, Microsoft, USA, 1995.
Fowler, Roger (ed.), *A Dictionary of Modern Critical Terms*, London, Routledge, 1973.
Gray, Martin, *A Dictionary of Literary Terms*, Harlow, Longman, 1992.
Halliwell, Leslie, *Halliwell's Filmgoer's Companion*, London, Granada, 1983.
Hart, James D., *The Oxford Companion to American Literature*, New York, Oxford University Press, 1978.
The Hutchinson Softback Encyclopedia, Stockley Park, Helicon, 1996.
Quid 1997, Paris, Robert Laffont, 1997.
Rodgers, Bruce, *The Queen's Vernacular: A Gay Lexicon*, London, Blond and Briggs, 1972.
Thomson, David, *A Biographical Dictionary of Film*, London, André Deutsch, Ltd., 1994.
Tuleja, Tad, *The New York Public Library Book of Popular Americana*, New York, Macmillan, 1994.
Tuttle, Lisa, *Encyclopedia of Feminism*, London, Longman Group Ltd., 1986.
Webster's Dictionary of Famous People, Random Century Group Ltd., 1990.

Promotion Audio Cassette and CD Interview

Hollywood Avenue / Columbia, promotion of the movie *A League of Their Own*, 1992.
The Life and Times of Madonna (two CD interview biography), 1996.

Selected Internet Sources

madonnafanclub.com
madonnacatalog.com
madonnaweb.com
maddymusic.com
madonnarama.com
madonna.com
madonna-online.ch
madonnamania.com
madonnasashram.com

Index

249